THIS INSURGENT GROUND

BLACK WOMEN'S HISTORY

Talitha L. LeFlouria, Ashley Farmer, and Daina Ramey Berry, editors

This series builds on and extends the research and teaching of generations of scholars who have developed the distinctive theories and methods that have made Black women's history a robust field. Works in this series engage with the archives, approaches, and themes elucidated by classic and cutting-edge scholarship to push the field in new directions. In a moment that demands a reckoning with the past and the tools historians use to recount it, the Black Women's History series meets this challenge, reshaping historical practice and transforming how historians and popular audiences understand the world today.

A complete list of books published in Black Women's History is available at https://uncpress.org/series/black-womens-history/.

This Insurgent Ground

BLACK WOMEN, MARRONAGE, AND REBELLION IN THE GREAT DISMAL SWAMP

Kathryn Benjamin Golden

THE UNIVERSITY OF NORTH CAROLINA PRESS

Chapel Hill

This book was published with the assistance of the Z. Smith Reynolds Fund of the University of North Carolina Press.

Set in Arno
by Jamie McKee, MacKey Composition

Cover art: *New Growth* by Rosalind McGary, 2009. Watercolor and 18K gold leaf on cotton rag paper. 4" × 6".

Excerpt from Alexis Pauline Gumbs, *Spill: Scenes of Black Feminist Fugitivity* (Duke University Press, 2016), used by permission.

The graphic of a woman holding a bundle that appears near the end of each chapter was used in a notice about a captured enslaved woman that was published in *The North-Carolinian* on March 20, 1841. Courtesy of the North Carolina Runaway Slave Notices project, Digital Library on American Slavery, https://dlas.uncg.edu/notices/notice/3641/.

LIBRARY OF CONGRESS CATALOGING-IN-PUBLICATION DATA
Names: Golden, Kathryn Benjamin author
Title: This insurgent ground : Black women, marronage, and rebellion in the Great Dismal Swamp / Kathryn Benjamin Golden.
Other titles: Black women's history
Description: Chapel Hill : The University of North Carolina Press, 2026. | Series: Black women's history | Includes bibliographical references and index.
Identifiers: LCCN 2026023867 | ISBN 9781469697963 cloth | ISBN 9781469697970 paperback | ISBN 9781469691565 epub | ISBN 9781469697987 pdf
Subjects: LCSH: Women, Black—Dismal Swamp (N.C. and Va.)—History | Maroons—Dismal Swamp (N.C. and Va.)—History | Free Black people—Dismal Swamp (N.C. and Va.)—History | Fugitive slave communities—Dismal Swamp (N.C. and Va.)—History | Dismal Swamp (N.C. and Va.)—History | BISAC: SOCIAL SCIENCE / Women's Studies | SOCIAL SCIENCE / Slavery
Classification: LCC E450 .G656 2026
LC record available at https://lccn.loc.gov/2026023867

For product safety concerns under the European Union's General Product Safety Regulation (EU GPSR), please contact gpsr@mare-nostrum.co.uk or write to the University of North Carolina Press and Mare Nostrum Group B.V., Doelen 72, 4831 GR Breda, The Netherlands.

For

JOHN HARDY,

BLANCHE DANIELS,

DAN BENJAMIN,

and

BARBARA SIMMONS

CONTENTS

ILLUSTRATIONS

FIGURES

MAPS

THIS INSURGENT GROUND

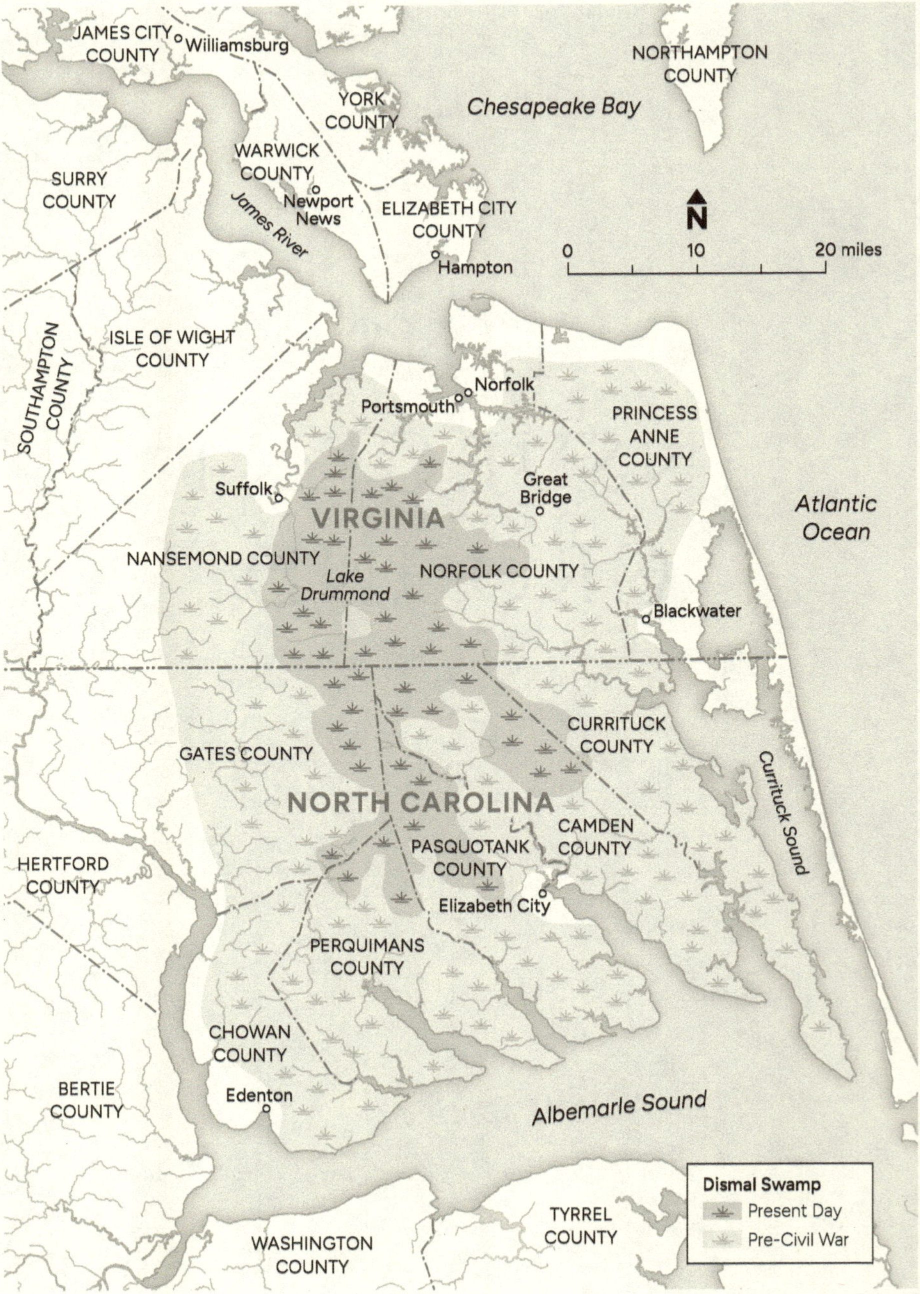

Map 1. The Great Dismal Swamp and the surrounding Tidewater key cities, towns, and counties.
(Map by Bart Wright, Lohnes and Wright GIS and Custom Mapping.)

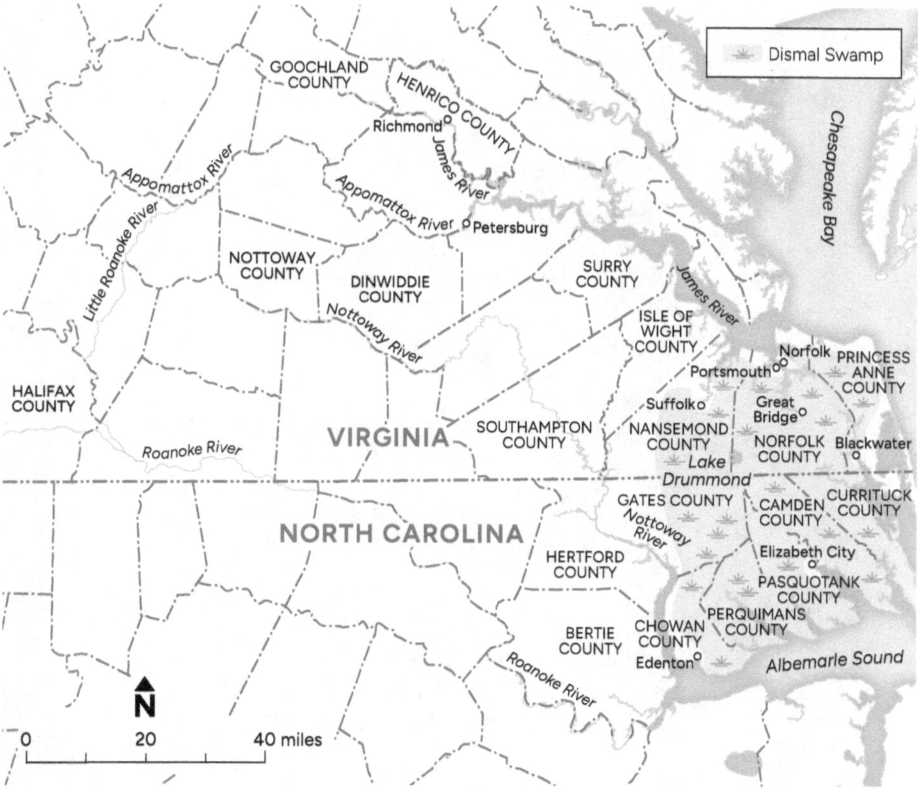

Map 2. The Great Dismal Swamp and connected waterways in the surrounding Tidewater during the Easter Rebellion of 1802.

INTRODUCTION

Women in Motion

the ground shakes with us
the gathering women
grows rich grows brown grows deep
the gathered hands women
grown brown grown women
the sure determined feet
the ground grows everything we eat
the graceful stomping women heading home
ungrateful women populating poems
the ground has everything it needs
we have never been alone

ALEXIS PAULINE GUMBS,
SPILL: SCENES OF BLACK FEMINIST FUGITIVITY

In 1864, less than forty miles west of the Dismal Swamp, Mary fled from the Pope farm in Southampton County, Virginia, and made her way toward Suffolk—a town on the western edge of the great swamp. Before she left, she had raided Amos Pope's storeroom for a few chickens, some fresh meat, and cornmeal; she then cautiously roused her children for the long journey ahead.

Mary had planned and plotted to escape together with six others who were to join her and her daughters Rachel (age sixteen) and Betsy (age twelve), and her sons Albert (seven) and little Amos (five). To Mary's advantage, it was wartime, and she was determined that her children would reach the Union occupied town of Suffolk—a destination she believed would offer them greater safety. Years later, recollecting her flight, Mary told her interviewer that the group had navigated and crossed the Nottoway and Blackwater Rivers before walking thirty miles, when they met "a rebel" named Jones. Armed with a revolver, Jones took the group four miles closer to Suffolk—a distance they "ran all the way." Having reached Union lines after four days of travel, Mary's "feet were so sore and swollen that she could not step." Still, she said "she did not mind her feet; her heart was light; she was free."[1]

Mary could not have known how many other women before her had stepped and moved through these wetlands and waterways that flowed into and out of the Great Dismal Swamp, but she did understand, as did those who moved along similar paths, that "locomotion was definitive of personal liberty."[2] It was not in or through her destination that Mary experienced something akin to freedom but, rather, through the audacious movements of escape; through her daring choice of itinerancy, roving, journeying, and fugitivity; through her movement toward places other than, elsewhere, and away. Informed by raced and gendered experiences, stakes, motives, and insights, Mary was not the only woman to move in ways that disrupted both slaveholding authority and the assumed supremacy of the white men in their way. In propelling herself forward and rejecting the imposition of boundedness, she joined other Black women in the Tidewater region surrounding the Great Dismal Swamp; these women's movements away also disturbed white society's racist and patriarchal demands that they remain in captive modes and locations for someone else's benefit and profit. Instead, Mary and women like her charted alternative directions toward new forms and possibilities of freer life—emancipatory movements toward "something else"—that both arose from and constituted insurgent ground.[3]

This is a book set in motion by the movements of Black women both to inhabit the world differently and to inspire and achieve a freer and more just world altogether. In serving their better interests and desires to aid, protect, and free their own futures and those of their families and communities, women's trekking, coursing, and striving plotted insurgency with their feet and in the spaces they chose to move through and reside in with conviction, dissidence, and noncompliance. This book begins and ends with women who, with great care, weighed and analyzed the ties between their bodies and their environment—and the places of both within the system of hereditary racial slavery—and decided to move otherwise. In doing so, *This Insurgent Ground* contributes to the ever growing field of scholarship that locates Black women's historical experiences, knowledges, and perspectives at the origin and center of the early modern world.[4] As people who knew best how the economics of chattel slavery and white supremacy depended on their productive and reproductive labor—on both sexual and maternal assault—it was Black women who "embodied both the apex of slavery's oppressive extractions and its potential undoing."[5] In the Atlantic-facing Tidewater region of eastern Virginia and North Carolina, Black women's movements shaped and contributed to a range of insurgent action against the plantation economy and slaveholding world; their actions spanned everyday ways of diminishing and escaping it; and their movements included fugitive lifeways, marronage, and rebellion. In these wetlands of the Upper South, these more transgressive practices of insurgency were options made more opportune by women's proximity and access to not only the abundant Tidewater river systems, which could channel into and out of the slaveholding world and the gradually emancipating North, but also the Tidewater's central feature, the abundant natural sprawl and teeming ecology of the Great Dismal Swamp.

The Dismal Swamp, which extended from the Albemarle Sound in North Carolina up to the James River in Virginia, was an expanse the size of Delaware at roughly two thousand square miles before the period of logging and canal development that intensified throughout the nineteenth century.[6] (See map 1.) The swamp was scorned and reviled by colonists and the enslaving class, who considered its miry, thick, and densely forested vastness a "horrible desart" or a "filthy bog," because its insistent unrestraint defied their capitalist demands for the domination and control of land, labor, and bodies.[7] Enslaved people knew well the connections between their own dispossession and bondage and the building of towns, farms, and plantations in the cleared or dry interstices between the untamable swaths of swamp. But unlike their captors, enslaved people viewed the swamp's indomitability much as they viewed their own. For them, the swamp was a refuge surging with opportunity for independent thought, action, and emboldened movements toward freer life. Thousands of once-enslaved women and men moved through the Dismal Swamp as fugitives on their way to other destinations, while thousands more opted toward maroon life and *marronage*—the process of sustaining flight and escape that accompanied alternative lifeways and resettlement, rooted in a symbiosis with wilderness and the natural world. Many more harnessed the insights of this motion while also practicing and promoting armed warfare

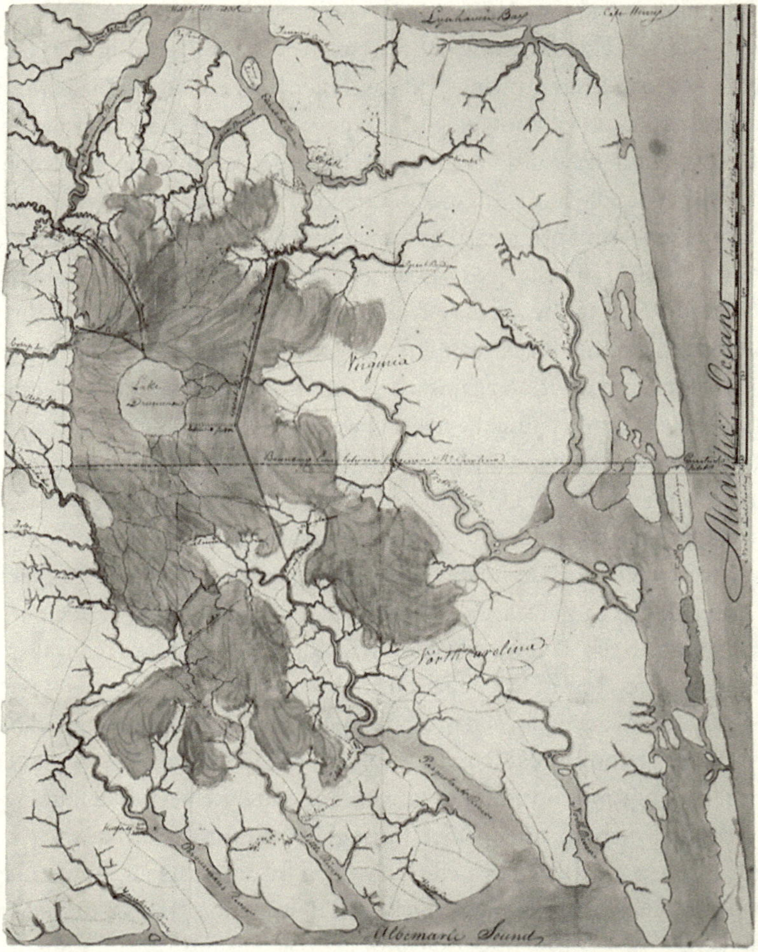

Hand-colored map of the Great Dismal Swamp, 1807.
(© National Maritime Museum, Greenwich, London, Caird Collection.)

or plotting and conspiring toward more transformative forms of organized rebellion.

The Dismal Swamp maroons were like the tens of thousands of other maroons in the Latin American and Caribbean colonies, for nowhere and at no time in the history of racial chattel slavery was there a place or a moment that was "immune" to the development of these alternative maroon societies.[8] Marronage was a hemispheric response to the plantation economies and slaveholding societies of the Americas, but it was also an African diasporic response to slavery and the transatlantic slave trade. Practices of marronage are known to have arisen on the eastern side of the Atlantic world, against the trade in African captives along the coasts of West Africa.[9] In the American colonies, the Spanish word *cimarron*—derived from the Taíno/Arawakan root—was originally used to refer to uncooperative, feral cattle that escaped to the hills and mountains. By the 1530s, colonists used the word primarily to describe "undomesticated," "wild," "fierce," or "unbroken" escaped Africans.[10] Throughout the Americas, slaveholders considered marronage to be "seriously annoying," the "gangrene" of the colonies, or the "chronic plague" to their exploits. Indominable maroons "struck directly at the foundations of the plantation system" by removing themselves from servitude to racial capitalism, by creating new life options for themselves, and by appropriating and subverting material resources and technologies typically used as apparatuses of state power. Maroons related to earth, water, and ecologies in ways that refused extractive capitalist logics, and in doing so they also inspired others to move, join, and help actualize rivaling insurgent spatial realities and ways of life.[11]

By the mid-nineteenth century, it was Black women's and Black men's own footwork—their subversive movement to, in, and through the Dismal Swamp over the course of more than two hundred years—that led the swamp to acquire its distinct national reputation as being a haven of "runaway slaves." The rise in abolitionist literature during this time also helped to promote the idea. The poet and educator Henry Wadsworth Longfellow, for example, wrote *Poems on Slavery* (1842), an antislavery collection that included the poem, "The Slave in the Dismal Swamp." Though it depicts "the poor old slave, infirm and lame," or else, "hunted," it gave the swamp national significance as a site of Black fugitivity and resistance. A decade later, Frederick Douglass wrote "The Heroic Slave" (1853), a short story that centers Madison, a fugitive who conspired with his wife, Susan, that he should live in the Dismal Swamp so that they could remain together. For five years, Susan met Madison weekly in the swamp's pine woods, each time arriving "laden with provisions" to support him. William Wells Brown's *Clotel* (1853), casts Nat Turner together with hundreds of insurgents, including maroon "runaways," who use the Dismal Swamp as an organizing space to plot the Southampton Rebellion of 1831. Harriet Beecher Stowe's *Dred: A Tale of the Great Dismal Swamp* (1856), tells the story of Dred, the fictive son of Denmark Vesey, who escaped to the Dismal Swamp and helped others follow suit. Martin R. Delany's *Blake; or, the Huts of America* (1859) similarly credits the swamp as being the birthplace of Gabriel Prosser's and Nat Turner's movements to eradicate slavery.

Though none used the term *maroon*, these writers described and confirmed a maroon ethos inscribed by and through the Dismal Swamp. Considering that each author lived in a time and place where maroon women and men were consistently reduced to "runaways"—or else routinely labeled "outlaws," "outliers," "lurkers," "banditti," and "gangs"—it is unsurprising that the term was seldom used.[12] Though colonists and enslavers throughout the American South reported with great alarm the presence of dozens of maroon camps, settlements, and communities, they refused to use the word *maroon*, preferring to unsee the phenomenon as it happened on their own turf. Instead, enslavers in British North America and the United States acknowledged only the *grand* scale maroons beyond their shores—those large, highly secluded, fortified, enduring maroon societies of Brazil, Jamaica, Suriname, Saint-Domingue, and Colombia that through unceasing armed warfare and populations regularly numbering hundreds, if not thousands, forced colonial treatises and negotiations. In the slaveholding South, there could be no other way to view predominately smaller, less secluded, less stable, and often roving or transient *petit* maroons than through a lens that diminished them as "desperadoes" and bands of "runaway negroes."[13] For Southern whites, to have acknowledged these maroons in the slightest connection to the *grand* maroons of the Caribbean and Latin America would have been an admission that the South, too, had its share of the "plague."[14] So began the contemporaneous denial of the existence of marronage in the United States that, in the words of the historian Sylviane Diouf, satisfied public opinion that "there were no maroon communities in the country" connected with or comparable to those of the Caribbean and Latin America.[15]

There was, however, at least one antislavery critic who, in 1852, openly recognized that although it was "not generally known," the Southern states contained "many communities of greater or less numbers, very similar to those of Jamaica and Cuba, though not designated by the name of Maroons." The affluent abolitionist and investigative journalist Edmund Jackson pointed to the maroons of the Dismal Swamp, who, he argued, exemplified the ways Southern maroons took to the abundant and "numerous extensive swamps and low grounds" in the absence of remote mountainous regions, cockpit country, or the impenetrable jungles of Amazonia and the Caribbean. His essay, "The Virginia Maroons," was featured in *The Liberty Bell*, an annual giftbook sold at antislavery bazaars and fairs, and published by the Boston Female Anti-Slavery Society. It was in support of the antislavery cause that Jackson wrote of the maroons of the "great Dismal Swamp," who "obtained their freedom" by "their own determined energy," and who sustained it through "invention," night forays, by cultivating "patches of corn and sweet potatoes, and not unfrequently rear[ing] a large family of children."[16] While his contemporaries refused to acknowledge the existence of maroons, Jackson placed the maroons of the Dismal Swamp and, by extension, North American marronage within a broader context of Atlantic world marronage and insurgency.

It would take historians far longer to begin to do the same. Herbert Aptheker is recognized as the first to take seriously the history of North American marronage. His "Maroons Within the Present Limits of the United States" (1939), and "Additional Data on American Maroons" (1947), both published in Carter G. Woodson's *Journal of Negro History*, were unprecedented in their reading of available documentary evidence against its trivializing and criminalizing terms for marronage, and in evidencing the existence of at least fifty maroon communities across the South between 1672 and 1864.[17] This number has since been shown to have underestimated marronage in the Southern colonies and states, since, as Aptheker himself noted, "notice of these maroon communities was taken only when they were accidentally uncovered or when their activities became so obnoxious or dangerous to the slavocracy that their destruction was felt to be necessary."[18] The successful evasion of the uncaught guarantees that there were more marooned communities than could have been recorded. But while some subsequent studies continued to dismiss North American maroons by perpetuating the view that only *grand* marronage is marronage in the "true sense," scholarship produced over the last three decades has paid slow but continued attention to marronage as a fixture within the history of Southern slavery.[19]

The maroons of the Dismal Swamp do not fit neatly within the categories of either *petit* or *grand* marronage, but there is scholarly consensus that everywhere, across the Americas, maroons ranged from tiny bands that endured less than a year to powerful states and sovereignties encompassing hundreds or even thousands of members that survived for generations and sometimes centuries.[20] Like elsewhere in the Atlantic world, the Dismal Swamp maroons included solitary individuals, small group communities, and more intensely populated communities, all of which varied between being ephemeral and maintaining evasion for many years. Though at no point was there any one unified, singular, concentrated community of swamp maroons, from about 1650 to 1865 there remained a great diversity of such groups; and maroons were varied, numerous, and constant as they ranged from individuals and couples to groups of fewer than ten, to communities in the dozens and even, over time, reaching the hundreds. Rather than attempt to measure these maroons through their scale, duration, or activities, examining the spatial opportunities presented within their environments reveals more about the ways maroons would have viewed, arranged, and experienced their own movements as well as the ways they deliberated and enacted contestations of power.[21] This thinking "beyond petit and grand" offers that maroons in the United States and beyond might be better understood through spatial frameworks such as Diouf's concepts of "borderland" maroons (those who lived and operated in the "wild land that bordered the farms and plantations, cities and towns") and "hinterland" marronage (maroons, "whatever their size," who took advantage of the presence of more remote wilderness accesses, farther from the borderlands)—both of which are recognizable through the "maroon landscape" or the social-spatial worlds maroons made and knew.[22]

In the Dismal Swamp, fugitives practiced both hinterland and borderland marronage. The most elusive, independent, enduring, and secluded moved and lived in the interior, hinterland, or deep swamps. These maroons established multigenerational communities complete with their own methods and practices of self-government and community organization, and they were the least likely to venture outside of the swamp. The less enduring, fleeting, and itinerant groups lived along the swamp's peripheries, fringes, or borderlands and maintained a constant local pressure on slaveholding society in the form of ambushes, the seizure of property and provisions, and by upholding mutually supportive networks with enslaved people at the swamp's edges. But regardless of where in the swamp they operated and lived, Dismal Swamp maroons, like their Latin American and Caribbean counterparts, acted in defense of the freedoms they gained. They gathered arms, created weapons, constructed palisades and defensive structures, practiced spontaneous and organized warfare—including reconnaissance, raids, ambush, and sabotage—and, at times, "supplied the nucleus of leadership for planned uprisings."[23] But marronage across the Dismal Swamp was not exclusively shaped by grit, fear, desperation, or warfare; it was also sustained by insurgent conspiring and spiritual communing with the swamp's natural world as well as by fierce and binding acts of love and the protection of selfhood, family, and other intimate relations where it was otherwise not meant to freely exist, or exist at all.[24]

This Insurgent Ground adds to four book-length studies on the history of these Great Dismal Swamp maroons.[25] Hugo Prosper Leaming's posthumously published *Hidden Americans: Maroons of Virginia and the Carolinas* (1995) leaves much to be desired in the dependability of his assertions and research methods, yet it is the first attempt to amass documentary evidence of the broad history of the Dismal Swamp maroons in any one study.[26] Daniel O. Sayers's pioneering archaeological study, *A Desolate Place for a Defiant People* (2014), brings invaluable material sources to the fraught and limited documentary archive of the internal dynamics of maroons in the interior swamp.

This book presents Sayers's archaeological findings from fieldwork conducted in just a small fraction of the swamp's greater expanse, evidencing beyond any prevailing disbelief that the maroons of Virginia and North Carolina maintained continuous intensive occupation in the swamp from the seventeenth century until "well into the nineteenth century."[27] More recently, Marcus P. Nevius's *City of Refuge: Slavery and Petit Marronage in the Great Dismal Swamp, 1763–1856* (2020) gives new focus to the illicit "internal exchange economy" between enslaved canal and timber laborers and the Dismal Swamp maroons networking despite the capitalist interests of slaveholders, industrialists, and white corporations running the swamp's canals and lumber camps.[28] J. Brent Morris's *Dismal Freedom: A History of the Maroons of the Great Dismal Swamp* (2022) is effectively the first comprehensive history of the varied and diverse swamp maroons, their motivations for marronage, and their movement in and locations throughout the swamp across the span of more than two hundred years. But while these works enrich the study of slave resistance and, specifically, "the most pervasive form of fugitive slave community formation, negotiation, and enslaver accommodation in the history of the Atlantic world," in failing to address the ways that gender, sexual economy, and reproduction lay at the core of chattel slavery and racial capitalism, each of these studies misses the significance of women's movements as those that could fundamentally offset slavery's perpetuation. Although these scholars recognize the swamp's self-emancipated "multigenerational families" and sometimes also acknowledge the fugitive and maroon women who appear in extant records, none of these works pays sincere attention to the motivations, risks, input, and contributions of Black women's insurgent movements throughout the Great Dismal Swamp and greater Tidewater region.[29]

While these studies have looked nearly exclusively at the most obvious actors found in the documentary archives concerning the swamp's history, *This Insurgent Ground* looks behind, alongside, and in front of apparently male rebels and maroons, and finds Black women in motion between geographies of bondage and containment and the woods and swamps, as well as in records where they have previously evaded historical detection and attention. It has been difficult for historians to locate rebel and maroon women in part because, as the historian Stephanie Camp has pointed out, women "enjoyed much less mobility than did men." Bound by both the plantation world and its patriarchal ideas about the place and the roles of (captive) women, most Black women were consistently confined to the homesteads of their enslavers and kept there—enforced by borders, patrols, curfews, and laws—under close surveillance. Faced with these conditions, women made up only a small proportion of those choosing to flee, and they "rarely participated directly in slave rebellions."[30] But the challenge of coming to terms with women's relationships to marronage and rebellion in the swamp is further compounded by the fact that records were produced by and through subjective omission—or by the sheer "unthinkability" of slaveholding men who could not believe Black women could or would be likely to act as willful participants in coordinated, sustained, forceful, or violent resistance.[31] Not a few historians have uncritically accepted these gaps and absences in contemporary documents, leaving untroubled the emergent assumption that fleeting mentions of women, or none at all, indicate their roles as inert, passive, and "unconscious observers of men's radical resistance," or warrant discounting them altogether.[32] Not long ago there was a time when historians widely considered all slaves to be male, or else the appendages of men. Against such disregard for the meaning and value of Black women's lives, there is no reason to doubt that, as Jennifer Morgan has recently shown, not all "rebels" and "rogues" were men, and "sometimes women were Maroons."[33]

While most of the maroons and rebels reported in slaveholding Tidewater Virginia and North Carolina were men, across the insurgent space of the Dismal Swamp's remotest accesses as well as throughout its borderlands, women can be traced aiding, supporting, leading, and nurturing oppositional community and resistive movement. They were collaborators in sustained evasion; bearers of liberated and enduring maroon life; makers and providers of alternative place, belonging, and home; as well as conspirators in ambush, plunder, and organized rebellion at the swamp's outskirts. In the pages that follow, Black women's visibility in such roles is sharpened and defined against archival hints not meant to further signify, guided by the core tenets of Black feminism that insist any analysis of power and human experience must emerge from the knowledges and perspectives of those who "live in the margin."[34] With these insights, this book prioritizes the truths, convictions, and experiences of Black women, who, as Deborah Gray White asserts, held "the least formal power and were perhaps the most vulnerable group" by the antebellum period.[35] This approach appreciates Black women as fully capable, conscious historical agents whose intersecting oppression in the slaveholding world made them the people in their communities with the most reason to oppose it. As Vanessa Holden has pointed out, the certainty of Black women's "ubiquitous resistive activity" and integral roles within their communities demands that we look beyond the obvious roles of men toward the ways premeditated resistance was "a product of interconnected community that includes enslaved women and children."[36] In beginning the history of enslaved and maroon insurgency in the swamp with women, *This Insurgent Ground* excludes no one and explores multiple, intersecting motives for enduring forms of fugitivity and rebellion that appear in excess of movement against productive labor and racial violence alone.

Throughout the Dismal Swamp, Black women acted not only against toil, hard labor, and corporeal violence but also against reproductive violence, sexual assault, and desecrated, "plundered" motherhoods.[37] Their movements established that maternity was not simply a hindrance or deterrent to flight, marronage, or rebellion, but sometimes it was a force that propelled them forward as insurgents in their own right. Though most enslaved women did not flee with their children in tow, some did. Others ran "very big with child," and still others knew that birthing and raising children in the swamp was preferrable to doing so within the grasp of their enslavers.[38] In the swamp borderlands, women transformed the limitations on their mobility into strategies of resistance by reappropriating the domestic, bound spaces of their confinement into the service of insurrectionary activity. Over the course of three conspiracies to rebel that involved the swampscape and maroons, enslaved Tidewater women, not unaccustomed to acts of defensive violence, were ready to support armed, organized rebellion by acting as keepers of secret and subversive knowledge, as providers of collective motivation and morale, and as those who fed and protected enslaved and maroon insurgency through the procurement and sharing of food. Though outnumbered by maroon men, borderland maroon women are also locatable as participants in violent defensive combat alongside men and as deep swamp maroons audacious enough to give life to their communities through the repossession of their bodies and themselves in profound defiance of the very economic workings of heritable slavery—dependent as it was on the labor of their captive wombs.

This Insurgent Ground is a testament to the ways that Black women shared in both everyday oppositional approaches and movements that were less visible, hidden, personal, informal, yet constant, *and* in the less frequent, more extraordinary, exceptional, and explicit practices of enduring self-theft, coordinated violence, movement by force, sustained collective escape, and the militant and political organization of uprise. Black women's insurgency in and around the swamp is situated in a continuous and persistent spectrum of resistive acts mounting from the quotidian and covert to overt and collective refusal. The everyday practices of property destruction, theft, "foot dragging," feigned illness, and short-termed flight constituted "the wide terrain between consent, on one hand, and open, organized opposition, on the other."[39] Daily acts of quieter, insular rebellion, or what Eugene Genovese has called "simple revolt," could yield to and precede more transformative forms of resistance, building along a continuum or escalating range of oppositional acts.[40] Black women's day-to-day mastery of dissemblance—willful acts of concealing knowledge or information, or in Darlene Clark Hine's words, "the behavior and attitudes of Black women that created the appearance of openness and disclosure but actually shielded the truth of their inner lives and selves from their oppressors"—could advance the aims of providing aid to fugitives and insurgents, or nurturing the otherwise clandestine, conspiratorial, and subversive as viable and achievable goals.[41] Verbal tussles and contestations of demeanor, or "insolence," were also insurgent testing grounds for bolder forms of opposition.[42] Out of the customary practice of temporary absconding, or truancy, more enduring forms of fugitive life could become conceivably attainable options. While it is far easier to locate women in resistance at the subtler, budding points of everyday insurgency than it is to find them recorded as either directly or indirectly involved in movements like marronage and organized rebellion, enslaved women and men nevertheless shared in the totality of this resistive scale, just as they mutually shared in the predicament of bondage.[43] Although men had the greatest opportunity to move and plot, and they did so in ways that were shaped and encouraged by masculinist standards for political leadership and the use of arms and force, acts of marronage, conspiracies to rebel, and rebellion itself were not possible without the daily insurgent motion present in preexisting rival geographies of subversive knowledge and use of space that Black women were integral in building and upholding.[44]

In this study, rebellion, insurrection, and revolt—beyond the "simple," quotidian forms—are synonymous with any deliberative, coordinated, organized act against the unlivable injustices of slavery, rooted in the lethal intent to destroy corporeal slaveholding authority or the untroubled continuation of systemic white domination. In the neighborhoods of the Great Dismal Swamp, Black women practicing marronage—sustained evasion and autonomous movement in self-banded, frequently "armed and officered," dissident groups—should fundamentally be understood as being engaged in a form of insurrection, revolt, or organized rebellion.[45] After all, the strategies of marronage to avoid capture, procure or create supplies, gather intelligence, and devise defensive or offensive plans are exemplary of the precursory steps necessary to form any organized rebellion plot. As Orlando Patterson has argued, "all sustained slave revolts must acquire a maroon dimension," such as the strategies of flight, ambush, attack and retreat, secret intelligence and exchange networks, and the defense of intended alternative futures.[46] Certainly,

Virginia lawmakers and authorities considered marronage tantamount to making insurrection, regardless of the relationship maroons had to actual armed self-defense or collective violent revolt.[47] As early as 1680, the Virginia Assembly passed "An Act for Preventing Negroes Insurrections," which mandated the apprehension and killing of any "negroe or slave soe lying out and resisting . . . lurking in obscure places, [or] committing injuries to the inhabitants."[48] Maroon women, who may or may not have engaged in violent combat, were nonetheless engaged in a state of prolonged revolt and organized rebellion, as they acted in support of insurgent groups and communities. Their self-extrication from the slaveholding economy was also crippling and destructive, if not fatal to the livelihood of enslavers and to the organizing principles of slaveholding society that depended upon the pillaging of Black women's bodies for its increase and perpetuity.

As for enslaved women in the Tidewater who considered and sometimes conspired to destroy their enslavers, with the above definition of organized rebellion, Black women's calculated, premeditated acts to "kill or attempt to kill slave owners or their agents" become recognizable as revolt once released from restrictive conditions suggesting that rebellion must entail "a minimum of ten slaves involved; freedom as the apparent aim of the disaffected slaves; contemporary references labelling the event as an uprising, plot, insurrection, or the equivalent."[49] Rejecting the quantification of rebellion as "the concerted action by a group of slaves with the settled purpose of and the actual destruction of the lives and property of local whites," as well as the qualification of revolt on the basis that "the activities must have been recognized as an insurrection by public officials who called out the armed forces of the locale to destroy the rebels" allows for the detection of insurrectionary actions that were more directly executed by enslaved women, actions that may otherwise have been dismissed as "merely a violent outburst against vicious local conditions."[50] This more expansive definition mediates against an undue reliance on both contemporary white authority and the subsequent interpretive assumptions of historians that together have too often denied, silenced, or ignored Black women's conscious and emboldened actions against injustice.

Looking past the long-standing notion that marronage, violent resistance, and outright revolt have been the primary if not sole domain of men, *This Insurgent Ground* joins a growing number of studies confronting, as the historian Aisha Finch has put it, "how deeply masculinity and male embodiment have structured the way in which we think about black opposition."[51] Finding women behind the show of highly visible armed and aggressive male rebels and maroons, this book is in dialogue with other works exploring the ways

The Hunted Slaves, by Richard Ansdell, 1862.
(Collection of the Smithsonian National Museum of African American History and Culture, 2009.34ab.)

that Black women contributed to the "presumed masculinist spaces" of militancy, armed defense, community control, and revolt.[52] Black women historians writing across time and place have shown that Black women, though often overshadowed by the obvious and expected actions of men, unfailingly "shared and helped organize larger critiques of white brutality" in a variety of ways—including through the active support and advocacy of strategies of violent protest, self-extrication, collective removal, and armed resistance.[53]

Given the slow and challenged development of scholarship on maroons and marronage in British North America and the United States, it is unsurprising that there are no books on Black women, gender, and marronage in these contexts.[54] While *This Insurgent Ground* is the first to explore women maroons and the implications of gender and marronage in the history of the slaveholding American South, this work adds to existing studies that raise critical questions about Black women's fugitivity, refusal by force, armed warfare and military strategy, reproductive justice, and the integral roles they held in their families and communities throughout the broader Atlantic world.[55] Fighting against the chokehold of paternalistic slavery and not merely colonial slavery—a system that made it easier to accomplish frequent, permanent marronage with its higher numbers of the African-born population;

the outnumbering of whites by Africans and African descendants; the perfunctory, depersonalized relationships between enslavers and the enslaved; and the higher rates of planter absenteeism—maroon women in the Dismal Swamp were far less numerous than they were in Caribbean and Latin American colonial contexts and as a result were also far more absent in records.[56] Despite these differences, combatant maroon women in Tidewater Virginia and North Carolina demanded notice at times, and even when notice missed them, their movements and contributions nevertheless shared in the Black radical tradition of maroon evasion, oppositional political consciousness, autonomous community, and armed, violent defense alongside maroon women engaged in similar, if not the same, responses to slavery elsewhere.[57]

Locating Black women of the Dismal Swamp within the larger diasporic context of Black radical action builds on historical scholarship employing Cedric Robinson's incomparable articulation of a linked and "essentially African response" against exploitation and oppression in the development of the modern era. Robinson named this "cauldron of Black radicalism" the Black radical tradition—a fundamentally liberatory, connective tradition across space, time, and geography—in which people of African descent frustrate, reject, and refuse the dehumanization, commodification, and reduction of Black humanity to property, items, or "things" of profit, market, trade, sale, and possession.[58] Robinson's excavation of the roots of Black radicalism reveals multiple forms of resistance—a "maelstrom," where very little separated minor acts of refusal from more serious rejections of Atlantic slavery and racial capitalism—among which marronage and insurrection were the "ultimate."[59] *This Insurgent Ground* joins other texts in asserting Black women's contestations of a *gendered* racial capitalism in the Atlantic world that was predicated on the intersections between race, sex, reproduction, and commodification.[60] Focusing on women maroons and insurgents in the Dismal Swamp affirms Black women as equal contributors to and as "primary agents" in this tradition of radical action in "distinctly gendered ways."[61] In so doing, this book's attention to Black women's multifaceted contributions to rebellion and marronage broadens and deepens Robinson's vocabulary for naming an insurgent Black tradition of opposition and claims to humanity; and it also bonds the maroons of Virginia, North Carolina, and the wider American South to radical movements across the African Diaspora as inherently and essentially linked responses to slavery, colonization, and its afterlives.

Fugitivity, a term that derives from the Latin root *fugere*, meaning "to flee," is the central principle of marronage. It is also a concept that scholars of the African Diaspora have used in the last two decades or more to elucidate the uncapturable, indominable practices of Black social life—including not only culture, cosmology, "critical mixes and admixtures of language and thought," convictions, speech acts, habits, and morality but also the physically and materially commutative practices, as well as mobility itself—all of which hinge upon persistent motion away from and against the force of zones otherwise dictating anti-Black corporeal violence and the commodification, exploitation, and social death of Black people.[62] As a pronouncement of constant defection in the pursuit of Black life other than and outside of racist, patriarchal, and capitalist exploitation, fugitivity is a lens that invites critical consideration of the creation of alternative modes and worlds—the elsewhere and otherwise—that are defined through ongoing movement. These rival worlds of fugitive making defy and evade captivity, carcerality, atrocity, and death.[63] In short, fugitivity has become a "metanarrative" for subversive practices and "modes of contestation and refusal" across time.[64] *This Insurgent Ground* views the history of Black women's subversive movements, marronage, and maroon dimensions of rebellion in the Great Dismal Swamp through such a lens, recognizing their motion as bold, formative assertions of fugitivity that hold "trans-historical utility" and value.[65] What proceeds here should be interpreted not as an isolated analysis of Black women's movements confined to the Tidewater swamplands but as an exploration of some of the origins of a tradition in "the artful escape of objectification," beginning with the ways gendered Blackness compels fugitivity, or, in the words of Fred Moten, the "modality of life's constant escape . . . the held and errant pattern, of flight," both in the period of slavery and its wake.[66]

Following this errantry—or the shifting footwork, motioning, and movement-building of Black women transgressing and defying borders, bounds, and limits of both spatial and temporal order—*This Insurgent Ground* must also be boundary-defiant and resistant to neat categorization and linearity in its treatment of time and space. This book finds women moving in and out of the swamps across time, between a period of years from 1650 to the end of the Civil War, during which time they navigated disparate and distinct areas of the swamp and sometimes moved to multiple places within it for varied purposes and lengths of time. These journeys were shaped by specific historical contexts but they also took place regardless and in spite of the period or historic moment. Through movement, women's engagements with space also suggest they understood the inner folds of the swamps to be the real spatial limits of where they were willing to move and dwell—a direct rejection of the slaveholding view that border spaces began where the plantation world met the insubordinate wilderness. Instead, maroon movements declared that these were not borders at all. Alongside the motioning of women who cut across expectations and impositions intended to limit where and when they might be found, this book moves across time and space, following traces of their flight and marronage, in order to locate and sit more fully with their interests and intentions. While this book does follow the swamp itself as it changes across time and affects the people in and around it, it also moves in and out of the colonial and antebellum periods, sometimes utilizing the insight of comparative time and place at different points and times within the swampscape and beyond the greater Tidewater region to arrive closer to the women in motion, where details about their activities and objectives otherwise evade documentary and material evidence.

The chapters to follow do not attempt to provide a comprehensive history of marronage and resistance in the Great Dismal Swamp. Instead, they offer a qualitative, experiential, and environmental history of women's insurgent movements and worldmaking that concerns three sets of actors: Black women, men, and children (the enslaved, fugitives, rebels, and maroons); capitalist slaveholding society and state apparatuses (enslavers, traders, swamp logging and lumber companies, patrols, sheriffs, justices, militia captains, jailers); and the living, breathing, and robust swamp itself. To ignore Black people's relationships with the natural environment would be to ignore, as the geographer Celeste Winston has written, how marronage is a "fundamentally spatial practice of building alternative worlds in service of liberation," and one that is rooted in multidimensional relationships with nature.[67] Black experiences of communion with and intimate knowledge of land and waterscapes is generated through movement, and, reflexively, ambulatory encounters with the natural world inspire and motivate sustained flight and fugitive lifeways.[68] As Katherine McKittrick and Sylvia Wynter have shown, whereas "the individual, the community, the land are inextricable in the process of creating history," Black women's actions "have *always*" inscribed their own geographies and spatialities of protestation, critique, their needs, and their stories, shaped by the raced and gendered struggles they faced.[69] Maroon women's decisive movements through the Dismal Swamp forged spatial claims to "social life, vitality, and cosmological integrity," as well as to their own reproductive labor in the advancement of insurgency, where such a world was otherwise not meant to exist.[70]

Though colonists, slaveholders, and industrialists considered the Dismal Swamp a geography of peril and refuse if not dominated and ravaged, the swamp's geographical and ecological properties—abundant in enclaves of natural refuge and plentiful in land and water resources—offered alternative options and opportunities to refuse gendered racial capitalism, plantation economies, and the exploitation of land and bodies, motioning closer to freer life. This maroon ecophilosophy directed Black terms of social life through the strategic arrangement of an insurgent ecology that was never bereft of Black women's contributions; after all, it was Black women who found the swamps and woods to be environments of their own "racial and gendered power, as well as [sources] of fear and control [for] whites."[71] The women whose footwork politics, creativity, and resourcefulness made the swamps places of kinship, home, and evanescent or enduring refusal, also modeled the right to rest, leisure, voluntary productive and reproductive labor, and holistic self-possession within their families and communities—by virtue of the swamp's natural provisions. Their insurgent communion with the swamp as mothers, healers, agriculturalists, spiritual guides, and fugitive strategists also provides that, as many of the scholars in the burgeoning field of Black ecologies have brought to light, Black women and men have always fostered relationships with the natural environment outside of and despite those defined by oppressive, extractive, and exploitative forces.[72] This book is a gathering of stories concerning these intimate, irrepressible, and insurgent environmental connections that have hardly been considered in either the historiography of Southern landscapes or in the fields of cultural geography and ecocriticism—particularly as they relate to the environmental and ecological imaginaries, negotiations, assertions, and experiences of Black women.[73]

The chapters that follow are based in archives, written and unwritten, emerging from searched and scoured woods, swamps, and centuries-old documents produced by those who did the scouring. It is because of the slaveholding priorities of intensive policing and surveillance of suspected geographies of enslaved subversion and marronage that documentary records useful to this investigation of gender, contested power, and Black placemaking in the swampscape are now available. But *This Insurgent Ground* entails a new scouring—this time, of records never intended to value or provide interpretive value and possibility for reading further into and against its own traces, fragments, mentions, and glimpses concerning Black women's lives. This book builds on studies at the intersection of Black feminism and Black women's history that have lent unprecedented methodological interventions for locating and recognizing Black women's significance against absence, oblivion, contemporaneous and archival violence. Women whose presence or actions compelled noting beyond their commodification, labor, and economic value appear infrequently in records, but women implicated in fugitivity, marronage, or insurrection are even more obscure, as they were fewer in number, subjected to raced and gendered bias, and further, because they were the women who intentionally moved clandestinely and with skill in stealth, elusion, and evasion. Yet, silences surrounding their activities, or even their very existence, do not preclude this history of the Dismal Swamp, since silences here are read "as texts unto themselves, often with gendered implications, by privileging utterances meant to be small and insignificant."[74] This book finds Black women by engaging documentary evidence with the understanding that sometimes, the apparently null or omitted "should be trusted and celebrated" as opportunities to treat the gaps as themselves indications of Black women's assertions, withholding, disruption, deception, or escape—and conversely, as indications of the duping of white authority, the limitations of slavery and patriarchy, or slaveholding failure outright.[75]

This Insurgent Ground subverts the scouring of the swamps commissioned and enacted by magistrates, justices, patrollers, volunteer "parties," militia, and cavalry to extinguish all hints of free Black life and instead uses the archive these actions produced to highlight the struggle and successes of Black women, their networks, and communities. As a result of intensive searching in places, in sources, and in ways that have previously not been examined, this work is the product of stretching and reading documentary accounts noting marronage and rebellion (including newspaper reports, runaway slave advertisements, court book dockets, coroner's inquests, and planters' and merchants' wills, deeds, ledgers, diaries, and correspondence) contrary to their own intended purposes. Slave narratives, enslaved people's testimonies recorded by the Federal Writers' Project and Works Progress Administration, abolitionist literature, traveler logs, and comparative accounts of women, insurrection, and marronage emerging from elsewhere in the Atlantic world are other vital documentary sources and methodological approaches wielded here against the otherwise unstated or unwritten. In addition, the use of unwritten archives cannot be discounted. These supplemental archives include not only the swamp's archaeological record and material culture but also the swamp's geography and ecology—or, the swampscape itself—a rich collection of unwritten texts comprised of defiant terrain, wildlife, reeds, cypress trees, and waterways that map conflicting knowledges, spatialized perspectives, and contested power and that evidence what is not, nor could have been, recorded in the documentary archive about the illicit movements, worldviews, and underworlds of fugitives, maroons, and rebels.

This history of Black women's insurgency begins on the ground, with dirt, soil, mud, groves, thickets, brackish water, and freshwater, flowing and still. Chapter 1, "The Insurgent Ecology of the Great Dismal Swamp," uses firsthand colonial and antebellum accounts of the swamp atmosphere and environment as well as the swamp's unmitigated vivacity to describe and introduce the insurgent ecology of the Great Dismal Swamp—the living force of the swamp's natural world, its geographical sprawl, and its profuse ecosystem that was fundamental in aiding and encouraging subversive networks, insurgent knowledge, rebellious movement, and overt resistance throughout the region. Slave narratives and testimony illuminate Black women's integral relationships and spiritual connectedness with nature—relationships that were often shaped by Indigenous American and African ways of knowing and understanding the sacrality of plants, animals, cosmos, land, water, and earth—foregrounding how and what women gave toward freer life as swamp maroons.

Chapter 2, "Venus's Choice: Tidewater Women on the Run," follows the movements of Venus—a repeated "runaway"—and other women from Tidewater neighborhoods surrounding the swamp who chose similar courses of action. Against an extremely limited set of options, Venus, and others like her, carefully weighed and strategized the decision to flee and consort with the Dismal Swamp in ways that protected and defended their loved ones and themselves. Women's refusals to remain captive, the gendered risks and motives involved in their decisions to escape, the kinds of lives they chose to leave behind, and the conditions they faced while on the run are each explored through Tidewater women's acts of flight. Venus fled the powerful and prominent Burwell family at least twice: first in 1771 when she escaped their Smithfield, Virginia, plantation; and then in 1778, when she again fled and was suspected of "lurking" in the swamp adjoining locations of Isle of Wight County, Virginia. Her unmistakable rejection of bondage in the Tidewater plantation world and her preference for flight and courtship with marronage in the swamps seams together diverse accounts of other fugitive women like her, who elected to move errantly around and through the swampscape. These women are traceable through a slew of runaway slave advertisements that give life to their stories and the insurgent motion of their footsteps as they gave new meaning to Tidewater wetlands.

Fugitive women like Venus, who were best positioned to become Dismal Swamp maroons, are explored in chapter 3, "'They Bid Defiance to Any Force Whatever': Maroon Women and Defensive Violence." Remaining at the swamp's edges, this chapter examines the activities of borderland maroon women, who sometimes elected lives of outlawry and brigandage. These women were unafraid of joining, supporting, and defending roving maroon groups principally composed of armed men. They can be found in moments of skirmishing and active combat, embracing defensive violence against the force of recapture, and otherwise acting as willing and invested participants in a subversive underworld of maroon foraging, pillage, and plunder. These lifeways were not easy, but some women preferred the hardship, danger, and precarity of maroon banditry at the swamp's borders to the hardship, danger, and precarity of captivity and enslavement outside the swamp. At least, for these borderland maroon women, there was some satisfaction to be derived from the time they passed in the swamp, effectively and self-sufficiently evading capture and raiding those who would otherwise raid and pillage them.

Following these brazen insurgencies that convened with the swamp as base and cover, chapter 4, "'Armed in the Great Swamp': Enslaved Women and Organized Rebellion," finds that enslaved women—those at the swamp's borderlands as well as those throughout the greater Tidewater—maintained supportive, collaborative roles with fugitives, rebels, and maroons during three organized conspiracies and armed rebellions. These insurgent movements gained traction through their connection to the natural environment and plotting ground of the Dismal Swamp between 1709 and 1802. The crux of this chapter—enslaved women's previously veiled contributions to the well documented Easter Conspiracy or Easter Rebellion of 1802—reveals how women like Pamba, Nelly, Nanny, Phebe, Jude, and others devised ways to support insurrection and helped sustain maroon militancy, warfare, and organized rebellion. This chapter draws primarily from newspaper accounts and county court books containing trial records and depositions held at the Court of Oyer and Terminer; and these records make clear that enslaved, fugitive, and maroon women alike sometimes viewed protective and defensive violence as the best course of action, or as a necessity in their movement toward securing alternative modes of freer life.

Consistent with the support and encouragement enslaved women gave to organized conspiracies and attempts to execute collective rebellion, chapter 5, "Hearthstones of Their Communities: Maroon Women and Insurgent Life in the Deep Swamp," traces the roles and the labor of women in the most enduring and fortified maroon groups of the deepest and remotest swamp settlements, and finds them to have been integral to their communities. Based on written accounts of deep swamp maroon mothers, twentieth-century accounts of abandoned but survived and remaining maroon settlements, oral and documentary records of enslaved and maroon descendants, the archaeological record excavated by Daniel Sayers and the Great Dismal Swamp Landscape Study (GDSLS) between 2002 and 2013, as well as a critical reading of the swamp as itself a living archive of maroon lifeways, this chapter explores how women formed and held deep swamp maroon communities together and helped make the swamp a space of lasting insurgency. Not unlike their roles within enslaved communities, deep swamp maroon women acted not only as placemakers, providers of hearth and home, herbalists, and spiritual leaders but also as fugitive strategists, life-giving forces of multigenerational free community, and conscious advocates for reproductive justice and freedom. By examining these women's roles and insurgent reclamations of intimacy, pregnancy, childbirth, motherhood, childhood, kinship, leisure, pleasure, joy, and love, this chapter underscores the core dynamics of insurgent Black sociality as well as women's gifts to community at the heart of the swamp.

Mary's decision to flee with her four children was aided by movements that aligned with the abundant wetlands at the northwestern edges of the Great Dismal Swamp. Though she did not maroon in the swamp, her fugitive motions away from Amos Pope are mirrored by so many other women's decisions to remove themselves, and sometimes their children and families, out of bondage and closer to the spaces and grounds they believed to be safer and freer. The same impulse Mary acted upon to set herself in motion was shared by other women such as Lucy Wiggins, who also used the shelter of the swamp to travel with her family to the Union camp stationed at a Norfolk farm adjacent to the Dismal Swamp. Lucy fled from Gates County, North Carolina, at the western edge of the swamp, where she too benefited from using the swamp and wetlands as cover and as routes toward nearby Union lines.[76] These fugitive women were also joined by maroon women like Larinda, who had fled her enslavers in Portsmouth, Virginia, and who lived in the more remote swamps for three years before deciding to leave her camp there once she heard word that the Union army was stationed at a reachable distance.[77] These women were just three of thousands who lived and moved within the thick swamp and woodlands that constituted the heartland of the Tidewater region. These women knew that freedom was neither a specific location nor a confirmed destination but rather "a spatial order grounded" in their continual motion and the plot they were forging through muddy waters and insurgent ground.[78] In these movements, their hearts and the loads they bore became lighter.

ONE

The Insurgent Ecology of the Great Dismal Swamp

My first step away from the old white man was trees. Then air. Then birds. Then other people. But one day when I was sitting quiet and feeling like a motherless child, which I was, it come to me: that feeling of being part of everything, not separate at all.

ALICE WALKER, *THE COLOR PURPLE*

When Moses Grandy believed himself to be fifty-six years old, he remembered that his mother "often hid us all in the woods, to prevent master selling us." Born enslaved in Camden County, North Carolina, in the year 1786, Moses, the youngest of his mother's children, lived in an emerging world of small rural towns and few cities wedged onto stretches of dry land located between the southern end of the Great Dismal Swamp at the Albemarle Sound and the swampy northern banks of the Pasquotank River. Moses's mother had more children than the four sisters and four brothers he could remember, but they were "dead" or had been "sold away" before Moses could know them. Their enslaver, William "Billy" Grandy—a "hard-drinking man" who claimed more than eighteen slaves—would not be stopped from selling the children he enslaved for a quick and sure turn of profit. But Moses's mother also refused to be stopped when she "often" took her nine children into the marshy woods at the ends of the great swamp, repeatedly concealing them there. When Moses and his eight siblings grew thirsty, she sought water "in any hole or puddle formed by falling trees or otherwise," and served it to them. Though it was "often full of tadpoles and insects," she "strained it, and gave it round to each of [them] in the hollow of her hand." When her children grew hungry, "she gathered berries in the woods, got potatoes, raw corn, &c." After "a time" in the wilderness, Moses's mother thought it best to return to the Grandy plantation. But after her final escape to the wooded wetland, Billy Grandy did not wait long before he pried Moses's brother, "a little boy," away from her in a fateful scene as his mother, "frantic with grief," made every resistance to prevent it. After Moses's brother was sold and gone, their mother continued to make "much outcry," prompting Billy to take her to a peach tree, where he subdued her by force.

At the outskirts of the forested swamp, Moses's mother demonstrated fierce acts of love and protection for her children, acts that were in no small measure guided and made possible by her shrewd understanding of her environment and the natural world around her. She knew that the offerings of food, drink, and shelter at the swamp's edge were bountiful, and she imparted this knowledge to her children. In doing so, she also instructed that they pay close attention to a crucial lesson in their young lives: The natural environment could provide insurgent means of escape and evasion, as well as preferable alternative to subjection and the viciousness of bondage. Her instruction must have resonated deeply with her children, as Moses grew to be a man who was "glad" of the "numbers of [his] coloured brethren" who, in his words, took themselves to the "woods and swamps" and stayed there "for months, and in some cases for years." Moses's sister Tamar also learned much from their mother's teachings about the insurgent meaning of the natural environment, as she would herself become a woman who joined countless others in marooning in the swampy woods.[1] Moses's mother—and, subsequently, her children—knew what innumerable enslaved women, men, and their children in the eastern Virginia and North Carolina counties surrounding the Great Dismal Swamp also knew: The essentially inescapable two thousand square mile, sprawling morass of swamp was a near and accessible place in which to design and devise new options and possibilities for their lives that better reflected their own desires, interests, and ideas about the future.

Extending from the James River in Virginia to the Albemarle Sound in North Carolina, the great expanse of the Dismal Swamp encompassed ten Tidewater counties and enveloped the backparts of Norfolk, Portsmouth, and Suffolk in Virginia, and Edenton and Elizabeth City in North Carolina, as well as dozens of smaller, more rural villages and townships in between.[2] Moses's mother and sister were just two of thousands—conceivably tens of thousands—of people who navigated the swamp as fugitives and maroons throughout the period from 1650 to 1865.[3] Their movements into and through the swamp both responded to and helped construct the dissident force of the swampscape, inscribed as it was by subversive Black knowledges, truths, their own insistent forward trek, and an insubordinate ecology. Their steps, pathways, and placemaking gave insurgent meaning to the swamp and is archived in its distinct spatiality that proved unconquerable and defiant, just as the intrinsically elusive swamp—neither land nor water—reflexively energized the forays and movements of dissidents themselves. Fugitive and maroon women and men conspired with the wetlands around them to demand the twin rights of mobility through space and a freer life, effectively subverting the careful spatial order of exploitative plantation economies and slaveholding interests. These contestations of power remain written in Tidewater mire, marsh, and wetland woods.

For people of African descent ensnared in the Tidewater's slaveholding, capitalist societies that rendered them expendable laboring property (subjects of "two zones of death—social and corporeal"), the swampscape invited insurgent imaginings of social life and possibility where it was otherwise not meant to exist.[4] It provided alternative resources and means to make elsewhere and otherwise not merely a state of mind, but a tangible and material space of home and belonging outside of and in conflict with the terrain of captivity. Enslaved people and the fugitives and maroons they became experienced and encountered the swampland in the context of this struggle. Contesting objectives between Black insurgents and colonists and enslavers made palpable the connection between nature and freedom. Though Black people's liberatory relationships to wilderness, woods, and wetlands first arose in response to plantation slavery and agrarian rule in the nascent American colonies, these connections would certainly prove central to Black political organizing and social vitality across time.[5] But in the system of inheritable racial chattel slavery that spared nothing to loot and pillage Black bodies, lives as well as land and waters, Black interruptions in this social-spatial order—or, as J. T. Roane offers, "the plot"—arose in the form of gardens, patches, and plots of soil the enslaved nurtured, enjoyed, shared, and ate from despite the spatial and temporal constraints imposed upon them. The plot arose as the twist in the story set into motion outside of and beyond the sites and modes of fungibility and commodification. It also arose as social and political deliberations strategized across the refuge of woods and swamp meant to further reject or undo the larger institution of slavery.[6] Black people's insurgent relationships with nature were generated through this continuum of defiant acts that together created new possibilities for attaining greater autonomy, sociality, and wellness. It was Black environmental knowledge—deep understanding of and even soul-connectedness to other ways, and to ways out, including communion with plants, trees, breeze, wildlife, water, creeks, swamps, rivers, earthen roads, paths, and woods—that constituted the intellectual, cultural, political, and spiritual building blocks of an insurgent ecology.[7]

Black geographies and Black ecologies are both critical frameworks for conceptualizing Black people's reciprocal relationships with the built environment and with the ecosystems that define the natural world. The joining of the two brings Black "fugitivity, improvisation, struggle, and place-making" into focus while providing a grammar for articulating how raced and gendered experiences, protestations, and assertions of power are spatial, cartographical, and capacious for producing alternative life options and competing worlds.[8] Contributing to these spatial analytics, scholars of slavery and of slave resistance have also applied conceptual frameworks for locating and describing the insurgent range of Black socio-spatial acts, including "rival geographies," "geographies of evasion and resistance," "insurgent geographies," the "maroon landscape," "maroon ecologies," "wetlands of defiance," and "forests of freedom."[9] Similarly, but beyond a purely geographic framing, insurgent ecologies name the relationships between subjugated people's social and political movements and ecosystems shaped by both built and natural spatial arrangements that yield solace, independence, and social vivacity and also new capacities for audacious, overt, and transformative subversive action against captivity, dispossession, and the fatal logics of gendered racial capitalism. In the context of plantation slavery surrounding the Great Dismal Swamp, the insurgent ecology scopes geographical *and* ecological opportunities for heightened enslaved mobility and a range of fugitive acts including sustained marronage and outright rebellion. It identifies the swamp's living, sentient ecological properties (both material and immaterial) as a sprawling and connective system, rich with topographical and natural provisions and opportunities for

Black women and men to breathe deeply, network, plot, evade, and—through gendered motives and options—to undermine and refuse slavery altogether.

The history of illicit and insurgent movement, marronage, and rebellion in the Dismal Swamp foregrounds and informs the broader radical tradition of Black placemaking, epistemologies, and poetics—the memories, stories, foodways, healing traditions, musics, ritual, poetry, and theory, or the "veritable archive of consciousness, subaltern visions, insurgent spatial practices and knowledges"—that create Black material spaces and sociosymbolic worlds.[10] In spatializing these knowledges and traditions and in calling attention to the ways these poetics are connected to flourishing and abundant ecologies, the history and practice of marronage throughout Tidewater woods and swamps further evidences Black worldmaking as ongoing resistance to depredating regimes of exploit, extraction, and disposability that began at the dawn of coloniality. Yet few have attended to Black women's environmental and ecological conceptualization, creation, and nurture of alternatives to these regimes, despite the fact that Black women have always been ecocritical and in tune with the natural world as a vehicle of their self-expression and worth, just as they have always maintained geographies of their protestations, critiques, needs, and stories.[11] This history of Black women's vision, creativity, and refusal in the Tidewater swampscape is one endeavor to do so. Venturing into the Great Dismal Swamp, Black women's fugitive movements and the geographies they produced and traversed can be located and explored, just as their ecophilosophies and "ecopoetics" also emerge as fundamental to arranging and giving sustained meaning to the insurgent ecology there.[12]

The American wilderness and nature itself have always been sources of imagination, expression, assertion, and creation in the lives of African-descended women. As conduits of African Indigenous cosmologies and conveyors of the wisdom in calling forth the natural world as material aid, spiritual animism, and intellectual guidance, Black women have always viewed living ecosystems in the natural environment as liberatory sites of transcendence and movement beyond multilayered and intersecting oppressions. In the words of Black feminist ecocritic Chelsea Frazier, Black women "have always developed their own alternative understandings of the interconnectedness of all things, and these ecological understandings have centered the health, well-being, and sustainability of Black, African-descended women across the Diaspora since time immemorial."[13] Against law, social custom, and the very economic underpinnings of slavery, Black women have long dared to conjure ways to care for and protect their bodies, hearts, and minds as well as those of their children, loved ones, and communities by connecting with water and woods by their own rites and through their own convictions about their rights to movement and to free life. The audacity of Black women to insert themselves as being a part of nature and therefore as part of something "beautiful, stable, and normative"—something greater than the ugly morbidity of the despoiling plantation world—amounted to an insurgency no one could prevent Black women from committing. Gesturing "beyond trauma," Black women viewed and encountered the natural world as a medium of quiet, reflection, meditation, critique, comfort, pleasure, and strategy. In these ways, they claimed a place in the advancement of their own interests as well as the interests of their communities.[14] Nature provided the cover, the calm, and the elsewhere from which Black women could theorize their next steps forward and reimagine and revise their lived experience, their objectives, and their futures.

In Black women's rendering of the insurgent ecology of the Dismal Swamp, the vast, forested, riparian swampscape nourished, channeled, and offered refuge to their active plotting of lives other than lives shaped by unending forced work, harm, and sexual and reproductive violence. Women connected with the swamp in autonomous moments of self-possession as ordinary individuals, as mothers, healers, herbalists and horticulturalists, spiritual leaders, and as designers of their own means of escape and well-being. As evidenced here and in the chapters that follow, women who made the swamp a place of home, kinship, sociality, and transitory or enduring refusal were also prepared to protect themselves and their claims to these aspects of free life by way of physical defense and retreat into the loophole of the swampscape. The natural world of the Dismal Swamp beckoned and outfitted women's abilities to implement a variety of insurgencies, including claims to and assertions of their natural rights to safety, rest, pleasure, leisure, health, and voluntary productive and reproductive labor in their lives. The ecological ethics, consciousness, and reverence for nature as a sacred, divine, and ancestral force among people of African descent also meant that Black women in the Dismal Swamp counties—women who could readily and frequently go to and revel in verdant boggy forests—did so equipped with these understandings of nature as interconnected to their own wholeness, being, direction, and quality of life. Their ties with nature helped direct them away from containment and captivity and positioned them to become at once among the first abolitionists, environmentalists, and advocates for reproductive freedoms, as their movements through and across the swamps were fundamentally protestations against extractive interference, exploitation, and the continued destruction of lands and waterways, as well as their own bodily harm, ill-use, and presumed disposability. From the standpoint of their eyes, wombs, and feet, the swamp signified a site of renewal, transformation, and transcendence.[15] It was out of these insurgent relationships with the imminent swampscape that untold and unquantifiable numbers of Black women in the Tidewater chose fugitivity, marronage, and rebellion.

SACRED WATERS: INDIGENOUS KNOWLEDGE AND THE SWAMP'S EARLIEST INSURGENT WOMEN

In 1619, after African women such as Angela and Isabell became the first to disembark the "floating dungeons" heralded as the *White Lion* and the *Treasurer*, they were followed by a slow but growing stream of Africans forced upon colonial Virginia and its eastern wetlands. Into the 1620s, women like Mary continued to be trafficked from the shores, watersheds, and rivers between the Gulf of Guinea and the Kongo-Angola region, across the open Atlantic, sometimes coursing first through Caribbean archipelagos before they reached the beaches and banks of the Tidewater.[16] The profitability of the tobacco plant and the chartering of the British Royal African Company in 1672 led to a population of Africans that grew slowly at first (from twenty-three in 1625 to three hundred by 1650), but that increased significantly by importations of more than one thousand Africans into the colony per year by the end of the seventeenth century.[17] By then, newly captive women such as Doll, Nanny, Kate, and Tulie joined thousands of other Africans and their descendants in the Tidewater. These women entered Surry and James City Counties at the northern fringe of the Dismal Swamp as "headrights"—literally—as colonial rights to land was determined by the number of persons, or "heads," aspiring landowners could claim, at a rate of fifty acres of land per head.[18] Though this system of colonial expansion and conquest of Tidewater land hinged upon the slave trade and slaveholders' claims to enslaved women and men, Black women were among those who would not be stopped from asserting their value differently. In uncontainable and uncapturable ways, they applied linked ecological and spiritual knowledge of their relationship with woods, water, and wetlands to consort with the swamp against the proprietary and extractive objectives of slaveholders—giving the tangle of flooded Tidewater forests a new insurgent meaning.

Born of the water, Black women entered the Tidewater world in which external claims to their bodies as well as rape and sexual violence against them could not be disentangled from conquest of land and capitalist attempts to conquer and control water. It took only fifty-five years following the first sustained English invasion at Jamestown and a little over four tenuous decades following Angela's and Isabell's arrival to the colony for Virginia to sanction heritable slavery and, jointly, the lawful and encouraged rape of women of African descent. By 1662, the first British North American colony had wasted little time in being first to enact and declare that "all children borne in this country shalbe held bond or free only according to the condition of the mother"—an effort to formally alleviate "doubts" as to the status of children "got by any Englishman upon a negro woman."[19] Though this was primarily an attempt to make profitable the "excess" of mixed-race children born to African-descended women, the law's insistent regulation of enslavability by way of (nonwhite) maternal descent also applied to Native American bondwomen. Thus was formalized a sexual economy in which customary rape and reproductive exploitation were wielded as implements of colonization, English claims to lands and waterways, and the establishment and continuance of extractive plantation economies.[20] The law licensed and even incentivized the already-regular occurrence of sexual violence against and exploitation of Native and Black women, effectively establishing white male access to women's bodies as natural and normative pronouncements of their rule and governance over both people and "country." As Sharon Block has noted, sexual violence against nonwhite women "extended far beyond desires for sexual satisfaction into a purposeful lesson about their cultural groups' degraded status," defilement, inferiority, and subordination—a veritable "sexual imperialism" of conquest, slavery, and war.[21] Black women in the Tidewater—like the Virginia and Carolina wetlands themselves—were to be plucked, taken, and expended as commodities of trade, sale, and ownership. As seizable, usable "things," colonial and slaveholding claims to their captive bodies were analogous to those made to the Tidewater itself.[22] Positioned alongside flora, fauna, woods, rivers, and swamps, Black women were rendered another kind of natural resource for the taking—one that, like the wetland soil they would traverse, was expected to reproduce and supply an increase of goods and chattel.

The Tidewater's first Black women met the rivers and swamps, rich soils, and teeming forests that characterize and give life to southeastern Virginia and northeastern North Carolina already well acquainted with marshy shallows, the currents, the yield, and the channeling of water.[23] The Tidewater they encountered was a rich ecosystem fed by tidal freshwater rivers and watershed from the Atlantic Ocean itself—the conduit of their entry. Black women found themselves amid this freshwater ecosystem that extended from the southern tiers of the Chesapeake Bay to the Albemarle and Pamlico Sounds of North Carolina and had been formed by regionally distinctive geological events in the course of the earth's natural life. The recession of the Tidewater's Atlantic shoreline during the last glacial period, some twelve thousand years ago, initiated ecological shifts that would set the stage for Black women's struggle to live during the crisis of English colonization and slavery at the dawn of the seventeenth century. The will of the earth left land escarpments and steep slopes kept saturated with remnants of the ocean, rainfall, and raised sea levels from rhythms of climate and weather. What resulted was a great accumulation of peatland forested swamp filled with clogged and slowly decaying organic matter (or peat), producing blackwater bogs and inundated wooded marshlands. These ancient wetlands enabled the maturation of massive swamps—the largest of which remains the Great Dismal—but also the formation of bays, lakes, extensive river systems, large freshwater and brackish sounds, and water-saturated forests supporting rich and diverse life. This Tidewater region became one of the largest freshwater wetlands in North America, "fully comparable in scale and biological wonder" to the Mississippi Delta, the Everglades, and the headwaters of the Okefenokee Swamp.[24]

But what separated the Tidewater from other swampscapes was the lapping of the tidewater at the Virginia–North Carolina eastern shores, as the swamps and rivers there convened with distant worlds of African homelands and maritime commerce and exchange, streamed and towed directly by the Atlantic Ocean—channeling the very epicenter of British North American colonization and slavery. The meeting of waters from the shores to the hinterlands and back again coursed and carried rising colonial desire for exploitable lands and labor capacious bodies, and the brutal rule of colonial Virginia with North Carolina following suit. A great deterrent to these courses of conquest was extant in the outstretching mass of concentrated marsh and woodland swamps colonists thought "dismal." Extending approximately sixty miles from north to south and forty miles from east to west, this Dismal Swamp formed the heartland of the 150-mile-long and 100-mile-wide greater Virginia and North Carolina Tidewater region.[25]

In Virginia, the northern swamp joins the Powhatan River, now known widely by its colonized name—the James River.[26] This river is the Virginia Tidewater's major throughway, flowing east into the Chesapeake Bay and Atlantic Ocean. Emptying into the James River are the Nansemond and Elizabeth Rivers, tributaries that themselves break into numerous upstream branches, creeks, and lesser waterways, each of which directly penetrates the northern reaches of the Dismal Swamp. In North Carolina, the Chowan, Perquimans, and Pasquotank Rivers as well as lesser rivers are fed from the southern ends of the great swamp and flow south into the Albemarle Sound before opening up to the Atlantic Ocean.[27] Forming the western border of the swamp, the Nansemond Scarp is the principal escarpment, featuring several ancient drainages cut across the swamp's western edge that direct tens of thousands of gallons of water into the swamp annually, from west to east, sometimes sourced from waterways as far away as the Virginia Piedmont.[28] Lake Drummond—named after North Carolina's first colonial governor and considered the "jewel" of the Dismal Swamp—is a 3,100-acre freshwater lake situated in the western center of the swamp. One of only two natural lakes in Virginia, its oval-shaped circumference is entirely surrounded by thick and densely forested swampland. The southern branches of the Nansemond and Elizabeth Rivers in Virginia, and the Perquimans, North, and North West Rivers in North Carolina (the latter two of which form the border between what later become Camden and Currituck Counties), flow out of Lake Drummond and into the Albemarle Sound to the south and the James River to the north, before meeting the Chesapeake Bay and Atlantic Ocean.[29] (See map 1.)

When Black women and men first met and encountered this landscape of swamps and wetlands, the Tidewater had already been the home of dozens of Native nations who, for twelve thousand years at least, defined themselves, their families, their communities, and their nations synonymously with these abundant waterways. The Powhatan, including the Appamattuck and Pamunkey, the Tuscarora, Secotan, and Pamlico were among some of the most prominent and earliest inhabitants of the wider Virginia and North Carolina Tidewater region. In the wetlands comprising the most immediate region around the Dismal Swamp, the Algonquian-speaking Weapomeoc (including the Yeopim, Poteskeet, Paspatank, and Perquimans), the Chowanoc, Warraskoyack, Nansemond, Chesapeake, and the Iroquois-speaking Meherrin were those to first understand the swamps and "pocosins" (an Algonquian word meaning, "swamp-on-a-hill") as vital to their social, political, and spiritual identities.[30] Connective rivers and wetlands shaped Indigenous people's kinship relations and politics—inseparable from their spiritualities and the sacred—in ways that manifested, as one scholar has shown, "*through* waterways and, often, through the Indigenous women who had specific relationships to them." The Powhatan, for example—a greater polity of thirty-two different Algonquian communities that had joined together before English arrival and that included the Warraskoyack and the Nansemond of the northwestern reaches of the Dismal Swamp—placed their towns along the inner curves of the Powhatan River, the Nansemond River, and each of the other major rivers of the region, as well as along their offshoots and tributaries. In this network of communities and wetlands they called Tsenacommacah, fishing, travel, communication, social life, and diplomacy were facilitated by way of water. This is also true of Native peoples in the greater Tidewater region outside of the Powhatan territory, such as the Algonquian peoples of North Carolina. Names of rivers were often the same words communities used to describe themselves (i.e., Chowan River/Chowanoc, Yeopim River/Yeopim, Nansemond River/Nansemond, Pasquotank River/Paspatank) while other crucial ecological features such as specific plants or animals were also used to name the tracts of lands and waters that communities considered important. Throughout, Indigenous nations and communities viewed themselves, their relationships with each other, with wildlife, and with the wetland ecology itself "in concert together as a community of relations" arranged by the natural bounty and flow of water.[31]

By the end of the seventeenth century, as the profitability of tobacco led the Royal African Company to increase the importation of captive African women and men, Indigenous Tidewater communities had been studying the possessive, accumulative, and dominating objectives of English colonists for nearly one hundred years. As the English claimed more of the Tidewater and established more plantations, Native people were the first to respond. Forced to confront the rising colonial order, these Indigenous communities collaborated with the wetlands in strategies of resistance and self-defense.

Native women—particularly knowledgeable about and expert in Tidewater plant life and wetland ecologies—consulted the natural environment to devise ways to undermine and refute the expanding plantation world. When a 1646 treaty dictated that the Powhatans would be restricted from accessing downriver lands they held as sacred, ancestral sites of ritual, memory, plant gathering, fishing, and oystering traditions, it was the women who "promptly" opposed.[32] Women across the Tidewater typically served their communities as those responsible for planting, producing, and preparing their family's food. They were the water bearers of their communities—fetching, hauling, and boiling water. But they were also expert foragers of wild plants that sometimes grew several miles away, in distant swamps and marshes. In these roles, women were highly mobile, "no woman was confined by her work to the house and its vicinity," and they were especially skilled and practiced in the use of canoes. These were vehicles necessary for transporting precious wild plants and food as well as "great quantities of reeds" for making mats, and marsh tubers for making bread in the absence of corn.[33] In pressuring their communities to demand new terms to the treaty, the women both rejected the colonial agenda and conveyed their environmental concerns about how the English terms would imperil the relationships their communities had with the wetlands and waterways. In the decades that followed, Native women's protests helped lead to subsequent concessions made by Virginia's House of Burgesses that permitted the Powhatans to gather roots, wild fruits, and other plants—but only if they had applied for and obtained a license to do so outside of fenced plantation boundaries.[34]

Yet these constraints did not prevent Indigenous peoples from utilizing their knowledge of Tidewater ecologies against colonial efforts to capture and contain them and to diminish and destroy their sacred and vital relationships with the wetlands. For example, Powhatan women, who were members of communities that recognized their value through matrilineal and bilateral inheritance and descent, lived in communities where they were in control of their own bodies, both before and after marriage. It is not surprising then, that these women took to the water with strong convictions about their own bodily autonomy that, guised as sexual overture, effectively overturned Englishmen's well-established beliefs about the twin obtainability of land and women's bodies for sexual use and exploit.[35] On at least two occasions, the Powhatan women employed their familiarity with and knowledge of Tidewater rivers to appear in places where they knew Englishmen would be susceptible to their lures and enticements. After seducing the men with propositions that they "barge" and row back into their villages to "make merry," the women then proceeded to kill the unsuspecting men, in one case chasing them into the forest before doing so. In another instance, women of high status such as Queen Cockacoeske of the Pamunkey Powhatan, along with her kinswomen and men, used their expertise of freshwater swamp and riverine ecologies to successfully escape, evade, and deliberate against persistent colonial violence and pursuit. In 1676, Cockacoeske and a young boy, together with a female elder and others from their community, fooled Nathaniel Bacon and his followers using their knowledge of a stretch of swamp the English called Dragon Swamp, just north of the Pamunkey (or York) River. Bacon was intent on destroying these "Indian enemies," as well as their rights to the land and resources he coveted and believed more Virginia colonists should claim and seize. Bacon believed he could achieve these objectives through "wholesale Native enslavement"—beginning with the symbolically important defeat of Cockacoeske, the heir to Powhatan leadership. Bacon and hundreds of his armed followers raided Pamunkey villages in search of Cockacoeske, before taking to the swamps and marshes to look for her there. Along the way, the men came across a Powhatan path and soon after encountered Cockacoeske's elder kinswoman. With ease and skill, this Pamunkey elder led the men astray, costing the white men a day and a half of wasted effort traipsing through the swamps. The elder's deception signaled the ultimate sacrifice she could have made for her people and for the vital wetlands, as the men thereafter took her life for it. While Bacon witlessly searched Dragon Swamp, Cockacoeske was moving deeper through it, accompanied by the young boy she traveled with, who was skilled in bringing her turtles for sustenance. There from her swampy post, so well concealed as it was in the cleverest of recesses, Cockacoeske outwitted her ungainly pursuers.[36]

Black women and men would soon become the primary inhabitants of these same swamps, bringing with them their own Indigenous African ways of knowing and understanding the natural world. Much like the Tidewater Native peoples, African women and men entering the region shared in a cosmology that understood nature as a spiritual home animated by soul, sacred entities, and energies such as ancestors and other divine spirits that were considered inseparable from their own being and sense of self. The natural world and its ecosystems were perceived not as removed concepts or things, but as actively connected forces informing the meaning of life and the source of all knowledge related to spiritual and social existence. For Africans, cross-culturally, nature was an experienced, pervasive reality that unified people with animals, plants, earth, water, weather, and skies through a strong collective sense of the sacred. Within this worldview, forests and waterways were at once both founts of essential ecological resources and sacred sites of spiritual significance and interaction.[37] Despite colonial efforts, the transatlantic slave trade, and the entrenchment of plantation slavery, enslaved African peoples' spiritual traditions and rituals—as well as the ways each was understood as tied to the ecologies of the natural world—were not knowledges easily bound, captured, or diminished. As scholars have pointed out, Africans and their descendants held closely their truths about the cosmos, nature, and the sacred—a reality that shaped both their adaptation to new and foreign ecologies, landscapes, and climes and their insuppressible reformation of self-determined life on American ground.[38] Their powerful faith in the spiritual and metamorphic potential of wilderness helped form the basis of an ongoing sacrality "ever poised to incite volatility" and disruption within colonial regimes that would give rise to a range of insurgencies against them.[39]

African descendants' uncontainable sense of the sacred and its inseparability from the natural world is evident in the significance Black women and men have placed on wetlands and on water itself. Rivers, oceans, streams, lakes, marshes, currents, channels, tides, shoals, and swamps have long been spiritually and socially meaningful connective spaces in the lives and movements of African people. This remained true of Africans and their American-born descendants in captivity, particularly as most captives entering the Americas came from societies oriented by a confluence of rivers and streams and the presence of plentiful wetlands and marshes.[40] Facing enslavement and bondage on the other side of the Atlantic, African descendants along the eastern shores of Virginia and North Carolina understood the Tidewater's essential boundlessness of water as the source and sustenance of life, and they responded to these wetlands with their own irrepressibility and mobility. The impossibility of capturing, containing, or preventing water's seep and flow evoked spiritual, social, and epistemic human connections to possibility and limitlessness—a power that Black people used against the imposed constructions of colonial and state borders and bounds.[41]

Water constituted a key element in African cosmologies about the natural world, and captive people first entering the Tidewater would have perceived it as a living spirit made up of varied sacred properties and forces. The Akan of the Gold Coast believed that some of the most powerful deities *were* the most important bodies of water—lakes and rivers and their outlets.[42] The Yoruba of the Niger River Delta distinguished the orisha (deity) Yemoja, the mother of all other orishas and supreme spirit of the water, for she protected sacred waters—from the rivers to the sea—and she commanded all other underwater women spirits. Through the ripple and breeze of their waters, Yemoja and other water goddesses gave and restored coolness, calm, and peace and soothed the environments they hydrated, fed, and nurtured. Oya and Oshun were other powerful riverine goddesses engaged in healing and giving by means of cool water, sweetness, and love but also cautioning with the wrath of their depths, storms, and destructive power, sometimes themselves brandishing swords against evil in the protection of sacred waters.[43] In Guinea and Sierra Leone, Temne women initiated intimate ritual relationships with river spirits to whom they appealed for the delivery of healthy children and protection for children already born.[44] Enslaved people in the Tidewater shared in this tradition of conversing with the spiritual essences of waters and wetland environments.

Through slave trade, the Atlantic Ocean became the fluid highway transporting these cosmologies as captive Africans carried these ways of knowing to American shores, modifying and adapting them along the way to accommodate new ecologies and to confront the extreme duress of colonial slavery. During horrific Middle Passages as well as along the banks of waters on both sides of the Atlantic Ocean, the bays, seas, rivers, and swamps became conduits of escape, and in cases when captives elected bodily death through self-immersion into rivers and oceans, water also signified a channel of return to kin and home through their spiritual belief that its sacred nature would carry them away to the world of ancestors.[45] The sacrality of waterways persisted and evolved among the enslaved in North America, the Caribbean, and Latin America through the resilient African-based spiritual practices of hoodoo, Vodou, Candomblé, and Santería, in which water spirits continued to bridge the material and spiritual worlds and offer sources of tranquility, inviolability, and power to a people who were otherwise systematically denied all.[46] Rivers, streams, bayous, and swamps welcomed Africa's descendants as sacred sites of spiritual guidance, renewal, cleanse, calm, and strength, but also as fluid avenues of flight, escape, resistance, and social vitality.[47]

Just as colonial forces could conquer neither the Tidewater swamps and marshes nor the cultural meanings they held among the Indigenous Americans, so too was the institution of slavery unable to conquer the beliefs of the Tidewater's African-descended women and men who maintained that the rivers, swamps, and waterlogged forests around them were spaces of spiritual significance, healing, protection, evasion, and opposition. Rooted in Indigenous knowledge, this manner of communing with this saturated environment presented insurgent potential, since it was a means of moving away from modes and sites of bondage and abuse toward lifeways and environments that invited enjoyment, spiritual guidance, soul centering, and the capacity for intellectual, social, and political deliberation. Rivers and streams flowing into and out of the Dismal Swamp became channels of information, news, and ideas; and they also signaled distinct opportunities for resistive movement, travel, and escape. The region's abundance of swamps, neither purely land nor water, provided "terraqueous terrains"—liminal spaces of insurgent possibility, defiant of categorization and control by virtue of their unpredictable and unruly dense vegetation, incalculable murky waters, and intrinsic indeterminacy.[48] In its constant state of uncontainable movement, transition, flow, and flux, the waterborne ecology of the Great Dismal Swamp and greater Tidewater welcomed Black women's and men's own uncontainable movements and associations with water—both "fluttering, stretching, and changing" against the tenuous claims of slaveholders and proprietors.[49]

With these unbound and irrepressible relationships with water and wetlands at play, Native peoples and African women and men sometimes worked together in consulting the Dismal Swamp for refuge, guidance, and strategies to counter colonization and slavery in ways that were collaborative and mutually beneficial. This is particularly true in the late seventeenth and early eighteenth centuries, when Indigenous Tidewater peoples still made up a significant population in their homelands, joined by the steadily rising numbers of captive Africans and their enslaved descendants.[50]

The 1730s saw Virginia's highest importation rates of Africans, with 15,700 captives forced onto its shores between 1730 and 1740 alone. African-born captive women brought to Virginia entered a male-dominant world; they represented only 30 percent of the enslaved individuals brought into the colony between 1710 and 1774. Yet other than the 1700s and 1710s—a time when African-born captives in Virginia constituted up to 52 percent of the total enslaved population—American-born African descendants were the majority of the Tidewater's enslaved population. This is because by the 1740s, Virginia planters had begun to cut back on direct imports of Africans into the region following a decrease in the profitability of tobacco farming and a surplus of enslaved laborers. This surplus was brought about by a combination of the heavy importation of Africans during the previous decade and the "natural" increase of the enslaved population through decades of enslaved women's reproductive labor and sexual exploitation. By 1775, at the dawn of the Revolutionary War, enslaved people in Virginia constituted 40 percent of the total population, with nine out of every ten enslaved individuals born in the colony. By 1800, enslaved people made up to 48 percent of the total population in Virginia—a number that would never again be as high—with less than 1 percent of this enslaved population born in Africa.[51] For these reasons, it was around the turn of the eighteenth century and during its first three decades that Tidewater women of African descent had the greatest opportunity to collaborate with the remaining Native peoples in consorting with the swamps and wetlands against colonial and slaveholding conquest of lands, use of indentured labor, and enslavement.

Examples of these collaborative relationships between Indigenous peoples and enslaved Black women and men have been documented. Women like Pamba—most likely born in Africa before she sailed the James River toward the northern Dismal Swamp region sometime before 1709—used the swamps to "escape by force," to maroon, and to conspire to "make insurrection" among the company of noted male insurgents. These men included her husband Peter, Salvadore "an Indian," Scipio, and others.[52] By 1728, at least one other woman of African descent was documented by a Virginia colonist who stumbled upon her family in an "Obscure Part" of the Dismal Swamp. The colonist described the woman as having been sheltering herself there, along with her husband and family, taking great "care to keep least in sight." The record also notes other "marooner" residents in secluded places in the swamp—a man and a woman—living a few days' walk from the woman and her family of "certain slaves." Notably, the couple was described not as fugitives from slavery sheltering themselves in the woods and swamps, but instead by their manner of habitation and "raiment," both of which reflected the style of "Indian fashion."[53] Only a decade earlier, following prolonged English invasion and a subsequent war with colonial authority in North Carolina, South Carolina, and draconian Virginia, remnant members of the powerful Tuscarora Nation were among the first to find refuge in the Dismal Swamp, moving from its southern edges toward the then-still-undetermined Virginia border in the swamp's interior. This violent unrest came to a head between 1713 and 1714, when the three colonies joined together in defeating the steadfast and defiant Tuscarora Nation and its sympathizing Old Albemarle settlers. In the words of the Virginia proprietors, these allies were also known as a "gang of tramps and rioters," made up of "running servants and all others that fly from the due execution of the laws" into the "sink" of the then largely unchartered North Carolina wetlands.[54] In the swamp, Tuscarora women and men joined other Indigenous people who had taken refuge there during the turmoil, such as the entire surviving Machapunga of the Secotan people.[55] During this tenuous early colonial period, Black women fugitives and maroons were among the swamp's inhabitants with the greatest opportunities to share African Indigenous knowledge and understandings of water and wetlands with the Native peoples seeking similar relationships with the swamp as an ecology of sacred life, refuge, and refusal.

Following the suppression of the Tuscarora and Old Albemarle settler society, which had been the greatest hindrance to cementing North Carolina as an effective plantation economy and slaveholding society, the colony's enslaved population grew from about nine hundred in 1710 to over one hundred thousand by 1790.[56] Swamp wilderness and the ecology of the harsh and markedly shallower northeastern North Carolina coastline also helped discourage colonization, seagoing trade, and plantation agriculture for lack of arable land and safe ports in which to harbor ships. The swamps and wetlands encroaching on the Albemarle Sound long remained resistant to plantation agriculture and the rise of tobacco and rice in ways the Virginia and South Carolina Eastern Seaboard had not. Instead, subsistence farming, small farm agriculture of staples like corn and wheat, and maritime trade in lumber, turpentine, tar, pitch, and other naval stores constituted North Carolina's primary industries and occupations. This economy meant that increasing numbers of captive Africans were very gradually brought into the colony.[57]

By 1800, Black women and men living in stewardship with the swamp's porous and immersive insurgent grounds had become the swamp's primary human population. Moving against slavery's extractive, exploitative, and commercial interests, the swamp's Black inhabitants had grown in number, becoming much larger than any other group.[58] African-descended women and men in the Tidewater approached the swamp bearing generations of Indigenous knowledge and relating to the sacred essence of nature in order to create spaces and modes of health and wellness, and to save and defend their lives. Their expertise of coastal waters, fishing, plant and animal life, seasonal cycles, and weather fluctuations—sometimes also benefiting from the aid of Indigenous people's ancient knowledge and respect for Tidewater ecologies—remained crucial assets to their insurgent arrangements of the great swamp and its surrounding wetlands.[59]

BLACK WOMEN IN FLUX: ARRANGEMENTS OF THE INSURGENT ECOLOGY

By the time Moses Grandy's mother fled with her children to the woods at the southern end of the Dismal Swamp at the dawn of the nineteenth century, Black women had been engaging the swamp through a range of similar insurgent acts for at least 150 years. When Moses was a child in the 1780s and 1790s, he received from his mother an education in the ways movement, changeability, fluidity, and flux were resistive modes and strategies that were invited and invigorated by the abundant forests and swamps adjoining the geography of their bondage. When his mother modeled flight and marronage in these woods and swamps, she and her children joined other women and children who also knew that their own willful motion, defiance, and errantry would be met by nature's response: ministering preferable and alternative lifeways and protection. Black women of the Tidewater knew that fallen trees signaled shelter, that rich vegetation meant healing and sustenance, that the flooded ground provided drink, and that the hollow of their own hands were the cups by which to sip and to soothe. Like Moses, his sister Tamar also learned from the example set by their mother. As a woman, Tamar returned to the swamp and moved through the same thickly wooded sprawls her mother had in an effort to escape sale and enslavers who "used her very cruelly." For several years she lived in the swamp, in a "den" she made for herself. Although Tamar marooned by herself, she was supported with provisions and encouragement provided by her brother Moses, her enslaved husband, and her mother, in addition to the sustenance and resolve she derived on her own.[60] Black women's willingness to shift and move alongside their reciprocal relationship with the living ecology of the Dismal Swamp helped compose and arrange its insurgent meaning.

Shallow swamp floor, Great Dismal Swamp, Gates County, North Carolina. *(Photo by the author, 2013.)*

The Tidewater's Black women in flux—motioning otherwise, elsewhere, and away, toward the Dismal Swamp—can be understood as both stewards of this wetland ecosystem and stewards of their own embodied futures. Both were insurgent arrangements within the slaveholding regime. As the labors of their feet and minds negotiated between water and land, these women maintained knowledge passed down to them by their foremothers and forefathers about the sacrality of their relationships with water, earth, and plant and animal life; they extended skill sets in healing and agriculture inherited from African and Indigenous American traditions and developed through their own work; and they upheld the core value of cultivating harmonious relationships with connective ecosystems.[61]

Black women moving in and through the Dismal Swamp communed with clumps of white cedar, juniper, gum, pine, oak, poplar, and bald cypress—some enormous and over a thousand years old, with roots and protruding knees shooting upward through the swamp water. Miles of aquatic plants such as duckweed, reeds, and cattails grew where dense forest canopies and pockets of open water allowed. Fugitive and maroon women knew and learned that the swamp also offered free life and sanctuary to black bears, raccoons, mink, deer, opossums, ducks, partridges, pheasants, muskrats, river otters, frogs, turtles, and snakes. They also knew that their movements through the swamp were shared with the courses of several species of fish, including pickerel, crappie, sunfish, catfish, longnose gar, and perch as well as with the flights and flurries of hundreds of species of birds, including geese, woodpeckers, swallowtails, and warblers.[62] Within the swamp's interior, Black women met these creatures as they traversed through lush vegetation; fresh, dark water described as "healthful, and pleasant to drink"; and drier patches of risen land, or "islands," sometimes spanning dozens of acres.[63] It was on these islands, which were not perpetually flooded and under water, that Black women could apply their agricultural knowledge to raise rice, grain, corn, potatoes, and other vegetation natural to the swamp.[64] Tamar was certainly someone who did so, as even before she marooned at the swamp's southern edge she was accustomed to clearing "a bit of ground" where she raised corn and flax—skills enslaved women and girls commonly practiced in the way of gardening and subsistence farming.[65] Conversant with the living, sprawling ecosystem of the Dismal Swamp, fugitive and maroon women joined and experienced it in gratitude for the bounty of its lush and lavish offerings that allied with their freedom to move, choose, and live differently.

Yet, the swamp's intense ecology also meant that it presented no shortage of difficulties and challenges to human habitation and navigation. Swarms of mosquitoes, sometimes as thick as clouds; innumerable land- and water-dwelling venomous snakes and spiders; the presence of sizable predatory animals; the density of vegetation; the vexing uncertainty of the depth of black water, including the trouble of anticipating the entanglement of tree roots and knobs submerged beneath the dark water, were all factors that made movement through the swamp challenging.

In 1835, for example, Harriet Jacobs—born enslaved in Edenton, North Carolina—escaped the sexual violence and persecution of her master and his wife and their designs to further torment her through the abuse of her two children. The town and its inhabitants shared the southwestern reaches of the Dismal Swamp, and Harriet knew that fleeing into a portion of the swamp known locally as Snaky Swamp was the best step forward in protecting herself and her children. She arranged for her aunt's "seafaring" husband—a waterman with crucial knowledge of the rivers and their connections to other wetlands—to row her "three miles" by river into this remote swamp. Although her stay there was fleeting, Harriet recalled "bamboos and bamboos of all descriptions" that were "so high and thick that it was impossible to see beyond a very short distance." She wrote that she had been "covered with hundreds

Reflection of water on forested swamp floor, Great Dismal Swamp, Chesapeake, Virginia.
(Photo by the author, 2022.)

Great Dismal Swamp at Gates County, North Carolina.
(Photo by the author, 2013.)

of mosquitos" before using the repellent of tobacco smoke to disperse them. Harriet could not forget seeing "snake after snake crawling round"—these "larger than any [she] had ever seen" before—yet in her words, "far less dreadful to my imagination than the White men" of Edenton.[66] Despite the environmental challenges of navigating the swamp, Black women's insistence that they move into and arrange themselves and their interests there anyway proved that these difficulties were surmountable and that the causes of their movements in the swamp were, indeed, urgent and dire.

The movements of Black women throughout the Dismal Swamp, and the presence of maroon women within the swamp, should not be overlooked as the primary reason colonists and slaveholders were frustrated with and threatened by the insurgent nature of the swamp's ecology. After all, Black women's investments in allying with the swamp helped make it an insurgent space that was not only defiant of colonial and slaveholding attempts to control, subdue, and exploit it, but also resistant to slavery's capacity to possess and exploit Black women's bodily futures and reproductive labor. Noting the swamp as a wild and untamable space, even before Black women and men made clear that the swamp would also constitute a massive loophole in their slaveholding authority and control, white stakeholders of the slaveholding regime consistently considered the swamp with great fear, trepidation, and scorn. During his 1728 expedition to survey the Dismal Swamp in an effort to determine the Virginia–North Carolina border at the Eastern Seaboard, the wealthy Virginia planter and distinguished Col. William Byrd II of Westover—one of the leading commissioners of the Council of Virginia between 1711 and 1744—wrote the first proposal to have the swamp drained to accommodate agricultural commerce and to provide easier passage between the colonies. He described the "mass of mire and dirt" a "horrible," "dreadful," and "filthy circumference," a "vast body of dirt and nastiness," a "mere quagmire, trembling under the feet of those that walk upon it." With "every impression instantly filled with water," the swamp was distinguishable by its "overgrown reeds, ten or twelve feet high," in which his company's "feet were perpetually entangled."[67] A 1784 account described the swamp as "indeed dismal far beyond description," for "no noise, clamour, or hallooing . . . can be heard," save for the unending raucous of insects, reptiles, and the constant rustling of jungle-like vegetation.[68] By 1805, the *Literary Magazine and American Register* reported that the swamp was "scarcely possible to pass through," for "the foot, at every step, sinks not less than twelve or fifteen inches deep into the soil. The trees . . . grow very thick together . . . and [are] composed of such tenacious, perplexing, and thorny wood . . . the flesh [is] wounded and torn at every point, and a path [is] only to be made by the incessant use of the hatchet." The report concluded that "no condition on the earth's surface [is] more wild and irreclaimable than this."[69] But the swamp was not only scorned because its ecological vitality could resist capitalist designs to commodify it, extract from it, drain it, and contain it. It also became a source of anxiety for colonists and slaveholders because its ecosystem fueled the fires and fanned the flames of Black subversion, nonconformity, and noncompliance—including that of Black women. In defending and embracing the subjugated, the swamp inverted slaveholding power so much that colonists and slaveholders suffered both the peril and impediment of an intolerant swamp ecosystem, reinforced by the constant threat it represented of lost property, lost capital, and loss of sexual access to enslaved women's bodies as well as the loss of their productive and reproductive labor.

The very attributes of the Dismal Swamp's natural environment that made it an insubordinate and perilous place in the eyes of propertied white men made it a sanctuary for Black women's assertions of self, safety, and independent interests. Despite its navigable challenges, Black women chose to relate to the swamp against the slaveholders' assumptions that the value of both Black women and the natural world began and ended as ownable, seizable

Swamp interior, Great Dismal Swamp, Gates County, North Carolina.
(Photo by the author, 2013.)

objects of use and plunder. But unlike those who would capture them and pillage the earth, Black women did not view nature as separate from their own sense of self and self-worth; instead, they understood it as a connective force that offered spaces of peace and beauty, and that transcended the world of plantation slavery and economies of extraction and harm. Black women fugitives and maroons arranged themselves in collaborative relationships with the swamp, as coconspirators in sustaining and protecting unconquerable lifeways shared with water, plants, trees, and nonhuman beings. Across time, they often gained confidence in their decisions to join the woods and swamps through strong sentient connection with the swamp's diverse living entities. As historian Sharla Fett has explained, across the Black Atlantic world, Africans and African descendants—including those in the US South—considered the forest a mysterious and impenetrable space of healing and transformation animated by spiritual life and power of its own.[70] This is true even as, for some Black women and men, wilderness within the context of chattel slavery may also have been associated with fear, danger, or the threat of concealable violence against them.[71] Nevertheless, the eco-spiritually connective capacity of Dismal Swamp woods and wetlands never stopped beckoning to enslaved women to move and to motion toward freer lives.

Perhaps, as Howard "Old Divinity" of the swamps of Bayou Pierre, Mississippi, recalled, it was "tree talking," or cultivating "friendship with a certain tree," and intent listening to the "murmurin'," windless rustling of leaves that helped reassure many Dismal Swamp women and men that this was a place offering connection to a spiritual and social world larger and greater than the contrived sites of their bondage.[72] After all, most African-descended societies in the Atlantic world maintained great reverence for trees, as trees were believed to be the dwelling places of spirits, portals between the material world of here and now and the spirit world of ancestors and deities, and the abodes of ancient wisdom, strength, and peace.[73] Rebecca Grant, for example, remembered that her mother would "all de time" take her and her siblings to the woods to collect firewood, "and we'd turn around to see her down on her knees behind a stump, a-prayin.'"[74] Besides these spiritual properties, maroons would also have related to trees as providers of shelter and protection. At the southern end of the swamp, one sizable group of Dismal Swamp maroons had "for a long time been depredating upon the property of the good citizens" of Edenton, North Carolina, before a faction of them were hunted down and their camp discovered to be "in a hollow gum, sufficiently large to contain six persons with much comfort." Although the report did not specify the genders of these maroons, one of them, "commonly called Jack Stump," died in an exchange of gunfire, but not before "he fired twice, and was in the act of loading again" from under the cover of the gum tree.[75]

Dismal Swamp maroon understandings of these spiritually and physically protective properties of trees and woods makes sense, given that enslaved people were already practiced in frequently connecting to forests and swamps as chosen sites to hold religious meetings, social gatherings and "outlaw parties" of leisure and community enjoyment, and as places to foster fugitive learning against antiliteracy laws—or, "stealin' a meetin'" in the woods to read and write.[76] In North Carolina, songs sung at prayer meetings held in the woods spoke to the import of nature in Black life, with words such as: "We camp a while in the wilderness, where the Lord makes me happy."[77] Peter Randolph, once enslaved in Virginia, recalled that "the slaves assemble in the swamps, out of the reach of the patrols" to preach and hold their meetings. Women and men knew the place they would convene, as they "br[oke] boughs from the trees, and ben[t] them in the direction of the selected spot."[78] It was through this range of forbidden, relational, and independent acts that Black women and men both inscribed and derived messages and meaning from and among trees and woods. Into the forested swamps and away from white surveillance and geographies of captivity and containment, Dismal Swamp maroons would also have enjoyed these ecological opportunities to nurture self-serving yet subversive relationships with nature, with each other, and with themselves.

In the Dismal Swamp, Black women fugitives and maroons likely communed with animal life in similar ways. If Moses Grandy's recurrent dreams of "flying over woods and rivers" indicate anything about the everyday ways enslaved women and men in the Tidewater might have thought about the wetlands they lived in, it is that nature's ascendency and otherworldliness mirrored their own deep fugitive strivings and flight toward elevated life and ways out.[79] Given this, there is little reason to doubt that their animistic understandings of Tidewater wildlife, such as the spirit and meaning of animals, especially birds or birds in flight, guided and aided fugitives and maroons in their movements across the Dismal Swamp.[80] In her discussion of fugitive-minded women, Stephanie Camp argues that as these women moved, they created a "rival geography"—a world of "alternative ways of knowing and using plantation and southern space that conflicted with planters' ideals and commands"—made possible by their careful readings of the natural environment, including "the events of the skies or the squawks of birds," as signs of opportunity or impending danger.[81] Outside the Dismal Swamp, fugitives and maroons shared distinct memories of the animated roles birds played as guides, messengers, and companions to their own flight through the woods and swamps.[82] On the run, moving north from Virginia through southern Delaware, Solomon Bayley was nearly caught by a pair of white men as he rested against a tree. Instead, a group of "little strange looking birds" that had descended from their flight and formed a circle around him "roused up all [his] senses," and he suspected "with great energy and force" that these birds had been sent as messengers warning not "to move out of this circle this day, [or] you will be taken."[83] A former maroon explained that while living in the swamps and woods of Alabama, he felt certain, "can't nobody come along widout de birds tellin' me."[84] As Kimberly Smith has pointed out, some of the most common memories shared by formerly enslaved people interviewed across the South under the Federal Writers' Project describe in "loving detail the flowers, trees, [and] birdsongs" of the places they lived and grew up in. In arranging and affirming the Dismal Swamp's insurgent meaning, the spirit, sounds, and songs of birds may have also served fugitive and maroon women in motion by emotionally bonding them to the swamp forests with their encouragement and reminders of their internal spiritual value, worth, identity, and belonging within something vast, beautiful, and free. Such bonds became insurgent, as this bonding functioned to counter the dominant notion that

Black women and men, like the woods and swamps themselves, were to be regarded exclusively as spiritually and socially dead objects of use and profit.[85]

Beyond the ways Dismal Swamp maroon women and men likely viewed animal life as spiritually connective forces within the swamp's ecosystem, animals also nourished maroon insurgency by providing them with a vital source of food. While enslaved women were accustomed to gardening their own small plots of crops and vegetables, and while they were commonly skilled in foraging for nature's bounty of wild fruit, greens, berries, and honey, they were also proficient in the art and skill of hunting. Animals offered a crucial source of protein that could supplement bondwomen's otherwise poor and lacking diets as bondwomen, and wild animals would have also been a staple in the sustenance of maroons. Although men generally performed the hunting duties in their families and communities, many girls spent their childhoods hunting in the woods, alongside boys, and remained capable and involved in hunting as adults. As E. D. Blum has shown, the "uncertainties of slave life necessitated that women be able to hunt if required."[86] Women like Alice Baugh of Edgecombe County, North Carolina, recalled there was "time off ter hunt an' fish"; and Adeline Cotton, also of North Carolina, remembered that her parents were "'lowed to hunt possums an' coons at night an' ketch rabbits in gums," just as they were accustomed to catching "birds in traps made of splinters split from pine wood."[87] In Greensville County, Virginia, John Brown remembered his mother carrying him from "down de woods" with a trail of fish on her shoulders after "she done bin fishin' dat day."[88] Elsewhere, Betty Brown, once enslaved in Missouri, proudly shared with her interviewer what others must have felt: "My Mamma could hunt as good as any man."[89] There is no reason to assume that any number of Dismal Swamp maroon women eschewed their hunting capabilities or ignored the need and opportunity to hunt and provide food for themselves, their families, and communities. For both women and men, hunting would have represented another form of active and appreciable connection with the swamp's ecology. It also would have afforded those procuring the food a great source of pride and sense of selfhood and autonomy; for the sharing of meals gained through the independent pursuits of hunting, gardening, and foraging also meant feeding Black sociality and sustaining fugitive and maroon livelihood and forward movement. These acts represented inherent insurgencies in the prevailing world of chattel slavery.

For women moving in and through the swamp, foraging and nurturing the Dismal Swamp's robust plant life would have served maroon appetites; but the swamp also would have provided means of healing, as both a source of medicine and a space in which to nurture spiritual wellness. In enslaved communities, the work of raising and gathering roots and herbs was highly specialized and highly valued knowledge kept particularly by women who practiced curative work in the service of their families and communities.[90] Enslaved women learned natural remedies, therapies, and effective medicine from their study of local environments, from Indigenous American peoples, from African-based traditions in hoodoo (conjure, use of charmed objects, herbal medicine, and ancestor veneration for health and protection), and from the wisdom and instructions of their own foremothers. As laborers, mothers, and healing practitioners with this expertise, enslaved women were very much at the center of health work, herbalism, and holistic wellness.[91] For example, May Satterfield, once enslaved in Virginia, told her interviewer to take "a good slug o' dem bitters—'bout dat much in a glass an' you ain't never gonna be sick a day in yo' life." May knew this since she "uster know ev'y weed and root in de woods"—her "grandma tole 'em" to her.[92] In North Carolina, Sarah Louise Augustus recounted that her own grandmother and namesake "was great on curing"—work the elder Sarah performed with herbs such as hops and other plants she grew to cure "many people."[93] Other women, who sometimes claimed "the Lord told . . . what roots to get," were respected in their communities for knowing "just what to do fer you," as their power and vision in giving health and protection to others was often trusted to be guided by a higher spiritual authority.[94] Polly Shine also recalled the "Negro mama" who "doctored . . . from herbs she got out of the woods," including "turpentine gathered from pine trees, honey, and onions, made into a syrup, mixed together." This "Negro mama"—as the role was sometimes called—was often an older Black woman skilled in the knowledge of plants, herbs, and roots. Polly remembered that the woman used "red oak, cami weed, and Jerusalem weeds for fever, chills, and malaria."[95] Moses Grandy—who had first spent time learning about the woods and swamps on the run with his mother, and then through his secret treks through swampy woods to support his maroon sister Tamar, and finally through his own experience as an enslaved canal laborer in the Dismal Swamp—was also sure to pay careful attention to Jerusalem weeds. This "strong weed," or the Oak of Jerusalem as he called it, grew wild throughout the swamps, and from these experiences, Moses had learned that it could also be used as a remedy to treat infected wounds. He likely shared in this knowledge with the women in his family, who may or may not have enlightened him as to the oak's healing properties to begin with.[96]

Fugitive and maroon women who made it to the swamp brought with them these knowledges and skill sets in relating to nature and select plant life, using them to educate, heal, aid, and create options for sustainable wellness within their escaped families and communities. After all, the swamp was rich with the natural ingredients necessary to promote healthy futures. Common diseases such as the agues, or intermittent fevers, coughs, dysentery, worms, and rashes could be treated with teas made from the root bark of the aromatic sassafras tree, found "everywhere" throughout the swampland and "used for almost everything." In addition to the Oak of Jerusalem, pellitory weeds, elm root, tulip buds, dogwood root bark, prickly ash roots, and the resin from gum trees were just a few of the swamp's plant offerings that fugitive and maroon women likely identified as essential ingredients for curative teas, lotions, and salves.[97] The bark and roots of the abundant juniper tree, saturated as they were in swamp water, could also produce a protective tonic against the ague and malaria. Maroons in the Dismal Swamp likely made their own drinks and solutions, as many enslaved women and men were already in the practice of doing so, both for medicinal use as well as for recreational consumption and enjoyment.[98] Archaeobotanical findings confirm that a number of wild grapes, berries, roots, and barks were used in the swamp, likely to make teas, tinctures, and liquors for the purposes of "treat[ing] diseases in ways very similar to whiskey," though these could also have been used to enhance pleasure, community sharing, and social life.[99] Comparative accounts add to the likelihood that Black women who were skilled and able upheld their roles as herbalists and healers within their communities of Dismal Swamp maroons, just as other women did so not only throughout the United States South but also throughout the broader Atlantic world.[100] One 1881 account of the swamp discusses the continued presence of the "Voudoo man or woman"—believed to be the "descendants of many a runaway slave"—still dwelling there in "a couple of lonely cabins."[101] Another report evidences the role of "wise wimmin'" in and around the Virginia swamps, including that of "ole Minta," a healer and conjurer to whom "de sperits" gave "de second sight" to work cures on behalf of her swamp community, suffering as it was from disease.[102] In sum, Black women's knowledge of Tidewater ecology, their reciprocal relationships with plant life, and their leadership in administering root work and herbal medicine would have been assets to the health and vitality of any and every Dismal Swamp maroon group as well as to other fugitives fleeting through the swamps. In providing this work, women helped arrange insurgent meaning in the swamp, since the wellness and holistic aid they proffered also supported noncompliant and oppositional Black life and vitality.

There is no doubt that there are eco-spiritual interactions, foodways, healing, and defensive practices Black women in the Dismal Swamp contributed that were never recorded; and as a result, they continue to evade the documentary archive and subsequent historiography about the roles and movements of fugitive and maroon women. The better-documented labor and lives of Tidewater enslaved women helps to inform reasonable conjecture about the variety of ways Dismal Swamp women gave the swampscape insurgent meaning. But the humming, living natural world of the swamp itself, as well as its inescapably central geographic position within the greater Tidewater also archives what might not be known about fugitive and maroon women's contributions to the insurgent ecology. Sacred waters, and every reed, plant, tree, and living, breathing being in the swamp presents an unwritten record ready for interpretation about how women communed with the wetlands underfoot and in their view. The swamp's profuse foliage, dense woods, and the observable freedoms of its nonhuman inhabitants is living evidence of how this space beckoned Black women who were considering or already determined to move, escape, and create new and collaborative worlds with the force of nature against the commodifying and extractive violence of slavery.

In addition to its spiritual animation and yield of abundant food, water, roots, bark, and herbs, the swamp also provided optimal shelter and concealment, the cover from reconnoitering and reconnaissance, and a ready retreat from which to dodge, ambush, and in which to plot against captivity and gendered dispossession. As will be shown in the chapters that follow, Black women did not only flee and abscond, pray, procure shelter and subsistence, or nurture their own health and the wellness of those around them in their contributions to and arrangements of the insurgent ecology; they also conspired with the woods and swamps as bases from which to physically defend their lives, their families, and communities. Across the swamps, maroon women often lived among men and sometimes also among other women who were battle ready—and this readiness for and closeness to open rebellion and the insight of defensive violence were strategies they both tacitly and actively supported.

Identifying Black women's flux, adaptability, and resourcefulness in the building and sustaining of the insurgent ecology reminds us that it is normal and appropriate to locate Black women in nature, to witness Black women in meditation and in concert with the peace, calm, sacred spirit, and refuge of the natural world. Through their errant acts of evasion and defiance, women are locatable in Tidewater woods, water, and swamps not only in moments of emergency, anguish, desperation, or defense but also, as will be seen, in modes of focus, pleasure, joy, care, love, and self-gratification.[103] Black women's connective relationships with the teeming swamp ecology were also declarations of their rights to rest and leisure, to voluntary productive and reproductive labor, to safety, and to security. These resistive alliances with the sprawling swamp were arranged by the movements, knowledges, and gifts of mothers, healers, agriculturalists, spiritual guides, fugitive strategists, and countless other ordinary women daring and inventive enough to endeavor the extraordinary pursuit of conspiring with the Great Dismal Swamp.

When Moses and Tamar Grandy's mother elected to maroon at a corner of the southern swamp, she likely breathed in and inhaled the forest air more deeply. It may have pleased her to look not at the face of Billy Grandy, but at the stillness or stream of waters, reeds, running vines, brambles, cypress, pine, and juniper trees, the patch of open sky peeking out between treetops, or the puddles of cool, peaty blackwater at her feet. We can imagine that she enjoyed some gratification in keeping her children close and together a while longer. The momentary peace and security the swamp afforded her must have offered her feelings of self-satisfaction—however fleeting—to be able to care for, feed, and shelter her children away from white surveillance, harm, and the agonizing threat of separation. From the flight and songs of birds, the beauty of the swamp's verdant vegetation, or from the ancient sanctity of woods and trees that mirrored her own worth and place in a spirited world far greater and vaster than the world of slavery and capital, Moses's mother may have felt encouraged to absent herself and her children in the swamp's recesses awhile longer.

In this communion with the swamp, Moses and Tamar's mother was not alone. There were women like Louise, who ran west of the swamp through the woods in order to escape her jealous mistress, whom she called "the meanes' white 'omen in de world." Perhaps her mistress envied her intimate yet uncertain proximity to whiteness, for Louise was light enough to pass for white—the legacy of rape and sexual coercion running through her veins. But Louise, perhaps like Moses's mother, did not merely run through the wetland wilds. Once "out of everybody's sight," she recalled that she stopped to rest, sat down on the bank of a spring, got a drink of "nice cool water," and spent time under the trees in her own thoughts and solace.[104] It was moments such as these—in the woods and swamps and away from the *un*natural world of slavery—that women like Louise, Moses's mother, Tamar, and innumerable others gave to themselves nature's soothing space of interior reflection, faith, health, protection, affirmation of their own universal belonging and value, and the promise of an unbound future.

But the first step toward achieving any of these liberatory objectives required Tidewater women to make a determined, studied, and calculated choice in the face of limited options and extreme risk and pressure. That careful choice was to break, move, and slip away in the hope of new outcomes and opportunities—on the run.

TWO

Venus's Choice

TIDEWATER WOMEN ON THE RUN

At times, running away was fun and exciting. At other times it was miserable, cold, and lonely. The part i dug about it, though, was surviving.

ASSATA SHAKUR, *ASSATA: AN AUTOBIOGRAPHY*

All her life, Venus knew well the flow of Tidewater rivers, swamps, and wetlands. Her mother, Hanah, had given birth to her sometime in 1739, somewhere between the York and the James Rivers, at one of the many estates of the prominent Burwell family of Virginia. Venus had been raised among orchards of apple, peach, and cherry trees, pastures of corn and wheat, large tobacco plantations, and small farms. She was one of more than three hundred Burwell "slaves" spread out across three branches of the Burwell family and their many properties located between Williamsburg and Yorktown. Her world was one connected by the course of major rivers, streams, wooded ravines, marshes, creeks, and an abundance of freshwater swamps. Venus may have been born at one of the Burwell's Gloucester plantations—a whopping 5,080 acres—just north of the York River. But by the time she reached adulthood, she was the property of Robert Burwell and laboring and living in one of his three Isle of Wight County plantations, just south across the James River at Warrasqueak Bay (properly, Warraskoyack, though also misnamed "Burwell Bay"), where it meets the northernmost sprawl of the Dismal Swamp. As most of the enslaved people Robert Burwell owned had been relocated from the Burwell's Gloucester properties to his Isle of Wight estates in Smithfield as part of his inheritance, it makes sense that Hanah and Venus were among those who traveled on foot and by water to get there.[1]

Venus lived at Robert's "home-house plantation"—a two-story brick mansion that was sixty feet long by twenty-six feet wide and flanked by two brick dependencies, each forty feet long and twenty feet wide. The estate had a "handsome," formally designed garden that extended in length and width a half a mile. The tobacco warehouse—where enslaved people readied and packed tobacco leaves in large wooden barrels for export—was another building that stood at the end of a road leading to and from the plantation and back up to the Warrasqueak Bay.[2] But Venus likely spent little time with the tobacco plants, since at the time of Robert's death in January, 1777, she, her mother, and at least one sister were laboring as domestics in the Burwell home. Robert Burwell's last will and testament, recorded just twelve days before he died, bequeathed to his wife, Mary Braxton Burwell, "all" his "house-servants"—a group amounting to "Zenith and her son, Hanah and her daughters Venus, Nelly, Rachel, Jack-dismal, Jemmima, Junius, Rachel and her children, Johnny the cook, David, Isaac, and Paul"—in addition to sixteen unnamed enslaved field laborers, his chariot and horses, house furniture, and "all the liquors in the house."[3] This intimate group of nine enslaved adults and several children lived with their families in the close quarters of the wainscoted manor house, in what would have been a very fragile, tentative state of togetherness. Venus knew that she could be moved and separated from her family and loved ones according to the slightest whim of the Burwell family. After all, such a fate had befallen others around her throughout her life, and she would have well remembered that she, too, had been forced to leave her Smithfield home in the summer of 1764. She would experience forced removal several more times in the coming decade.

Venus may have been at work alongside her mother and sister(s) when the newly formed Dismal Swamp Company (DSC) held its first meeting on Thursday, November 3, 1763, on the other side of the James River in the town of Williamsburg. The company—previously called the Adventurers to Drain the Dismal Swamp—consisted of twelve propertied men, including Virginia Councilman Robert Burwell and thirty-one-year-old representative of the Virginia House of Burgesses George Washington. After twice presenting a petition to begin the work of "taking up and Improving a large Tract of waste Land lying in the Counties of Norfolk and Nansemond bounded to the Southward on Carolina and commonly known by the name of the Dismal Swamp," the Governor's Council finally approved the DSC its requested land patents, which granted the company rights to 150,000 acres of the swamp for the profit-driven purposes of surveying, draining, and developing it to accommodate the industries of tar and lumber production as well as the cultivation and export of hemp, rice, and corn. The success of the petition, written in Washington's own hand, was certainly not hindered by the insistence of its 151 signatures—all DSC members plus six Washingtons (three of them George's brothers and three his cousins). Two days after its approval, while Venus labored at Burwell's plantation, the company held its inaugural meeting to apportion the newly patented Virginia swampland among the shareholders and to devise plans for the immediate transformation of the swamp into a profitable zone of commerce and capital—a feat they easily decided would be undertaken by enslaved labor. As the men talked and noted their plans in their meeting books, Venus could not have known that Robert Burwell had pledged her as one-half of his financial contribution to the fledgling enterprise. In under a year, Venus would be moved from her home in Isle of Wight County to an uncertain life of labor in the Great Dismal Swamp.[4]

By July of 1764, Venus, then in her twenties, and twenty-eight-year-old Jack, the other half of Robert Burwell's contribution to reduce the company's expenses, were both taken from the Isle of Wight plantation and brought to the grounds of another plantation soon to be known as Dismal Town, or Dismal Plantation. They arrived at the 402-acre tract of land, just six miles south of the town of Suffolk, in Nansemond County, along with dozens of other enslaved people sent by the other eleven DSC investors. There, Venus, Jack, eight other enslaved women, forty-two other enslaved men, a boy named Toney, and a girl named Hannah encountered the prolific wetlands spilling and sprawling from the northwestern edges of the great swamp. Mills Riddick—a prominent Suffolk planter and resident—had rented these lands to the DSC for the purposes of establishing a headquarters for their operations in the swamp.[5] The men of the DSC agreed that trees and certain other defining natural features, such as a "burnt stump" or a specific stretch of marsh, were to serve as borders marking the bounds of land and ecosystems they now presumed to own. The DSC thus designated a set of imagined perimeters that would become Dismal Plantation—hundreds of acres "beginning in the great swamp at a maple running thence due west . . . to a small red ash on the edge of the white marsh . . . to a pine on the side of back branch . . . then along the said line . . . to a red oak . . . then to a white oak corner tree."[6] For two years, until Robert Burwell withdrew from the DSC in 1766, Venus was held captive within the limits of these grounds to serve and to work. Under the direction of John Washington—the resident overseer and George Washington's younger brother—the group of fifty-four enslaved people were set to the initial tasks of hacking and cutting down reeds, vines, and brush to create navigable paths; hand-digging ditches to pool and collect water for irrigation and to facilitate easier passage; clearing woods of trees for the building of structures, houses, and fields for subsistence farming; and ultimately, performing the everyday labor of the plantation's upkeep and the extraction and production of goods for use and export.

Almost four decades before Venus walked onto the land that would become Dismal Plantation, Virginia Councilman Col. William Byrd II had led an expedition into the swamp in order to determine, once and for all, the precise "Dividing Line betwixt Virginia and North Carolina." The year was 1728, and Byrd—the first to do so—wasted no time in writing a proposal full of suggestions for "Draining the Dismal," following his conclusion that the swamp was a "vast extent of bogg, which is now of no value to the crown, nor ever can be, in the condition it lyes at present." Byrd's proposal called for the creation of drainages, such as ditches and canals, and he envisioned using these newly drained lands for the cultivation of hemp, which was then widely used to produce a variety of commodities including rope and fabrics. He strongly cautioned against letting such a "corrupt" mass of unruly swampland "lye to wast, and continue a nusance to perpetuity," and so he proposed that "10 seasoned negros be purchased, of both sexes," to work at clearing and trenching the ground, planting and tending crops, and otherwise "improving" the land. Byrd insisted that despite the expense of purchasing at least five men and five women to labor in this manner, "their breed may supply the loss." He urged that care be taken "to buy as many women as men," not only because "provideing wives for the men" would assuage the concern that enslaved men would otherwise go fleeing and "rambling abroad," but also because enslaved women's reproduction was part of a strategy to guard against the expected loss of profits due to fatality among those men and women undertaking the arduous work of toiling in the swamp. The anticipated financial loss caused by the illness and death of the enslaved laborers, according to Byrd, could be alleviated and "fully supplyd by their children."[7] Colonel Byrd was also confident that the labor of these men and women would ensure the taming, containment, and submission of the Dismal Swamp. By his estimation, enslaved labor would transform the swamp into a commodity of commerce and capitalist exploit. Like the members of the DSC after him, Byrd failed to understand that attempts to drain and control the swamp were as futile as efforts to prevent the fugitive designs of rebels and runaways.

Despite what Venus thought about the waterways, woods, and swamps around her, the DSC shareholders and enslavers she suffered unequivocally believed that her worth and value was akin to that of the abundant swamp itself—no more consequential than the use and profit to be gained. As someone who arrived to Dismal Plantation with experience as an enslaved domestic worker, Burwell and the DSC would have demanded that she continue to serve their enterprise not only in the maintenance of their houses—by cooking, cleaning, and washing—but also in plowing and tending to crops and livestock as some of the "negro girls" at the plantation were compelled to do. It is also possible that Venus would have been forced to become more directly involved in the company's efforts to destroy, subdue, or else bring the Dismal Swamp to heel.[8] The crew of fifty-four men, women, and children were, after all, tasked with cutting clear to the ground the oldest white cedar trees, and they were also required to shave tens of thousands of eighteen-inch shingles from the felled lumber within the first five months of their time at Dismal Plantation.[9] A group that probably consisted entirely of men was to dig a massive drainage ditch—three feet deep and ten feet wide—that began at Dismal Town and ran almost five miles long before it drained into Lake Drummond.[10] John Washington and his brother, George—the latter of whom visited the plantation only briefly "to receive & set ye People to Work"—watched as the enslaved people labored in these ways.[11] Although the DSC and its overseers believed it "proper" to teach the "negro *men* to saw, make shingles, burn tar, draw clap-boards, and set up tight casks" (emphasis added), and although most of the enslaved laborers forced to work in the swamp were men, enslaved women were sometimes also compelled to work at clearing the underbrush, felling trees, cutting and trimming shingles and staves, and keeping the waterways clear.[12]

Venus may have been among the women at Dismal Plantation tasked with such work. But, as the DSC viewed each of the women they held as objects to be fully used for accumulating profit, women's gendered labor in the swamp would have been subjected to more than just keeping house,

"Washington at Lake Drummond, Dismal Swamp," 1880.
(From the New York Public Library, Digital Collections, https://digitalcollections.nypl.org.)

cutting shingles, or yielding crops. Another set of expectations overlapped and intersected with these productive labor demands: sexual labor. Venus and the other enslaved women were also expected to perform the sexual labor of ensuring male gratification—that of the enslaved men and the enslaving men alike—as well as the reproductive labor of delivering a perpetually enslavable and profitable labor force. As Saidiya Hartman reflects on the life and fate of another Venus in her seminal essay, "Venus in Two Acts," captive women and girls can be found "in exactly the same place" throughout the history and archive of Atlantic slavery, either as the romanticized "Sable Venus," the wicked and wanton whore, the witch, the drudge, the unrapable wench—or not at all. The Venus that Hartman writes of, whose compulsory "pet name licensed debauchery and made it sound agreeable," died in 1792 of the pox (gonorrhea) at the hands of slavers aboard the ship *The Recovery*. The Venus who found herself at Dismal Plantation in Tidewater Virginia and "every other Black Venus" are linked both literally and symbolically to all captive women and girls, since "all of them" shared in the unutterable corporeal and sexual violence of chattel slavery as well as in the ubiquitous violence of archival oblivion.[13] At Dismal Town, the DSC extracted its fullest use from the bodies of Venus, Bella, Rachel, Minne, Nan, Hannabel, Bab, Penny, and Molly as part of the company's scheme to diminish, dominate, and extract profit from the Dismal Swamp. The DSC shareholders were so sure that these Black women's presumed sexual availability and readiness would temper the enslaved men's inclination toward absconding, or else satiate their own lusts, that by the end of December 1764, the DSC had vowed to send an additional twelve enslaved women to accompany forty-eight more enslaved men.[14]

At Dismal Town, Venus likely stood at the edge of the Dismal Swamp contemplating that it harbored a world capable of defying the rules, authority, and interests of the plantation regime she was brought there to help build, serve, and reproduce. In spite of the DSC's efforts to mollify enslaved men with the lure of Black women, the company nevertheless continued to be "mutch plagued with the runaway negroes" who occasionally robbed the company's barns and stores, and sometimes remained at large for years.[15] Venus would have taken note of the obvious disappearance, flight, and marronage of people like Tom, who escaped John Washington and Dismal Plantation in April 1767, choosing instead a life in the refuge of the swamp he had been ordered to destroy. Tom was one of three men named Tom employed by the company in July of 1764—the same month Venus arrived. Described as having a "roguish look" and bearing his "country marks, (that is, four on each of his cheeks)," he was reported to be a runaway by both John Washington and his owner, DSC member Samuel Gist and his associate John Mayo, and thought to be "about the *Dismal Swamp*" as late as June 1768.[16] Tom seems to have eluded capture, as there is no record of it. Despite the company's attempts to use Black women as both laborers and sexual pawns, the women's presence at Dismal Plantation proved no deterrent to flight and marronage; in addition to the DSC's recurrent problems of "worn out negroes," drowning crops, and considerable deaths among the enslaved, the absconding and escapes continued to be a primary concern.[17] Although Venus was not one of the women who "fully supplyd" the company enslaved children to defray the losses incurred by adult mortality, there may have been some success in this part of the shareholders' plans, as there is indication of a continued presence of children among the dwindling labor force as late as 1783.[18]

By 1766, Robert Burwell, struggling with debt, decided to pull his shares from the DSC and return his enslaved investments to his Smithfield plantation. Venus and Jack left Dismal Town and moved back to Isle of Wight County. But neither would have been able to forget the Dismal Swamp, the work they had performed there, or the insurgent practices of evasion and

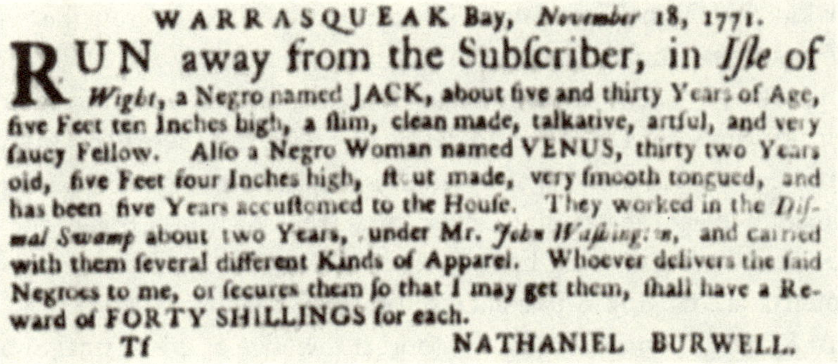
WARRASQUEAK Bay, *November* 18, 1771.

RUN away from the Subſcriber, in *Iſle* of *Wight*, a Negro named JACK, about five and thirty Years of Age, five Feet ten Inches high, a ſlim, clean made, talkative, artful, and very ſaucy Fellow. Alſo a Negro Woman named VENUS, thirty two Years old, five Feet four Inches high, ſtout made, very ſmooth tongued, and has been five Years accuſtomed to the Houſe. They worked in the *Diſmal Swamp* about two Years, under Mr. *John Waſhington*, and carried with them ſeveral different Kinds of Apparel. Whoever delivers the ſaid Negroes to me, or ſecures them ſo that I may get them, ſhall have a Reward of FORTY SHILLINGS for each.

Tf NATHANIEL BURWELL.

Venus and Jack, *Virginia Gazette*, December 5, 1771.
(Courtesy of newspapers.com.)

marronage they would have witnessed and considered throughout their time there. It also would have been hard for Venus to forget the gendered threats to her person she likely experienced alongside the other women at Dismal Town—women who had at best composed 20 percent of the people there (both enslaved and white). What is more, the pair's return to Burwell—a man even the governor and members of the Virginia Council believed lacked "mental Qualifications" and had "an unwarrantable Impetuosity of Temper"—must have compounded Venus's and Jack's weariness and concerns about the future.[19] If Burwell suspected this, he may have tried to placate or reward the two for having sent them away to labor in a swamp widely considered "intolerable," "dreadful," "dirty," and "horrible," by assigning them both "to the house" at the time of their return.[20] Burwell would have known that work in the swamp was "very severe," as laborers who worked at digging the ditches and canals could be "up to the middle or much deeper in mud and water, cutting away roots and baling out mud: if they can keep their heads above water."[21] Yet there had been some reason that he had not minded sending the young, healthy, and capable Jack and Venus to join in this grueling labor, while other company shareholders had been reluctant to risk the health of their valued laborers, sending instead "the worst" of their enslaved people and the "refuse of every one of the[ir] Estates."[22] Whatever the reason was, it did not deter Venus from her "very smooth tongued" retorts, nor did it affect Jack's behavior. Robert and his only son, Nathaniel, concurred that Jack remained a "talkative, artful, and very saucy fellow."[23] Perhaps it was this very cunning, this defiant conduct, inclination, and countenance that had conveyed to Robert Burwell the pair's dispensability to begin with. Whatever the case might have been, five years after her return from the Dismal Swamp, Venus carefully weighed her circumstances, designed a plan, and made a strategic choice: flight.

FLIGHT RISK: RUNNING AGAINST THE GENDERED ODDS OF ESCAPE

Venus's decision to leave the home of Robert Burwell was motivated by an impulse shared by African women and women of African descent across the Atlantic world since the dawn of slavery and throughout its duration. That impulse was, in short, a matter of self-liberation. It was both a refusal to stay and a determination to move on and out; and it was shaped and motivated by gendered predicaments, risks, and options for gaining greater control over one's life.

As in other places in the slaveholding South, in Tidewater Virginia and North Carolina, thousands of enslaved women made the choice to flee their enslavers and the sites of their bondage. But what separated fugitive women sojourning and moving through the Tidewater's eastern seaboard from those who chose flight in other Southern landscapes and wetlands was, on the one hand, that the risks they were willing to take had to contend with and measure plantation societies that were (1) the stronghold and absolute center of British North American colonization, and (2) had remained the seat and model of early national and antebellum slaveholding authority since the Revolutionary War. In addition, as a leading market in the domestic slave trade, the Tidewater also presented an intensive and unparalleled threat of sale, as hundreds of thousands of enslaved people from Virginia's exhausted tobacco soils were routinely and forcibly relocated to source the new labor demands in the expanding Deep South and in southwestern slaveholding states.[24] On the other hand, despite these regional forces of pro-slavery vigilance, Black women in the Tidewater also had uniquely significant access—by way of elaborate connective and proximate waterways—to emancipatory destinations in the nearby Northern free states *and*, for the fugitive-minded, to the Tidewater's centrally defining feature of the Great Dismal Swamp.

In the Tidewater, as in most places at most times, the majority of enslaved people did not attempt to flee at all. Most of those who did, did not do so with the intention of making a break for it forever. Called "runaways" by their contemporaries throughout the colonial and antebellum periods, most fugitives were what historians have described as "truants" or "absentees"—those "lying out" within the vicinity from which they came, seeking temporary escape and relief from the grip of bondage.[25] While both women and men generally found this form of fugitivity and protest to be the most readily achievable, and though "men made up the majority of truants most of the time," as a group, enslaved women became transitory fugitives and absentees at rates higher than those of men, and women were more frequently truant than they were able to sustain long-term or permanent forms of evasion and escape, such as flight to the northern states and enduring practices of marronage. As Stephanie Camp has pointed out, because the geographies of containment "did not hold women and men in the same ways, nor to the same extent," fugitive women were more prone than fugitive men to move and stay away temporarily over a period of days, weeks, and sometimes months, concealing themselves in places such as neighboring slave quarters, nearby woods and swamps, and, less often, in local towns.[26]

Unlike Venus, most of the Tidewater's fugitive women had not previously spent time hired out and moving across the counties and forested wetlands beyond their owner's homes. Certainly, as more lumber companies entered the swamp during the canal construction era (ca. 1790–1829), companies "hired" nearly exclusively enslaved men and boys to dig canals and haul shingles and wood staves out of the swamp. Venus was one of very few women who chose to flee who also had firsthand knowledge about the insurgent possibilities of the great swamp in mind.[27] The vast majority of the Tidewater's fugitive women reached the determination to flee with much different and far more limited set of geographical experiences and knowledge about possible destinations and routes out and away. Unlike enslaved men, who were granted greater opportunities to exercise mobility, in the Tidewater and throughout the South, enslaved women's labor was predominately confined to the home of their enslavers as well as to their own assigned quarters, or to the fields, pastures, yard, kitchen, and other outbuildings on their enslavers' farms and plantations. For the most part, enslaved women were not given passes to run errands, ride horses, or drive coaches transporting goods, correspondence, or the slaveholders themselves, nor were they hired to row skiffs and canoes or steer and lighter boats.[28] Thus, enslaved women had less knowledge of and experience with the outside world than enslaved men did, and they must have known that their presence on the roads and waterways would have raised more suspicion than the less-conspicuous sight of an enslaved man doing the same. The gendered nature of this "spatial illiteracy" proved a strong deterrent to women's decisions to flee, and it remained one of several obstacles hindering their attempts to reach more strategic, out-of-reach, and potentially enduring destinations.[29]

Like Venus, Tidewater women who did elect to run shared in the awareness that they were choosing to risk terrifying encounters with dogs, slave patrols, hunger, cold, and heat as well as the dangers of finding themselves lost or without direction. Whether absconding into their owner's backwoods or moving toward other local hideouts, toward the free Northern states by way of water, or toward the abundant Dismal Swamp, fugitive women knew that if they were captured, the worst kinds of punishment was almost guaranteed to be inflicted upon their bodies. If their efforts failed, they knew they would face a punitive system of surveillance and correction upheld and maintained by watchful enslavers and overseers, jailers, justices of the peace, sheriffs, newspaper publishers who placed ads for their capture, and the vigilant friends and neighbors of slaveholders everywhere. It is unsurprising that a system of justice concocted by such a wide net of players sanctioned a slew of punishments for apprehended fugitives, including forcing them into carceral devices such as shackles, iron collars and mouth coverings called bits, horns and bells attached to the head and neck; sending them to stocks and gaols; leaving them in jail for prolonged periods; and commissioning the most common form of correction—private and public whippings at the pillory, between "nine to 100 lashes" each—among ear croppings, and other corporeal mutilations.[30]

Venus and other bondwomen knew the extent and depth of this violence better than anyone. As women, not only were they subjected to routine lashings aimed at regulating their productive labor, but they were also—and sometimes simultaneously—the regular targets of sexual violence exacted against them by slaveholders, overseers, and non-elite men. If caught, fugitive women would have anticipated punitive cruelty and corporeal violence that was commonly crossed with sexual machinations meant to degrade and humiliate. Many enslaved women were too often "stripped, tied down, and thrashed" in totalizing displays of domination and control. On top of this, women who were caught for choosing to flee were frequently punished more strictly and severely than men were, since enslavers and overseers typically maintained gendered assumptions about Black women's place and resistive capabilities that contrasted with their assumptions about masculinity. On that view, Black men's inclination toward insubordination was somehow more understandable. Fugitive women troubled, disturbed, and transgressed white men's misguided expectations that Black women would neatly comply or behave as cowed, submissive females—and insubordination needed to be punished accordingly.[31]

Enslaved women had to imagine and deliberate the potential losses and gains of fugitive futures in each of these ways, but they also had to weigh other risks and hesitations. Paramount among their concerns were the consequences that departing from their respected roles as mothers, sisters, daughters, aunts, laborers, and nurturers might cost the entire communities they left behind; they also faced the gendered pressure of being mothers and women who were expected to dedicate and commit their laboring lives to home, family, and the raising of children.[32] These concerns and constraints were by no means alleviated by the difficulties mothers faced while considering fleeing during pregnancy, or while making other impossible decisions such as whether to leave infants and children behind and accept the pain and heartbreak of separation, or whether to take them along and subsequently add to the demands and risks of feeding, quieting, carrying, or hurrying them to keep pace in flight.[33] Together, each of these factors significantly limited how many women felt prepared to make, or were even capable of making, the choice Venus made in 1771.

Yet, even with these constraints, some women chose to flee anyway. Thousands of Black women in the Tidewater practiced truancy, while untold numbers became maroons, and others fled from the region entirely. Enslaved women chose from a range of opportunity-based fugitive acts. A useful way to distinguish between those who practiced absenteeism and those who practiced marronage, is that unlike absentees or truants, all maroons—including the *petit*, short-term, and borderland variety—practiced flight to destinations decidedly outside of dominant, inhabited spaces and for a number of days, weeks, months, or years sustained their escape through resettlement and the construction of alternative lifeways relative to wilderness and the natural world.[34] Though slaveholding authorities in the US South referred to both absentees and maroons as "runaways," another distinction between the two is that most truants were neither captured nor caught but instead returned of their own accord, as they generally had meant to do to begin with.[35] It is impossible to quantify how many ephemeral maroons were caught compared to how many successfully evaded discovery and capture, but the activities of *petit* maroons often penetrated (if not built) the underground world of clandestine Black economies, brigandage, and outlawry, and they were not, on the whole, noted for willingly returning to the sites of their bondage. As will be seen in the following chapter, fugitive women became these maroons too, though again, far less often than men. Overall, despite the region's insurgent advantage of the Great Dismal Swamp and other nearby waterborne avenues of permanent escape, in the Tidewater and beyond, there were unquestionably more male fugitives—absentees, northbound escapees, and maroons alike—than there were women fugitives.[36]

The small numbers of women who did manage to move themselves out and away were frequently listed and described in advertisements published in local newspapers, in the hope that they might be found and returned to their owners. Venus, for example, was described in an ad the Burwells repeatedly placed in the *Virginia Gazette* as a "Negro Woman," at "thirty two years old, five Feet four Inches high," and "stout made," whose premeditations enabled her to carry off "several different kinds of Apparel" before she fled the Burwell home.[37] But she was one of few. Of runaways whose return was advertised in Virginia between 1790 and 1816, 85 percent were men, while 15 percent were women. Between 1838 and 1860, 91 percent of runaways were listed as men, while just 9 percent were women.[38] Another estimate shows that between 1730 and 1805, just 11 percent of escapees in Virginia were women.[39] The numbers in North Carolina are comparable. Between 1790 and 1816, only 18 percent were women; and between 1838 and 1860, only 14 percent were women.[40] Another study corroborates that a total of 2,179 enslaved men fled from North Carolina between 1775 and 1840, while just 482 enslaved women did the same during those same years.[41] Although quantitative studies of advertisements do indicate the kinds of people who chose flight and their probable methods and rates of doing so, exclusive reliance on ads to determine the frequency or numbers of women in motion risks distortion by missing, "perhaps to a great degree" the archival omission caused by the commonly held gendered assumptions of slaveholders who were less likely to pay for ads in newspapers or to offer rewards for the return of women they believed would soon return voluntarily, or who would otherwise be unable to sustain their escapes as women out on their own.[42] While accounting for this bias in runaway slave advertisements can to some extent help explain the lower number of fugitive women (as opposed to fugitive men) who appear in these records, overall, these ratios remained strikingly uneven, and women's propensity toward flight remained strained compared to that of men who benefited from dominant notions of male capability and mobility. Yet, those women who did manage to escape for any length of time should not be ignored. Instead, people like Venus merit closer attention, particularly as it was women like her who dared to flee in any capacity who were also closest to realizing and achieving bolder and more enduring forms of fugitivity and marronage across the Tidewater's inviting stretch of the Dismal Swamp.

Testimonies of formerly enslaved men and women from Tidewater communities in Virginia and North Carolina reveal much about the factors and final pushes that propelled their choice to turn their backs on the plantation world and set their feet to forward motion. Of course, at the core of any decision a woman or man would make to run was their human will and innate desire for personal safety, the right to protect their family and kin, and simply the freedoms of independence, mobility, self-determination, and self-possession. While this is irrefutable, the immediate concerns and conditions enslaved people faced such as overwork; sexual and corporeal violence; cruelty; lack of food or clothing; the threat of sale, relocation, separation from family and community; and injurious or life-threatening changes made by enslavers, employers, or overseers most commonly triggered and ultimately compelled their decisions to flee and to leave their former lives behind.

In Tidewater Virginia, enslaved women were overworked, overtaxed, and exhausted primarily from their work as agricultural laborers—cultivating and harvesting tobacco, wheat, corn, and cotton—or from their positions as domestic laborers who were expected to provide their masters and mistresses whatever service they demanded, including cooking, cleaning, nursing and keeping watch over white children, spinning, weaving, and working the loom, on top of bearing the frequent sexual demands of white men. Women in Tidewater North Carolina took on these same roles, as the economy there shared its colonial efforts to sustain profitable tobacco production; but the production of wheat, corn, cotton, and naval stores (tar, pitch, turpentine, lumber) remained the most lucrative markets well into the antebellum period.[43] Women were rarely employed in naval and maritime trades, save for those who occasionally cut and shaved shingles and staves, or who assisted on barges, locks, and dredges during the canal era that developed in the first half of the nineteenth century.[44]

Formerly enslaved in Virginia, Jordan Johnson explained that both men and women worked in the same tobacco fields, "plantin', settin', and hillin.'" He recalled a time when a woman named Annie—"big wid chile an' gittin' near her time"—was at this work when she "made a slip" and accidentally chopped down a young tobacco plant. For this, the overseer came "runnin' up screamin' at her," took his rawhide, and beat her "'cross de back an shoulders 'till she fell to de groun.'"[45] Susan Mabry of Southampton, Virginia, remembered picking "four or five hundred pounds of cotton a day"; and Jane Arrington of North Carolina recalled that her "Aunt Chaney runned away an' mother run away" after "wurkin' all day" at the "task of cotton to be picked an' spun."[46] Elizabeth Sparks of York County, Virginia, brought herself to return to unnerving memories of her enslaver's father, who beat enslaved women and men alike "until they couldn't work," and who also gave them "more work than they could do," assigned to "wheat or other crops," six days a week, from "sun to sun." This was the same man who had bought her own mother to serve him "when he was married" and her mother just "a little girl." Elizabeth also recalled that the man's wife—"a mean ol' thin'"—ordinarily forced her Aunt Caroline to knit all day and night, and when night fell and she became sleepy, the woman made her continue on after dark. In Elizabeth's words, her aunt was worked "so hard" that "she'd go to sleep standin' up an' every time her haid nod an' her knees sag, the lady'd come down across her haid with a switch."[47] Enslaved women, including pregnant mothers, field laborers, and domestic laborers, suffered strenuous and grueling physical labor that mingled with the pervasive economy of sexual exploitation. Their layered experiences of overwork and drudgery constitute one of the primary factors leading to women's decisions to flee.

Women also turned their backs on their constant exposure to routine explicit violence, the harrowing anticipation of punitive violence, and the ways that both sources of harm were very often further polluted with sexual terror. Fannie Berry, once enslaved in Appomattox County, Virginia, remembered a woman in her community who "was gonna make uh try fo' freedom," and chose to run one night because she had "been beat so bad." The woman made it "'bout 5 miles" before she was caught.[48] In Camden County, North Carolina, Moses Grandy spent time working in the cornfields alongside women, whom he noted could not be spared from being flogged, or seen "taken home at night, stripped naked, and whipped before all the men" for giving offense in the field. Moses mourned for those women who were still nursing infants left in the quarters as they worked endless hours—their breasts painfully growing full with the milk their babies hungered for—and all the while, they were subjected to the overseer's rawhide so much so that "blood and milk flew mingled from their breasts."[49] Elizabeth Sparks also implied these sexual overtones of enslaving men's violence when she recalled seeing, with her "own eyes," the perpetual beating of women stripped "naked an' wash[ed] down in brine," sometimes beaten "so bad, they jes' couldn't stand it an' they run away to the woods."[50] In Virginia, Katie Blackwell Johnson remembered the "moans and groans" of runaway slaves, including those of her mother, who was made to "straddle a big log" face down, her clothes held "over her head" while "they whipped her" for some infraction.[51] Though she didn't "like to talk 'bout dem times," Minnie Fulkes of Chesterfield County, Virginia told of her mother's sufferings at the hands of another overseer. But Minnie left no confusion with her interviewer as to the sexual nature of this violence when she shared that "this ol' man" used to tie her mother in the barn "with a rope aroun' her arms up over her head" before he would begin "beatin' her nekkid 'til the blood run down her back to her heels." Minnie remembered asking her mother what she had done to be beaten so, to which her mother replied, "nothin' tother than she refused to be wife to dis man."[52]

Fugitive women also chose to run to protect their families from torment and separation, and to protest slaveholder interference in their family lives. For example, after repeatedly refusing the sexual overtures and lewd advances of her enslaver, Harriet Jacobs of Chowan County, North Carolina, chose to run away from the plantation he sent her to after banishing her from the alleged comforts of life in his household—a punishment he intended to remedy her resolute rejections. It did not. Out of vengeance for this, James Norcom removed Harriet and her two-year-old daughter Louisa from their home in Edenton, separating her from her six-year-old son and sending them instead to labor at his son's plantation outside of town. There, at the Norcom's cotton plantation, while Harriet was forced to leave Louisa unattended while she labored long hours in the great house, the toddler "wandered about" with no one to look after her, "cried herself sick," and eventually fell asleep in a space two feet off the ground, underneath the house. It was the same place a "large snake" had crept from and had been killed that same afternoon. These punishments and tribulations did not end, and Norcom continued to pursue and intimidate her, first promising to send both of Harriet's children to labor indefinitely on the plantation if she did not comply, then by threatening to sell the children away for a "handsome sum." Between the pain of these schemes and threats, nineteen-year-old Harriet, exhausted from dodging the man's harassment and assaults, "resolved to leave them that night" so that she might altogether remove herself from Norcom's taunting manipulations, as his lust for power over her was now affecting the lives of her children and loved ones. When Harriet fled, the incredulous Norcom again retaliated against her family so that she might be forced into submission, this time by jailing her uncle, aunt, and children—still six and two years of age—to force her return. But Harriet was committed to her choice of flight—evading Norcom first temporarily, hiding in the homes of friends, "a thicket of bushes," and the refuge of Snaky Swamp at the southern end of the Great Dismal Swamp. She then fled to the garret underneath the roof of her grandmother's small house, where she remained for seven years, before finally reaching Philadelphia and New York

City. Although Norcom claimed Harriet had absconded "without any known cause or provocation" in the ad he listed for her apprehension, it was his own unhinged pursuit and malicious intervening in her loved ones' lives that led to Harriet's decisiveness. For in her prolonged absence and successful flight, Norcom lost interest in meddling with Harriet's family members and turned his attentions instead to hunting her down. Harriet's choices thus protected her family and kin and, above all in her mind, the well-being of her children.[53]

Just two counties east of the Dismal Swamp county of Chowan, at much the same time that Harriet duped Norcom in the town of Edenton, Moses Grandy was in Camden, witnessing the sunrise as enslaved mothers lay their young children down by the hedge-row at the ends of the cornfield, gave them "straws and other trifles to play with," and began their long, full days of work. Moses remembered the dangers that awaited those unattended small children, and the helpless anxiety of the women working in the fields under the threat of the lash. On one occasion, he saw "a large snake found coiled round the neck and face of a child, when its mother went to suckle it at dinner time."[54] Nestled as they were so near the lower swamps of the Great Dismal, the same danger had nearly befallen Harriet's daughter, Louisa, at the Norcom plantation after Harriet too, was ordered to neglect her maternal instincts, "steel [her]self" against the cries of her little one, and suffer the excruciating deprivation of the right to act in her natural role as a mother.[55] Given the accumulation of multiple forms of extreme violence, unremitting danger, and the psychological and emotional terror Black women faced, it is little wonder that women like Harriet, Moses's mother, and his sister Tamar preferred to flee and contend with the snakes they might encounter in the nearby Dismal Swamp rather than remain among the vipers of the plantation world, filled as it was with the bite and sting of anguish, grief, and certain dispossession.

When Venus took her leave from Robert Burwell's plantation in Isle of Wight County sixty-four years earlier, affairs in the Burwell family were in disarray. His Isle of Wight plantations were too small and were not profitable enough to provide for the many enslaved laborers who lived there. During the late 1760s, the Burwells actively contemplated minimizing their Tidewater operations and began earnestly to consider moving to fresher and more lucrative holdings. Robert had already sent Jack and Venus to the Dismal Swamp in the hope that his shares in the DSC business would turn a profit that could help him recover from mounting expenses. But by 1766, as increasing debts kept him pressed for funds, he pulled his shares from the struggling DSC venture, forcing Venus and Jack to move back again at his behest. It was during this time that he also acquired new land in Frederick

County—some two hundred miles northwest of Smithfield and the James and York River deltas—and began moving some of the enslaved people from his Isle of Wight estates to Frederick County to labor there instead. During this time of financial woes, Robert's wife Sarah grew ill and died of a stroke in March of 1770. After twenty-eight years of marriage, her death caused Robert to display a hard, lonely, and unhappy demeanor that some of his acquaintances made note of. Soon after, he sent two enslaved women as wedding gifts to his daughter in Gloucester County and turned the management of the Isle of Wight farms over to his son, Nathaniel.[56] On May 16, 1771, father and son posted an advertisement in the *Virginia Gazette* listing for sale three plantations on a "very good tract of land" amounting to a space of 3,500 acres "in good order of cropping, sufficient to work thirty five Hands."[57] Like so many other women before and after her, Venus paid careful attention to these matters that so affected her life and her future as she made decisions about her next steps. Just five months later, she was gone.

Although by the time Venus chose to run in November 1771 she had been "five Years accustomed to the house" and, back in Isle of Wight County after two tiresome years at Dismal Plantation, she would also have been reunited with her mother and family—Venus was not content. The Burwell family's financial struggles brought the threat of more forced relocation and disruption to her social and familial life, and this would have been of great concern to her.[58] On the verge of another uprooting, Venus kept in mind the education she received during her hire in the swamp as to the insurgent value of mobility, the resistive potential of the wetlands around her, and the successful escapes she had witnessed others achieve there. She chose not to look backward but to forge a new way forward, leaving behind the peril she experienced subjected to hard labor, violence, and the sexual economy of slavery. Like so many other women who responded in similar ways, Venus's decision to flee also signaled her rejection of slaveholders' unending disregard for and interference with her relationships with loved ones.

"SHE WAS SEDUCED AWAY": RUNNING WITH MEN

There was something about Jack that made Venus choose to run away with him in November 1771. Though there are no records confirming the nature of their relationship before they were ordered to the swamp the summer of 1764, that Venus was twenty-five and Jack twenty-eight when Burwell sent them there could suggest that the two were already a married couple and romantically involved before their tenure at Dismal Plantation. Given their prime age, and the fact that most enslaved women were partnered or with children before they reached their twenties, this would not be implausible. Still, it is also possible that the two did not know each other well before their time together at Dismal Plantation; and it is possible that once there, they bonded over arriving from the same place and provided each other a sense of comfort through their mutual familiarity with the same people, their dealings with the Burwells, and life in Isle of Wight County. However their relationship unfolded, five years after their return from the swamp to the Burwell home, Venus felt strongly enough about Jack to decide to abscond with him shortly after Robert and Nathaniel Burwell placed the estate they lived on up for sale. By the time Venus and Jack made this decision, the two were most likely married, as seven years later, after this first attempt to flee together did not go according to plan, Robert's second wife, Mary, listed Venus and "Jack Dismal"—her "husband"—as missing together, yet again.[59]

Fugitive women like Venus chose to run with men for a variety of reasons. For one, men generally knew more about the world outside the geographies of captivity and containment, and this knowledge would have proved invaluable for escape attempts likely to last. Many women may also have believed they would be safer fleeing beside men, since the societies they lived in largely assumed that "men could better defend themselves and were willing to resist recapture."[60] As the historian Sylviane Diouf has shown, "few" of the women reported to be at large or caught as fugitives and maroons in the areas bordering plantations and slaveholding towns were moving and living as individuals on their own. Most fled coupled with men, with their families, or in mixed groups so that they could benefit from mutual aid and the support and protection of others.[61] Of course, the pull and bond of romantic love, partnership, and the voluntary choice of one's intimate partner were also significant factors that should not be overlooked in women's decisions to take off, plot, and strategize their futures alongside men.

However, the actions of women like Venus who chose to flee with men they knew, trusted, and cared about should not be mistaken for women's lack of initiative; nor should these decisions overshadow women's own leadership and personal investment in escaping. Though racist and patriarchal assumptions about Black women led slaveholders to frequently imply and complain that their "negro women" ran off only because they were "seduced" into doing so by enslaved and fugitive men, Tidewater women nevertheless demonstrated their own capability, insistence, and desire to devise and sustain plans of escape—both long- and short-term—even if in collaboration with men.

In North Carolina, for example, Sall and Eve fled their enslavers in Hertford County and were believed to be keeping out of sight "at or near Elizabeth [City], and from there to the head of the Pasquotank River"—which is, unquestionably, the Great Dismal Swamp itself. The women's enslaver, John Wood, advised that Sall had been "seduced away" by her husband, George, and he was also sure that "Eve was seduced away" by her husband, "that noted villain Manuel." Both men were enslaved at another estate and belonged to a man by the name of Mathew Cluff. When Wood listed his $200 reward for the women's return in July of 1833, Eve had already been a fugitive for nearly four years—a testament, he surmised, to the "assistance of white persons" and her obtaining a free pass. Sall, a "tall, stout woman" with "smooth skin," had fled under the cover of night on July 2, 1833, after a visit from George. Wood suspected that wherever Eve was, she had "a child or children" with her, and that George had meant to "place" Sall with Eve, somewhere near Elizabeth City, so that both of the women and the child[ren] would be protected by Manuel "and his brothers"—fugitives who appear to have escaped after a failed attempt to transport them to New Orleans. John Wood could not conceive that Eve and Sall might have had even more reasons of their own to commit themselves to devising, supporting, and executing a plan to get away from him and their life of bondage at his estate in Hertford than the men might have had to flee from Mathew Cluff. Moreover, that these women were clever and intentional enough to support and place themselves and their children within this fugitive network that also seemed to be eyeing sustained evasion at the swamp's southern edge should call into question the role of Sall's and Eve's own ideas about their futures and cast doubt on the notion that they were merely passive followers behind what Wood believed to be the exclusive designs of male vision, capability, and leadership.[62]

Two sisters enslaved in Halifax County, North Carolina, wanted to escape Bassett Smith and Mush Island Plantation badly enough that they plotted to flee on Christmas Day—a holiday they knew would keep their captors unsuspecting and much distracted. Yet, Bassett reduced the sisters' calculated decision to leave him to his assumption that the "tall and spare," toothless, and "thin visage[d]" thirty-two-year-old Amey and her "very likely and well grown" ten-year-old sister Eliza had been "seduced away by a negro fellow named Adam." But given Smith's admiring description of the pre-teen and the protectiveness Amey displayed for her sister in ensuring that the child was included in the escape, the two must have had ample reason to plan and conspire to abscond together, including the very real prospect of sexual predation and the coercive "seductions" of young girls by overseers and slaveholders like Bassett.[63] These reasons would have been compounded by the obvious lack of health and nutrition Amey, at least, suffered at Mush Island. While Adam may well have provided aid and supported the two in their flight, the sisters themselves found sufficient cause to flee and set their own minds and feet into motion.

Like Sall, Eve, Amey, and Eliza, Chloe too was described by her pursuer as having, "upon hearing that she was to be sold, immediately eloped, or was seduced away." The subscriber, H. Potter, in placing his ad for the return of his troublesome property, believed that Chloe endeavored to move closer to her children, who lived in Edenton, but he maintained she must have had "the aid of some person, probably some negro fellow" in order to do so. Like so many other enslavers who wrote most of the documentary archive concerning the history of Black fugitivity, Potter was unable to credit an enslaved Black woman with the wherewithal to devise a plan of her own to escape and avoid sale. For Chloe, however, the slightest threat of being dragged farther away from her children and all that was familiar to her seems to have been enough to motivate her "immediate" resourceful action—even enough for Potter to inadvertently acknowledge that her "immediate" resourceful action suggested that her flight may or may not have involved or necessitated the assistance of "some negro fellow."[64]

As it pertains to the broader history of Atlantic world slavery, the recurring question of whether women's decisions to flee and maroon with men resulted from their being "seduced" or coerced, physically forced or "simply abducted by men," or whether they voluntarily *chose* to join fugitive and maroon ranks is one that should be revisited.[65] While there is some evidence of fugitive and maroon men luring or capturing enslaved women in colonial slavery and notably through *grand* marronage in the Caribbean and Latin America, consensual and voluntary flight and marronage among women prevailed nevertheless.[66] In colonial and antebellum Tidewater Virginia and North Carolina, there is no evidence of fugitive men raiding farms and plantations for women; yet, the dominant belief that enslaved women needed to be convinced one way or another to flee and embrace fugitive lives resonates and is largely a consequence of racist and patriarchal disbelief in Black women's personhood, competency, and will. Despite the incredulity of slaveholding authority that women held insurgent ideas about their own lives and futures other than continuous injury, labor, and use, Black women showed they were prepared to act upon their own fugitive convictions about forward movement and greater freedoms—even if they accompanied or were accompanied by men. After all, there is overwhelming evidence that enslaved women directly supported fugitives and shared in their rejection of the slaveholding world, just as there is irrefutable evidence that Tidewater women absconded on their own, sometimes doing so with their children, and sometimes doing so in the state of pregnancy.[67] While women like Venus benefited from male company and often chose to flee with men they knew for a variety of reasons, their minds and hearts were still at work on their own accord, making informed calculations about the direction, movement, and next best course of action needed to protect, evade, and construct new life possibilities.

Evidence of the mutual and cooperative initiative taken by fugitives like Venus and Jack, Eve and Manuel, and Sall and George is found in everyday and ordinary resistive action and in ever-present rival geographies—the contesting and competing worlds enslaved people made in their own interests—that informed enslaved thinking and decision-making. Just as men aided and assisted women seeking routes out, so too did women feed, protect, and help conceal fugitive men in their daily lives. Even if they lacked the opportunity to flee themselves or chose not to do so, enslaved women remained essential and ubiquitous supporters of fugitives because of their convictions about justice, because of their care for and investment in others in their communities—particularly those whom they loved—and because they recognized that the suffering and fate of other enslaved women and men was also theirs to share, oppose, and undo. Though gender, labor, and status differences factored into enslaved women's outlooks about what was in their own best interests, and while the appeal of individual protection or power was also a social reality that could result in division, mistrust, and betrayal among bondpeople, for many enslaved women and men alike, supportive acts toward or alongside fugitives were both personally gratifying and politically contributive to community safety and collective protest.[68]

In the Tidewater, enslaved women like Mamy Lou in Virginia, for example, built and upheld the insurgent potential of such enslaved-fugitive supportive networks by hiding her friend John one evening when patrollers arrived at her cabin door in search of him. On the other side of the door, what patrollers could not see, Fannie Berry remembered well. Inside the cabin, Fannie recalled the awesome sight of John running "between Mamy Lou's legs" where she hurried to spread her quilt "across her lap and kept on sewing an', do you kno', dem pattyrollers never found him?"[69] Other women were known to feed, harbor, and protect the whereabouts of fugitives. In Edenton, North Carolina, Harriet Jacobs's grandmother, Molly Horniblow, certainly did, when she hid, secured, and defended Harriet in the garret below her roof for over seven years. Similarly, Cornelia Carney of Williamsburg, Virginia, recalled that her mother used to send her eldest brother "out to de woods wid food fo' father," who was beaten so much and so bad that after a while "he run away an' lived in de woods." Her father was never caught, but it was her mother's hand in this arrangement that impressed upon Cornelia a lasting lesson: They were "too smart fo' white folks to git ketched."[70]

Fugitive men headed for and moving through the Great Dismal Swamp also directly benefited from the support, confidence, and nourishment provided by enslaved women. Charley, for one, had been so set against the promise that he was to be sold at market in Richmond, coupled with the unfairness he felt at having long been separated from his wife, Lizzie, that he decided to "make clear." He remembered: "I jest let my legs be 'sponsible for my heels, till da bringed me and my heels to de woods." After traveling for miles, all day long, Charley reached his wife, before walking fifteen more miles to see his mother at her house. He left the woman "frettin' mightily" over him, before she bid him her goodbye. Charley then moved on to the house of a friend, whose wife, in her husband's absence, "knowed I was hungry, and so she ga'en me a right smart supper, and arterwards I intired." These Tidewater women did not balk or turn Charley away; instead, they were ready to offer him affection, news, victuals, counsel, and a place to rest and shelter before he set out to maroon in the Dismal Swamp.[71]

A similar scenario may have graced Stephen's travels toward the swamp. In 1811, twenty-two years before Sall and Eve were reported to have been "seduced away" from the estate of John Wood, the very same John Wood learned that Stephen was likely splitting his time between visits with his mother, Franky—"commonly called Old Frank"—who lived in Pasquotank County, and the "Shingle Swamp" at the Dismal Swamp Canal, where he was suspected to be working. When John posted the reward notice for Stephen's return, Stephen had already been missing five years.[72] What's more, sixteen years after Sall and Eve fled to the swampy head of the Pasquotank River from Wood's estate, Solomon, too, ran from the Wood family, this time escaping John's wife, Mary. Mary wanted the thirty-to-thirty-five-year-old apprehended and jailed for robbing her of his labor, and she was willing to pay a thirty-dollar reward to make it happen. She believed Solomon was "lurking about" the neighborhood of his wife or mother in Elizabeth City, but she was also worried he "may endeavor to make his way to the Dismal Swamp."[73]

Another man, Daniel, also thirty-five years old, took to the swamps and waterways outside Elizabeth City to be near his wife, who lived near Newbegun Creek—a stream originating from the Dismal Swamp and emptying south into the Pasquotank River. Between Daniel's "lurking about there," it was expected that he, too, was spending his time "endeavoring to make his way to the dismal swamp."[74] Aaron was believed to be "lurking thereabouts" in the swamps near Nixonton, North Carolina, where his wife lived, but besides this destination, he might have been seeking "employment as a shingle weaver, on the Virginia side of the Dismal."[75] Fleeing from Chowan County, near Edenton, North Carolina, Diver was thought to be "lurking about among his relations," either in the lower part of Pasquotank County, "near the shingle-Swamp," or nearby on the Virginia side of the Dismal, "having a mother in Nansemond County."[76] Bev, a literate man described as often wearing a "broad grin upon his face," escaped from Gates County, North Carolina, where he had been seen "lurking around" the house of a woman, though he would probably soon be "aiming for the Dismal Swamp."[77] These associations between fugitive men and enslaved women suggest that Black women provided supportive networks, intelligence and information, protective secrecy, resources, encouragement, and morale that would have been vital in sustaining escape and achieving enduring and worthwhile flight and marronage at the swamp's borderlands.

Frederick Douglass was wise and experienced enough to know how true this was. It was probably his personal journey as a fugitive who escaped slavery in Talbot County, Maryland—an accomplishment he owed much to the support and aid provided by his wife, Anna Murray—that inspired him to write the short story, *The Heroic Slave*, in 1853.[78] The novella imagines Madison, a fugitive who conspired with his enslaved wife, Susan, to prolong his escape in the Dismal Swamp so that they could avoid imminent separation and remain together. For five years, Susan—whom Madison "knew might be trusted with [his] secrets even on the scaffold"—met him weekly in the swamp's pine woods, each time arriving "true to her word . . . laden with provisions." Douglass wanted his readers to envision the two meeting and deliberating in the forested swamp "at that dark and lonesome hour of the night," where together they came to an understanding and devised a plan. Madison would: "make the woods my home, for if I gave myself up, I should be whipped and sold away; and if I started for the North, I should leave a wife doubly dear to me. We mutually determined, therefore, that I should remain in the vicinity. In the dismal swamps I lived, sir, five long years."[79] Douglass knew firsthand that such an enduring feat of flight, evasion, and what amounted to borderland marronage, often depended on the preexisting rival geography and resistive ground that Black women were instrumental in creating.

The mutual aim and reciprocal support Venus shared with Jack is also corroborated by the commonplace assistance even enslaved men, who were decidedly not fugitives, offered the rarer and more vulnerable company of fugitive women. Enslaved men like Moses Grandy went to great lengths to support and help protect the fugitive women they knew and loved. When Moses's sister Tamar fled to the "den" she made for herself in the folds of the Dismal Swamp in Camden County, North Carolina, he "tied pieces of wood or bundles of rags" to his feet so that no track would be made when he delivered her provisions and news about the world outside the swamp. Although he was enslaved some twenty-five miles away, Tamar's husband also extended great effort to support her. He ventured the long distance to visit her in the swamp as often as he could after his day's work, or on a Sunday, bringing with him whatever he could save.[80] If enslaved men and women stood at the ready to help conceal, provide for, and protect fugitive people, it should be no surprise that fugitive women and men did the same for one another. Black men and women benefited from these relationships of care, service, and aid both before and during flight and escape.

Just as many enslaved women did not flinch at giving and extending their support to those on the run, many others did not hesitate to take off on their own, with little other than the expedience of their own two feet. Enslaved by none other than Councilman Col. William Byrd II, the tenacity of one enslaved woman to escape him—though unnamed in the diary he kept—is exemplary of this. Byrd and his family lived at Westover Plantation, not far from their friends and neighbors the Burwells, who lived at the time between Merchant's Hundred Plantation (later Carter's Grove) in Williamsburg, and the Gloucester estates along the York River.[81] The enslaved woman had had enough when one day she refused to tolerate Byrd and her labor at his tobacco plantation any longer, and she conspicuously discarded her hoe and left it "by the church land" before taking off. According to Byrd's diary, the woman had run from him repeatedly between June and November of 1709, breaking away at least four times on record. Steadfast, she made good use of the cover of night to make her escapes, and she even managed to do so after she was repeatedly "found and tied." She did not let being forced to wear the humiliating iron bit (muzzle) stop her from running either. She was found on July 8, a week after her second attempt to escape, and though she still suffered the iron bit, she wasted no time in fleeing a third time that very night. Sometime between that moment and November, she was again captured, because on the sixth day of that month, Byrd reported that she "ran away again." It would seem, nothing but death could prevent the woman's flight from Westover and her refusal to remain under Byrd's command, as her fourth escape attempt was her last. Before the "prayers, good thoughts, good health, and good humor" that Byrd appreciated at the end of his November 13th entry, he wrote, with revelatory dismissal, a fleeting mention that the "negro woman who ran away was found dead."[82]

Across time, other Tidewater women chose not to wait for the guidance, protection, or any other perceivable benefit that running with men might have afforded. Evidence of this abounds. At eighteen years of age, Mary escaped John Baley of Pasquotank County, North Carolina, who had grown too familiar with her "large fleshy" body, "very large breast," and the "scar on the calf of one of her legs," for her to stick around a moment longer.[83] After being sold to a new man, Nelly—the "mild tempered" seventeen-year-old noted for her "pleasant countenance"—was also wily enough to move through Norfolk and escape, despite her new owner's assurances that in his service she would find "all due indulgence, and a good home."[84] Charles Grandy, of the same enslaving family who claimed ownership of Moses, Tamar, and their mother, listed the "likely" and "young" Ruth a runaway from his home in Camden. Charles believed that the twenty-year-old might be found across state lines in Virginia, "lurking about Norfolk," a distance that would have required bold passage through waterways and portions of the Dismal Swamp.[85] From Chowan County, North Carolina, Clarissa and Mariam decided to run together and managed on their own to evade Elizabeth Pettijohn for at least two weeks.[86] John Cornick of Princess Anne County, Virginia, did not believe that twenty-seven-year-old Pendar would return to him without the help of the white public on alert, after she fled from him on her own just eleven days before.[87] Nell, at age eighteen, chose to flee John Hutchings of Norfolk, despite, or perhaps as consequence of the fact that she had "a few stripes on her shoulders."[88] Described as a "mulatto wench," Sukey absconded on her own, braving it with her three-year-old "mulatto" daughter Matilda.[89] A forty-year-old woman named Nancy stole a bay mare and rode her way to Pasquotank to escape her recent purchaser, James Burrow.[90] Even a child named Maria, "about 11 or 12 years of age, flat nose, short but strongly built," fled from the man she was hired out to in Princess Anne County. The young girl had been spotted alone "about Deep Creek"—a small town about eighteen miles west of there, at the edge of the Dismal Swamp.[91]

Black women were ready and positioned to make choices like Venus's, without the compulsion of male seduction. Though they did not evenly experience the same opportunities to choose flight, men and women mutually provided aid and received support both as enslaved people and as fugitives. As people who were already invested in the competing world of dissemblance, clandestine knowledge, and fugitivity throughout the Great Dismal Swamp and surrounding Tidewater region, women and girls, mothers and daughters, proved their readiness to foster new worlds of dissent and alternative life both through their support of fugitives and through escapes motivated by their own sense of urgency, safety, and desire for better futures. In these roles, Venus and others like her were integral to inscribing these wetlands with insurgent meaning.

"LURKING" AS KINSHIP AND ROMANTIC LOVE

If anything is indicated by the three separate advertisements for the return of Venus and Jack, posted and paid for by multiple members of the Burwell family, it is that the two made very clear their unwillingness to be apart. After their shared experience as laborers in the Dismal Swamp, Venus and Jack decided to take control of their own lives and futures, and they meant to do it together. Just as other enslaved men and women had, the couple desired an independent intimate life removed from white interference and surveillance and a marriage and family untethered to hereditary bondage. Though generally a permitted and allowable custom, enslaved marriages were not recognized by law and were further strained by the extreme precarity and vulnerability enslaved people faced from sale, relocation, being forced to live at different homesteads, and from injurious, ongoing sexual violence that devastated couples.[92] Venus and Jack had other plans. The "talkative," "saucy," and "cunning" man had much in common with the quick-thinking and "smooth tongued" woman, and together, the two knew they would fare better on the run than they would remaining at the sale-pending plantation in the hands of new management or hanging on to hope that they would stay together after the plantation was sold. They knew it would be only a matter of time before Nathaniel Burwell announced their fates, along with the fates of the rest of the human property held at the Isle of Wight estates. As prospective fugitives, Jack and Venus would have been encouraged by the experience they already had in moving through the woods, rivers, creeks, and swamps that characterized the Tidewater. When they fled from the Burwells in November 1771, they would have made logical and good use of these fugitive spaces both as destinations and as means of travel. However they managed to flee, they did so successfully for at least six months, well into April of 1772, at which time the Burwells stopped listing their reward of forty shillings for the return of each of them.[93]

Testament to Jack and Venus's cunning, there is no way to know where they stopped and slept, or how they arranged meals, how they stayed warm during the winter, or with whom, if anyone, they communed during those months of sustained escape. What can be known, however, is that somehow, and for some reason, the pair returned to the Burwells in Isle of Wight County in the late spring or summer of 1772. Given their repeated escapes and assertions of intelligent defiance, the two were less likely to have surrendered than they were to have been caught and apprehended, particularly as the Burwells were intent on punishing the two for their insubordination. Within months of their recapture and reinstatement at the plantation, Robert and Nathaniel Burwell banished Jack from Isle of Wight County—separating him indefinitely from Venus and other loved ones—by sending him to northern Virginia to work at their Frederick County plantations. There, Jack was to be assigned to labor he knew well: Trees needed felling, fields needed clearing, timber needed to be cut, shingles needed to be made, houses and buildings needed construction, fences were to be erected, orchards were to be planted, livestock needed care, and of course, tobacco, corn, wheat, flax, and hemp needed to be cultivated and harvested. For Jack, this forced journey would have meant traveling a distance of roughly 180 miles by a combination of horse, water, and his own two feet. The trip required travel by ferry and the crossing of several major rivers, beginning with the James, the Rappahannock, and finally the Shenandoah River, near the town of Fredericksburg. It would have taken Jack up to two weeks to reach the Burwell properties in Frederick—if he had gotten that far. Instead, days if not weeks before Robert Burwell solicited the return of "Jack Dismal" in the *Virginia Gazette* in February 1773, the "slim made" and "artful fellow" had already fled from the overseer of operations in Fredericksburg, refusing to take another step toward Frederick. The latter was a destination Jack would have viewed as one of no return. Robert Burwell supposed that Jack had found his way back to the Rappahannock River "in some vessel," with the aim of reconnecting to the more-familiar James River. He wasn't wrong. Jack had waited for the right opportunity to flee, and when he found it, he went downriver. His next steps were to return to Venus.[94]

Enslaved people like Venus and Jack could not be stopped from moving and running for love, and women and men did so throughout the duration of chattel slavery. Across the archive of runaway slave advertisements, fugitives are commonly suspected of taking flight in order to locate and reach friends and loved ones; and at other times, they are described as absconding as couples, families, and kin in order to stay together. Fugitive men and women alike were accused of "lurking" in certain neighborhoods, towns, cities, or along rivers, creeks, and swamps where they might be nearer the people they loved and trusted. Yet the favorite slaveholding descriptor "lurking" falsely depicts Black kinship, family, and the intimate, binding ties of romantic love as nothing more than mindless skulking, or else senseless loitering and criminal prowling. Ignoring and invalidating the legitimacy of these ties altogether, this language intentionally fails to account for affective interpersonal connection, amorous relationships, and the strength of blood and fictive kinship bonds that comprised the very fabric of Black social life and community, and that so often motivated escape.

Venus and Jack were one of countless Tidewater couples who shared the impulse to reject captive intimate lives and choose collaborative flight instead. Polly and Carter, too, were thought to be "lurking about" in the vicinity of Halifax, North Carolina, after the "yellow" and "genteel" looking Polly had made threats that the two would soon make their escape to the free states. Even though her enslaver, Lunsford Scott, recognized that the twenty-eight-year-old "wench" was "an expert hand at roguery, and is well calculated to deceive," he also maintained that she had to have been "seduced away" by the likes of her beaux, Carter. The two made good on Polly's word and were not to be found.[95] Ben and Celia chose a Sunday night in the springtime to flee their new enslaver in Salmon Creek, in Bertie County. From there, the husband and wife decided to cross the Chowan River and together traverse the Dismal Swamp leading into Chowan and Gates Counties, where they had once lived, were "well known," and where Celia's mother, still enslaved there, might offer them her support.[96] When Polydore and Nelly met and joined as husband and wife, the couple was determined to honor and secure their future together, free from the interfering demands of the Adams and Hare families of Surry County and the town of Hampton in Elizabeth City County, Virginia, respectively. The two had very clearly plotted and deliberated their plan together with tremendous strategy, foresight, and care, for Polydore had already fled the Adams family in Surry and was waiting in Norfolk for his wife to leave the Hare family at Back-River, in Hampton, and join him there. To Thomas Hare's immense frustration, Nelly was unwilling to remain with him, and she left no uncertainty about this when she absconded from his service to join Polydore in Norfolk instead. To add insult to injury, Nelly brought with her a vast collection of clothing she had stolen from Thomas and his wife, as well as thirty dollars in silver she figured the Hares owed her, to fund and support a promising journey north to the foreseeable free states, beside her devoted husband.[97]

While these women "lurked about" as strategies to sustain flight and fugitive futures with the men they loved, other women were accused of "lurking" to ensure their physical nearness to enslaved husbands, who were otherwise unreachable or separated from them, without necessarily aiming to flee with them to other destinations. Women like Azzy, who was "so well known that a description is deemed unnecessary," was probably lingering in the neighborhood of Chowan, where her husband lived.[98] Similarly, a "pretty black woman" named Tamer fled a new enslaver who lived in the North Carolina Piedmont before she traveled a distance of over three hundred miles to reach her enslaved husband back in Elizabeth City, where it was believed she was laying out.[99] The "yellowish" and "slim spare made" Dinah also took flight to reach her husband, Hews, an enslaved river pilot who had already brazenly informed her enslaver that he "would keep his wife out eternally." At twenty-five years of age, Dinah chose to embrace her own direction and reject her status as Philip M'Guire's possession; as a result, M'Guire informed the *Edenton (NC) Gazette* that the "wench is lurking in and about Edenton, for the purpose . . . of better effecting her escape, together with her husband, who has threatened to march off, and take her with him." The two may have preferred to remain near Edenton—a town so pervious to coursing rivers and the swamps of the Great Dismal that it was known to be "a place more noted, than any in the state, for the concealing and harboring of runaways."[100]

Some might have described Jack as lurking around the Burwell farms after his return to Isle of Wight County from Fredericksburg, sometime after February 1773. When Venus learned of his reappearance, she had likely felt both overjoyed and moved by deep concern. She would have known that Jack's latest daring could result in yet more trouble, with consequences they both would feel. Since her escape with Jack the previous year, Venus had returned to housework alongside her mother and sister(s), and during the time Jack was away, her work was likely consumed with thoughts of whether she might ever see him returned. But she might have also kept in mind that Jack was driven and fearless enough to make a run for it a second time. Thoughts like these would have proven true, as "Jack-dismal" was among those still enslaved and in the service of the Burwells, alongside Venus, in the years that followed.[101]

While there is no record of the undoubtedly harsh punishment Jack received for such bold and repeated escapes undertaken to remain by Venus's side, he was not forced to endure another journey north to Frederick County and was instead eventually assigned to work in the Burwell home. By December 31, 1774, Robert had married his second wife, Mary Braxton, and the two had taken their Isle of Wight household—including a total of fourteen adult enslaved domestic laborers—along with them to Newington Plantation in inland King and Queen County, where Mary had lived prior to marriage. Among this group of transferred enslaved laborers were Jack, Venus, her mother, sister(s), and presumably other friends from the Smithfield plantation. Throughout this time, Jack and Venus would have been together, first reunited at Isle of Wight County, and then at Newington Plantation following Robert's second marriage. Even after their move to King and Queen County, the Burwell's Isle of Wight holdings remained on the market; the estate was not sold until 1782—a delay caused by the eruption of war throughout the decade. The Revolutionary War interrupted much, and by 1775, Robert Burwell and other James River planters like him moved their families to locations farther inland where less vulnerable to British attacks. The war also caused Nathaniel Burwell to temporarily pause his efforts to develop the Frederick estates in earnest, a factor that might have contributed to the Burwells' decision against sending Jack back to Frederick County after his escape at Fredericksburg. Throughout most of the war years, Jack and Venus remained together at Newington alongside family and friends from Isle of Wight, until the fateful aftermath of Robert Burwell's death in January 1777, when the threat of separation and forced movement once again disturbed their lives. Venus weighed her heart and mind against an uncertain future without Jack, as well as an unfree future with or without him, and when the opportunity presented itself in the summer of 1778, against all risk, she chose to flee with him a second time.[102]

Venus wasn't the only enslaved woman in the Tidewater to use the instability of war and conflict among the slaveholding class to her advantage. Throughout the Revolutionary War, women gained additional means and opportunity to execute escapes they may have only imagined in the years prior. Corroding surveillance and authority resulted in many enslaved people choosing to flee more frequently than they had before.[103] What's more, the fugitive and resistive actions enslaved women and men were already taking in pursuit of their liberty before the war now played a key role in pushing the last Royal Governor of Virginia, Governor John Murray, the Earl of Dunmore, toward issuing his Proclamation of 1775. In November of that year, Dunmore recognized the freedom of enslaved people on the condition that they serve the Loyalist cause, offering further encouragement and a new sense of security to Black women's already-established and pronounced interests in escape.[104] With this added incentive in place, thousands of Black women, men, and children fled slaveholders in Virginia, Maryland, and the Carolinas to join the British. Since New York City was occupied by the British between 1776 and 1783, it became both the headquarters of British military operations and the most secure destination for Loyalists—white and Black alike. Of the three thousand enslaved people who fled the southern colonies and arrived at British camps in New York, 1,336 were men, 914 were women, and 750 were children.[105]

Hundreds of fugitives from Virginia were among those documented there by name, age, and brief description of labor, status, origin, and date of arrival. Of these, the Tidewater region was represented by women like Hannah, who at twenty-two fled Norfolk with no one but her one-year-old daughter, Nancy. When Hannah arrived in New York in 1776, she was appointed to the British Wagon Master General's department, where she spent seven years driving the carts hauling British military equipment and provisions. At thirty-five, Bridget left on her own immediately following Dunmore's Proclamation and also joined the Wagon Master General's department. Funky Hancock, "25, ordinary wench," fled Princess Anne County in 1781; and Rachel Jordan, "30, stout wench," took her eleven-year-old son and nine-year-old daughter out of the reach of her enslavers in Nansemond County, in 1779. Sukey fled Norfolk with her five-year-old daughter, Nancy, and her eleven-month-old son, George, in 1778. Once in New York, she also worked for the Wagon Master General's department, until 1783, when she boarded the *Nisbet* along with 250 other fugitives bound for Nova Scotia. When registering herself as someone due formal emancipation before boarding, she gave the name "Sukey Dismal." At least one other person boarding the *Nisbet* did the same. Though Sukey may not have known him, Sam registered himself as another Tidewater fugitive with probable connections to the northern edges of the Dismal Swamp, when he reported his name to be Sam Dismal from Somerset County, Maryland—just a boat ride north of the James River and the northern swamp by way of the Chesapeake. Many registrants failed, declined, or were for other reasons not given last names in the registry. But Sukey and Sam—perhaps not unlike Venus's Jack—made clear their connection with the Great Dismal Swamp when they styled their names and maintained that the "dismal" would continue to signify who they were and how they envisioned themselves. These Dismal Swamp references and associations may have been Sukey, Sam, and Jack's identifications of fugitive pride to have worked, lived, or moved agentively through the swamps of the Great Dismal, and they could have also been ways of linking to or reminding themselves of their places of origin and the home spaces they knew and that were meaningful to them as they charted new, emancipated lives during the Age of Revolution.[106]

Although Venus was never called "Venus Dismal" in any of the records surrounding her life, Jack himself was first noted as "Jack Dismal" when he fled Fredericksburg in 1773, nearly a decade following his time spent with

Venus in the swamp at Dismal Plantation. The name was used again in 1777, when Robert Burwell noted "Jack-dismal" as someone whose "use" would belong to Mary Braxton Burwell following his death. The following year, the appellation appears again in a third and final runaway slave ad concerning Jack and Venus, published by Mary in the *Virginia Gazette* for the apprehension of "three negro women, named Venus, Zeny, and Nelly, and a negro man named Jack Dismal"—the "husband of Venus," who was "probably with her."[107] Three of Mary's domestic bondwomen had run away—one, Venus, a known repeat fugitive, alongside her husband, a "saucy" figure known for at least three escape attempts and a seemingly willful association with an insurgent swamp—and Zeny (also Zenith) and Nelly, a mother and daughter who had also been employed in the Burwell home. The widowed Mary had moved her enslaved household from Newington in King and Queen County yet again, this time to a farm in Prince William County, in northern Virginia, along the Potomac River. Although Zenith left behind her son, Nelly's brother, and although Venus parted with her own mother and sister(s) to be with Jack, something about Mary, her intentions, or the recent move to Prince William County disinclined them to stay put. Mary's expectations that Venus and the others would comply and remain with her were no match for the group's own will to flee and get on the move; and soon after their uprooting to a destination so far north, Mary reported them "lurking" in the neighborhoods of Williamsburg or Isle of Wight.[108]

Beyond the prospects and parameters of war, Venus and this fugitive troop set off from the Burwell holdings because they had other ideas about where, how, and with whom they wanted to live. Their links and relationships show that "lurking" women on the run were protecting and upholding not just romantic love but the affective bonds between mothers and daughters, family and kinship, and that they were willing to assert these intimate connections as most important to them. Into the early national and antebellum periods, running and lurking as practices of love and togetherness continued. Examples abound. Although the fugitive-minded Flora and Chloe were not blood relations, the two were kindred souls and friends enough to choose to flee John Lanston together to reach their respective family members in Edenton, North Carolina. Lanston, who cruelly described Flora as a "slender, raw boned ugly negro . . . well known in Edenton to be as bad as she is ugly," and Chloe as "black, tall and likely," was certain that Flora would be found near her mother or her sister, who each lived in different places near the town. Lanston thought Chloe would be found either near her husband, her father, or her one-month-old baby, who might have been at the residence of her sister. All these family connections had been viciously torn from these two women, who consequently decided to lurk, linger, and move to restore and nurture them anyway. Against their enslaver's wishes, Flora and Chloe escaped to be near those they loved in ways that soothed and rectified the hurt and pain of this excruciating harm.[109] Harriet also considered lurking to be the safest way to stay close to her mother while also ensuring that she, too, was protected. The "audacious and impudent" nineteen-year-old "bright mulatto" had an unimaginably slim set of life options. Yet out of these, she chose to reject and run away from John Davis and the demands he made of her. These seemed to include his dependence upon her "slothful and dirty" habits as a noted "great favorite of some people who call themselves gentlemen." Harriet fled Elizabeth City and was "supposed to be lurking" in her mother's neighborhood between Nixonton and Newbegun Creek, where she could escape the pangs of kinlessness, dispossession, sexual violence, and coercion and might instead be nearer the console, support, protection, and strength of a mother's love.[110]

Wherever Venus and Jack chose as their destination in the summer of 1778, they fled from Prince William County during the war, at the moment they thought most opportune; and they did so with a wealth of faith, trust, courage, and love. Traveling a distance of nearly two hundred miles back south, the couple would have fled along the currents of abundant and interconnected waterways that joined physically and likely conceptually to their own significant knowledge of the Dismal Swamps of Isle of Wight and Nansemond Counties, both just south of the James River. It is possible that Jack and Venus, Zenith and Nelly opted to move together as one group, heading for the same destination or safe places. But as Mary Burwell suggested, it is also possible, if not probable, that Jack and Venus separated from their friends and chose fugitive life in the forested wetlands of Isle of Wight County, nearer the swamp where they had lived and worked, and where it was reported they had been seen. Knowing definitively where the fugitives decided to go is an impossibility, but given the steadfastness of their repeated determinations to flee, their fugitive education and "artful" careers in the Dismal Swamp, their persistent association with the Dismal Swamp, and the absence of any record of their capture, it would not be unreasonable to deduce that Venus and Jack were among those in the Tidewater who viewed and used the woods, waters, and swamp recesses as places of refuge, kinship, and fugitive insurgency.[111]

The interruption of war, the unending problem of flight and marronage, and the irrepressible nature of the Dismal Swamp itself led to the failure of Dismal Plantation and the slow demise of the DSC's efforts to subdue and control the swamp. Following the war, capitalist demands to establish more and more local extractive economies led to the rise of collaborative efforts between incorporated slaveholding companies intent on draining the swamp and making it more navigable for the purpose of exporting wood shingles, staves, and other natural resources. Primary among these was the Dismal Swamp Canal Company, established in 1791, which began employing enslaved laborers to hand-dig what would become a twenty-two-mile-long "Great Canal" extending from Deep Creek in Norfolk County to the Pasquotank River in North Carolina. Completed in 1829, the canal resulted in an increase in travelers, company men, overseers, and enslaved laborers—primarily men and boys as young as ten—who were present within the swamp after the year 1800.[112] Yet all ongoing efforts to dominate and tame the swamp, and even the increase in white citizenry and authority in areas of the swamp claimed by companies, did not prevent fugitive-minded women and men from relating to the swamp ecology differently; nor did it stop them from continuing to choose flight toward and through it. Even with the passage of legislation such as North Carolina's 1847 "Act to Provide for the Apprehension of Runaway Slaves in the Great Dismal Swamp and for Other Purposes," women and men employed in or near the swamp as well as in the surrounding Tidewater counties continued "setting at defiance the power of their masters, corrupting and seducing other slaves, and by their evil example and evil practices, lessening the due subordination, and greatly impairing the value of slaves in the district of country bordering the said great dismal swamp."[113]

Venus and other captive women in the Tidewater had choices to make. Whether as enslaved or as fugitive women, the decisions they made out of care and concern for themselves, their families, and their loved ones were always in contest with the most limiting and violating raced and gendered terms and options. More than anyone else in the societies they lived in, Black women, as bondwomen, faced the fullest and most frequent forms of sexual, corporeal, and emotional violence as well as gendered constraints on their mobility and exposure to geographies outside of white paternalistic surveillance. Still, they maintained resistive roles within their communities and helped build and sustain competing worlds of Black social life and insurgent action; and they often began doing so through their ever-present aid to and support of fugitives. On the run, women also chose to risk personal harm, getting lost, the endangerment to their children, violent punishment, and the difficulties of weather and the elements. Despite all threats against them, both before and during flight, Black women were in conversations with themselves, they were in communication with their supportive networks, and they also consulted and deliberated with the uncontainable natural world around them in ways that offered encouragement and conviction above fear, doubt, and anxiety. With a mix of their own shrewdness, determination, trust, and belief in justice and the right to free life, they chose to move elsewhere through other routes and paths.

Although most Tidewater women and men who chose to run did not become Dismal Swamp maroons—some did. Women who chose the swamp outskirts bordering slaveholding towns as well as those who chose the swamp's more remote and inaccessible interior retreats, carried with them experiences and backgrounds similar to those of Venus and the other Tidewater women whose stories have shaped the preceding pages. These are the women who would continue choosing to elect, to birth, and to defend—sometimes by force—more enduring forms of fugitive and insurgent life in and surrounding the great swamp throughout the antebellum years ahead.

THREE

"They Bid Defiance to Any Force Whatever"

MAROON WOMEN AND DEFENSIVE VIOLENCE

> One tried to throw me, but he couldn't. We tusseled an' knocked over chairs an' when I got a grip I scratched his face all to pieces; an dar was no more bothering Fannie from him.
>
> MRS. FRANCES "FANNIE" BERRY, 1937

Fugitive women and men who became maroons in the swamp edges nearest Tidewater cities and towns were those least likely to know and experience nonviolent lifeways and most likely to embrace the insight and value of armed defense. These *petit*, "borderland," or "fringe" maroons were often notorious for ambushing white citizens, stealing and destroying property, and inciting and encouraging enslaved people to join them in support of these insurgencies.[1] Newspaper reports published in Dismal Swamp–adjacent towns make clear that slaveholding society both loathed and feared these maroons who were determined to act in their own defense and fortification against capture. In their firm stance to resist captivity and enslavement by means of force, the activities of these peripheral or swamp edge–dwelling maroons also presented a nearly constant reminder that the social and economic order enslavers sought and desired was openly defied by "runaway" warfare.[2]

Black women might have been party to maroon men like General Sampson, Pompey "Pomp" Little, Shadrack, and Bob Ricks when white male authorities failed to notice them, but readily took to their pens to note that it was these men who were responsible for "set[ting] the world at defiance plundering, mustering, feasting & frolicking almost in public view, in open day, corrupting, [and] poisoning the minds of every slave."[3] Shadrack, a "runaway for over two years" near the swamps surrounding Edenton, North Carolina, was reported to have been "discovered lurking" after a "long" career of "depredating upon property of the inhabitants of this town and county."[4] Three years later, in the summer of 1822, in the Dismal Swamp county directly north of there, a white traveler quickly gave his account of an encounter with a maroon man to reporters with the *Portsmouth and Norfolk Herald*. The outraged traveler stated that he had been "leisurely riding along" in a Gates County, North Carolina, pine forest along the western swamp when he was "shocked" by the sudden appearance of a "heavy-set, full-faced, six-foot-tall" maroon "brandishing a long two-edged knife." The maroon, who had for seven years remained at large from Littleton Plantation in Hertford County, North Carolina, "professionally" informed the man that he was welcome to call him "Pomp," as he began to rob the traveler for all of the money he held.[5] Two years later, operating in the woods and swamps in the same county, Bob Ricks and other "runaway desperadoes" shot, stabbed, and slit the throat of their pursuers just three months before the "six negro men armed with guns" attacked two slave traders driving a coffle. The maroons "demanded the release" of the ironclad captives while "presenting and snapping their guns" at the slavers, who were then "compelled to run for their lives."[6]

Without question, maroon men were the "runaways" most likely to pose the greatest and most apparent threat to slaveholding society across the Dismal Swamp counties and towns. Their visibility in documentary records is in part a testament to the fact that young men made up the overwhelming majority of these outlaw groups as well as fugitives more broadly.[7] But white male authorities also more readily noted and attributed the leadership and execution of borderland maroon activities to male insurgents—even in the few documented cases of Dismal Swamp borderland marronage in which the presence of edge-dwelling maroon women is acknowledged. The logic of patriarchy and paternalistic slavery required slaveholders to view and understand physical, intellectual, and political capability as belonging to men and to male rule. But in this patriarchal haze, what Tidewater authorities missed was that sometimes the progenitors, advisers, participants, and supporters of these seemingly all-male "outliers," "assassins," "lurkers," and "banditti"—were women.

In refusing their enslavement, maroon women in outlaw groups at the swamp's outskirts were not only outnumbered by their male counterparts, they also had to move between the underworld of the swamps and the perilous world of male supremacy and sexual domination they knew might be found inside the swamp, but was certainly found outside of it. On top of these vulnerabilities, women's decisions to join these fringe maroon groups were also dangerous, as these groups were itinerant, on the run, and swamp bound. These were the maroons most likely to be caught—reliant as they were on plunder, the theft of arms, and constant readiness for violent self-preservation. It is little wonder that so few women appear to have joined these "brigands." Yet, that women appear to have done so in a handful of documented accounts, necessitates our looking behind, underneath, against, and through their presumed passivity and inaction following insubordinate men, or their otherwise scant mentions for more about their own possible motives, actions, and approaches to sustaining evasion at the fringe. These women joined and helped shape alternative, fugitive worlds in the swamp alongside men like Sampson, Bob, Pompey, and Shadrack, attesting to the ways that overt insurgency and violent defense were also endeavors undertaken by maroon women.

FUGITIVE WOMEN AND VIOLENCE

However discomfiting it may be, violence has always been integral to Black people's liberatory strategy, and this is *because* it has always been integral to captivity, enslavement, and state-sanctioned violence.[8] In the words of Frantz Fanon, "violence is a cleansing force" for "those who have nothing to lose and everything to gain."[9] It is a force that frees from the clutches of despair, inaction, fear, and degradation when all other options have been exhausted. Against the ongoing warfare that was chattel slavery, it was also an intellectual and political deliberation that was a reciprocating, dialectical, and direct response to violent means of domination and control.[10] For the enslaved and the maroons they became, the use of violence was defensive, protective, and meant to motivate and engender radical change against the force of unabating injury. Carried out by fugitives and maroons, defensive violence—forceful or deadly acts of self-preservation and self-possession, including the imperative of community protection, control, and perseverance—was a political declaration as well as a critique meant to weaken, dismantle, or otherwise reject and expose the fragile order of slaveholding power.[11]

Although until recently, the history of slavery has tended to interpret violent rebellion "as the prerogative of enslaved men," enslaved women had as many, if not more, reasons to resort to physical confrontation as enslaved men.[12] Not only were they subjected to routine lack, loss, overwork, and all manner of corporeal abuse, they were also faced with sexual violence and exploitative reproductive labor. It is impossible to separate enslaved women's decisions to flee and embrace defensive violence from the compound and intersecting realities they faced as gendered commodities. Enslaved women's conviction that it was time to run—and sometimes time to run while armed, or in armed company—and fugitive women's willingness to participate in defensive combat, were flagrant rejections of the institution of slavery as well as of patriarchal gender norms, sexual violence, and notions of femininity dictating submissiveness, docility, timidity, and restraint. Nevertheless, it is also true that captive and fugitive women generally avoided violent conflict, particularly conflict with those who might have had the benefit of greater physical strength or size. But as Kali Nicole Gross reminds us, although violence structured Black women's worldviews and was "typically a black woman's undoing," it did not mark the end of the story for all.[13] In the context of chattel slavery, some Black women were prepared to physically fight to defend and protect themselves, their families, and their larger communities in ways that exceeded feminized strategies of dissemblance or other forms of passive, covert, or "everyday" resistance.[14] Violent resistance has never been an exclusively male pursuit, despite how maleness and masculinity has directed prevailing understandings about Black opposition. Locating maroon women at the swamp's edges reveals that Black women have always shared in the full spectrum of resistant acts in the fugitive underworld, including defensive violence.

In Tidewater Virginia and North Carolina, bondwomen contributed to insurgent culture not only through everyday, quiet, or secret acts of refusal and opposition such as insolent dispositions, impudence, or withholding labor or information; they also sparked and fanned the flames of collective rebellious intent by arming themselves and openly using the force of their bodies against enslavement.[15] Fannie Berry remembered fighting against sexual violence at the hands of one of "dese here ol' white men," when she was enslaved in Appomattox County, Virginia. She recalled that after she "tussled" with him "an' knocked over chairs," she "got a grip" and "scratched his face all to pieces; an dar wuz no more bothering Fannie from him" after that.[16] When Phoebe was roused "after midnight" by her enslaver so that he could "get some seed Irish potatoes out of the cellar in the floor" kept underneath her bed, she "refused to let him." He then offered to give her "a dram," which she took, but she still refused him and his access to her bed. As her three-year-old and one-year-old children tried to sleep through the "considerable noise" that ensued, Phoebe calculated her own defense by selecting a grubbing hoe to "indent" and "break" his skull. It wasn't the first time the "frequent runaway" had resisted her enslaver—but Phoebe made sure it was the last.[17] Near the northeastern swamp edge in Hampton, Virginia, William Hughes offended Polly to the point that she felt compelled to take "a certain pair of fire tongs and a knife made of iron and steel" into her right hand, causing him to "instantly" die with the ensuing force of her blows.[18] In Nansemond County, Celia stood before five court justices for "feloniously murdering" her enslavers while they lay in bed one June evening. She chose to wield "the eye of the axe" to strike repeated blows on both Mr. and Mrs. Powell, then took their orphaned infant "out of doors," before Abel—her partner-in-crime—set fire to the house with "split lightwood and fodder."[19] It would seem that Celia and Abel found cause to collaborate in the use of force and arms against those who had used it so often against them; yet, they spared the defenseless infant.

The wielding of poison—"the most common weapon enslaved women used"—should also be "recategorized as a form of armed resistance due to the damage it does to the human body."[20] Enslaved women in the Tidewater, too, held to this course of violence. In 1803, Charity of Princess Anne County was publicly hung at the usual place of execution, near the county courthouse, "for administering medicine for the purpose of destroying" her master "and his whole family."[21] In Norfolk, an enslaved woman held by the family of the "humane" and "indulgent" Benjamin Ham was committed to prison for killing his infant and toddler by way of "a quantity of arsenick," which she concealed in their food and drink.[22] Friends, kin, and entire enslaved communities surrounding each of these women would have witnessed, heard about, and deeply considered each of these acts of violence as well as the political stakes involved in the physical rebellion these women were willing to wager. Enslaved women's contemplations of and decisions to embrace defensive violence contributed to collective insurgent thought and potential in the rival Black geographies of the Dismal Swamp borderlands.

"Mrs. Frances Berry—86 Years Old," February 26, 1937.
(Photograph by Susie R. C. Byrd, Virginia Writers' Project. Printed in Weevils in the Wheat: Interviews with Virginia Ex-Slaves, *edited by Charles L. Perdue Jr., Thomas E. Barden, and Robert K. Phillips [University of Virginia Press, 1976]; credited to the Roscoe Lewis Papers at the Collis P. Huntington Library, Hampton Institute, Virginia.)*

If enslaved women, some of whom were already repeat truants, were willing to resort to defensive acts of violence, it is unsurprising that fugitive women did not recoil at it either. This is certainly true and perhaps best documented in the border states of the Upper South, where enslaved people were most likely to perceive the bold actions needed to reach northern cities as achievable aims and objectives. Harriet Tubman, perhaps history's most famous fugitive woman, made twelve or possibly thirteen trips back into Maryland to help liberate nearly seventy people from slavery. She did so armed, with "guns ready."[23] General Tubman, as she became known, later supported and helped strategize armed rebellion at Harpers Ferry in 1859 and served as the military brainpower behind the Combahee River Raid against the Confederacy near Beaufort, South Carolina, in 1863. The raid was instrumental in the liberation of close to 750 people from the rice plantations along the river.[24] Like Tubman, women like Leah, Alice, and Daffney—all once enslaved in Cambridge, Maryland—held fiercely to the insurgent belief in three options to reach full and immediate freedom: flight, fight, or both. In 1857, they fled alongside at least ten fugitive men, one unnamed woman, ten children, and one baby, armed with "three revolvers, three double-barreled pistols, three single-barreled pistols, three sword-canes, four butcher knives, one bowie-knife, and one paw," as they made their way to Philadelphia.[25] Two years earlier, Mary and Emily left Loudon, Virginia, alongside four men, all armed with pistols and dirks. They had traveled about a hundred miles toward Philadelphia with the aid of their enslaver's "best horses and carriage," when they were stopped in Maryland by "six white men and a boy," one of whom pointed the muzzle of his gun at one of the women. Without hesitation, the woman took "a double-barreled pistol in one hand and a long dirk knife in the other," and ordered her party, "Shoot! shoot!! shoot!!!"[26] Daunted by this, their pursuers retreated, making it possible for four of the six fugitives to escape, including both Mary and Emily. Fugitive women, like men, were determined to stand their ground against bondage and captivity by any means necessary.

Yet for the most part, in Tidewater Virginia, North Carolina, and beyond, fugitive women were not brandishing pistols. However, it is also probable that more fugitive women were armed with concealed weapons than was reported in runaway slave advertisements or in accounts left by authorities. For example, the report that was printed in Maryland's *Frederick Examiner* made by Mary's and Emily's pursuers altogether omits the women's swift use of dirk and pistol, already carried as they were, on their persons. It is only because of the painstaking archiving and recordkeeping of William Still, the Black abolitionist and chair of the Pennsylvania Anti-Slavery Society's Vigilance Committee, that we even learn of the women's part in the group's defensive violence—a credit to the fact that the fugitives relayed their versions of the incidents once safe in Still's offices in Philadelphia.[27] It is unsurprising that the accounts left by authorities, emerging from the intersection of racism, paternalism, and patriarchy, decisively ignored or were otherwise unable to conceive of Black women's injurious proximity to violence or to acknowledge the physical, intellectual, and political roles they shared in combative resistance and militancy.[28]

What fugitive women successfully withheld and concealed, and what authorities failed to report will never be ours to know, but if Charity's "medicine," Phoebe's grubbing hoe, Polly's fire tongs, and Celia's axe tell us anything, it is that Black women in the Tidewater were highly resourceful when they decided it was time to arm themselves and commit acts of defensive violence. At the edge of the swamp, West Turner, formerly enslaved in Nansemond County, recalled the time that "Ant Sallie," the nurse for their enslaver's children, was put in the cotton fields after their mistress accused her of causing the baby to fall ill. Opposed to this order, Aunt Sallie decided that she would no longer report to work at all, and she proceeded to make her protest while concealed in the quarters, aided by Turner's own father. When their master banged on the door and demanded Aunt Sallie come out or else the entire enslaved community would be whipped, she "grabbed up a scythe knife f'om de corner an' she pulled de chock out dat do' an' come out a-swingin'." Repurposing the senior Turner's scythe—an implement used to turn hay, harvest wheat, cut away weeds, thistles, and brambles, or else cut paths in tall foliage—Aunt Sallie transformed the instrument of captive labor into an instrument of defensive violence. Turner described how she then "cut her way out" of that cabin and "backed off into de woods." Focused as she was on evasion or the fight to come, she was "still swingin' dat scythe" despite the frantic promises, "screamin' and cussin'" of her enslaver, when she ran, unfollowed, "into de bushes."[29] Driven toward the logics of both flight and defensive force by their own unimaginable discontent and critical understanding of the intersections between labor, sex, violence, gender, and race, it was women like Aunt Sallie who were most likely to have helped form the notorious maroon groups at the edges of the Dismal Swamp.

THE WOMEN "BANDITS": OUTLAW MAROON GROUPS AT THE SWAMP'S EDGE

At the southwest corner of the Dismal Swamp, in Chowan County, North Carolina, two maroon women were reported among a "nest of robbers, who nightly infested" the town of Edenton. A party of white men who had set out to "scour the pocosin" came across them one Friday in 1811.[30] This area of the Dismal Swamp, known as Cabarrus's Pocosin, or "Snaky Swamp," was ten miles wide, and thirty miles long, stretching north toward the Virginia state line.[31] The men's hunt through Snaky Swamp was not unusual, as there were many civil and military expeditions against runaway slaves throughout the region.[32] In this "negro camp," the men reported they discovered "5 runaway Negroes, 2 wenches and 3 fellows, who were armed." The *Edenton (NC) Gazette* informed the citizens of the town that upon discovery, "each fellow stood with his musket pointed, watching a favorable opportunity" for the "resistance they were about to make." The white men hurriedly fired upon the group. A battle ensued, and "these fellows," it was reported, "bid defiance to any force whatever, and were resolved to stand their ground." Two of the maroon men, Arthur and Solomon, were identified as runaways from as far away as Fayetteville and Montgomery County, North Carolina, some two hundred miles west of the swamp. Both were killed in this battle, while the third man managed to escape, "though shot through the arm." The two unnamed maroon women were both "taken," and their fates—beyond servitude, near "certain rape, and probable death"—cannot be known.[33]

Ignoring the women almost entirely, this account exclusively specifies the forceful actions taken by the "negro fellows," casts the women into a fog of passivity and inertia, and also qualifies sole male leadership by claiming that "the risk run by these men was great."[34] While it is true that the risk these maroons ran was great, the report altogether discounts that the women present shared in these risks, as if their motives, deliberations, and contributions to the activities of the group did not exist at all. Just three years before their discovery at Cabarrus's Pocosin, Edenton residents had been so disturbed and distressed by the unrest and disorder caused by the town being "surrounded by desperadoes," "clans of negroes," and so much "villainy" that they called for the establishment of "a more permanent and efficient system of police," a more sufficiently "vigilant" and "trusty" regular watch, and additional Black codes.[35] In this moment of heightened watch, the five at Snaky Swamp moved in and out of Edenton from their marshy base—stealing not only food and resources but also themselves as a way of life. No matter how imperceptible the two women of the group were in the eyes of the authorities, the risks they each took as participants in the group's activities were great, and no one would have considered more than these marooning women the ways discovery and capture at the swamp's edge would practically guarantee continual raced and gendered retributive persecutions.

The fates of women like Catharine, a "runaway" from Hertford County, North Carolina, would have been foremost in the minds of women pursuing enduring escape when they considered the possible risks and consequences of capture. Catharine traveled through the rivers and swamps at the southwestern edge of the Dismal Swamp until she crossed into Princess Anne County—at the northeastern edge of the swamp—where she was caught, arrested, and confined to jail. She was imprisoned on March 23, 1834, and kept in the company of Edward Fentress, a local slaveowner and the county jailor.[36] Sometime in the year between her confinement and the following spring of 1835, Catharine gave birth to "a male child."[37] On April 6 of that year, the sheriff was ordered to advertise her sale toward the benefit of the state, as no one had come to claim her. It is possible that Catharine was already pregnant when she was brought to the Princess Anne County Jail, but given the perilous world of slavery and sexual violence from a Black woman's standpoint, it is just as likely, if not more so, that she was violated, raped, and abused following her capture and her incarceration, leading to pregnancy.[38] Possessing common knowledge about stories of women like Catharine would have cemented for maroon women the need to avoid capture at all costs—including the use and strategy of physical force and defensive violence.

Although the account of the maroons at Cabarrus's Pocosin tells us virtually nothing about how the five maroons operated and functioned together at the swamp's fringe or even in the moment of their discovery and recapture, the ease by which the *Edenton (NC) Gazette* assumes the women's inaction, or apathy, at being "taken" and fired upon, should give pause. Did the maroon women say nothing, do nothing, or otherwise respond so slightly that the "scouring" white men had no other course than to deem them insignificant, unimportant, and unworthy of note besides their discovery and seizure? If the women appeared merely as shadows behind the white men's assumptions about the threat of Black masculine capability, did the party believe the women had been simply lured or seduced into the swamp by the maroon men, and therefore merited only fleeting reference? Or, on the contrary, did the women themselves consider marooning in Snaky Swamp a defensible best option toward survival and freer life? We are left with uncertainty as to how the women might have helped "bid defiance to any force whatever" in this moment of great emergency, but what is certain is that they had every reason to try. Despite how inconceivable it may have been in white men's minds, given the raced and gendered stakes the women faced if recaptured as well as their intersectional motivations for fleeing to begin with, the probability that these women, too, "[stood] their ground" against recapture is great.[39]

This likelihood is also supported by maroon women's frequent embrace of force, as documented across space and time. In colonial Louisiana, for example, the maroons of Bas du Fleuve, including fifteen women (or 47 percent of this particular community), were known to "never walk about without arms" when scouting, trading, and securing provisions—activities that women there sometimes joined.[40] According to one scholar, the "maroon's violence was almost entirely defensive" against the threat of capture and against organized raids led by Spanish authorities, who were in active battle with both the maroon women and men.[41] Celia (or Cecelia)—the wife of St. Malo, the purported leader of Bas du Fleuve, known to arm himself with "gun, machete, and big knife"—was noted by authorities as being his "inseparable companion in all his exploits."[42] In Alabama, a "nest of runaway negroes"—fourteen in sum—who had for "several years" lived between the Alabama and Tombeckbe Rivers, had "committed many depredations on the neighboring plantations" before nine white men decided to attack them with guns and cannon. The maroons, consisting of women and children, "fought like Spartans, not one [giving] an inch of ground."[43]

But beyond the Snaky Swamp women's confirmed presence and definite closeness to raids, arms, and violence, the two women may also have aided the group in other ways. Authorities declared them responsible for the theft of a "vast deal of plunder," including at least three guns and "a great number of keys" found among their possessions. The group likely used these keys to open locked cellars, warehouses, and stores of nearby farms or plantations to secure their subsistence and provisions. The presence of the keys, items commonly kept in domestic spaces where enslaved women were often assigned to labor, suggests one possible way the women could have asserted themselves as active and willing contributors to the group's "nightly" plunder.[44] Had the two maroon women—motivated as they were to flee and stand their ground against capture in the refuge of a swamp—also contributed their familiarity with and knowledge of local domestic spaces to steal the keys and advance the insurgent activities of the group? Other women did not hesitate to do so. Urana, an enslaved domestic at Silver Bluff Plantation, South Carolina, for example, was "punished" after her enslaver discovered that she took and "gave the key" to his cellar to Frank and Abram—two enslaved men. Following Urana's actions, the men stole "wines & other spirits, corn, glass, meats &c."[45] Lindsey Faucette of North Carolina remembered that her "gran'mammy toted de keys to de pantry an' smoke house, an' her word went wid Marse John an' Mis' Annie."[46] Thavolia Glymph has argued that in the contested realm of female domestic authority, "control, even symbolic, of the keys to smokehouses, corn cribs, and other stores of supplies" signaled a "vaunted exercise of power" that white women performed while Black women carefully watched; though sometimes, as in the case of Lindsey Faucette's grandmother, Black women were granted access to keys and their holding places.[47]

The two maroon women reported in 1811 were not the only women to use and understand Snaky Swamp as a space inviting fugitivity. Harriet Jacobs, a native of Edenton, also experienced the pocosin as an insurgent refuge.[48] During one of her first attempts to escape her master, Dr. James Norcom, Harriet fled to Snaky Swamp, and found it "covered with hundreds of mosquitos . . . snake after snake crawling round."[49] She was assisted in reaching the swamp by two men: her aunt's "seafaring" husband—a waterman with invaluable knowledge of the swamps, creeks, and riverways—and her longtime friend Peter. The men were armed with a dagger, a large knife, and an awareness of the undertakings of maroons and those in flight at Cabarrus's Pocosin.[50] By the 1830s, the "legendary" Snaky Swamp was well known in local lore for its chief characteristics, though few wanted to or knew how to reach it. It was described by contemporaries as a place where "snakes are to be found anywhere—along its jungle-like shorelines, in the frequent clumps of grasses and bushes, upon fallen tree trunks, in branches outstretched arm-like over the water . . . and everywhere there is a patch of spring sunshine or a mottled summer shadow."[51] By 1842—after Harriet had moved from her temporary hideout in the swamp to the nine-foot long, seven-foot wide, and three-foot high garret above her grandmother's home, where she eluded Dr. Norcom for seven years—even the captain who would afterward ship her to Philadelphia knew and described Snaky Swamp as a "slave territory that defies all the laws."[52] Harriet and the two maroon women at Snaky Swamp before her were three among countless other women who successfully avoided detection there and who aptly concluded that, in Harriet's words, "those venomous snakes were less dreadful to [the] imagination than the White men in that community called civilized."[53]

On the Virginia side of the Dismal Swamp, maroon women—like those in Cabarrus's Pocosin—were also familiar with plunder and defensive violence at the swamp outskirts. A rare glimpse of a maroon woman living among "a gang of desperate wretches" in the woods and swamps neighboring Black Water—a town in Princess Anne County that shared its southeastern border with the northeastern edge of the Dismal Swamp—stands as further evidence that Black women joined edge-dwelling maroon bands and were not afraid of violent outlawry. Although unnamed, the Black Water maroon woman emerges from an 1818 report, published in the *Norfolk Herald*, warning that this "band of ruffians said to be 28 in number, all armed and officered," had "openly proclaimed themselves at war with the inhabitants of Black Water." The group—composed of "runaway negroes" and at least two poor "white men"—had "for some time past" kept the citizens of the county "in a state of alarm." Not only had they dragged a "negro man who had offended one of the party" into the swamp to beat him to death with "clubs," but they had also grown so bold that "they would enter enclosures and shoot down cattle, hogs or poultry at noon day." The report does not elaborate on the leadership of the sizable group, but it does mention that "a detachment of the gang" was busy at the work of hog stealing, under the direction of their "captain," when they were shot at and attacked by "a volunteer guard of citizens." Authorities noted only that "the captain and an old woman who belonged to the gang, were killed." The rest were committed to jail, but the maroons not included in this "detachment" remained at large.[54]

We cannot be certain how the woman came to join this large community of "rogues," just as we cannot be sure whether the ungendered group of "runaway negroes" contained other women who may or may not have been left out of this particular mission to catch, tie, and steal hogs.[55] But what is clear is that the maroons collectively understood the role of the "old woman" in their acts of aggression against the inhabitants of Black Water. They had, after all, decided upon, agreed to, or requested her presence and her help. Although her race is not specified, the only white people associated with the maroons are described as "men," and it is far less likely that the white men who appointed themselves to protect the town's white citizenry would have gunned down an "old" white woman.

Age lends much here as an analytic for reading against what we cannot know about the woman and her role in this community of maroons. That she is described as "old," in combination with the fact that she is accounted for at all, suggests that she responded to being ambushed by the guard with such force, prominence, and distinction, that in their accounting of the violence that took place at the hog pen, authorities could not ignore her presence among the most notable members of the group. That the "old woman" is the only other maroon referenced beside a more recognizably male leader also points to the highly revered "leadership roles older women of African descent have assumed" throughout the African Diaspora.[56] In Jamaica, for example, Queen Nanny, or Grandy Nanny of the Windward Maroons—a group comprising "three hundred or so" men, women, and children—was the maroons' chief and obeah woman, or spiritual leader, alongside the "headman" Quao.[57] The two collaborated in leading the maroons against the British in the Maroon War of 1739. Nanny's leadership as a respected military and political strategist in this society of maroons was inconceivable to the colonists, who sought to diminish her position by refusing to directly interact with her in their attempts to entreat them, preferring instead to deal with Quao.[58] One junior officer in the British militia described Queen Nanny, who was likely in her middle years, as "the old hagg"—an attempt to belittle, reduce, or unsee her status and importance among the maroons—perhaps not unlike the account reported by the guard of the concerned citizens of Black Water, Virginia.[59]

In this early national period, the Atlantic-facing swamp borderlands in Princess Anne County and adjoining Norfolk County had seen a rise in marronage, probably brought on, at least in part, by the War of 1812. As Herbert Aptheker notes, the possibility that military activity during the war years, and "particularly, the withdrawal of bodies of armed men from a given area, would be likely to encourage slave unrest." This has been shown to be the case in Tidewater Virginia and North Carolina.[60] Five years before the Black Water maroon woman ventured out of the swamp with her comrades to steal hogs, a report made in 1813 cautioned against "runaway negroes" prone to "desert to the enemy from Princess Anne." Citizens of Princess Anne County in the neighborhood of Lynnhaven Bay urged the patrol to guard against "those deluded wretches," and established a "large number of citizens" to voluntarily patrol "the desert [swamp] that skirts the southern boundary of Lynnhaven Bay, and in which the runaways and outliers secret themselves." Patrols had already discovered, "in a recess of the desert, an encampment of nearly 20 negroes, who, being apprized of their approach, had time to disperse; not, however, until 5 or 6 of them were shot."[61]

By September 1818, not long after the Black Water maroon woman was killed, another faction of maroons, or possibly the remaining members of the same faction of the woman's own "formidable gang of ruffians," were reported responsible for "many atrocities." The maroons were accused of continued plundering and the shooting, wounding, and killing of several white men. The report, one of many, states that "it is notorious" that "these ruffians occupy the pocosins along the Southern boundary of Norfolk county, from Black Water to North West River Bridge." One small farmer in this neighborhood "was seeking a stray horse in a contiguous swamp, when he accidentally stumbled upon the camp of these desperadoes." In defense of their base, it took the maroons a matter of minutes to locate and shoot their unsuspecting discoverer dead—concealed as they were at the edge of his farm, in the dense and swampy woods.[62]

These Black Water maroons remained at large, and no maroon activities were reported again until December of 1818. At that time, 663 white citizens in the Princess Anne County neighborhoods of Pungo, Kempsville, and Black Water signed a petition pleading with Virginia Governor James Preston to execute "the murderous Mingo" and his accomplices.[63] The petition states that Mingo, who had "long been a runaway associated with a gang of others like him in open war against the property and even lives of our citizens," had "repeatedly threatened the life of the Sherriff or of any and all persons."[64] The petition also alleges that Mingo—"commonly armed with a gun, sword"—committed arson, having set fire to Henry Capps's smokehouse.[65] A letter from the justices of the peace to the sheriff confirms that "the negroes Mingo and Ned, and other runaway negro slaves whose names and owners are unknown, are lying out hid and lurking in the swamps, woods, and other obscure places committing murder, killing hogs and doing other injuries to the inhabitants." The maroons also were accused of shooting at and threatening the life of Peter Land, the sheriff, and his son, William K. Land, a justice of the peace.[66] On December 11, 1818, a detachment of the Princess Anne militia consisting of "140 infantry and cavalry"—"set off, in squads, to scour the different swamps and forests."[67] The militia had no luck finding the maroons until the following day, when one of Mingo's confidants betrayed him and delivered him to the authorities. The whereabouts of Ned and the other maroons—whose genders remain in question—remain unknown. Following his capture and trial at the start of 1819, Mingo was condemned by the Princess Anne County court, but not by the executive seat in Richmond. The white citizens of Princess Anne were outraged. On February 18, 1819, as Mingo was being transported to the Norfolk jail from Kempsville to await the steamer that would ultimately bring him to the state prison for trial in Richmond—frustrated, impassioned, and impatient "unknown" white vigilantes fired upon him on the road, bringing him to what they considered a timelier execution.[68]

About ten miles west of where these events were unfolding, at the exact same time, at least one maroon woman lived and worked alongside a "party of outliers" at Great Bridge—a neighborhood in the lower part of Norfolk County, nearly entirely engulfed by the outreaching Dismal Swamp. Maria (also referred to as Mariah), her husband Nelson, a man named James, and the "notorious and even formidable" Bob Ferebee had been living "in the cypress swamp" there for at least five years.[69] Bob, "late the property of Matthew M. Ferebee, deceased," was reported missing in an ad placed by his new master, Wilson Butt, as early as March 1, 1818.[70] Butt described Bob as being about twenty-three years old, "stout and well made; rather of a dark yellow," with "relations at Captain Ree Land's, in Princess Anne County," a sister in Norfolk, and "many acquaintances about the Great Bridge and Canal, in one of which places he is now lurking."[71] That Bob was so connected to these neighborhoods in the northern portion of the Great Dismal Swamp as well as to people enslaved by the Land family—the same family that could claim the Princess Anne County Sheriff Peter Land, whom Mingo had attempted to kill that very year—suggests that these Great Bridge maroons were likely in network with the Black Water maroons, operating at much the same time. What stood to connect them was the cover and stream of a short stretch of swamps and tributaries there at the northern edge of the Dismal Swamp. The likelihood of these connections makes the "old woman" one of at least two maroon women who actively contributed to the Norfolk and Princess Anne County maroon insurgency in 1818. Maria, the other documented woman, lived in a "tent" in the swamp with at least three men, including the tobacco-smoking, gun-toting Bob Ferebee. In their swamp den, these maroons kept at least one gun, bullets, and "several buck shot."[72] The group successfully avoided capture until June 1823, when the Norfolk militia, composed of "200 men, cavalry and infantry," was ordered to "scour the country" and "patrole the forests and swamps" in the hope of relieving "the neighboring inhabitants from a state of perpetual anxiety and apprehension."[73] This scouring resulted in the discovery and capture of Bob, Maria, Nelson, James, Lewis, and Jasper.

While we will never know precisely how these maroons lived and interacted with each other and the world at the edge of the swamp, what is certain is that defensive violence was integral to their claims to free life. Although there is no record of Maria giving testimony after her recapture, depositions left by Nelson and James make clear that she was no stranger to the use of force as a practice of survival and in the interest of community protection. Both men's accounts, given in 1823, state that the group, including Maria, had been fugitives for more than five years and had decided to continue living as maroons despite the fact that Bob had shot and killed a white man who had discovered them one October day five years earlier, in 1818. Bob had told his comrades that the man was David Manning, a slaveholder of St. Brides Parish in Norfolk County, near Great Bridge—the very same parish in which the

Butt plantations and estates were located and from which Bob had escaped.[74] Manning had been accompanied by Josiah McCoy, another slaveholding neighbor living near "the poquoson land adjoining" the property of Robert Butt.[75] Bob was certain that these men—with whom the maroons were clearly familiar—would come "shortly to hunt them out," and he meant to beat them to it. The next day, Bob took his gun, loaded "with sundry buck shot," and left their camp in the swamp. He returned to the swamps after only fifteen minutes, having already shot Manning and scared McCoy away. James and Nelson reported that after the maroons "heard the report of a gun" from their hideout, they soon heard someone "running thro' the woods." It was not until after Maria's husband, Nelson, heard Bob "blow" the secret signal, that he "got upon a log to see to greater advantage" and saw it was Bob approaching. They quickly hailed him. Later that night, after Maria had spent the day contemplating the sound of the report of Bob's gunshot, and every new risk of recapture the group faced, she decided against withdrawing passively into her tent in the swamp. Instead, she chose to work actively alongside Bob and the others to gather intelligence from the nearby estate of yet another member of the Butt family—Charles. Nelson and James stayed behind "at the fence" at "the rear" of this Butt property, while Maria and Bob worked together to determine whether anyone in the neighborhood knew what had happened to Manning. This reconnaissance came to a head when Maria "quickly returned" and came "running back" to her crew at the fence with the news that Manning was confirmed dead. Bob joined them soon afterward to share he had discovered the same.[76]

Although Maria did not pull the trigger, she was no passive spectator in these events. Instead, she used her knowledge and her connections with people in the neighborhood to help protect and defend the maroons.[77] Moreover, it was not without *her* help that the group remained at large until their apprehension five years later. During that time, Maria would have been a supporter of more "daring outrages" that were associated with Bob Ferebee's growing "banditti," that by 1823, also included Lewis and Jasper (who is also referred to as Jerry or Jesse).[78] Her inclusion in this "band of lurking assassins" meant that she was an active member of a community of "desperadoes," regarded by the white citizenry as "monsters in human shape," whose "first object [was] to obtain gun and ammunition, as well to procure game for subsistence as to defend themselves from attack."[79] By May of 1823, the group had become so bold in their movements in and out of the swamp, that one of them even wrote and delivered a note threatening the life of a "gentleman at Great Bridge," should he come out of his house after nightfall.[80] Like Mingo, the maroons seem to have made targets of the enslavers and authorities they knew personally, or whom they knew were directly involved in hunting them down. On May 5, 1823, the maroons also shot and killed another white man, William Walker, who was the postmaster at Great Bridge. On May 23, they attempted, but failed, to assassinate Gen. Nehemiah Foreman, a Norfolk County magistrate, justice of the peace, and militia officer in the 9th Brigade, 4th Division, who was also James's enslaver.[81] By the end of May, Lewis, once enslaved by Alexander Foreman of Norfolk County, and Jasper, once enslaved by Lemuel Butt at Great Bridge, were captured, tried for the murder of William Walker, and sentenced to be hung "at the usual place" in June and July.[82]

While Lewis and Jasper were imprisoned, it may have been Bob, Nelson, James, or Maria—all then still at large—who fired the shots at General Foreman from a spot "concealed in the bushes" as he "rode along a path way through a swamp."[83] The group avoided apprehension until they too were captured and tried in June. In the end, it was none other than General Foreman who issued the warrant for Bob's arrest and who personally saw to his confinement in jail awaiting trial.[84] Bob was executed in July, but the fate of Maria and the other collaborators is unknown.[85] An enslaved man named David, accused of consorting with the maroons, was transported out of state after he served as a witness against them.[86] Perhaps a similar outcome such as sale or transport, if not execution, befell Maria, Nelson, and James.

Without question, Maria and the unnamed "old" Black Water maroon woman were just two of any number of maroon women at the edges of the Dismal Swamp who, unlike them, never got caught. But borderland maroon women's successful evasion of capture signals more than their victory. It also means that their presence and activities in the swamp will never fully be known. This is why pointed attention to any and all accounts of captured maroon women read alongside records of wanted fugitive women—such as Rachel, Violet, Sarah, and Phillis—who also ran away from their enslavers in the neighborhood of Great Bridge, can help illuminate the possible movements and motivations of Maria, her Black Water counterpart, as well as the women at Snaky Swamp at the other end of the Dismal Swamp.

In 1818, Rachel escaped a (unnamed) member of the Butt family. She was described by her solicitor as someone who was "very stout and black, about 23 or 24 years old," who had "very unnaturally left her infant child (about 16 months old) behind, when she took herself off."[87] Whatever untold sufferings Rachel experienced at the Butt estate, she believed her best move was to leave her one-year-old child behind and flee through the swamps surrounding Great Bridge. Like Rachel in her dissent, thirty-year-old Sarah—though bearing a "pleasing countenance"—was determined enough to flee Mary Ann Miller's home in Great Bridge, from where it was suspected she and her nine-year-old daughter, Polly, fled by way of the wetlands to reach the Elizabeth River, after which Mary believed the two might be found "lurking in Norfolk or Portsmouth."[88] Though her enslavers in Currituck County, North Carolina, knew her as Hannah, eighteen-year-old Violet rejected the name her enslavers gave her and ran away, true to the "bold countenance" her mistress described her as having. Violet's pursuers suspected she had set off across the length of the Dismal Swamp, toward "the neighbourhood of the Great Bridge."[89] There was Phillis, "formerly the property of Mr. Silvester, near the Great Bridge, where it is supposed she will make for," who was described as being "between 40 and 48 years of age" at the time of her departure.[90] Phillis ran south into the swamp-abundant neighborhood of Great Bridge to get away from the prominent Hutchings merchant family, longtime residents of Norfolk.[91] These women likely ran to Great Bridge so that they could be nearer to family or loved ones who might protect them, or so that they could remain with those they could not stand to live without. Of course, each of these women's movements was also aided and guided by the ecologies of the forested swamps and woods that they preferred to traverse and engage with more than they were willing to stay put. What relatable sacrifices had Maria and the other maroon women at the northern swamp made as the price of their own sustained escapes? Certainly, taken together, these accounts reveal that women of all ages and attachments were among those driven to run through and to the Dismal Swamp borderlands, escaping, as they were, the residual trials of girlhood, captive labor (productive and reproductive), overwork and fatigue, sexual assault, and tormented motherhoods.

Women who meant to stay at the swamp borderlands and within the swamp's fringes considered armed outlawry in a male-dominant criminal economy their best bet. Their intimate knowledge of violence did not deter their decisions to join the prowling bands of edge-dwelling maroons—instead it solidified the imperative of desertion and their own willingness to live by way of defensive force, banditry, and outlawry. These maroon women defined their own safety and protected themselves within the swamps, alongside men and women who understood that violence "can be preemptive, in that sometimes people—particularly people in areas that lack appropriate protection—'kill simply to avoid being killed.'"[92] This philosophy of defense was shared by the women who chose to live on the edge rather than face a lifetime of atrocity and death. Examining the movements of women whose stories have long been buried beneath dismissive traces in records and in subsequent studies reveals that maroon women at the swamp fringes were not only present, but they also did not merely cower behind the leadership or protection offered to them by maroon men. Rather, women like Maria, the Black Water maroon woman, and those in Snaky Swamp acted in ways that supported the logic of defense by force, and they actively contributed liberatory labor to advance maroon collectivity and survival.

The strategy of defensive violence has never been the sole domain of men. Women responded to the raced and gendered conditions of their enslavement by constructing their own insurgent roles based on their committed study of the politics of their subjection, their best interests, and the interests of their communities. Through flight, they defied bondage and welcomed fugitive lives of outlawry, even in an underworld dominated by men. With forethought and care, borderland maroon women supported, protected, and defended alternatives to captivity and to capture by any and all means. While it was not pleasant or ideal, they helped sustain emboldened insurgency and shared in its armed defense, actions guided by their insight that articulations of justice sometimes require force. Produced in part by this continuous maroon warfare and armed struggle at the tenuous edge of the swamp borderlands, the ensuing insurgent culture of the Great Dismal Swamp was also produced through enslaved women's political thought, intellect, cunning, and militancy over the course of several planned and organized armed rebellions set across Tidewater wetlands and swamps.

FOUR

"Armed in the Great Swamp"

ENSLAVED WOMEN AND ORGANIZED REBELLION

> Women resisted and advocated challenges to slavery at every turn. Given the unceasing repression of women, "no wonder," said Herbert Aptheker, "the Negro woman so often urged haste in slave plottings."
>
> ANGELA DAVIS, *WOMEN, RACE, AND CLASS*

While fringe maroon women worked in roving groups that frequently navigated the world at the edge of the Dismal Swamp by force, enslaved women still bound to Tidewater farms and plantations supplied insurgent thought and action toward other forms of rebellion. Not only did innumerable enslaved women labor to aid and conceal the whereabouts and plans of maroons and insurrectionists who were predominately men, but they also worked in active support of outright revolt or organized rebellion intended to undermine, overthrow, and eradicate slavery.[1] In the Tidewater, at least three plots to do so involved maroons and the insurgent ecology of the Great Dismal Swamp as the organizing space and ground by which to advance these insurrectionary designs. These plots—known by historians as the conspiracy orchestrated by Angola Peter in 1709, the conspiracy of 1792–93, and the Easter Conspiracy or Easter Rebellion of 1802—were underwritten by the collective insurgent efforts of male insurgents together with the support of some noted enslaved women, whose names and contributions have, until now, hardly been considered.[2] While it is clear that these plots were most visibly and primarily the undertakings of men, the appearance of women in records concerning the constituencies of these conspiracies indicates enslaved women's invested contributions to organizing, sustaining, and executing revolt across the swampscape.

The ingenuity of enslaved women who worked to guard, plot, and sustain insurrection as it unfolded can be detected by means of careful inspection of the historical record—an effort characterized by a sincere commitment to Black women's social, political, and intellectual contributions. Rereading these three best-documented rebellions involving marronage and the insurgent expanse of the Dismal Swamp reveals that enslaved women like Pamba, Daphne, Nelly, Phebe, Jude, and others have long been dismissed and overlooked in both contemporaneous and subsequent accounts of insurrection arising from the localities surrounding the swamp. Yet, guided by Black women's transhistorical capaciousness and full humanity, these women can be found not merely as marginal spectators or as the auxiliary wives of rebels, but as sources of inspiration, confidence, and intelligence; they provided strategy, stamina, and encouragement to the collective and community undertaking of revolt.[3] In a number of resourceful ways, including by feeding and harboring insurgents, by working as secret messengers or guardians of privileged information, by transforming motherhood and domestic space toward insurgent ends as well as by pressuring, agitating, and affirming the place of arms and defensive violence in struggle, enslaved women supported insurrection and revolt, contributing both discreetly and overtly to the broader culture of insurgency in and around the swamp.

PAMBA, "HIS WIFE": LOCATING THE WOMEN BEHIND MEN IN TIDEWATER VIRGINIA'S EARLIEST ENSLAVED CONSPIRACY

As early as 1709, and most assuredly earlier, white inhabitants in the neighborhoods of the northernmost Dismal Swamp counties were kept in a state of anxiety over their suspicions that the Africans and African descendants they sought to hold in bondage were plotting to make insurrection. Their suspicions were correct. Along the lower James River, colonists were already vexed that their fledgling townships adjoined the unsteady terrain of an encroaching and defiant swamp. In Isle of Wight County, Virginia, for example, colonists as early as the mid-seventeenth century acknowledged the foreboding Dismal Swamp by naming its numerous reaches the Ballase Marsh, Beaver Dam Swamp, Bows and Arrows Swamp, Cypress Swamp, Duck's Swamp, Gale's Pocosin, Kinsale Swamp, and Great Swamp.[4] There, at the swamp's northern fringe in Isle of Wight County, in Surry County directly to the west, and even across the James River in James City County, enslaved people also took careful note of these swamps. Though James City was the very seat of Virginia's draconian colonial government—with the colony's capital in Williamsburg—enslaved people were nevertheless aware of the nearby swamp's insurgent advantages. (See map 1.) Between 1709 and 1710, authorities in these three counties reported that "a late dangerous conspiracy, formed and carried on by greate numbers of ye said negroes and Indian slaves for making their Escape by force," had "destroy[ed] and [cut] off Such of her Majesties Subjects as Should oppose their design."[5] That design was, in part, a shrewd and studied movement toward "permanent escape into the Great Dismal Swamp."[6] It was also, as Virginia's House of Burgesses noted, a "conspiracy of The Negro's in Surry County and Their Accomplices for Levying Warr" against the colony.[7]

Reports of the plot first began to circulate among authorities on March 19, 1709, in James City County, after several investigations of enslaved people led three slaveholding colonists to conclude that three enslaved men—Jamy, Essex, and (Mr. Jaquelin's) Will—were "very instrumental in the designe and are doubtless great rogues."[8] Gripped in alarm by this disturbance, and unsatisfied with the men's subsequent imprisonment in the public gaol at Williamsburg, Edmund Jenings, the president of the Council of Virginia, responded to these reports of unrest the following day by dispatching the guard and signing a warrant for the arrest of "several negros" named and listed as locatable at plantations in Bruton Parish—in the neighborhood of Williamsburg.[9] The warrant "ordered and required" the guard to "apprehend and secure" Angola Peter, "Pamba his wife," Bumbara Peter, Mingo, and Robin.[10] At the plot's inception, it was these individuals' knowledge of and implicit contributions to the rebellion that were of utmost importance to Jenings and the authorities. No doubt, Jenings as well as the guard dispatched to find the five believed them to be at the helm of plans to advance the "late dangerous conspiracy."[11]

On March 21, 1709, the day after he issued the warrant for the arrests, Jenings met with the council and wasted no time in issuing a formal proclamation that was to be followed throughout the colony "according to the Strictest Severity & Rigor of the Common Law." In this order, Jenings announced that he had "received Intelligence of Severall Illegall and unusuall and unwarrantable Concourses Meetings & Assemblings together of Negro, Mulatto & Indian Slaves at Quarters where there are noe white or Freemen Overseers and more particularly of a Notorious Insurrection Intended & Contrived at Such Meetings by Severall Slaves." Concerned by these unlawful gatherings, Jenings forbade all white subjects to "knowingly permitt any slave not belonging to him or her" to be absent from the homesteads of their owners "above four Hours at any one time." Failure to enforce and adhere to this would result in imprisonment and a fine of 150 pounds of tobacco, to be paid to the informant of the offense. With this fresh vigilance, the proclamation also reinforced that "no slave goe Armed with Gun, Sword, Clubb, Staff, or other weapon" or leave the appointed place of their servitude "without a Certificate of Leave in Writing for soe Doeing from his or her Master Mistress or Overseer."[12] The dictate's adamancy and inferred connection between Black evasion, organized action, and use of force further suggests that the possession of arms and the means of escape were believed to be key ingredients of rebellion shared among suspected and accused insurgents, if not an already notable colonial problem giving rise to the threat of future plots as well as to the plot currently underway.

By March 24, 1709, the investigation had expanded well into Surry and Isle of Wight Counties, where the commission directed further examinations of several others thought to be involved in this "Conspiracy of divers negroes." While there is no record of the apprehension, testimony, or even the discharge of the five wanted in James City County, statements made by accused insurgents at courthouses in Isle of Wight and Surry Counties led the court's subscribers to "very clearly" find that Salvadore, "an Indian," and the "very rude and insolent" Scipio, Tom Shaw, and Peter were the "principal contrivers" of the plot. Though Tom and Peter had been enslaved by the same man and had considerable opportunity to collude, investigators found Scipio and Peter to be the "first and chief promoters of [the] wicked and pernicious designe."[13] Statements made by both Scipio and Manuell—another enslaved man—convinced the court of this as well as of Manuell's guilt of "knoweing of the designe of the negroes goeing away." As a result, Manuell was subjected to forty lashes "upon his bare back." The Isle of Wight County court also found that the "free negroe" James Booth "entertained" some of the insurgents at his house and knew of their "Intentions of goeing away." For this, Booth, like Manuell, was "punished and Discharged" after suffering twenty-nine lashes in the same manner.[14] In Surry County, the investigation determined that Salvadore had promised his assistance to the insurrection and had reassured the insurgents of "the probability of Effecting their design" to escape by force. While Salvadore, Tom Shaw, and Scipio were committed to the Surry County jail to await sentencing, Peter, "now outlawed," had escaped, and was evading capture somewhere in the vastness of the swamp's northern edge.[15]

More than a year later, Peter remained at large, while Scipio and Salvadore were still imprisoned at the General Court in Williamsburg. In the midst of what appears to have been another stirring of insurrection intended to have begun on Easter Day, a council was held at Williamsburg on April 18, 1710, concerning the whereabouts and activities of Peter, who was still believed to have been an active and principal leader of the previous year's rebellion.[16] On that day, Jenings ordered a "speedy" trial of those jailed for the conspiracy, and the council offered a reward of ten pounds sterling for the capture of Peter, if alive, and five pounds to "any person that shall kill the said Negro." The Virginia Assembly again named Peter "one of the chief actors in the late Conspiracy of the Negros to rise and levy war."[17] It would seem that Will, a man enslaved by Robert Ruffin of Surry County, had been "signally serviceable" in the discovery of the renewed plot, had given the "first information of the Negro's Designs," and had "Continued from time to time to Make Known Their Consultations." For his betrayal of this persistent plot, Will was manumitted.[18] Three days later, on April 21, 1710, Jenings signed a proclamation to be published "in all Churches Chappels & Courthouses" throughout the colony, requiring all persons "to use their Utmost Endeavors to take & apprehend the said Negro Peter," and promising payment of the sterling reward upon delivery of Peter to the public gaol at Williamsburg. Jenings added that Peter had been "Notoriously Active in Stirring up & abetting the Negro's in the County to Levy Warr," and that, being "conscious of his Guilt," he had made his escape, "fled from Justice and is Lurking in or about the said County or the County's of James City Prince George or Isle of Wight."[19] It was during this time that Salvadore and Scipio were tried and found guilty of high treason and were subsequently condemned to be hung, drawn, and quartered—their heads, limbs, and torsos to be distributed and "sett up in the most publick place[s]" in Surry and James City Counties as well as in the neighboring counties of New Kent, Gloucester, Middlesex, Lancaster, and King and Queen. The two were sentenced on April 27, 1710, to be executed in May; Jenings signed warrants for their execution on April 29; and by early June, Jenings had written to the Lords of Trade that "two of the ringleaders of the intended Negro insurrection" had been executed.[20]

While it is clear that Jamy, Essex, and (Mr. Jaquelin's) Will were among those who were corporeally punished and then discharged, there is no record as to the fate of Tom Shaw, other than that he was at one point held alongside Scipio and Salvadore at the Surry County jail in March 1709, awaiting further orders from Jenings.[21] There is also no record of the apprehension or securing of Angola Peter, Pamba (his wife), Bumbara Peter, Mingo, or Robin—the five wanted in Bruton Parish, James City County, at the time of the insurrection's initial discovery.

Yet, just four days after the warrant for the five was issued in 1709, the Surry County Court warned that a Peter who belonged to Mr. Samuel Thompson of Surry County was "now outlawed," and was considered one of the "first and chief promoters" of the plot.[22] Records do not clarify whether this Peter—outlawed and accused of instigating and perpetuating the plot well into 1710—was the very same Angola Peter, or perhaps Bumbara Peter. To complicate matters, Angola Peter, and presumably Pamba, whose only recorded location is under her husband's name, were listed on the 1709 warrant as being at the Bruton Parish plantation of Albortus Warren, and not at the Surry County homestead of Samuel Thompson. In the warrant, "Bumbara" Peter, a blundered reference to his Bambara background, was described as being "at [Colonel] Brays old plantation"—and not at Samuel Thompson's.[23] Notably, Jenings's warrant does not specify the precise ownership of the wanted five; it directs only that they each should be looked for at the given plantations in Bruton Parish. It is possible that Angola Peter or Bumbara Peter were owned by Samuel Thompson but could also be found at the plantation of Warren or Bray across the James River in Bruton Parish. An arrangement like this would most likely result from the practice of hiring out enslaved people's labor—the temporary leasing of the enslaved that was customary during Virginia's late colonial period but that had also been practiced at least "occasionally" during the first half of the eighteenth century.[24] However, it is also possible that a third Peter—neither Angola Peter nor Bumbara Peter—provided leadership to the insurrection. Despite this uncertainty, historians have credited

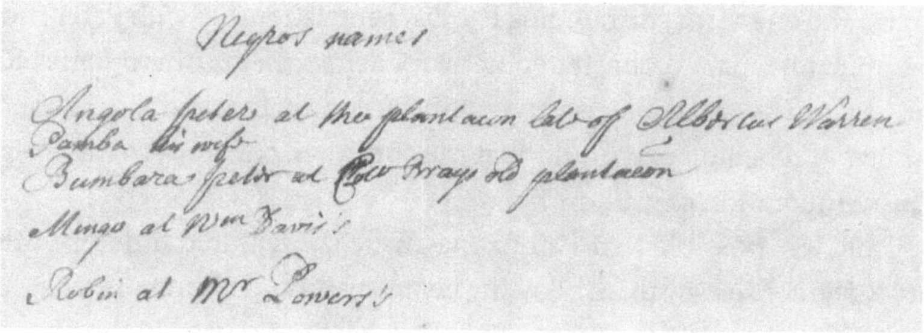
Negros names
Angola peter at the plantacon lat of Albertus Warren
Pamba his wife
Bumbara peter at Mr Brays old plantacon
Mingo at Wm Davis's
Robin at Mr Powers's

Order of Edmund Jenings, March 20, 1709.
(Courtesy of the Library of Virginia.)

the rebellion to the vision and design of "Captain," or Angola Peter, nearly exclusively.[25] This is likely because Angola Peter is the very first and immediate name listed on Jenings's expeditious 1709 warrant, issued and signed only a day after the first investigations had ended.[26] Numerous subsequent urgent and outstanding mentions of Peter at large in James City, Surry, and Isle of Wight Counties lend further visibility to the name. But whether or not Angola Peter and Thompson's Peter were one and the same or two distinct people, repeated accounts seeking the capture of such a person far outweigh the categorical absence of the arrest or apprehension of any enslaved man named Peter. In the end, it was the evasion and elusiveness of insurgents in Peter's camp—moving within a network of towns, swamps, and rivers—that gave momentum to the plot.

Across the surviving records of events that gave way to the insurrection, the singular—and tantalizing—reference to Pamba stands as evidence that there was at least one woman whose knowledge, action, and intimacy with the rebellion received the notice of the authorities. Jenings's warrant demanding that she be apprehended and "br[ought] forthwith before [him]" suggests that he considered her in league with the four male conspirators, an aid to or accessory in the plot, and otherwise notably valuable to the council's preventing further resistance.[27] Yet, other than Jenings's prudent naming of "Pamba his wife" as the second wanted person on the warrant, she subsequently disappears from both primary and secondary sources—with the exception of one historian's acknowledgment that among those "suspected blacks" was "*Pamla*, his wife" (my emphasis), a misreading of Jenings's hurried script.[28] But this marking of Pamba's presence among "great numbers" of insurgents need not end her place in the history of the plot.[29] Instead, it is an entry point from which to understand the collective work of organized revolt and Black women's roles therein. The questions surrounding Pamba, her relationship with Peter and the predominately male-orchestrated network across the southern James River counties, and her probable resistive contributions before and throughout the planning of rebellion cast doubt that the conspiracy of 1709–10 was ever the exclusive operation of just one man.

While it is possible that Pamba may have contributed little or nothing more to the conspiracy than following her husband and his friends, or keeping their secrets, there is good reason to believe that she shared in the plans and played an active role of her own. Motivated toward opposition by the raced and gendered predicament of compounding violence only Black women could experience in the burgeoning plantation society, Pamba also likely gave to the rebellion because of her strong ties to life and memory outside of racial chattel slavery—in Africa. Her place in the warrant alongside her husband, Angola Peter, Bumbara Peter, and Mingo suggests that an African-born constituency shaped the plot.[30] The name Pamba itself derives from the matrilineal Ovambo—a Bantu people of southern Angola. The deity Pamba, or "chief," is considered the mother, creator, and sustainer of her people and of life.[31] If Pamba was born in West Central Africa, she would have carried with her the meaning of her name when she received her first education in European tastes for the trade and flesh of African women and girls, boys and men along the African coast and into the sea.[32] In Virginia, she would have known that any children she produced with Peter, or with any man, would inherit her enslaved "condition" according to the 1662 law codifying perpetual hereditary slavery through Black women's reproduction and sexual exploitation.[33] Even if Pamba was not born and named in Africa, the rise in slave trade and the increasingly profitable tobacco economy meant that she lived and worked alongside many—such as Angola Peter—who were. The colony saw such an increase in captive Africans during the early 1700s, that not long after Salvadore's and Scipio's executions, Governor Alexander Spotswood cautioned that the "Negro's dayly encrease seem to be The Most Dangerous, and the tryals of last Aprill Court shew that we are not to Depend on Either their Stupidity, or that Babel of languages among 'em."[34] That "babble" of languages—an amalgamation of Igbo, Mande, and Bantu—invigorated tongues in the dialogue of the plot. It makes sense that Pamba, too, had her ears filled with such talk and was proficient in the articulation and exchange of the language of dissemblance and resistance.

Pamba, Angola Peter, Bumbara Peter, Mingo, and Robin never appear to have been located, arrested, or examined in extant records; whereas those *without* the formality of a warrant—Salvadore, Scipio, Tom Shaw, James Booth,

Manuell, Jamy, Essex, and Will—do. This raises several questions about why members of the former group were so urgently searched for, and why the discovery and capture of persons considered so significant to the plot would later be omitted from the council's documents and correspondence, whereas the arrests and examinations of those less intensely pursued were not. Perhaps Peter, Pamba, and the others listed in Jenings's warrant fled and evaded detection and capture together, and thus they remained absent throughout the conspiracy, its aftermath, and in the record produced from both. Surry County land patent records, wills, and deeds show that William Edwards of Jamestown Island—the same man identified as Scipio's enslaver in Surry County Court proceedings at the beginning of the conspiracy—claimed land in Surry that listed Mingo and Robin as headrights. The following year, in 1692, Scipio joined the list of Edwards's holdings.[35] The likelihood that the Mingo and Robin—included in Jenings's warrant alongside Pamba, Angola Peter, and Bumbara Peter—were in the same network as Scipio and other insurgents in Surry County increases as by 1709, the three men appear to have known each other for over a decade because they shared the same enslaver. This connection between Scipio, Mingo, and Robin indicates that the five names appearing on Jenings's warrant likely reflected individuals working together and also working with other named and apprehended insurgents in the neighborhoods of Surry, James City, and Isle of Wight Counties—particularly as Scipio was known to be directly associated with Samuel Thompson's (perhaps Angolan) Peter as the rebellion's "first and chief promoters."[36] These cross-county connections, the lack of evidence that (any) Peter was ever captured, Jenings's belief that Pamba was with Peter, and the culminating unlikelihood that she and the others were ever seized suggest that the insurgents' "unusuall and unwarrantable" meetings in places "where there are noe white or Freemen Overseers" were concerted forays intended to lead into more enduring forms of evasion and opposition.[37] In 1711, a year after the plot's 1710 resurgence, Governor Spotswood wrote that the "country" between the colony and North Carolina—or, the swamp—had "long been the sanctuary of all our runaway servants."[38] Perhaps he was not far from the mark.

If Pamba and Peter, their Bambara comrade, Mingo, Robin, and others were accustomed to holding insurgent meetings in spaces uninhabited by whites, they joined ranks with significant numbers of African-born absconders and maroons who were among the first to take their chances in the colony's woods and swamps. In Virginia, Africans constituted nearly 30 percent of fugitives fleeing between 1730 and 1787—a period of time when "their share in the enslaved population fell from 30 to 10 percent."[39] The council's conviction that conspirators in the plot were going "off of the plantation" to places outside of the gaze of whites, coupled with the resounding silence surrounding the outcomes and whereabouts of the wanted five, together support the likelihood that the group fled into the plotting ground of the near and inviting forested swamps around the time that Jenings ordered the guard to arrest them.[40] This is even more likely considering the striking number of Africans who were inclined to take to such places, fleeing in groups of two or more. In colonial Virginia, "a little over half" of the African people who ran did so in pairs or in groups of more.[41] Although runaways—including those born in Africa—were predominantly men, Pamba seems to have been one African woman who joined in their numbers.

While it is impossible to quantify what Pamba's insurgent labor included as a female participant in the plot, it is possible to move closer to what her role could have been, and plausibly was, based on the fact of African and African descendant women's fully capable personhood, their traditional roles of authority and reverence within their communities, and based in the resistive contributions of enslaved and fugitive women elsewhere. For example, at the dawn of the Revolutionary Age, in 1775, when a plan involving "near forty" accused of plotting to rise and "effect a massacre on the white people" arose along the Tar River between Pitt and Craven Counties, North Carolina, a "negro wench" was discovered to be the author of rumors exaggerating these numbers even more in the hope of effecting the plot's success.[42] A few decades later, in 1791, Molly planned and plotted with two enslaved men on neighboring farms—her husband, George, and Ben, a known "conjurer and fortune teller"—and convinced them to set fire to *her* enslaver's house in Fauquier County, Virginia.[43] Enslaved women like Celia and Hannah were also instrumental as initiators, decision-makers, advisers, and strategists to an 1812 rebellion involving "thirty or forty" conspirators. In the western counties of Henry, Montgomery, and Franklin, Virginia, Celia "instigated" Tom to kill their master by chastising that a braver man would "not serve [their] master any longer." She advised that Tom wait until the man "came home drunk" before ensuring that the deed was well and truly done, and she then directed Tom to flee. Meanwhile, Hannah incentivized two enslaved men to destroy her enslaver with promises that she would compensate them with two hundred pounds of hemp. These acts were part of a wider revolt, planned to coincide with the distraction, chaos, and uncertainty of the War of 1812. It was a time when Tom felt confident enough to follow Celia's instructions that he "take a horse and clear himself" of killing their enslaver. During his escape he met another enslaved woman whom he told he was on the run, that he had killed his master, and that "the negroes would shortly" seize arms to "rise and kill the white people." The unnamed woman replied that "they could not rise too soon for her, as she had rather be in hell than where she was."[44]

Though these women lived in different Virginia and North Carolina neighborhoods, and at different times, each shows how enslaved women like Pamba may have also given life and leadership to earlier swamp-adjacent movements, such as the 1709–10 plot, its momentum, and the mission and determination of her comrades. The late historian Rosalyn Terborg-Penn has emphasized how African women and women of African descent certainly placed their spoken word, urgings, calls, and outcry in the service of collaborative opposition. She points to African women's traditional use of "ridicule"—a tool of critique and criticism providing a means for women to question or motivate men—that could take the form of "direct taunts, group pressure, or ritual satire."[45] The use of their "mouths as weapons"—in expressions of self-defense, self-advocacy, but also of community interest and collective agitation—is one way Black women contributed to the planning and the execution of rebellion, usually outside of white surveillance.[46] It is not difficult to imagine Pamba conversing and conspiring with the men in tones and tenor of similar pressure. Her gendered investment in the group's success would have been paramount in the urgency of her fugitive and insurgent thinking. In addition, as Peter's wife, Pamba would have had his ear as well as his intimate trust. These dynamics could have lent Pamba's input about safety, justice, and forward steps greater weight and influence among the mostly male insurgents in their shared deliberations, plans, and execution of the plot. It is also true that Pamba's presence may have contributed to the insurrection merely through her refusal to betray the plot, or through the affirmation and reassurance even her passive complicity could have offered the men. But given all evidence that the insurgents in the movement of 1709–10 moved to sustain flight and rebellion "by force," Pamba's inclusion as an active contributor to the unfolding plot, if not her very leadership, should astonish no one.[47]

WITH "GREAT FURY": TIDEWATER WOMEN AND THE REBELLION OF 1792–93

Further into the eighteenth century, the Dismal Swamp continued to serve as an organizing space of insurrection. By 1730, the northern swamp counties of Princess Anne and Norfolk witnessed "above three Hundred" non-gender specific "Negroes"—thought to be substantially of Congolese backgrounds—who had joined together in the "woods and desarts" where they caused "a great deal of Michief." These insurrectionists intended to launch a surprise attack against their enslavers on a Sunday when they were unarmed and at church. The rebels' plans, however, were foiled. The militia was called up and the insurrection was suppressed, but not before the insurgents had used their "sanctuary in the woods" and swamps to conspire and "commit many outrages." Two dozen were captured, but the vast majority escaped, peopling the swamp's deeper retreats.[48]

Although women and men continued to plot and evade in and across the Dismal Swamp throughout the eighteenth and nineteenth centuries, after the rebellion of 1730, it was not until the dawn of the nineteenth century during the Age of Revolutions that the swamp was again decorated by flight, marronage, and organized revolt. It was during this period that enslaved people in the Tidewater brought the swamp to its high point in harboring and assisting organized Black rebellion and conspiracy to overthrow the slaveholding regime. Throughout the 1790s and into the 1800s and '10s in particular, the explosive impact that news from revolutionary Saint-Domingue had in the bustling port centers of the greater Chesapeake was certainly felt across the Dismal Swamp's eastern shore and throughout the wider Tidewater, as "every vessel brought its tidings" of the burning fires of Black revolt that refused to be extinguished there.[49] Like a cancer or unremitting contagion, the revolutionary determinations that only war could dismantle oppressive systems, win a trampled people their independence, and achieve total and immediate liberty were spreading with invigorated confidence across the Atlantic world. The fact that the American Revolution (1775–83) maintained and espoused these ideals and objectives was one thing, but for a revolution led by uprising Africans and their descendants to do the same was another. The Haitian Revolution (1791–1804) incited and encouraged the already-smoldering embers of Black rebellion that defined a relentless African diasporic tradition and shared experience.[50] While the French were embattled in their own revolution that began two years prior, enslaved people still bound to the crown jewel of the French empire—Saint-Domingue—burned thousands of sugar and coffee plantations and seized their own liberty in mass revolt. News of this Haitian Revolution could not be prevented from spreading among enslaved communities across the Atlantic world, particularly as captives were continuously being moved between Caribbean and North American ports for sale and transport; all the while they shared what they knew and sought what they could learn as a matter of priority. This rattled whites throughout the new American states, since the overpowering prospect of "total onslaught by angry Black people" threatened to reorder the racial distribution of power that slavery, capitalism, and white accumulation of wealth depended on.[51] During these years, slaveholders in the Tidewater and proximate Dismal Swamp neighborhoods were terrified, too, and for good and well-evidenced reasons.

In November 1793, Virginia authorities reported that "since the melancholy affair at Hispaniola [Haiti], the [white] Inhabitants of the lower country"—the northern reaches of the Dismal Swamp—had been "repeatedly alarmed" by the "dispositions," "suspicious conduct," and "different behavior" of "some of their slaves having attempted to raise an insurrection."[52] Since at least May of 1792, enslaved people plotting in Norfolk and Portsmouth appear to have joined together with enslaved people in the town of Hampton and in Northampton and Warwick Counties, just north of the James River and west of the Chesapeake Bay. (See map 1.) From these neighborhoods and towns, authorities exchanged a series of letters expressing their disturbance and alarm concerning Black organizing and insubordination. Officials wrote and appealed directly to the governor to send reinforcements. They then arrested, whipped, executed, and transported dozens of accused insurrectionists, and they gave depositions of their own evidencing not only their fear of a plot but also of the rebellion's validity and the actual danger the conspiracy posed.[53] Authorities reported "bodies of negroes collecting in numbers not less than 300," while newspapers informed that "about 900" in Hampton and in Northampton County alone had "assembled in different parts, armed with muskets, spears, clubs, &c." While these numbers likely reflect fear-induced sensationalism meant to garner white vigilance, authorities were nevertheless confident that insurgents in these areas had "concerted a plan" with enslaved people in Norfolk and Portsmouth to seize and destroy the Norfolk arsenal and "massacre the inhabitants."[54] Significant numbers of insurgents were said to have been crossing the bay under the cover of night and using the connecting waterways and swamps to strategize and spread the rebellion across the lower wetlands. Though a "considerable number" of rebels were apprehended and detained alongside their "barrel of musket balls, about 300 spears, some guns, powder, provisions, &c," authorities failed to suppress the plot. The following summer, in their continuous commitment to "get[ting] free," the movement pressed on.[55]

Flight and insurgent networks—inclusive of maroons and marronage—were crucial to sustaining this plot for nearly two years. This is evidenced by frequent reports of "banditti," persons described as "eloped" and fleeing from "different plantations," and others noted for being armed with "spikes fixed on sticks," swords, reap hooks, and clubs, who "lay in ambush" throughout the area and across these events.[56] While these bold acts may have been inspired in part by the success of the Haitian Revolution, the fact that most of the 1792–93 Tidewater rebellion took place in, or was said to have commenced in the immediate vicinity of the Dismal Swamp's northern edge must also be considered as influencing the formation of these insurgent designs.

Though no records specify the genders of the "banditti" or the "bodies of negroes," surviving documents do show that the few dozen who were accused and apprehended were entirely men. In Northampton County, Jack, Matthew, and Daniel were hung for conspiring and attempting to kill three members of the patrol. Armed with "large clubs," they had worked alongside other absconders in ambushing the patrol.[57] For their part, Peter and Stephen were sent to the "common whipping post" to receive thirty-nine lashes each, while authorities believed other male insurgents had acted as the "chief speaker" or "ringleader" in the plot to "burn all."[58] Moving between ports and across waterways, enslaved and free Black watermen—river boatmen, fishermen, stevedores, canal laborers, and draymen, or "Black Jacks," as they were also called—were instrumental in the plot, acting as messengers, lending the benefit of their exceptional mobility to pass along pertinent resources and information, and providing potential means of human transport.[59] Yet, while the confluence of slaveholding racism and patriarchy makes the total absence of Black women in these records unsurprising, women's probable undertakings as colluders and conspirers within the plot should still be considered, particularly as slave revolts—both intended and achieved—are collective efforts rooted in burning mutual interest, which Black women shared in equal parts with Black men.

Toward the end of May 1793, while male insurgents operating in the northern Dismal Swamp region were causing white authority much panic and alarm, Nelly and Daphne were also busy. Word of the rebellion underway had spread up the James River, and by the time it reached James City County, where the two women lived, they had decided they were ready to fight and to take matters into their own hands. Nelly (sometimes called Nell) and Daphne were in the field working with plows when their overseer, a man named Joel Garthright, accused Nelly of leaving the fence open and causing the sheep to disturb the young corn there. Nelly denied the charge and used some "impertinent language," to which Garthright responded by "repeatedly" striking her with a cane. Nelly then "quit her plough" and ran, but Garthright pursued her and continued to strike her, even "after she had fallen" to the ground. Daphne, also in the field "a small distance away," saw that Nelly's struggle had grown deadly. She too then abandoned her plow and "ran to the place where they were engaged," and together the women "seized and threw" their overseer to the ground, where they proceeded to beat him using "their fists and switches with great fury a considerable time." Their alleged "malice aforethought"—or calculated, coordinated, and lethal defensive action—was indeed a concerted rejection of the raced and gendered violence against Nelly, who was, at the time Garthright beat her to the ground, unmistakably "quick and big with child." The women's furious use of sticks, stones, and "other weapons of no value" to thoroughly bash Garthright's skull and also, notably, to assault his "loins" exudes the sexual undertones of undocumented crimes against Nelly and Daphne that exceeded their forced labor, and helps to explain their determination that Garthright should die.[60]

Although at the time of this incident there is some chance that Daphne and Nelly may not have heard about the greater insurrection plot of 1792–93, and it is also true that they may not have viewed themselves as insurgents contributing to it even if they did, the "subscribers, freeholders, and Inhabitants of the County" (or white citizens) certainly did not fail to make the connection. While Daphne had been promptly executed, Nelly was imprisoned for about three months, during which time she delivered her baby in jail, at the beginning of September 1793. Responding to a petition for Nelly's pardon signed by six of the county's subscribers who believed she had already "suffered sufficiently in a state of pregnancy," sixty-four others signed a contrary petition insisting that Nelly's "dangerous" actions were especially so "when we consider the alarming commotions which have lately existed among the negroes in this neighborhood."[61] By September 24, 1793, just two days after the petition for Nelly's "hastened" execution reached the governor's desk, more reports of "runaway" warfare and "intended rising" among a "number of negroes," rumored to amount to "three hundred" at least, again made their rounds.[62] Records documenting Nelly's near-certain execution were either lost, destroyed, or never produced. While the fate of her newborn is also unknown, we can surmise that Nelly—like other pregnant and incarcerated enslaved women before and after her—would have understood the "political weight of her pregnant body in her historical moment" and used this, along with the economic value of her childbearing, to leverage and negotiate her immediate conditions, her future, and her life.[63] In the days and weeks following the petition to see Nelly brought to the gallows, heightened surveillance and vigilance against Black people throughout the region must have proved effective, as reports concerning the conspiracy subsequently dwindle.

Whether the insurrection that began along the swamps and waters at the Eastern Shore in 1792 motivated Daphne and Nelly to kill their overseer and contribute to the uprising, or whether it did not, the women's joint and coordinated use of deadly force that summer day in the field stands as evidence that Tidewater women were willing to advance and even lead in deliberate, intentional, and cooperative rebellion and defensive violence. It also reveals how some enslaved women knew that their interests in and demands for safe and unbound intimacy, pregnancy, and motherhood required deadly insistence. Daphne's and Nelly's convictions about the transformative potential of acts of war, and their embrace of violent rebellion in self-defense and in support of their ideas about what was right, wrong, and just, helped fuel the fires of insurrection already blazing around them, regardless of whether they knew it. Though, it bears stating that just as the sixty-four subscribers in their neighborhood knew it—Daphne and Nelly likely did too.

Tidewater women would aid and instigate organized rebellion again not a decade later. This time, they helped strategize and sustain the greatest conspiracy of concerted revolt yet—a movement that intended to eradicate slavery in the state of Virginia, with North Carolina to follow. Like those before it, this rebellion was orchestrated by Tidewater enslaved women and men, fugitives, and edge-dwelling maroons who convened in and arranged the plotting grounds of the Great Dismal Swamp, the insurgent base and ultimate center of operations.

"In the House of a Negro Woman": The Easter Rebellion of 1802

In August of 1800—thirty-one years before Lucy, Charlotte, Ester, Cynthia, Venus, Nat Turner, and others in the Southampton County community of slaves sustained the rebellion that would become "the most famous slave revolt in American history"—a plot said to involve hundreds, if not potentially thousands, arose near Richmond, in Henrico County, Virginia.[64] Though Gabriel Prosser, an enslaved blacksmith there, was named the "spring and chief mover" of the conspiracy to take and "subdue the whole of the country where slavery was permitted," the plot was, in fact, upheld and supported by many in the enslaved community centered in the neighborhood of Henrico.[65] For months, meetings to plot, recruit, and strategize were held in the predominately male spaces of grog shops and taverns, or at Gabriel's blacksmith shop; but the meetings also frequently took place at Sunday community gatherings such as fish feasts, barbeques, and "preachings" in the neighborhood. At a bridge or near a spring, enslaved men and women in Henrico came together to play games, share food, drink—and exchange ideas. After the plot was betrayed, testimonies given by both enslaved witnesses and the accused confirmed that "the purport of the barbecue[s] was to concert measures for raising an insurrection."[66] Throughout the development of these plans, women were present and participating, which reflects their roles as wives, mothers, daughters, and sisters, but also as people invested in the life and future of their communities.

Natty—the only woman who testified at the Henrico County courthouse—said that on the "Sunday of the last Barbacue which she heard of," she and Isham, her husband who stood accused, spent the morning and afternoon together, before they "set off to the Barbacue after dinner from her house." Upon arriving, the two determined that "the women had eat up all the Fish," so they both returned to Natty's house between "sunset and dark." Natty also told the court that she had been "unwilling" for Isham to go to the barbeque to begin with—a statement that is corroborated by her having fed him at her house beforehand. Natty was sure to add protectively, that Isham was "persuaded to it by his brother George." But despite this supportive testimony, the court sentenced Isham to death on charge of conspiracy and insurrection.[67] Natty was charged with no crime. Her innocence was assured, no doubt, both by the court's assumptions that her gender made her least prone to conspire and "make insurrection," and by her professed reluctance to move closer to the plot, even though her testimony also guaranteed that she was part of the rival geography of insurgent knowledge. By the warning she issued to Isham, she showed that she clearly knew of the unfolding plans; but according to what she told the outraged court, she remained too cautious to support it.

Although Natty's testimony could have been a cover for her own involvement, there is clearer evidence that other enslaved women aided and gave rise to the rebellion. Natty's admission that "the women had eat up all the fish" before she and Isham arrived at the barbeque certifies that she was not the only woman present and participating in these gatherings.[68] Nanny, Gabriel's wife, would have been another participant. Although not much else is known about her, she actively worked alongside her husband and other male insurgents to plot, recruit, and otherwise encourage the men's manufacturing and collecting arms with which to storm and take the capital.[69] Daniel, an enslaved witness testifying against the accused Isaac, conceded that Isaac told him it was Nanny who had recruited him by informing him "that 1000 men were to meet said Gabriel near Prosser's Tavern the ensuing night, and that he [Isaac] also was to be one of them, for the purpose of murdering the White Citizens."[70]

Other women may have supported the rebellion in less obvious ways. At the fish feasts and barbecues, those preparing, cooking, and serving food were most likely women. Some, if not many, most, or even all these women must have been aware of the plot as they served, enjoyed, and cleaned up from these shared meals. In addition to what Natty and Nanny knew, visits with the "wives" of male insurgents are mentioned in multiple testimonies in connection with meetings to plan the rebellion. For example, the accused Ben Woolfolk found George and William, also accused, with their wives directly following a Friday night meeting, which Ben was late for and had therefore missed. Beyond this, another woman, unnamed, relayed to her enslaver a very detailed account of the intended insurrection. She confessed that the rebels "did not meet last night" and "would meet to-night" in the number of "300 or 400, some from town and some from the country, and that a number of them were to be mounted on horseback, who were to go at a distance and kill and destroy all as they went," before moving "on to Richmond."[71] Women in Henrico were aware of the plot as actively involved and invested members of the enslaved community who would have been interested in organized revolt under the rallying cry, "Death or Liberty."[72] Feeding and conversing with men whom they knew were close to these plans was also a way to feed and give sustenance to the rebellion itself. Through their support of their husbands, brothers, fathers, and sons, the women who spoke toward collective action, listened carefully, and shared with the men in the exchange of food, intimacy, and ideas, were active contributors in the shaping of the plot.

Yet, historians of "Gabriel's Rebellion" of 1800 have chosen to dismiss and overlook enslaved women's participation, place, and noted presence in the documentary evidence concerning the conspiracy of 1800.[73] Douglas Egerton writes plainly that "Gabriel chose no women," while James Sidbury stunningly concludes that "Black men did not include women in their plans for violent rebellion."[74] Sidbury also suggests that "the conspirators may not have trusted Black women," citing as his exclusive evidence Ben Woolfolk's testimony that he recruited King by telling him to keep the plot "a profound secret," and "not to mention it to or in the presence of any woman."[75] Not only does this assumption reproduce troubling beliefs about women, it also denies the totality of offsetting evidence that women like Nanny, Natty, and others were, in fact, trusted and were consulted and purposefully engaged in the making of plans. Egerton at least, acknowledges the gendered constraints on Black women's mobility as a key reason that women appear to have been only at the plot's "periphery," and did not take on what he considers to be the most important or central roles.[76] Both, however, miss the ways the rebellion was a collective pursuit of liberty and justice shared and sustained by the maneuverings of an entire community.

It is true that it was enslaved men—highly mobile, skilled artisans, several of whom were literate and able to pass on and receive written correspondence—who were most capable and prepared to execute the plan directly. Gabriel himself was a well-traveled blacksmith who made "500 bullets" for the revolt, while other male insurgents made crossbows, and manufactured swords out of scythe blades.[77] These men were able to produce, conceal, and distribute these weapons, along with word of the plot itself, as they moved between agrarian and urban centers. One weary official was right to notify the governor that he had placed "stationary patrols along the [James] river, the chief danger to be expected being from the batteaux men"—watermen or "negro boatmen" who were crucial in connecting the plot across far distances, using the region's intricate waterways.[78] Throughout the trials, frequent references were made by insurgent men that the "boys" had joined; "the boys on the Brook were going to fight"; "the Boys in Town" were "nearly ready to do the business"; had "Enlisted as a soldier"; "wanted to be a captain to fight"; or had "appointed" and "voted" Gabriel to be "General" with the "title and command of Captain." These references suggest that the male insurrectionists themselves may have understood their "meditated war" as the business and duty of men—brothers in struggle.[79] Gendered norms of dominant patriarchal society that excluded women from warfare and politics, along with the reality of male military and political authority in conventional displays of power, would have shaped these men's outlooks as well as their organizing. However, the ease by which these gendered customs and norms make deducible enslaved men's prominence in the documentary archive surrounding the plot should no longer license or produce new historical dismissal of women's inhibited and often veiled, but no less significant, offerings to building and sustaining rebellion.

The 1800 insurrection was intended to signal rebellions planned jointly in other counties throughout Virginia. The extensive web of rivers and their many offshoots of creeks, ponds, and swamps served the insurgents in channeling the rebellion across the state. Enslaved people in Henrico and Richmond spread word south of the Appomattox River (an offshoot of the James) to Petersburg; west of Richmond following the James River to the Tuckahoe Coal Pits and Goochland County; north to Caroline County, and also back down the James River to the eastern Tidewater and Dismal Swamp counties of Nansemond and Norfolk.[80] (See map 2.) After the plot's discovery, Gabriel himself fled south on a three-masted schooner—"armed with a bayonet"—eluding capture for nearly a month before being apprehended in Norfolk Harbor at the end of September.[81] On October 3, 1800, officials in the town of Suffolk reported, "There can be no doubt but about the time the insurrection was to have commenced at Richmond, the same was to have taken place here." The report continued, stating that at the start of September, there had been "150 blacks assembled near Whitlock's Mill." Among them were "20 from Norfolk" besides "the negroes that came from Carolina," of which there were "a great number." There, at the northwestern corner of the Great Dismal Swamp, fugitives from as far south as North Carolina had crossed the expanse of the swamp and joined those in Suffolk "to do what those in Richmond were about to do."[82] It would not be the last time that organized rebellion in the Tidewater would be advanced by the illicit movements of fugitives and Dismal Swamp maroons.

The insurrection of 1800 was an undertaking made possible through the extraordinary mobility and organizing capability afforded by enslaved watermen, skilled artisans, and enslaved women who nourished, nurtured, and held down the movement in ways that have previously been ignored. But besides these actors, "the vitality of Black folklore around the Dismal" also indicates that maroons may have worked in support of Gabriel's plans on the outskirts of "Virginia's primary mythic locus of black freedom"—or, the Dismal Swamp.[83] Some, including Martin R. Delany, one of the earliest proponents of Black nationalism and the political position of flight or fight, believed or imagined that Dismal Swamp maroons had acted in support of the Prosser conspiracy.[84] While those tried in Henrico County were only twice recorded as being runaway slaves, it remains possible that some borderland swamp maroons passed correspondence, hid arms, harbored insurrectionists, or planned to fight themselves—without detection.[85] This possibility becomes even more likely when considering the broader history tying marronage and insurrection throughout the Tidewater, and when considering that elsewhere in the Americas, maroon groups eagerly assisted or provided direct leadership in conspiracies, armed struggles, and organized warfare against the colonies.[86]

Although by October 1800, Gabriel Prosser had been hung and killed "before a horde of vengeful whites," the plot and plans he and others fought for to their death could not be thwarted.[87] By December of 1800, authorities in Norfolk requested additional patrols after "some seditious speeches" concerning the subjects of "cowards and liberty" that "only required a beginning" were "several times expressed" by Black people talking together on the street. These reports followed more of "the most alarming accounts" that another intended insurrection was to begin in Norfolk.[88] The following August 1801, Norfolk was again on alert after the "extremely artful" and "dangerous fellow" Sam had been jailed and transported for his "tendency to excite insurrection."[89] By

Christmas of 1801, insurgents declared "the insurrection was not done with" as insurgents planned across Nottoway, Amelia, Powhatan, Prince George, and Southampton Counties at least, to proceed "immediately" to Petersburg and Richmond, where they would be met with reinforcements. A "number of arms" were discovered, and arrests were made, but this did not stop others from trying.[90] By February of 1802, the plot had spread even further west, and the court in Brunswick County, Virginia, tried Phil and Isaac for making insurrection. Isaac, who "had been in North Carolina," just over the Brunswick southern border, had reportedly been "doctering and raising men (meaning negroes [*sic*]) to kill the white people," and planned to begin in the household of his own enslaver—"old Randolph" Hagood. As Isaac made plans to get rid of Hagood "and then the rest of the white people," he went to see his mother. There in her house, she "advised him" to stay with her, or else she foresaw "they would raise a company and take him," to which he consulted with her and confided that "he would raise a Company too."[91]

These uprisings must have also inspired Phebe, who by the spring of 1802 stood before the Halifax County court justices (two counties west of Brunswick)—the only woman formally charged and tried for "feloniously consulting and conspiring to make insurrection." Phebe, regarded by the justices as a "negro woman slave the property of Daniel Price," also stood accused of "wickedly and maliciously plotting the death of Daniel Price," in connection with the rebellion.[92] Sworn witnesses gave statements against her in support of the Commonwealth, though these were not deemed worthy of a single note on record. Whatever the evidence was against her, the court, in the end, did not find Phebe to be a danger to the safety of white Halifax as much as they found Sancho, Abram, Absalom, Frank, and Martin to be. While Phebe was acquitted, substantial evidence was presented and recorded in trial against these men, who were subsequently sentenced to die together at the gallows in May, for their part in the conspiracy that would become known as the Easter Conspiracy or the Easter Rebellion of 1802.[93]

Sancho, an enslaved ferryman who in 1800 had "tried to induce others to join the insurrection under Gabriel," tried again the following year. By November of 1801, he had recruited about sixty men, notably watermen, committed to "rising and destroying the white people."[94] Sancho's plan was to begin in Halifax, where he worked along the Roanoke River—a waterway that empties into the Albemarle Sound and also leads upstream directly into Petersburg as it joins the Appomattox River, and thus into the eastern Tidewater region where the Appomattox River meets the James. (See map 2.) "Companies" were to collect in Halifax and "assemble by the sound of a horn, trumpets,

&c and to begin on Friday night before Easter," or on Easter Monday, 1802.[95] The strategy was to use the holiday—an occasion when it would be the least unusual to see Black people traveling on the roads to town or otherwise doing independent activities with their time off—to advantage.[96] The Halifax plans, well underway by the fall of 1801, inspired and were inspired by coordinated plots arising similarly across southeastern Virginia to organize defensive violence, to plunder for vital resources necessary to sustain the insurrection, and to proceed onto Petersburg and Richmond during Christmas of 1801 and into the months of January and February of 1802. While uniformity and consensus across the various plans made in the various counties that winter of 1801 and spring of 1802 was not achieved, all these plots were related and connected—as one historian has pointed out—by the insurgent flow of wetlands and the many "river arteries that bound the region together."[97]

Amid these currents, Phebe—brought to the bar alongside Sancho and eleven other accused men—had somehow attracted the scrutiny and attention of the authorities. The Halifax County court justices had supposed her willing and capable of advancing the insurrection. They also suspected that she had already begun to do so by setting into motion the elimination of her own master. Though she did not possess the same freedom of mobility or opportunity to contribute to the plot in the same ways as the trained, skilled, and traveled bondmen at the bar, something about her, something she said, or an action she took made local authorities find it necessary to arrest and jail her, turn her in to "the custody of the Sheriff," and push her case forward with formal charges.[98] Considering that women were less likely to stand trial for crimes because of gendered assumptions about women and girls, and about their inclinations toward lawfulness and subversion, Phebe's trial is even more striking.[99] Phebe pleaded "not guilty," just as the accused men beside her did. But while the justices were less concerned with her, or were perhaps less willing to execute a woman for a crime that resulted in the loss of no white lives, her master may have had good reason to be more concerned than they.[100]

After Phebe was acquitted in April 1802, it would seem that Daniel Price—a husband and father of seven white children—held more serious suspicions about her than the judge did, for soon after the trial he appears to have rid his household of the "wicked and malicious" bondwoman. Whatever had happened between Phebe and Price, or whatever it was he knew or suspected about her interest in violent rebellion, rattled him enough that he believed he and his family were better off without her. For while Phebe had been one of four adult slaves he owned in 1801 and 1802, she was no longer his claim in the Halifax County property tax lists by 1803.[101] By the time Price lay on his deathbed at the end of February 1804, Phebe was also not to be found among the human chattel he willed to his children for their "use," "management," and "increase."[102] Despite her acquittal, Phebe must have displayed enough discontent with, deviation from, or rejection of Daniel and the Price family's interests and demands in order for them to have expelled her from the Price estate in the aftermath of her trial and of the Easter Rebellion.

As more arrests and trials in Dinwiddie, Nottoway, and Richmond continued into May 1802, plans that had once been devised primarily by hired out, sometimes literate, enslaved artisans and watermen, began to take new shape.[103] By May and into June, the coordinated efforts of conspirators were centered farther east and south as reports of insurrection grew increasingly adamant that the activities of insurgents in Norfolk and Princess Anne County, Virginia, were connected to simultaneous plots in at least seven counties in North Carolina—Bertie, Hertford, Chowan, Perquimans, Pasquotank, Camden, and Currituck. These, notably, are the same counties constituting the southern ends of the Great Dismal Swamp where it meets the Albemarle Sound. The plot now irrefutably emanated not only out of the Tidewater's elaborate and connective river systems, but also from the great expanse of the swamp. Now, some of the conspiracy's more brazen and emboldened acts were made possible by the plotting ground the swampscape provided, and by the leadership and support of swamp maroons.[104]

As early as March 1802, Norfolk officials had been kept busy in their appeals to Governor James Monroe, urging him to heed reports that "frequent meetings are held in the neighborhood of this place; that those meetings have consisted of from one to three and four hundred"; and that "a correspondence is held by these meetings with similar ones in North Carolina."[105] These numbers were most likely exaggerated to provoke and restore white vigilance and control, reflective again of the fear and terror authorities felt when confronted with real and mounting evidence of Black organizing and armed defense.[106] Unsurprisingly, white citizens did grow more vigilant, "strong" patrols of the militia were ordered up each night, and by April 15, the confessions of Will, a hireling of Princess Anne County who had been "a runaway for nine of the past twelve months," led to the discovery of the plot to "burn and plunder the town and murder the inhabitants" on Easter Monday night.[107] This coincided with the discovery of papers Norfolk officials found stuffed in a jug on a boat, confirming their suspicions that insurgent communications were being held across state lines via connective waterways and the states' shared, massive swamp.[108] On April 20, "five or six negroe men [were] taken up and confined in gaol," and by nightfall the guard also "took up" and arrested a "black girl."[109] She must not have gone to trial for her suspected involvement, as there is no record of it. But by April 26, just three days after Phebe's trial in Halifax for her part in the movement, Ned and Jeremiah were brought before the Norfolk court, found guilty of attempting to "make insurrection," and were condemned to hang. Three other men were tried but acquitted by the first week of May. In the end, Ned convinced the court that his sentence should be reduced to transportation. The Norfolk justices concluded that he was "a simple fellow," "almost an idiot, little capable of acting for himself."[110] Jeremiah was executed on May 28, 1802. His wife, Mary, brought him a pen and paper as he waited in his jail cell, and made it possible for him to write down his dying words: professions of innocence and prayers for Mary and their "dear little Ones."[111] Minutes before he died, Jeremiah was "pressed" a final time to confess "whether he had any knowledge of any conspiracy or not intended by the Slaves." He "refused to answer, and nothing would extract an answer."[112] There at the gallows, among the jeering crowd gathered to watch the spectacle of his last earthly moments, stood Mary, pregnant, alongside their two children, as Jeremiah "took leave" of them.[113]

It was hoped that Ned and Jeremiah's executions in Norfolk would be "sufficient warning" against continuing "nightly meetings" that were concurrently reported to be "very general among the negroes" in several North Carolina counties.[114] It was not. Although the month of May saw more trials and executions in several North Carolina counties—"two negroes" tried and executed at the Camden County Courthouse, and "two more hanged" at Currituck—the insurgents were not deterred. The determined still swore that while it had been a "Warm Winter, a dry Spring," it would be a "Bloody Summer."[115] By May 12, in Pasquotank County, the Elizabeth City jail was "full of negroes" after authorities suspected a plot concerning "a chain of those horrid savages running through this state and Virginia." The rebellion was no longer expected to rise on the belated Easter holiday, but instead, sometime during harvest. One of the persons jailed was Tom Copper, the named "general to command this county in a plot to kill the white people." Nothing is known about the circumstances surrounding his arrest, but not more than a day after it happened, Copper escaped with the help of "six stout negroes, mounted on horseback," who broke him out of jail. During the breakout, four of these men were caught and arrested, but Tom and one other escaped. Shaken by this, Charles Grice—a magistrate of Pasquotank County and the mayor of Elizabeth City—alerted the public that Copper had "a camp in one of the swamps, and is outlawed."[116] Grice learned of the swamp camp from testimonies given by Copper's imprisoned associates. Mingo, the "property of Jesse Reding," confirmed that he had visited the camp in the swamp and that Copper carried a paper with the names of sixteen men that were to join the rebellion. Bob admitted that Copper had planned "to write to Virginia for arms and ammunition."[117]

In the aftermath of the jail rescue, Grice also took the testimony of at least one woman, Silla, the property of Benjamin Powers. Silla testified that she knew well about the plans to rise up and had known since April 27. On that day at the Powers estate, she had been in discussion with Davis and Tann, two enslaved men who told her of the plot, added their support of it, and stated "they would Kill all the Black folks that would not join them." Tann anticipated that during the rebellion, "he would have that Neck to himself," and meant to have a piece of the action. Up until Silla was committed and brought to testify against the men and, ultimately, against the plot, she had been a participant in this exchange of insurgent knowledge, plotting, and conspiracy. Davis and Tann wanted to share what they knew about the plot with her. Clearly, they valued her ideas and trusted in her confidence, which she did not betray until she was seized by officials and coerced under the implicit threat of violence.

The spirit of the conversation Silla was invited to join was one of agreement that in the impending rebellion, the discussants would not be those, nor did they view each other as those who might oppose it.[118] Silla's decision to omit all indication of her own dissent and to share with Grice and the rest of the Pasquotank County Court what Davis and Tann "told her," earned her being discharged. Her cooperation makes sense, given the force of retaliation sweeping across so many counties. Silla would have known that transport, extreme violence, or execution would follow a conviction for conspiring to "make insurrection." Mingo, the prime witness in the case against Tom Copper, for example, was sentenced according to the law of 1741: that the sheriff take him "to the public pillory and have one ear of him the said Mingo nailed there to a [the post] and there stand for the space of one hour, and then the said ear to be cut off, and thereafter the other ear to be nailed in like manner and cut off at the expiration of one other hour, and that he more over then receive thirty nine lashes well laid on his bare back."[119] In addition to his marronage and accused role in the insurrection, the court found Mingo guilty of perjury for failing to effectively take the captain of the cavalry to Copper's swamp camp, as he was ordered to do. Despite Mingo's strategic misguidance, the Pasquotank authorities did their best to search the swamps; but there is no evidence that they ever found the camp, or that Copper was ever captured. But by the end of May 1802, in Pasquotank County alone, twenty-four people were committed and released, four men were whipped with thirty-nine lashes, and one man, Mingo, was whipped and suffered the brutal severance of both of his ears.[120] Women like Silla knew, just as men did, that even the hint of insurrectionary association risked provoking white bloodthirst and vengeance that would affect whole communities as well as bring personal pain, loss, and suffering upon themselves.

Yet women continued to decide to act in ways that supported the persistent Easter Rebellion throughout its duration. On June 2, 1802, after weeks of newly appointed patrols in the North Carolina counties of Hertford and Bertie were spent conducting searches of Black people's homes for weapons and other signs of "hostile design," authorities felt compelled to search the home of Jude. There, "in the house of a negro woman," the party of white men discovered a letter with detailed plans of the insurrection's latest turn. Jude lived in Colerain, Bertie County, a township about twenty-five miles north of Edenton, directly across the Chowan River from the Dismal Swamp's southeastern edge. (See map 2.) She had placed the letter in a "barrel where there was some cotton," which she kept in the kitchen of her home. There the patrols found it, "curiously concealed."[121] During the confrontation in her home, Jude told the men that Fed had left the letter with her that morning and told her it was given to him "the night before by [David] Sumner's Frank, to carry to [James] Brown's King."[122] Fed, who belonged to a Mr. Fitts, was soon apprehended and testified before the Bertie Court sometime on June 9 or 10. He said that he had been visiting his wife's house on Tuesday night, June 1, when he met Frank "on the road." Frank handed Fed the letter and "told him to give it to King," for on June 10—harvest, or "reaping time"—they were to "make a Start & come down to the Ferry & plunge & destroy." The following morning, Wednesday, June 2, Fed found reason to take the letter to Jude who lived at the property of Miles Rayner, instead of delivering it to King. When Fed approached Rayner's property and saw Jude there, he called to her—though, perhaps more alert than he, "she did not come." Instead, she "sent her little girl to him," and he then "put the letter in the girl's bosom and told her to give it to her mother."[123]

That Fed went to Jude to hand her the highly privileged letter suggests the possibility that King, the addressee, was her husband or other close kin. In either case, Fed trusted that Jude would know what to do, and that she would get the "small piece of paper" promptly to King.[124] When Fed concealed the letter in the child's dress, he simply told the girl to give it to her mother and that he would be back "in the evening"—a time Jude would recognize as safer to share in the plot. But Fed did not return at nightfall, because the search party that had been making rounds "in all the negroes' houses and other suspected places" had discovered the note earlier that day, and quickly rang the alarm.[125]

The letter was not long with Jude that morning, but while it was, she did know what to do. She did not destroy it, discard it, disregard it, pass it on to someone else, or turn it over to Miles Rayner. Instead, she chose to cautiously avoid unwanted detection until she saw a favorable opportunity to conceal it, first in the unsuspected hands of her child, and then in her own home. In doing so, Jude transformed both captive motherhood and the feminized and presumed apolitical space of domestic interiority into political sites of insurgent effect. Her decision to wage her own maternal authority by instructing her daughter—an apparently harmless young girl—to go to Fed, served the rebellion by protecting insurgents and preventing the plot's discovery and undoing; but her decision also reveals that the interests and objectives of women and children were active forces sharing in the demands of what so many male rebels were calling "the birth of liberty."[126] Jude's actions gave the rebellion fuller meaning, inclusive of acts of protest against violated, suffering, and shattered Black motherhoods as well as childhoods.

When her daughter dependably handed Jude the letter, Jude may or may not have read it before tucking it deep into the cotton barrel she kept in her kitchen.[127] Although "literate slaves appeared everywhere," most enslaved people were illiterate, particularly those who had not learned a skilled trade, or who lived on isolated, restricted farms and plantations, far removed from towns and cities.[128] As to the latter set of circumstances, Jude did not live in an isolated or far removed location in the neighborhood of Colerain. She could have learned to read, as did Harriet Jacobs, born a decade after the Easter Rebellion in the nearby town of Edenton, where she had been taught to read.[129] Although Jude was a woman, and thus likely not considered "skilled" in a trade, she was clearly very close to and trusted by a community of skilled and traveled men—many of whom could read, write, and impart that knowledge onto others, including her. Frank's own writing, after all, had made its way into Jude's home. The letter read:

> Frank Sumner, Captain will command Hosea Sumner, Ned Sumner, Cromwell Sumner & Harry, Bob Moore, Ned Moore, Jink Wateridge, Tom Simon, David Fitt, Peter Harrell, Buck Seal, Simon Hunter, Peter Hunter, Ganse Surry and we will rise at the tenth of June. Men won't join us we will kill them and all make to Colerain and get together and kill all, this is the line let you no Capt King Brown or you may get men in order, my gun is hid.[130]

Whether or not Jude read the message there in her kitchen, her decision to bury the tangible evidence of the plot under cotton until it could be of further use to King, Frank, Fed, and the conspiracy, was itself an act of insurrection. And if she had read it, Jude's actions are even more perceptibly political, since in that case, her deliberate labor to conceal and protect the movement also would have marked her knowing service to and support of organized and armed rebellion.

Jude's "little girl" may have been present when—after the patrol discovered the letter—Jude decided it was best to tell the men threatening her and ransacking her house that Fed had given it to her, and that Frank had given it to him the night before to give to King. Despite her careful measures to keep the letter hidden, its discovery and her reluctant admissions were devastating to the plans. Six days later, on June 8, 1802, Nansemond officials back on the Virginia side of the Dismal Swamp wrote to Governor Monroe that after a very brief period of some relief following the recent trials and executions, citizens of "the Town of Suffolk particularly" received "fresh and more alarming" news of insurrection "in consequence of the movements of the negroes in this and neighboring Counties." The Nansemond County militia captain requested backup from Richmond after officials in the adjacent North Carolina counties of Bertie and Hertford had—following the tip provided by swift circulation of Jude's letter—warned their northern neighbors to be on guard, for a "total destruction of the whites" was to commence on June 10.[131]

Within days of the discovery of the letter, trials began in Bertie County, and by June 16, nine men, including King Brown, were executed. Meanwhile, Frank was tried and executed in Hertford, the county of his enslaver.[132] The Bertie County Court, believing Jude incapable of posing any real threat and unlikely to be of any further aid to the insurrection, did not find it necessary to try her. The evidence presented against King and Frank, however, was damning. Testimonies, though often given after the inducement of whippings, nevertheless repeatedly and consistently confirmed that King and Frank were to command a group of men on the east side of the Chowan River—which is the southwestern edge of the Dismal Swamp—and that they were also working to recruit more insurgents.[133] On June 10, officered "companies" of men were to use "clubs, with nails drove through them," as well as guns hidden "in the wood on the swamp." An "outlaw" named Tony was to provide a sword, Bob had powder and a "sword made of a scythe" hidden in a log, Salem was ready with his sword, and it was reported that Frank "had powder and ball." Harry said, "The negroes were going to rise in Virginia & would carry it on here." Davy corroborated this, admitting they were to "get encouragement from Virginia," and when the time came, they would receive guns "from the neighborhood around," in addition to the fifteen or so guns they knew they could take from the magazine. These testimonies also revealed that "five or six negroes were in the swamp to guard the magazine and ammunition." It was believed that Tom Boston or Salem knew more about where the ammunition was located. Simon testified that Boston told him he "expected to get arms as they slay the country," and that "the runaways from the other side of the sound had brought over a case of guns and 20 lb. of powder which were hid in the swamp."[134] From the vantage of Bertie County, the other side of the "sound" (the Albemarle Sound) was the Chowan County corner of the Dismal Swamp. (See map 2.) Enslaved watermen, who made up at least 14 percent of all skilled Virginia runaways, were vital to these plans to move arms, information, and people across these connective wetlands.[135] But these testimonies, taken together with the analogous activities of Tom Copper's maroon camp in the Pasquotank County swamps, also suggest that *maroons* aided the rebellion by trafficking, concealing, guarding arms, and exchanging correspondence across the expanse of the Great Dismal Swamp.

Authorities in both Virginia and North Carolina certainly believed so. At two o'clock in the morning on June 10, Charles Grice received a hurried dispatch warning that "the negroes have embodied in Hertford County and are under arms." A second dispatch, received at midnight in Nixonton, Pasquotank County, reported that insurgents in Bertie County had "committed great havock" before they moved eastward toward the Chowan River, where they were in fact "embodied and armed at the ferry." Five days later, excerpts from these two letters were published in the *Norfolk Herald*. A new letter of alarm dated June 13, 1802, also appeared in this notice. Wilson Butt of Great Bridge, a neighborhood in the lower part of Norfolk County, nearest the northern stretches of the Dismal Swamp, had penned the letter. Wilson Butt—the very same man who, along with his prominent family at Great Bridge, would hunt down the maroons Maria, Nelson, James, and Bob Ferebee sixteen years later—reported that more insurgents had "embodied in large companies, armed, in the Great Swamp, near the Virginia line."[136]

Across these movements, enslaved women in the Tidewater asserted themselves as actors, collaborators, and sometimes as leaders or instigators of insurrection and organized rebellion. Although the swamp-based conspiracies and intended revolts of 1709–10 in Isle of Wight County and the Revolutionary Era rebellions of 1792 and 1802 were most visibly the primary endeavors of enslaved and fugitive men, careful attention to the recurrent mentions of women allows new questions to be asked about their presence, stakes, interests, criticisms, and insurgent labor throughout. A leading dimension of these rebellions follows Black men's privileged mobility as well as the undeniable opportunities they were afforded as men within a "southern white masculine culture" that ensured militarism, fighting, providing, and defending were male pursuits, while childrearing and domestic responsibilities were identified as women's.[137] But in spite of the raced and gendered limitations they faced, Black women throughout the Dismal Swamp counties and greater Tidewater were fully and equally invested in the pursuit of freedom, and they worked whenever, wherever, and however they could to mobilize protest and make rebellion a realizable and attainable option within their communities.

Women like Pamba, Daphne, Nelly, Nanny, Phebe, and Jude were among innumerable others who studied and remained alert, listened intently, spoke up about justice, and otherwise agitated, urged, and inspired insurrection in any way they could, given the options they had at their disposal. They might not have trailed the edges of the great swamp armed with guns, scythes, and swords, but they served their communities by weaponizing their words; by feeding and nourishing dissent; by laboring with stealth as secret messengers, recruiters, or gatherers and guardians of prized and privileged information; by lending their homes to the cause; and by directing their gendered roles as mothers, wives, sisters, and daughters toward insurgent and transgressive ends. In doing so, they affirmed the place of arms and defensive violence in struggle, while also playing active roles in political mobilization and organized action that required their interest, collaboration, and support.

The gendered constraints enslaved women faced, such as often near-totalizing confinement, routine reproductive and economic exploitation and use, bodily harm, punitive violence, rape, sexual assault—but also a lack of rights to safe and voluntary pregnancy, childbirth, and secure and undisturbed motherhood—provided compelling motivation enough to reject slavery and invest in rebellion, if not more so than whippings, starvation, withheld pay, toil, and the threat of sale alone. Tidewater women who chose more enduring practices of marronage, or who were born into multigenerational maroon communities in the deepest and most secluded interiors of the Great Dismal Swamp, most assuredly agreed. Preferring the difficulty and hardship of life in the wetland ecology of a forested swamp to pervasive oppression and lives shaped by pain and terror outside the swamp, deep swamp maroon women took their rejection of slavery and captivity beyond insurrection. In their sustained flight and creation of long-lasting alternative lives in the swamp, these maroon women birthed, cultivated, and heartened fugitive communities that opted out of the slaveholding world altogether.

FIVE

Hearthstones of Their Communities

MAROON WOMEN AND INSURGENT LIFE IN THE DEEP SWAMP

Women are like hearthstones, men like axe handles. Once placed in a house, a set of clay hearthstones may never be moved; they endure. But an axe handle is made to travel, and once worn out from use, it is discarded on the spot; it leaves no traces.

SARAMAKA MAROON PROVERB, SURINAME

Away from the swamp's edges and into the deepest and remotest parts of the Great Dismal Swamp, the singular human factor that made possible the capacity for the least detectable groups of insurgent maroons to become enduring, multigenerational, and even thriving communities was provided by the gifts and labors of Black women. Just as the continuation of racial chattel slavery fundamentally relied and depended upon the productive and reproductive work carried out by captive women and girls, so too did any lasting future of self-liberated maroons. Formed synergistically with the purest and most inaccessible ecologies of the Dismal Swamp, families, groups, and communities containing women demonstrated that the very undoing of the social and economic order of the slaveholding Tidewater could come from Black women's decisions to remove themselves from it and to reconstitute their lives and labor differently, within the interior swamp's protection. Living in daily consultation with the most isolated wilderness, maroon women recast their energies and their bodies to be made effectively inaccessible and unattainable to white men, and in doing so, they transformed themselves into a corps of perpetual loss for slaveholders and slaveholding capital. Women's determinations to permanently or indefinitely maroon are thus readable not merely as self-interested decisions but also as insurgent political choices capable of crippling and undermining enslaving power and the system of slavery. Through marronage, Black women pronounced inheritable free life where it was never meant to exist. Maroon women of the most elusive and mysterious inner swamps were those most likely to have achieved relatively secure and stable lives, just as they were those best positioned to repossess and reconfigure their own social, economic, reproductive, and embodied values and futures—this time, in the service of innately dissident Black community.

Although maroon women were fewer and generally outnumbered by men across the Dismal Swamp, and despite the less frequent success of their evasion and elusion, the names and personal backgrounds of most of the women who did shape the more permanent and potentially sizable maroons of the deeper swamps will never be known. Nevertheless, these women left their marks in documentary, archaeological, and material archives of the swamp's history. Women like Tamar, Larinda, and Minta entered into written records alongside other women whose names were not recorded, and possibly hundreds of others who between the mid-seventeenth century and the Civil War were neither discovered nor captured by their pursuers and their record keeping. In addition to this slight and limited documentary archive, excavations led by Daniel Sayers between 2003 and 2013 of less than 1 percent of a twenty-acre island inside the deep swamps of Gates County, North Carolina, unearthed strong material evidence that there lived "potentially hundreds" of maroons between the period 1600 and 1860 in this one area alone.[1] Sayers's groundbreaking Great Dismal Swamp Landscape Study (GDSLS) concluded that intensely populated, multigenerational communities reproduced and persisted through their own methods and practices of self-government and community organization, including the division of labor, "social expectations, dispute resolution, community safety and defense systems, and daily subsistence practices."[2] Central to each of these pursuits was the work of maroon women, whether or not their names can be credited.

Although deep swamp maroon families and self-regulating communities were the most established, steadiest, self-reliant, and therefore the least likely to encounter strangers or engage the world outside of the swamp, movement and motion—the basis of all fugitive practice—was nevertheless constant and unquantifiable. Sustaining maroon life in even the most obscure parts of the swamp required deep swamp maroons to occasionally move, plot, and foray away from any definitive home base. Through their movements in the fluid, unfixed, sprawling swamp, there arose limitless possibilities for partnerships, mutual aid, social and economic exchange, and collaborations between and among disparate deep swamp groups, between maroons of the remotest recesses and those more ephemeral "banditti" at the swamp's fringes, and between all the varied and diverse maroons and supportive networks of enslaved people in the towns and counties neighboring the swamp.[3] Insurgent networks of intelligence and exchange between male *petit*, or borderland, maroons and enslaved male canal laborers who worked the swamp's canals and lumber camps also constituted a long-standing illicit economy in which maroons—who may have sometimes included those of the deep swamps—traded their own labor in retrieving wood and manufacturing shingles in exchange for vital correspondence, goods, and resources they otherwise lacked.[4] Hinterland swamp maroons, not unlike the most elusive and enduring *grand* maroons of the Caribbean and Latin America, did not neatly remain in one place indefinitely, but embraced flexibility and errantry just as they employed careful and methodical strategies to secure and protect their home settlements.[5] Fugitive knowledge of the necessity of movement and the constant readiness to move meant that even the women and men of the deep swamp could have maintained or developed relationships with other maroons outside of their communities, with transient fugitives scattered throughout the swamp, as well as with enslaved people still connected to them through kinship and family ties at the ends of the swamp. Although these men and women were generally self-sufficient and most concerned with securing and protecting self-isolated and autonomous life in the swamp, the endless capacity of fugitive movement helps explain how these interior communities were initially formed, how they grew in ways that supplemented the reproductive labor of maroon women, and how they may have been supported in networks within a broader insurgent wetland world that included both women and men alike.[6]

Women of the deep swamps may have lived in maroon communities that were influenced by dominant patriarchal ideas about gender and the roles women should serve and occupy, not unlike the enslaved communities in the world outside the swamp from which they fled. This would have been especially true by 1800, when the majority of enslaved people in the Tidewater were American-born and had been American-born for at least a half a century. The imposition of Western culture on enslaved people included the foisting of white patriarchal and hierarchical gender roles that certainly shaped the experiences and understandings of power and authority held by enslaved men and women outside the swamp. The expectation that inside the swamp, maroon social organization would not have perpetuated aspects of these norms is an unreasonable one. Though they were liberatory in nature and in essence, maroon communities across the Americas were not egalitarian utopias.[7] The maroons of the Dismal Swamp were no exception to this. In fact, the mirroring or replication of dominant designations of gender roles may have been even more common among maroons of the Tidewater and broader US South, because maroons fleeing these slaveholding regimes were fleeing from settler slavery, and thus they were generally (in most places and at most times) escaping from the yoke of close and interpersonal relationships with patriarchal *and* paternalistic enslavers who were highly invested in their human property as possessions for their personal grooming and heritable and bequeathable economic gain. Paternalistic slavery required enslavers (both men and women alike) to model and instruct that white men were the fathers and pinnacles of hierarchical power; that women's work was to be place-bound and tied to childrearing, caregiving, and the home; that femininity was reducible to docility, submission, and subservience; and often, that women inherently lacked intellectual interest and capacity for critical and political thought.[8] These influences on African descendants should be considered, because they resulted in uneven and distinctive gender roles within enslaved communities, and differing experiences of subjugation between enslaved women and men.

However, despite the patriarchal ideals, demands, and customs that paternalistic slaveholders enforced and imposed onto enslaved people, an aspect of

African cultural precedent did survive. Enslaved women maintained within their communities "a great deal in common with their African foremothers," who in many precolonial West African and West Central African societies shared not passive, submissive, inferior, or subordinated roles, but dual, complemental, and parallel positions of shared value, power, and authority alongside men.[9] Dismal Swamp maroons, who were descended from primarily matrilineal and matrilocal African people, most assuredly continued to place high value on women's integral roles and capabilities as respected and necessary social, political, and spiritual leaders and actors within their communities. In this regard, the maroon women and men who navigated the deep swamps of Virginia and North Carolina may not have been entirely dissimilar from the *grand* matrilineal Saramaka maroons of the swamps and jungles of Suriname. Although these Caribbean-facing maroons rebelled against depersonalized Dutch colonial slavery, numbered in the thousands in any one generation, and consequently retained much of their African language and culture across time, multigenerational interior Dismal Swamp maroons may have shared the Saramaka's belief in the social sacrality of the "bêè ('womb' or 'belly')," and in their general honoring of women as vital contributors and leaders.[10]

More likely than not, deep swamp maroon women would have been highly respected figures among their families and kin, not only for the essential work they performed as child bearers and mothers, but also for the crucial value of their minds, their knowledge, and their savvy. They may have continued to perform or been expected to perform the usual labor of housekeeping, raising crops, preparing food, and childrearing; and they may have remained less mobile and perambulatory than maroon men; but deep swamp maroon women occupied central positions as stabilizing forces of home and belonging both to themselves and to their communities. As contributors to and providers of sustenance, pleasure, joy, and social vibrancy, they fed and nurtured the collective rebellion of free life. Their love, labor, skill sets, critiques of white domination, and active participation in defending and protecting the insurgent ground of the swamp also encouraged the overall collective morale and spirit of determination and assurance. In these roles, women acted as the "hearthstones" of their communities.[11] Like the very foundation of a home's hearth and fireside, Black women gave warmth and light to the place and purpose of fugitive motion and insurgent gathering, to life in an otherwise desolate swamp; and in so doing they made possible enduring movements of Black autonomy, resiliency, and refusal in the very midst of entrenched chattel slavery.

"I JES' TUK MY CHILE, AN' I NEBBER STOP TILL I COME TER DE SWAMP": MAROON WOMEN'S RECLAMATIONS OF INTIMACY, REPRODUCTION, AND MOTHERHOOD

Days after the Civil War ended in early April 1865, a woman emerged from the Dismal Swamp. For about a week, she had traveled north out of the deep swamps by foot, by boat, and by wagon in search of work. When she arrived in the area of Norfolk County, she relayed to her new employer that she had been living with others in the "big swamp" south of there but had decided to come out when she heard the news that Black people "b'longed ter darselves now." Although her name is not recorded, she was described by the woman who hired her as "dirty, ragged" but of a "radiant good-nature," and someone, it was quickly determined, who had been accustomed not to domestic servitude but to that of the "cornfield." The former maroon woman shared a story of such anguish and grief—a story her employer described as a "great mother-love"—that the white woman was moved enough to hire her, but just for the span of the day. The ex-bondwoman, who had been a wife and mother to six children, had been tormented by her enslaver's sale of each member of her family, save for her youngest child, a young boy. The boy had worked in the fields alongside his mother, until one day he fell miserably ill. The woman pleaded with the overseer to let her son stay home that day, but her pleas were viciously ignored, and the man whipped her and cut her on the head as a result. The woman recalled she would "nebber forget de look dat chile gib me," when she had to tell him he would have to work after all. Mother and child went to the fields, where he "kep' along till mos' ebenin" before he collapsed "right whar he wor a pickin.'" The overseer beat and whipped the boy while his mother was forced to watch, and when he finally stopped, the woman carried her limp son home, where he soon died in her arms. After that, the woman remembered going "crazy or suffin" before she marched to the overseer's house and "gib him my tongue." The man laughed and promised her a whipping "mos' ter deff," the following morning. Instead, she responded with firm and decisive movement of her own; she waited for the night to be "all still," and as soon as it was, the woman "jes' tuk my chile, an' I nebber stop till I come ter de swamp."[12]

This unnamed maroon woman's unimaginable pain and loss was horrifyingly common within plantation contexts, and the profound suffering, grief, and trauma she must have experienced was surely familiar to countless other women. The brutalities of rape and forced breeding, profitable reproductive labor, and captive mothering was met with varied responses from enslaved women, including the use of abortives, maternal dejection, apathy, detachment, infanticide, resignation to enduring personal harm and strife so as to protect their ability to parent, as well as defensive violence; but some women also made the decision to create new modes of life, securing the right to possess their own wombs as well as to protect the lives of the children they had labored to deliver.[13] The woman's choice to flee into the swamp and to live with others "dat had runned away diffe'n' times" was an action plan shared with women across the hemisphere and across time who also decided that maroon life was preferrable to remaining, even in the face of new possible dangers, difficulty, and lack.[14] While in slaveholding societies, women's intimate lives, reproduction, and motherhood were sites of conflict between violence, domination, and dispossession on the one hand, and self-gratifying reproductive and maternal relationships on the other, women who chose marronage opted out of this struggle altogether and instead created new possibilities for intimacy and motherhood rooted in choice, connection, joy, and love. As the historian Crystal Eddins has argued in her discussion of the maroons of Le Maniel, Haiti, women in marronage knew that maroon settlements could be the ground on which to claim their own "complete wellbeing" based on their "human right to decide when and how to have—or not to have—children, and to parent existing children in safe and sustainable communities."[15] In this sense, women's sustained movement as maroons can be understood as some of the earliest practices of reproductive justice, as it was through their fugitivity that they were able to remove their wombs and progeny from exploitation and ill-use and remove themselves from further emotional injury and bodily harm. Through this womb resignification and the reclamation of their intimate lives, Black women in marronage committed, in the words of Jennifer Morgan, the most "profound rejection of the totalizing logic of hereditary racial slavery."[16]

The woman who ran into the northern swamps carrying with her the body of her slain son found her way to a community of maroons who held her in her grief, offered her a space to cope, to mourn, to express sorrow; and they helped her "bury my chile" and perform the important death rites necessary to ensure his peaceful transition.[17] Maroon aid and support in what must have been an all-too-familiar scene of tragedy suggests that part of deep swamp insurgent worldmaking hinged upon practices of love as well as on reverence toward motherhood. In lifting the woman in her final earthly act of motherhood toward her last and youngest child, the maroons also demonstrated how acts of care and love are key to engendering collective movement, purpose, and the potential for greater and more capacious community action. After all, it was through this act of aid and relief that the woman was invited to join the fugitive community in the more remote swamps and remain there until the close of the Civil War. When the maroons discovered the woman ragged from exertion in her flight from whomever or wherever she had come, and when they saw that she was holding onto the lifeless body of a young boy, they may not have been very surprised. As studied as maroons were about the workings of violence and power in the slaveholding regimes they had deserted, they may have known firsthand that motherhood did not have to be a hindrance to marronage but rather, "a powerful motivating factor."[18]

Across the Dismal Swamp, maroon women reclaimed their rights to safe and voluntary intimacy, reproduction, and motherhood through continual flight and evasion meant to secure their own desires and best interests, as well as to ensure the best interests of their families and loved ones. Their movements away and into the inner swamps were rooted in decisions they made about how they loved and valued themselves and their families, kin, and children—both born and yet-to-be born. Through acts of love, maroon women worked to protect marriages and romantic unions they had chosen to enter into either before or after marooning in the swamp; and it was also through love that they worked to ensure they could care for themselves and deliver, raise, nurture, and safeguard their own children. While Black women's intersectional vulnerability meant that it was possible that forced or coercive sex and the resulting reproductive labor could be abuses that followed them into the swamps—only this time, at the hands of maroon men rather than at the hands of their enslavers—there is not even a single suggestion of this in documentary evidence or in oral testimonies. There is, however, substantial evidence of mutual intimacies and pregnancies consequently conceived, as well as a strong indication that deep swamp maroon women had decided for themselves that their personal safety and sense of self-worth, sexual and reproductive lives, and the future of their children and families were better off in marronage deeper within the swamp.

The amorous bonds between Isle of Wight County repeat fugitives Venus and Jack Dismal as well as their refusal to be apart indicates that women's needs and desires to love and be loved freely, and to live with intimate partners in reproductive and familial futures of their own choosing was motivation enough to flee and maroon in the Dismal Swamp.[19] But while there is no record of Venus and Jack bearing any children that may have motivated them to conspire with the wetlands to sustain their escape, other women leave no doubt that they chose marronage to gain control of their intimate lives, to attain safe and consensual pregnancies, and to claim liberated motherhoods.

For example, in 1820s Camden County, North Carolina, Tamar Grandy had had six children "very fast," presumably with her enslaved husband, though he was owned by "hard owners" and lived at a distance, some twenty-five miles away. Before she "put herself in the woods," five of her six children had been sold away from her as soon as they were considered "big enough"—an age that usually meant between five and ten.[20] While grieving the boundlessness of this loss, Tamar and her remaining sixth child, just over a year old, were sold to traders who were to sell them on at market in Savannah or New Orleans. Although Tamar could not manage to "obtain" and rescue her infant, she made her escape from the coffle, which had by then already traveled one hundred miles south. Tamar knew that conversing with the natural world could save her life, and so she partnered with night's starlight and concealed herself in thick woods by day. When she finally reached her old neighborhood, she would have appreciated the welcoming sight of the woods and marsh of the Great Dismal Swamp. Deciding that was where she would go, she got word to her mother, her brother Moses, and her husband that she, like her mother before her, would go to the swamp. As often as he could, Tamar's husband journeyed the long distance to visit her there in the "den" she made for herself. Even though he had to return to work by sunrise following the many Sundays he visited, sharing as much private intimate time together as they could was so important to them that they both agreed Tamar's husband should "spend part of the night with her" on each of these occasions. Through marronage Tamar protected her own intimate life and the affective bonds she shared with her husband. In doing so, she also committed the insurgency of reclaiming her right to choose the future and the progeny of her own womb. As a maroon, Tamar conceived at least three pregnancies and experienced the nine months of aches and swelling as well as the awe and uncertainty of her physical transformation throughout the course of each. In her den, she labored to deliver three babies and then nursed the newborns as she saw fit, into the healthiest children possible. For Tamar, this began with her ability to love and parent them freely and to keep them away from the greedy and grasping hands of slave traders. These reclamations of intimacy, reproduction, and motherhood were made possible through her movements to and communion with the secluded swamp.[21]

Other women also chose marronage in the deeper swamps as a means to defend their rights to their bodies and to protect their choice of whether or how they would birth children and raise families. One observer, writing in 1817 about "frequent instances" of marronage in Tidewater North Carolina, recalled the news that "a woman was discovered in the center of the Great

Dismal Swamp. There she & her six children had lived for years."[22] Another account tells of a maroon couple who lived together in the remote swamp for more than seven years. There the woman brought seven pregnancies to full term and labored to deliver her body of seven children she would protect from recapture and bondage. During the Civil War, when the family vacated the swamp and emerged from it at its northern edge, the Union company stationed there was surprised to find that all seven children "had never looked upon the face of a white man before."[23] When a fire of "unparalleled fury" ravaged portions of the northeastern deep swamps in 1845, a maroon mother and her eleven children knew that movement was again the only way to save their lives. Due to an unprecedented dry season, the fire had spread from within the swamp and reached as close as "five or six miles" from the towns of Bower's Hill and Portsmouth, in Norfolk County, Virginia. The woman, described in the report as "an old black woman, being burnt out of her capacious home," returned to her enslaver, bringing with her each of her children. After such a long time without the woman's use as laboring property, her owner considered her return—and her return with an increase of so many children—an "indemnity or remuneration," since the woman's free intimate life and subsequent pregnancies in the swamp had turned her enslaver a great profit after all, despite all losses incurred during her decade-long absence. The woman was one of "a large number of runaway slaves" who had reportedly "in many cases, been secreted for years" in the Dismal Swamp but were driven from it by this fire that raged there for "some two weeks."[24]

Larinda White and Abraham Lester were another maroon couple who, after having met in the swamp, "agreed to live together" there. Abraham had fled from "hard" enslavers nearby not long before Larinda fled in January 1860. She chose the swamp to escape overwork, the pain of the recent sale of her (unnamed) then-husband into the Deep South, her mistress's threats to sell her as well, and the daily torment of beleaguered motherhood to their nine-year-old son. Larinda ran from the household of Dr. William White of Portsmouth, Virginia, judging it best to leave her son behind, who during her absence in the swamp was, she later learned, inevitably sold to South Carolina. The trauma and suffering of families besieged and broken apart by slavery had also affected Abraham's decision to leave behind a wife and seven children of his own. In addition to the cruelties of an enslaver who swore "he would be the death of [him]," Abraham had been routinely separated from his wife and family by hires that removed him from them so much that he was accustomed to seeing them only at Christmas. Out of these strained and severed bonds, the pair found solace in the swamp, and in each other.

Before meeting Abraham in the swamp, Larinda fled first to the home of her mother in Suffolk and then to "friends" at the swamp outskirts. She then spent some months on the run, living at the swamp edges, sawing and piling shingles for a small company of poor white men in exchange for a few cents, food, and supplies. One of the men—who owned no slaves—lived on a small farm at the edge of the swamp. Apparently accustomed to offering friendship to fugitives such as Abraham, but less so to solitary women fleeing their bonds, he introduced the two in the hope that he might offer her protection from the "bushmen"—or maroons—known to live farther within the swamp. Larinda was never accosted by any such person, but Abraham, whom she also described as a "bushman," did promise to offer her his aid and protection on condition that she would "go only when and where [he] said." Not viewing this arrangement as any more repressive than her life as a bondwoman under the rule and thumb of the White family, Larinda preferred it to any and all other options within her grasp. She agreed. The two then traveled farther into the swamp to live together, for Larinda recalled that she had grown "almost tired" of living at its outskirts by herself, "it was so lonesome." Over the course of three years, the couple built several camps in the interior swamp, each "always in the water," by creating shelters from piles of blocks of wood to house them, provide them with a "bed," and keep them dry. In these floating shanties, if Larinda and Abraham "stepped out of the door," they could go from "knee deep to almost waist deep in water." They were able to build fires atop "a large block of wood" and thus cook on these nearly submerged camps, and by scraping the resulting ashes into the water, "in time" they would "fill up" so that "a solid hearth" was formed for the comfort of warmth and dryness to temper the perpetually wet environment. In this way, the two went nearly two years without seeing "but two white men." Larinda admitted she had become "so used to stooping" to get through reeds and brush that she had become "almost wild" from living in the swamp and wading through "shoe-deep to waist deep" water so long that she could "hardly walk on dry land." Eating opossum, raccoon, the beef of wild cattle, wild honey, and fish, the two enjoyed so many meals together that Larinda "got so fat"—though this condition was also the result of intimate time the couple spent together freely in the swamp, resulting in one pregnancy and the birth of a child she had made certain she could mother and protect on her own terms.

When Abraham and Larinda emerged from the swamp in 1863 to take what they hoped would be new refuge with the Union army they had learned was camped in Suffolk, the two considered themselves husband and wife. Their child, who was at that time nearly a year old, had "scarcely ever seen a white

Fugitive Slaves in the Great Dismal Swamp, by David Edward Cronin, 1888.
(Courtesy of Wikimedia Commons.)

person, and would scream and try to hide away when white folks came." Though in Larinda's words, the swamp was "wild" and "never dry," she still maintained that life there with Abraham and the family they made together was preferable, safer, and also more fulfilling and enjoyable to the mix of subjugated intimacies and sexual violence, maternal loss, and perpetual servitude she had experienced in slavery and rejected in marronage.[25]

MAROON MOTHERS AT WORK: NURTURING ALTERNATIVE BLACK CHILDHOODS AND INSURGENT FAMILY

Deep swamp maroon women not only asserted and reclaimed their rights to voluntary and consensual intimate relationships, to safe and self-elected reproductive labor, and to unbound motherhoods; they were also instrumental in creating alternative childhoods for their children and in raising family against the demands of the world beyond the swamp that remained intent on degrading the human significance of both. As the historian Wilma King has shown, children born to enslaved mothers in captive spaces "had virtually no childhood" because they were forced into extractive labor very early in their lives and were subjected to violent white authority, surveillance, punishment, and separation, just as enslaved adults were.[26] One of the first lessons enslaved children learned was that their own parents lacked authority over their children's lives, lacked the unquestioned right to parent, instruct, care for, and protect them, and that their mothers and fathers were vulnerable themselves to cruelty and harm should they try to do so anyway in ways that conflicted with the interests of enslavers. Women who became mothers through enduring practices of marronage, and enslaved women who chose to take their children into the swamp knew these realities well and would have weighed them very carefully as they made decisions about which conditions, environments, and ways of life were least harmful and most beneficial to their futures and the lives of their children. Against uncertainty, potential suffering, isolation, and privation in the wilderness, scores of women asserted that no matter how challenging life in the deep swamps was, providing different childhoods and outcomes for their children and their families there was preferrable and more advantageous than remaining in the brutal grip of slaveholding power.

Larinda's "wild child"—as the people at the Union Camp in Suffolk referred to her swamp-born infant in 1863—was far from the only child who had learned to babble, eat, crawl, play, and begin to understand the world and its possibilities from within the swamp depths.[27] As early as 1728, when Col. William Byrd II of Westover, Virginia, first set out to survey the swamp to charter and propose its draining, he pushed through the deep swamps and encountered what he described as "a Family of Mulattos, that call'd themselves free, tho' by the Shyness of the master of the house, who took care to keep least in Sight, their Freedom seem'd a little Doubtful."[28] Charley, who had marooned and worked near the Juniper Swamp shingle camp more than a century later, spoke from experience when he confirmed: "Dar is families growed up in dat ar Dismal Swamp dat never seed a white man, an' would be skeered most to def to see one. Some runaways went dere wid dar wives, an' dar childers are raised dar."[29] In 1856, when the Connecticut-born journalist Frederick Law Olmsted traveled on the road from Portsmouth to Deep-River, along the northern swamp, he met an enslaved man named Joseph Church, who told him "children were born, bred, lived, and died" in the Dismal Swamp, and that there were people who still lived there who were "the children of runaways, and who had been runaways themselves all their lives."[30]

Mothers of these children—sometimes their sole or primary caretakers—envisioned and provided new childhood experiences and forms of family life that were swamp-dependent and rooted in protective vigilance and insurgency. A strong example of this comes out of Tidewater North Carolina, where a woman, whose name was not deemed important enough to record, fled her enslaver with a baby girl in her arms after he promised to move them West, away from her husband and the baby's father, who was enslaved separately on a property near the Dismal Swamp. Rather than comply with these plans, the woman took to the swamp with her infant daughter and "found means to conceal herself" in the abundant marshes and fens there, "overgrown with weeds, and interspersed, in some places, with clumps of pine trees." Her enslaved husband, who knew where his young family was, visited her in the swamp as often as he could, bringing them bread, meal, corn, and other supplies whenever possible. Between his visits, the maroon mother kept her family satisfied on her own by hunting and roasting frogs, terrapins, and snakes. When her husband could come, the couple used the refuge of the swamp to shelter their bonds of marriage and intimacy, and the woman soon conceived a second child. During her time in the swamp, spent primarily as a lone adult, she managed to care for herself and her two-year-old daughter, all the while laboring to carry out a successful pregnancy. She bore a son sometime during her second year in the swamp. This remarkable feat was almost certainly accomplished without aid or childcare for her toddler as she worked hard to bring the girl's infant brother into the world. It was the woman's own sheer determination and focus as well as her previous knowledge of and experience in delivering babies and their afterbirth that led to the successful birth of her son. By 1814, after a total of seven years spent in the Dismal Swamp, the woman, her seven-year-old daughter and five-year-old son were discovered by a man traveling with a cart on a road at the swamp's edge.

Though this unnamed maroon woman's recorded story ends with her leaving the swamp, followed by the recapture and jailing she and her children endured, it also sheds light on the kinds of maroon childhoods and insurgent family women made possible through inarticulable ingenuity, tenacity, and love. After her husband was no longer able to come to her in the swamp (whether because he was sold, sent away, or otherwise prevented, or whether he deserted her), the woman considered her children's changing needs and growth and decided the best course of action for their futures was to set off on the move again. The "little family" left the swamp, was soon after apprehended, and was ultimately taken about ninety miles south to the Newbern jail in Craven County, North Carolina—where she had likely originally been enslaved.

The woman and her children were confined to the jail for more than a month as they awaited her owner to come claim them, but the man had then been "about seven years previously removed to the western country." The alternative was to await sale and transport that would turn a profit over to the state. In this situation the woman and her children remained "lodged" in the Newbern jail, where white townspeople "crowded to see" them, as the children had gained a reputation for never in a single instance raising "their voices higher than a soft whisper." The girl and boy visibly struggled, initially, to stand or walk erect without "great difficulty," a "low stoop," and a "hasty step." The children were noted for this "favourite" squatting position that they could remain in for hours, and like this they could move when directed with such skill and "caution, that not the least noise could be heard by their footsteps." Clearly, their mother had taken great care to educate them about the real threats lurking outside of their swamp home. With the "strictest discipline" she had instructed her children against making clamor and noise and created ways to compel them to "stifle their little cries and complaints." The woman had also done whatever she could to quell and soothe their "pinching hunger, or the severest cold." To the best of her ability, she fed, entertained, and occupied her children's time by teaching them to hunt and catch mice that could be used for protein, but also to knit pairs of gloves and stockings from fur, skins, and the use of sticks—an "art" that even the little boy had learned to manage with "surprising dexterity." On very cold winter nights, when she deemed a fire absolutely necessary, the woman had reminded her children how important it was that they take turns staying up to keep watch and listen intently, in case the flames or smoke attracted danger. For seven years the woman raised her children in this manner, creating and offering them what she knew to be a more livable upbringing in the swamp than any that might be found in the slaveholding world she had determined to leave.[31]

The price of self-possession and the right to mother and to parent autonomously in the swamp was steep. But despite the unimaginably challenging, stressful, exhausting, and painful measures the woman was driven to take to keep her family together as safely as possible for as long as possible, she knew their strain and striving there also salvaged the natural human bonds between mothers and children as well as the human dignity intrinsic to unrestricted relation to and care of one's own offspring. As for the woman's maroon children: Although their watchfulness, crouching, and whispered tones might be taken as signs of devastation and destitution, it is unlikely that they lived in an exclusively crippling state of simple and perpetual fear, distress, or alarm. After all, their parents felt strongly—with due reason—that any childhood they could provide inside the swamp was preferrable to the violated and stolen childhoods produced and held captive through chattel slavery. The woman, and others like her, gave to their children new norms that exceeded terror, unease, and anxiety. They also provided outlets of everyday creative expression: the wonder of nature around them; the art and skill of self-sufficiency and self-satisfaction, self-serving labor; and space for leisure, rest, and play.

In addition to providing their children with the best education possible about movement, caution, vigilance, and the meaning of danger, deep swamp maroon mothers also taught them about courage, responsibility, self-determination, the unending lengths of maternal and parental love, and the significance of family and kinship removed from slaveholding interference and domination. What separated these lessons and the childhood experiences they paved from comparable instruction enslaved mothers provided their children was that maroon mothers were able to model maternal love, respect, and authority in positions effectively removed from the near constant meddlesome interference of enslavers. Maroon women knew that the children they brought into the world were, as Joseph Church disclosed to Olmsted, "born outlaws" and "educated self-stealers," and so on the one hand, for their children's own safety and security, they trained them from infancy to be "constantly in dread of the approach of a white man as a thing more fearful than wild-cats or serpents, or even starvation."[32] But on the other hand, they had created free and insurgent spaces in the swamp that provided their children an essential, liberatory education about legitimate and pervasive Black knowledges that rivaled the norms and demands of the white slaveholding world, and about geographies and ecologies of health, trust, protection, and critique as to the function and injustice of racial slavery and white hegemony.

Women in the swamp not only taught their children how to converse and consort with the swamp's rich ecology to create clothing, build shelter, and procure food, they also transferred to them experience and knowledge of medicine and healing that could be gleaned from the natural world in which they were immersed. Enslaved and maroon mothers alike would have adopted remedies to aid their teething babies, such as giving them necklaces made of rattlesnake rattles, animal teeth, and other chewable objects they might find in their environment. In Dinwiddie County, Virginia, for example, Louise remembered how common it was to "keep de babies from hollarin' by tying a string 'roun' a piece of skin an stickin' it in dey mouth. You see if dey got choked, we pull out de meat skin wid dis string. Lord, yes! I've done it many time."[33] Traditional remedies such as teas made from herbs or the bark of abundant plant and tree life also would have soothed sick and ailing maroon children.[34]

Maroon children, while strictly disciplined to guard against discovery and capture, would also have imagined ways to play safely and in accordance with their parents' teachings and approval. Near the western swamp in the town of Emporia, Virginia, Allen Crawford recalled inventing games "chillun-like" in the woods that could occupy him and his friends for hours; while near Hampton in Elizabeth City County, Virginia, Candis Goodwin remembered making "houses in de woods" out of "brown pine needles" and grass for the houses out of the green ones.[35] Enslaved descendants still living near the swamp in the town of Suffolk as late as the 1950s remembered their parents making toy helmets out of turtle shells for their play.[36] With water that could submerge a grown man "up to the middle or much deeper" surrounding their homes, it is not difficult to imagine that some maroon youth in the remotest areas of the swamp may also have enjoyed swimming and water play, particularly in warmer weather.[37] Interactions with and sightings of insects, animals, and wildlife would have provided children both opportunities to learn and sources of entertainment. Although they cannot be known, the stories and songs maroon mothers and fathers told and sang to their children likely ranged from family histories to lore, to trickster tales, fables, and stories embedded with morals and life lessons that also would have offered maroon children sources of amusement, calm, and reflection, shaping their minds and the ways they understood their place within the world.

There is more to learn about these lived experiences in the most obscure swamps. Oral history and documentary evidence read together with the material record unearthed by archaeology has proven essential to advancing what is and can be known about the internal dynamics of deep swamp maroon communities. This mixed method, interdisciplinary approach also aids in the directed study of maroon children and women of the Dismal Swamp's remotest locations. Artifacts and soil features uncovered during Daniel Sayers's GDSLS digs in Gates County, North Carolina, for example, suggest "intensive settlement and population" at this site alone throughout the period from 1600 to 1860. The remnants of a "nucleated" cluster of five different cabins, evidence of a porch-building tradition with communal structures spanning "at least a couple of generations," the presence of three water-catchment pits or basins a few meters away from these, and at least one "definitive," centrally located fire pit indicate heavy collective usage, occupancy, and enduring social life. Evidence of rotted structural posts that were replaced with newer supportive posts also suggests cross-generational reworking and the repair of dwellings over time. Sayers concludes these structures would have been "raised" by floor posts and had wattle-and-daub siding (mud or clay cementing between wood-planked walls) or possibly solid wood walls. The strategic geographical location of these structural arrangements within the deep swamp at this site should also be considered here because it meant that its inhabitants planned and plotted enduring autonomous social lives protected by miles of swamp water and nearly impenetrable brush to separate these communities, built on drier islands, from the swamp edges and outside world. With the rise in canal digging, lumber company activity, and the industrialization of the swamp throughout the first half of the nineteenth century, populations of these deeper and more permanent communities would have increased as maroons at the outskirts of the swamps moved increasingly into the interior areas to escape these developments. In short, the dozens of people who lived together at this singular location in Gates County—during any one of the several generations it was inhabited—were women, men, and children who meant to stay.[38]

Documentary evidence on the housing and structures constructed by deep swamp maroons reveals that these communities built and maintained different kinds of dwellings, based on specific environmental and ecological opportunity. For example, on higher knolls within the swamp "huts" were built, while in other remote recesses "cabins elevated upon stilts above the water" were more suitable.[39] Another account reveals that in one secluded area of the Dismal Swamp near Princess Anne County, Virginia, maroons "arranged around a square" on raised ground "eight or ten log houses on stilts" with "floors a foot or two from the ground." In this particular community, a cabin contained a "rude bed" filled with moss, a "sedge broom on the hearth," and a "home-made chair and bench."[40] Yet another record explains that tree stumps were used to elevate wood and planks set atop them to create solid flooring. The elevation protected the structure from flooding and pests, and it also would have provided for the circulation of fresh air.[41]

Picturing children, their mothers, and their fathers within settlements such as these means that childhoods here were not spent in harsh dens whispering or "stooping." Children were also less likely to have been estranged from their fathers and other relatives, or isolated from other children, than the maroon mother and children who ended up in the Newbern jail. Loud noises and unnecessary prolonged clamor would have been avoided, but in the deepest swamps, the distance between these hinterland islands and the encroaching slaveholding world would have made it less necessary to stifle the sounds of community and social life. At the Gates County site, so far removed and protected from the plantation world, maroon children and their parents would have been able to enjoy the warmth of community fires, especially with the use of drier hardwoods known to produce the least possible smoke.[42] In a long-enduring community such as this one, maroon families—consisting of fathers, mothers, and children—were most likely to have been able to care for each other and remain together throughout their lives. Adult men and women who were among the earliest to escape to this site could have lived long enough to have experienced becoming the grandparents and great-grandparents to generations of children born against captivity on this insurgent ground.

While the earliest people to maroon in deep Dismal Swamp locations may initially have settled as individuals, couples, friends, or families, eventually more people would have joined such inchoate communities, having learned about them through clandestine networks of trusted contacts and illicit economies of information and trade. Maroon women in locations like the Gates County site would thus become central to the development of multigenerational communities.[43] Within such enduring communities, individualism and personal gain would have been antithetical to the shared, communal endeavor of building and sustaining collective evasion and alternative life. At the same time, it would be against the clearest understandings of humanity, and what is known about the dynamics of enslaved and maroon communities elsewhere, to assume that selfishness, discord, disagreements, disputes, and division did not exist.[44] It makes sense that the organization and function of government or authority within these communities depended primarily on

Excavation of a cabin structure, Great Dismal Swamp, Gates County, North Carolina, GDSLS Archaeology Field School, 2013. *(Photo by the author, 2013.)*

how populous the settlement was and who was in it. Deep swamp maroons of a dozen or more inhabitants could have officered and titled themselves in ways that emulated the European and Anglo-American government and military systems they had learned about—appointing male leaders roles such as "general," "chief," or "captain."[45] They may also have reinstated the more gender complimentary West African and West Central African distribution of power, such as the matrilineal Asante's organization of authority by mirroring the dual positions of the *Ohene* (king or chief) and the *Ohema* (queen mother). In this model, the queen mother advises the king or chief in all matters; serves as spiritual leader of rites and ritual on behalf of her people; mediates social disputes and conflicts; advises women in matters of marriage, sexuality, and motherhood; and also leads with the *Ohene* alongside a council of sub-chiefs headed by community-appointed elders.[46] With the passing of enough time, the presence of both women and elders in communities like the Gates County site would have been guaranteed, and customs set forth by people whose African forebears had made sure would uphold deep reverence for women, for mothers, and for elders would have continued to influence community formation. This was certainly true in the shaping of enslaved communities.[47]

All considered, remote swamp communities produced in part by women and hereditary marronage and consisting of families and elders would have modeled a "community democracy" based in collective accountability, complemental specialized roles, and division of tasks and duties in which children, women, and elders would not have been excluded or diminished.[48] Such community praxis would have been fundamentally cemented by the powerful mutual interest and commitment to the organizing principle of free life and sociality the maroons worked to protect and sustain.

Without question, women and mothers in deep swamp communities such as the one excavated by the GDSLS would have benefited from the ability to collaborate with and join other mothers in kinship and in support of their intellectual and creative interests; their liberated intimate relationships, pregnancies, childrearing, and familyhood; and in their shared work toward the cohesion and future of the larger group. As mothers and bearers of life, opportunities to give to and learn from other women who possessed understanding, knowledge, and expertise about the physical and spiritual properties of childbirth would have been fundamental, if not the greatest distinction characterizing deep swamp marronage in the Dismal Swamp. Considered the most critical rite of passage and source of female power among the enslaved and their West African and West Central African predecessors, childbirth was viewed as a sacred and cosmologically significant event that required the care and support of "women in fellowship" to administer the necessary ritual and specialized knowledge of its physiological and spiritual dimensions. Laboring women were to be held, supported, and surrounded by other women, and a woman's pregnancy and childbirth was to be under the care and counsel of aged, wise, and seasoned women venerated in their communities for their life experience and skills in healing, ritual medicine, and midwifery.[49] While it is true that many deep swamp women entered motherhood and delivered babies in the absence of these crucial traditions and supports, without them, women and their babies were more prone to illness, injury, or fatality. Tamar Grandy, for example, lost one of the three babies she delivered on her own in her "den" in the swamp.[50] Larinda too, lost her "wild child," not yet the age of one, shortly after leaving the swamp.[51] The supportive spheres of women's knowledge in the life-giving work of healing and childbirth were thus essential to ensuring the vitality and continuation of entire communities. In this regard, enduring marronage fundamentally began with and depended upon women's health, wellness, knowledge, and work.

Deep swamp maroon women in community with each other would have shared more than the indispensable labor of their childbirth. Motherhood, parenting, and best practices for the care, instruction, and discipline of children would also have been viewed as shared work toward community goals and collective benefit. Even in tightly surveilled Tidewater enslaved communities, Black people maintained an ethos where the instruction of children was treated as collective work and responsibility. In Norfolk, Virginia, Marriah remembered that enslaved children in need of discipline could count on the fact that "your mammies didn't have to do it either; any ole person would and send you home to git another lickin.'" Marriah also recalled that evenings were special times grown folk would "talk, tell jokes" and together provide life teachings, pass on knowledge, and impart skill sets to children.[52] Enslaved mothers, generally the closest people to their children, also "seized every opportunity" to teach them how to negotiate between compliance with slaveholders' demands and protecting themselves from harm, as well as the important insights of self-worth, self-defense, critical thinking, and other strategies of survival.[53] Rev. W. P. Jacobs's mother, enslaved near Hampton, Virginia, made it her duty to instruct her young son about geographies of subversion and fugitivity as well as about the art of deception when she made certain he knew how she "used to slip away" at night, sometimes walking up to eight miles without their slaveholder's permission to go to camp meetings to meditate, pray, and deliberate the next steps forward.[54]

In communities of maroons where women could share together in disciplining and instructing children, these customs and traditions in bringing up children would have persisted, likely with even greater subversive emphasis concerning justice, independence, and the necessary commitment to a range of fugitive and insurgent acts as the only option to life. As Barbara Bush has pointed out, maroon mothers in the broader Atlantic world were instrumental in working together to provide their children instruction in the strategies of resistance, and in generally promoting and maintaining a spirit of opposition by way of their parenting. In an exchange between Philip Thicknesse—an English army officer on expedition against the Windward Maroons of Jamaica—and the maroon children he encountered there, he noted their immediate display of disdain for him and his presence among them. According to Thicknesse, they "could not refrain from striking their pointed fingers as they would knives" against his chest while repeatedly shouting "*becara*"—a pejorative for "white man."[55] Fear and caution would not have been the only education mothers of the interior swamp imparted to their young. Another, no less important lesson, was that maroon children too, were to be active and conscious participants in their insurgent families and the wider communities they held together. Children among enduring maroon groups would have learned that this instruction was the business of everyone to ensure and assist—but, it began at the hearthstone.

MAROON WOMEN IN COMMUNITY DEFENSE

Just as the preceding chapters have shown that enslaved women in the Tidewater and maroon women operating at the Dismal Swamp fringes did not shy away from defensive violence, militancy, and the politics of force, the maroon women of the deep swamps would not have shirked from it either. Black women's investments in defense, offense, and the protection of themselves, their children, families, and communities meant active support of, if not direct leadership in, the totality of insurgent movements, including the collective strategies of rebellion and marronage. While the lack of documentary evidence concerning deep swamp maroon women's internal activities makes it difficult to know definitively what their contributions and positions were within their communities' military approaches and defense systems, comparative study of hinterland maroon women in the broader Atlantic world, alongside the environmental and archaeological record of the Dismal Swamp interior, provides a helpful place to begin.

Deep swamp maroons were varied, small, and populous collectives that went to great lengths to avoid outsider detection and remained steadfast in their isolation and effective removal from the slaveholding world. Guided by the pursuit of long-term escape, the women who traversed miles of marsh, who trekked through waters of varied depths, who encountered insect and animal life, and who then crawled along narrow islet paths verdantly buried under thick and seemingly impossible vines and brush had, in doing so, demonstrated that they were people who were interested, willing, and resolutely committed to defending the goals and purposes of themselves and their people in such a place.[56] Further, since maroon women born unto the deep swamp were born and raised by women who had fled through the remote swamps and had already proven their investment in a future of self-possessed life, family, and community there, there is very little reason to believe that any women within the deep Dismal Swamp would have been uninvolved, inattentive, or generally indifferent toward the shared necessity of community defense, offense, security, and any or all preparations for emergency resistive and combative action. In order to educate and encourage an understanding of the collective nature of defending enduring marronage, deep swamp women may also have reminded themselves and warned their daughters and sons of the raced and gendered perils of dispossession, of girls being subjected to the lusts of white men, of punitive violence and the violence of forced productive and reproductive labor, and of the pervasive precarity of family and kinship that awaited them on the other side of capture and defeat, should they resign to passivity in the defense of their lives.

Trends in the broader history of Atlantic world marronage show that when communities were threatened or attacked, maroon women who lived among remote and enduring groups were not only ready and prepared to act in the interest of collective defense, but also sometimes offered strategy as military-minded leaders or fought in combat themselves. For example, a report made in 1748 warned that "all the Negroes and Negresses" in a maroon community in the tropical swamps of French Guiana were collectively readying themselves and were "equipped with axes and machetes" in preparation for battle.[57] In another case, when a detachment of soldiers attacked a maroon settlement in 1826 consisting of about fifty people, a woman named Zeferina "fought fiercely" alongside men, doing her best at urging on the others and "keeping them on line." However, having no more than a bow and some arrows to make her resistance against superior slaveholding artillery, this battle proved fatal for Zeferina and the other Urubu maroons of Bahia, Brazil.[58] Besides the physical use of force, maroon women devised other ways to contribute to military strategy and to actively participate—along with their children—in defending their communities. As the matrilineal maroons of Suriname, numbering in the few thousands, planned to confront the colonial expedition against them during the 1770s, it could have been a woman's idea to completely dupe and outsmart the encroaching militia, resulting in the maroons' victory.[59] But however the maroons arrived at the decision, they assigned male warriors engaged in active defensive battle the additional task of distracting the attacking enemy with a commotion of ceaseless shouts and "war-whoops," loud songs of victory, reports of gunfire, and the additional clamor of horns. Meanwhile, as one English soldier present at the battle later recalled, it was by this ingeniously dispatched "unremitting noise" that the colonists were prevented from discovering that the other maroons "were employed, men, women, and children," in another part of their villages preparing "hampers filled with the finest rice, yams, and cassava, for subsistence during their escape, of which they had only left the chaff and refuse for our contemplation."[60]

While militias were called up numerous times at various ends of the Dismal Swamp to suppress and subdue the more obvious activities of less stable and less enduring borderland maroons, there is no record of any equivalent military campaign or attack expedition against the more sizable, isolated, and lasting deep swamp maroon communities of Virginia and North Carolina. This is largely because the geography of the Dismal Swamp was never one singular concentrated swamp for militia to begin to scour and navigate in search of any one fugitive community. Instead, the swamp spread between and adjoined many settled areas and towns interspersed across its borderlands and two disparate colonies and states, making it difficult for concerted colonial and state efforts to prevent, locate, and eliminate deep swamp maroons and known or suspected occurrences of permanent marronage. Military campaigns against multiple and diverse hinterland maroons were also strained because of the broader demographics of the area. In Tidewater Virginia and North Carolina, Black people were nearly always outnumbered by slaveholding whites, and negligible ratios of African-born (hence free-born minded, and motivated by distinct and sharable African cultural and ethnic backgrounds) to American-born (primarily captive-born and acculturated) African descendants across time also made the formation of hundreds or thousands of maroons operating in solidarity or as a united front highly unlikely. Thus, in the Dismal Swamp, hinterland maroons were less likely to attract exhaustive military attention, manpower, and expense. Nevertheless, the enduring and more populated maroon communities that spanned generations in the innermost areas of the Dismal Swamp were, without question, prepared to do battle and meet their pursuers—should they ever find them.

Archaeological evidence brought to light by Sayers and the GDSLS proves that deep swamp maroon women lived in communities that were armed and that contained structures built for the express purpose of self-protection and defense. The dig unearthed munitions artifacts such as lead shot, and fragments of British and French gunflint—though these were few in number, and the flint showed it had been such a rare yet precious commodity that it had been whittled away down to its last possible spark. The excavation also found evidence of a large landscape feature that Sayers has called a "community defense structure," wall, or palisade, behind which these maroons would have "stored and developed their defensive or offensive capacities."[61] The discovery of three-thousand-year-old arrowheads, spearheads, or projectile points found in soil from the period dating between 1700 and 1800 indicates that highly self-reliant and resourceful maroons constantly reworked and reused available swamp material objects—in this case, objects they had unearthed that had been left behind by ancient Indigenous Americans, which would have served resurrected use and purpose for the maroons as instruments of defense, knives, scrapers, or other sorely needed tools and utensils.[62]

Documentary evidence concerning the deep swamps corroborates this material archive. Though it has already been established that maroons possessed firearms, secluded hinterland maroons did not come by them easily, and consequently they also created their own weapons, such as bows and arrows, that would have served both as weapons with which to hunt and procure food and as a means for self-defense.[63] One maroon man ventured too far from the recesses of the swamp and had the misfortune of being "shot at several times, but was little hurt. He had on a coat that was impervious to shot, it being thickly wadded with turkey feathers."[64] As to the question of acquiring guns, Larinda's husband Abraham shared that he had carried two guns and a broken drawing knife while the couple lived together in the inner swamp. He had procured the guns through illicit trade with shingle workers in exchange for his own labor.[65] Perhaps most famously was the rare 1856 sighting of the interior maroon Osman, who, in the words of the swamp outsider who caught a glimpse of him, was a "gigantic negro" wearing little other than a pair of "ragged breeches and boots" and carrying nothing more than "a tattered blanket wrapped about his shoulders, and a gun in his hand." The journalist and illustrator David Hunter Strother, or, as he preferred, "Porte Crayon," had "long nurtured a wish to see one of those sable outlaws who dwell in the fastnesses of the Swamp," and so he walked alone "a mile or more" off the causeway at a lumber camp where enslaved shingle laborers were at work, until he heard the sound of footsteps. Strother studied the maroon he spotted "thirty paces" away, whose expression, he noted, was one "of mingled fear and ferocity" before the man retreated back into the thicker swamp. Strother rushed back to the shingle camp and immediately drew a sketch of the maroon, leaving it out in plain view for the enslaved laborers there to see. He then overheard the men whispering "Osman," though when Strother further pressed them on the matter, the men each firmly denied knowing anything about the man in the sketch.[66]

Other than Larinda's closeness to and awareness of her husband's weapons, women in these accounts are altogether absent. Deep swamp maroon forays outside the swamp, carried out by men, occurred seldom enough to begin with, since risking detection of permanent settlements that had taken great work to build and establish would have been counterproductive to sustaining life in isolation. Interior maroon women, then, would not have often ventured far from their communities unless it was a matter of safety, or unless it was considered helpful or necessary for them to go out on select forays, scouting, or other rare missions. For the most part, deep swamp maroon women would have remained committed to securing, protecting, and uplifting their homes in the inner swamps, right at their heart and center.[67] And just as

"Osman," by "Porte Crayon," or David Hunter Strother,
Harper's New Monthly Magazine, September 1856.
(Courtesy of the Library Company of Philadelphia.)

countless other hinterland maroon women throughout the wider Atlantic world had been, the women of the deep swamps were mindful as well as actively supportive of their own best interests and those of their families and communities, inclusive of the strategy of armed defensive violence against recapture and attack.

HEART AND CENTER: MAROON WOMEN'S EVERYDAY ESSENTIAL LABOR

Deep swamp maroon women were central figures within their communities not only for the life-giving work they performed as child bearers and mothers, or as invested participants and partners in sustained escape, but also because of the essential contributions they made to everyday life through their labor for all. Maroon women would have been instrumental in the upkeep of homes and yards (where yards were possible on drier settlements), the raising of crops, the procuring and preparing of food, and the washing and making of clothes and other fabrics. Certainly, maroon men may have performed some of these same tasks, but given that there were at no point neatly egalitarian maroon societies, it makes sense that self-secluding inner swamp communities assumed a gendered division of labor.[68] This distribution of labor would have reflected the collective interests and ideals of complementarity, mutual aid, and the need for specialized skill sets shaped by gendered norms and customs practiced by both their African forebears and by African descendants in the surrounding Tidewater enslaved communities from which the maroons came. Women of the deep swamps probably expected to—and probably were expected by their communities to—occupy positions that kept them less mobile than maroon men and in roles that may also have meant serving men and children in domestic capacities. But rather than interpret the possible reproduction of patriarchal notions of place and labor within maroon communities as simply oppressive to maroon women, it is more generative to consider how the women themselves made judgments and decisions about their own futures and about the slaveholding societies they were escaping and evading, as well as about how they likely thought about their own roles and value as actively invested members of swamp communities. While it is true that there has never existed an egalitarian maroon utopia, women in maroon societies had more opportunities to lead and assert themselves in ways that were illegible to and forbidden in colonial and slaveholding spaces. In the words of one scholar, despite any evidence of gendered inequality among maroons, women still "played significant, and on occasion outstanding, roles in maintaining the integrity of these communities and contributing to the quality of life in them."[69]

If the proud words "Kin do most anything; I kin do a heap of work," spoken by the former maroon woman who buried her slain son in the swamp and then marooned there until the Civil War, indicate anything about how other women in the deep swamps may have felt about the value of their work and skills within fugitive communities, it is that settled maroon women likely derived a sense of pride and purpose from performing daily chores that were aligned with their own interests, their families, and the greater collective they believed in and were committed to.[70] The same servile tasks that might have been considered loathsome drudgery in the context of forced labor and enslavement would have signified differently in the service of self-emancipated fugitive communities. For example, women who were already practiced at weaving, spinning, knitting, and sewing would have applied these gendered skill sets toward meeting new needs and demands within the swamp. Women like Larinda, who while enslaved had been accustomed to sewing, washing, scouring, field work, and cutting wood, and the unnamed North Carolina maroon woman who, using sticks, taught her daughter and son to knit gloves and stockings out of mice fur, possessed expertise that would have been invaluable to manufacturing alternative materials such as skins and pelts in lieu of other fabrics to serve their families and communities as clothing, blankets, or other coverings.[71]

Other essential daily labor, like porch and yard sweeping or gardening may have been work that inspired new satisfaction, pride, and pleasure among the women who performed it. Within the swamp and removed from white surveillance and control, women also likely viewed these tasks as gratifying since they were carried out to accommodate their own use and purposes, and to improve the quality of life in their communities. Thanks to discoveries made by the GDSLS, it is evident that porch-building was an architectural decision maroons made at the site in Gates County, indicating that deep swamp maroons there structured their communal values of social exchange, interaction, and shared daily life activities into the built landscape, including designated outdoor work and rest areas such as porches, yards, and gardens.[72] As some studies have suggested as it relates to slaveholding Virginia and North Carolina, the work and social significance of sweeping, gardening, and raising poultry within these central community spaces was typically the domain of women.[73]

Not only were Dismal Swamp maroons who resided in the swamp for "twelve, twenty, or thirty years and upwards" known to raise animals such as hogs, fowls, and even goats, as one 1784 account notes, they also planted a variety of crops—including corn, sweet potatoes, rice, and grain—that could also have been supplemented by the planting of peas, beans, squashes, gourds, sunflowers, and melons.[74] Certain reeds as well as the abundant lupine flower bore seeds and shed grains that, if collected, could yield a "palatable cereal dish" or be worked into a "tolerably good bread."[75] Given that "women usually did most of the agrarian" labor in many West African and West Central African societies, and given that the same can be said of the many enslaved and maroon communities across the Americas, in the Dismal Swamp, this work was also likely under women's command.[76] West African women such as the Igbo and Ibibio performed a wide range of agricultural labor—such as weeding and planting vegetables and crops like pumpkins, maize, okra, beans, pepper, and taro yam.[77] Similarly, among the Mende, women were the primary producers of rice and experts at rice growing and cultivation within their communities.[78] As was often customary, enslaved families were permitted "a little patch o' garden stuff," and it was common for women to feed their families from these gardens to supplement meager and otherwise negligible diets.[79] From this, as Karen Bell Cook has deduced, it makes sense that where women were present among the deep swamp communities, it was they who did the work of maintaining the small "kitchen gardens" in the yards and on the dry grounds of settlements.[80] Tamar Grandy had certainly wasted no time clearing ground of her own to raise corn and flax in the swamp, and her mother before her had used the swamp during her own escapes to feed her children by collecting berries and raw corn.[81] As it has been shown in chapter 1, the insurgent ecology enabled other women across the swampscape to gather wild fruit, berries, grapes, greens, and honey to do the same, while others still may have served their families and communities with proficiencies in hunting and fishing.[82]

In truth, many of the few existing reports of sightings of the mysterious and elusive hinterland maroons describe maroon men as "bushmen," "ragged," or "wild men."[83] Enslaved witnesses to these maroons disclosed that "dey look strange," while others described them as downright starving—their desperate appearance driving some to be "scared to deaf of 'em."[84] Perhaps these men did not emerge from communities where women were present and conducting the daily tasks and work of cleaning, fashioning clothes and fabrics for dignity, warmth, and comfort; or growing, procuring, cooking, and sharing food; or else generally creating and chartering geographies and economies of care. It was through this work that women heartened alternative life in the swamp, making it less ragged and more certain and sustainable for all.[85]

WOMEN AS SPIRITUAL LEADERS

Part of the heart and spirit of enduring community that deep swamp maroon women provided also came from their spiritual guidance, leadership in meditation, prayer, and in the work of the soul. There is some evidence that these women upheld their roles as healers, "conjurers," and preachers within their fugitive communities, and this is supported by the fact that enslaved and maroon women occupied similar positions throughout the United States South and broader Atlantic world.[86] Religious practice in the swamp likely followed the spiritual customs and traditions of the plantation world, where the language of Protestant Christianity covered the spiritual orientations and sacred views of West Africa and West Central Africa. Christian tenets and biblical scripture interacted with African beliefs in the seen and unseen spiritual power of human and nonhuman beings, spirits, and the natural environment as well as in the fundamental belief that spiritual practitioners held the power to manifest or conjure real material and immaterial outcomes, including healing, protection, and harm.[87] Christian preaching and praying together with African-based traditions in North American hoodoo—or the summoning of spirit and energy, the use of charmed objects, herbal medicine, and ancestor veneration to achieve health, safety, and wellness—were both practiced in the swamp, sometimes under the direction of gifted women.[88]

Prayer, or the purposeful willing of positive effect, was a critical part of the lives of deep swamp maroons. During Larinda's time in the swamp in the 1860s, for example, she noted that "regular prayer meetings" were held at "different camps in the swamp."[89] This collective worship, praise, and faith would have been highly important to people boldly creating life outside the oppressive force of the law. Women like Mary Perth, who preached and prayed hard and often, indicate how women of the deep swamps may have led their communities in prayer and spiritual deliberation. Mary was enslaved near the Dismal Swamp in Norfolk, Virginia. During the 1770s, she made it her mission to preach to fugitives at the swamp edges from the Book of Exodus and on St. Paul's advice to the Galatians the word of liberty and deliverance from "the yoke of bondage." Wrapping her infant daughter on her back, Mary used the cover of night to walk ten miles from her enslaver's home to reach the swamp, where she carried out this ministry, and she soon earned a "considerable" following.[90]

Among Tidewater enslaved communities, it was common for women to work and serve their families and communities in the creole hoodoo tradition of healing and conjure. Many women possessed plant and herbal knowledge that was essential to spirit and health-giving cures. For example, George Harris recalled that his mother, enslaved in North Carolina, "doctored us with herbs she had in the garden."[91] In Virginia, Marrinda Jane Singleton also knew that "the brewin' of certain concoctions composed of herbs, roots and scraps of cloth with certain fowl feathers was believed to wuk charms or spells on persons desired and yet not affected by other persons."[92] In the deep swamps, evidence of the presence of a "Voudoo man or woman" follows in this tradition.[93] Lore insists that "witches" and "conjures" sought out the "deep recesses" of the Dismal Swamp to do the work of the spirit.[94] But the role of "wise wimmin" reported to live in and around the swamps included the leadership of at least one woman whose name was recorded as "ole Minta"—a healer and conjurer to whom "de sperits" gave the "second sight" to work cures on behalf of her swamp community, suffering as it was from disease.[95] Minta may have been one of the community leaders whose cabins were reportedly outfitted and decorated with roots and herbs gathered from the bounteous swamp ecology or with other "native remedies" that hung "in festoons" from the smoke-blackened rafters of maroon homes.[96] The GDSLS dig offers more supportive evidence of maroon worldmaking in health and spiritual care in the swamp, in which women would have shared a part. At one structure, Sayers unearthed remnants of a clear glass vessel, believed to have been reworked into "fetishes or charms" in the rituals and rites of the women and men who lived there.[97]

Belief in the presence of spirit and ancestors in nature and the ritual practice of spiritual communing with the swamp's diverse and vibrant ecology gave to women a soothing space of interior reflection, faith, health, protection, and soul affirmation in their own universal belonging and value. As spiritual thinkers and practitioners, women would have been able to breathe more deeply and fully in the deep swamps, but they also would have been able to provide spiritual guidance and support to others in their communities, offering collective emotional, spiritual, and physical wellness and health. These spiritual relationships with the natural environment as well as with other maroons held insurgent potential because they provided a space for intellectual, social, and political reflection. Additionally, they vitalized movement away from sites of bondage and modes of extraction, exploitation, and abuse, toward lifeways that invited alignment, soul centering, and enjoyment instead.

MAROON WOMEN IN PLEASURE AND AT REST

Although deep swamp maroons were people sustained in the labor of ongoing escape and evasion, they were also women and men invested in building and creating alternative lifeways and other worlds they determined were more agreeable, livable, and actually enjoyable. While hardship, the challenges of navigating muddy swamps and saturated wetlands, the lack of manufactured material resources, the constant risk, and the vigilance required to protect and maintain self-emancipated life would not have been easy, there is no reason to assume that enduring maroon communities lived in a state of perpetual fear, anxiety, or desperation. The bounty of ecological offerings among the swamp's ample natural resources provided maroons the "luxury of self-sufficiency" that was not only conducive to their perseverance but that also opened space for pleasure, leisure, and rest.[98] Through the sharing of food and drink, women and men built social lives that served their needs for human connection in remote and isolated places; they fostered collective engagement and enjoyment; and they also literally fed the insurgency of continual escape and their own self-possession. Not only was full possession of one's own body particularly gratifying for maroon women who otherwise suffered intersecting forms of dispossession, but women's consciousness of the fact that they were actively "stealing" themselves, their labor, and their bodies from the use, profit, and wealth of enslavers also would have been a source of profound satisfaction and even mirth at their effective resistance at slaveholders' expense. The ability to work, rest, and recreate with chosen intimate partners, children, family, and fictive kin would have also provided women respite, laughter, and the sentiment of joy that would have palpably uplifted their communities.

The most secluded and uncapturable women of the deep swamp attained the strongest possible understanding of themselves and of their bodies, not as commodities or objects of use, but as their own, to feel, express, nourish, treat, give, move, and to value as they desired and pleased. Conversely, enslaved women embodied experiences shaped by external valuation and dispossession from their physical, sexual, psychological, and emotional interests and needs. Bondwomen, then, were in a state of internal struggle and conflict between at least "three bodies": the first, a site of domination; the second, a subjective "vehicle of feelings of terror, humiliation, and pain"; and the third embodiment, a competing "political entity" of "pleasure, pride, and self-expression."[99] This third body—always present—reclaimed and made possible practices of self-possession and was itself a source of insurgent potential, including movement toward perhaps a fourth body—that of the liberated maroon. Once a maroon, a woman could altogether reject the other two-thirds of the embodied experience that enslaved women suffered. Fugitive women who chose marronage as a way of life made it their business to be able to enjoy their bodies and their lives in ways that were capable of providing purer and unfettered feelings of pleasure, satisfaction, and selfhood because they had entirely detached from and escaped conflicting and ruinous bonds to slaveholders and their demands.

Removed from such prying interference and surveillance, maroon women afforded themselves the ability to more fully enjoy and experience their intimate lives, their families, and daily activities of rest and leisure such as sharing food, drink, conversation, and reflection. The insurgent ecology of the Dismal Swamp provided an abundance of plant life and proteins maroons could access, prepare, and share together in an environment of independence and communal peace. Maroons sipped "sweet" drinking water filtered from the swamp to accompany their meals, absent of the stress and worries associated with forced reproductive and productive labor, and without the expectation or demand that they hurriedly share in their victuals only to return to grueling toil and violence. Savoring the pleasures of eating, drinking, and community is evidenced in one 1881 account describing the lifeways of "swampers" believed to have descended from maroons. The observer noted that the swamp water was considered "wholesome" and "excellent," particularly by those who shared in the custom of drinking it with a "strong admixture of whisky."[100] The GDSLS excavations of sparse amounts of ball-clay tobacco pipe fragments, along with fragments of clear and olive glass from bottles at the Gates County, North Carolina, site is also an indication that deep swamp maroons took pleasure in smoking and drinking spirituous liquors.[101] Glass bottles containing alcohol could have been obtained through trade with enslaved lumbermen and canal laborers who were known to frequent grog shops at the edge of the swamp at the end of their five-month hires.[102] As was common throughout the Caribbean and Latin America as well as throughout the US South, maroons in the deep swamps could also have made their own liquors, both for recreational consumption and enjoyment as well as for medicinal use.[103] Archaeobotanical findings in the swamp show that a number of berries, roots, and barks were present with which one could make brandy and liquors. These could have been used for pleasure, community sharing, and sociality as well as to soothe and treat ailments in ways very similar to whiskey.[104] As for smoking tobacco, it was habit for enslaved women like May Satterfield to "smoke ma pipe" because the "'lief [relief] takes keer o' me"; while maroon women such as Maria at the swamp's northern edge moved and lived among maroons noted for carrying pipes and smoking tobacco.[105] Through foodways, imbibement, and enhanced inhalation, maroon women and men created space for personal and collective respite, enjoyment, recreation, and social vibrancy.

Maroon women and men's claims to relief and reprieve from endless forced labor and the "grind culture" of capitalism and chattel slavery is what artist, poet, and activist Tricia Hersey has called "rest as resistance."[106] Practicing the rights to self-care, rest, and leisure can be understood as a necessary step toward liberation, or toward any forward movement capable of disrupting and opposing violent systems of harm. Put plainly, rest and relaxation are essential to stamina and sustained insurgency. Further evidence that deep swamp maroon women lived in and helped create communities positioned to honor and uphold these priorities emerges from a rare account recorded by two Norfolk merchants who visited the swamp to trade in clapboards and shingles. There they encountered "a negroe man ran away from his Master" who for thirteen years had "rais'd Rice & other grain & made Chairs Tables &c. & musical instruments" from the abundant juniper, cypress, gum, or pine trees. The man claimed to have "lived by himself," though the doubtfulness of this is clearest in the communal nature of these objects of leisure, comfort, and pleasure not typically built for solitary use but for the benefit of collective sharing, rest, and enjoyment.[107] If the maroon's assurance that he lived alone was meant to distract from or conceal the fact that such a community existed, this was undoubtedly a protective strategy the maroon employed to forestall the discovery and downfall of what surely must have been a plentiful, lively, yet restful settlement.

Women might have been members of this furnished and musical deep swamp community, and the sounds of their laughter, the sight of their smiles, and the experience of witnessing or sharing in their joy and satisfaction in this and in similar communities would have provided greater collective cohesion, purpose, encouragement, and morale. As Kellie Carter Jackson has explored, the spiritual basis and essence of joy—"a conscious conjuring of pleasure that transcends one's circumstances"—is a calling or an incitement to change the atmosphere, and it is usually tied to difficulty and the felt experience of oppression.[108] Distinct from happiness, joy need not deny pain. Instead, it creates the space in which to laugh and smile, all the while recognizing and holding space to push beyond and through that which harms and injures. Joy has liberatory potential because it alleviates while also creating the moment and the space to feel better, to feel good, to persevere, hold on to faith, and to administer to one's needs as a fully worthy and deserving human being. For these reasons, rest, pleasure, and the good feelings that follow have often served as necessary revelations and sources of clarity preceding political action or resistive movements.[109]

Maroon women, who through their own shrewdness had effectively outsmarted and evaded the slaveholding world that denied their abilities to do more than labor and serve, would have experienced joy, humor, and pleasure, not only in everyday life shared with their families and greater communities, but also in the active process of duping enslavers and in the making of resistance itself. As uncaught maroons, many if not all deep swamp women would have enjoyed satisfaction in their own self-claiming, and also in the very act of outwitting, conning, and escaping their racist and patriarchal enslavers who thought so much of their own cunning and supremacy, and so very little of the value and capability of female "slaves"—aside from the profits to be gained from them. As Carter Jackson has offered, "Black joy as refusal" has historically looked like quitting, walking off the job, leaving without permission—or, the great delight in taking flight.[110] Enslaved women and men and the maroons they sometimes became also used laughter, mockery, ridicule, and joke telling to feel and to express pleasure but also to defend themselves from pain and harm, to critique injustice, and to incite change.[111]

Deep swamp maroon women may have felt and shown a kind of joy akin to that of enslaved Tidewater women like Minnie Fulkes, who exclaimed, "Ha! ha! ha!" when recalling the pleasure she and members of her community felt when they caused slave patrols on horseback to "stumble and fall" over the grape vines they laid on across the roads.[112] West of the swamp, in Emporia, Virginia, Ishrael Massie recounted how his brother Bob, Bob's wife, and two boys lived underground in a covered "vault," or hole in the woods, where, unbeknownst to white authorities, the marooning family had shared with him "many er good meal of vituals," as well as the exchange of laughter that: "Ha, ha, ha. Ya could stan' right over dis hole an' wouldn't kno' hit."[113] While Harriet Jacobs was waiting in the Dismal Swamp, her uncle was constructing the crawl space that would become her "loophole of retreat" in the small garret of her grandmother's house. With the gimlet her uncle had left in the garret, Harriet bore holes in the sides of the roof space to give herself air and light, but also to create a means to turn the gaze of surveillance onto Edenton's slaveholding class. Despite spending seven years confined to the nine-foot-long, seven-foot-wide crawl space, and despite the hardship and pain of her struggle against capture there, Harriet had also "rejoiced" and derived pleasure from her loophole in being able to hear the "merry laugh" of her children and to look upon their "sweet little faces" so near to her in the street below. But it was her own sharp intelligence and victorious outsmarting of James Norcom that, in Harriet's words, was the "greater satisfaction" of her flight, as all the while she looked out from her retreat, the man's obsessed pursuit of her had failed and yielded nothing.[114]

These were the kinds of moments of pleasure, joy, and satisfaction that maroon women would have shared and felt in their possession of themselves; in their achievements of family togetherness, rest, and safety; and in their outwitting, fooling, and refusing enslavers. Despite the reality of chattel slavery and the threat of discovery and recapture, women's modeling of good feeling, good humor, and good faith would have contributed significantly to the cohesion and holistic wellness of their communities. In these ways, maroon women's contributions to creating positive sentiment also uplifted the overall spirit of collective action and mutual support that sustained insurgency, which free life depended upon.

Though not all interior swamp experiences were the same, women were essential to the more enduring, lasting, populous, and frequently multigenerational communities that the deeper Great Dismal Swamp harbored and concealed. Women's everyday labor, care work, creativity, and astounding resourcefulness as mothers and as women, birthed the very life force of fugitive gathering and prolonged marronage. As maroon women arranged and rearranged the swamp's natural resources toward emancipatory and, thus, insurgent ends, their spiritual and medicinal knowledge of and communing with the swamp's healing properties and dimensions afforded their communities wellness, protection, and vitality, just as their procurement, preparation, and sharing of food provided the very "currency for forms of insurgent Black social life."[115] As people who evinced the absolute and categorical rejection of unending toil, the sexual use and exploitation of their bodies and intimate lives, the commodification of their wombs, and the pillaging of their motherhoods, deep swamp maroon women instructed their families and their communities in the most thorough lessons in self-ownership, self-worth, and strategies of self-protection and defense. Despite trace documentary evidence concerning people who never intended to be traced or even found, the certain immeasurable and unquantifiable *un*documented actions maroon women took—including extensions of romantic love, maternal love, love and care for their kin and community, and the love they showed themselves—when considered, adds to what we can know about how deep swamp women fortified their communities by providing and instilling warmth, mutual responsibility and respect, motivation and morale, rest, joy, pleasure, home, and belonging. Women who extended themselves in these ways engendered and encouraged a deeper sense of collective identity and direction, while encouraging perseverance and integrity in the shared and ongoing imperative of refusal, and the potential for greater and more transformative community action. These named and unnamed women were the hearthstones of the insurgent deep swamp.

EPILOGUE

Black Women's Insurgent Movement and the Future

When I found I had crossed dat line . . . I looked at my hands to see if I was de same pusson. There was such a glory ober ebery ting; de sun came like gold through the trees, and ober the fields, and I felt like I was in Heaven.

HARRIET TUBMAN, *SCENES IN THE LIFE OF HARRIET TUBMAN*

In the autumn of 1849, after Harriet Tubman set off from the family that enslaved her on the Eastern Shore of Dorchester County, Maryland, she trekked through more than 120 miles of woods, rivers, and marsh and blazed a trail across the length of two states before crossing the invisible border to the emancipated state of Pennsylvania. At twenty-seven years of age, a lifetime of forced labor outdoors and daily immersion in the natural world would prove invaluable to her success in completing twelve or thirteen trips back into Maryland to guide nearly seventy other fugitives out of slavery's grip.[1] Harriet crossed creeks by night and used the woods for refuge, respite, and concealment by day. As she recalled it, she told time "by the stars," studied and grew literate in rivers and trees, and often "lay alone in the forests all night," her soul "filled with awe of the mysterious Unseen Presence" tying nature to spirit and lifting her "up above all doubt and anxiety into serene trust and faith" in each of the next places her feet would meet ground.[2]

Harriet Tubman was extraordinary. Most women in the Tidewater, or anywhere, never accomplished such a feat, much less their own flight or escape. Yet the impulse and instinct to get away, to refuse to remain, or to remain in ways that undercut, transgressed, or defied was shared by too many women to count. Tidewater women who lived in the vicinity of the Great Dismal Swamp had an advantage, and as a result, they sometimes moved boldly and with daring, not unlike Tubman. Tidewater bondwomen benefited from the unique invitation and source of protection offered by the inescapable nearness and natural abundance of the great swamp, which encouraged them to act on indomitable fugitive instincts. Black women and men alike took note of the fact that the region's core *was* the mighty stretch of the Dismal Swamp, and that this swampscape was also inseparable from an extensive river system linking disparate Tidewater communities and channeling into the Chesapeake waters leading into the free north. Despite their gendered constraints as enslaved women, untold numbers accepted the swamp's invitation, moving closer to realizing their interests and objectives through interactions and arrangements they made with these exceptional wetlands.

Black women have never been inert. There has never been a time or place in the history of British North America, the United States, or the broader Atlantic world that the stirrings and movements of African women and women of African descent did not intervene, disrupt, or redirect the machinations and the yoke of slavery's raced and gendered hold. Through movement and motion, the women who conspired with the Tidewater woods and swamps as they ducked and flew through, in and out, and fled deeper still into the natural refuge of the Great Dismal Swamp gave new meaning to both the captive spaces they rejected and the grounds of vibrant wilderness they chose to consort with instead. Their stewardship of and journeys through these environs gave footing to other, contesting, more livable worlds they imagined and helped create. Black women's insistence on moving in ways that actively supported networks of fugitives, maroons, and enslaved people in acts of enduring escape, coordinated force, and organized rebellion also helped make these liberatory efforts possible. Across the Tidewater's heartland of the

Dismal Swamp, a most totalizing insurgency was afoot, for the women who traversed it mapped not only their opposition to the imposition of bound place, unending lack, loss, toil, and corporeal cruelty; they also charted refusals of sexual violence, unwanted and unsafe intimate partners and pregnancies, plundered motherhoods, and the overall profitability of their reproductive labor they knew was the bedrock of heritable enslavement and perpetual slavery. Their flight, marronage, and rearrangements of time and space following their own interests and visions of when and where to go, in addition to their shrewd political and intellectual undertakings that moved and shook the terrain of captivity around them, together inscribed the Dismal Swamp and its connected and surrounding Tidewater as insurgent ground.

The stories of the women in this book do not stop at the end of the Civil War. Women who fled through and marooned in the swamp, or who joined and sparked rebellions emanating from collaborations with the swamp—women like Phebe, Maria, Jude, Harriet Jacobs, Tamar Grandy and her mother before her, Mary, Lucy Wiggins, Larinda, and many others whose names still evade and were never recorded—maintained lives after their movements in and around the swamp that helped shape the places and the communities they moved through next. Exhausted returns to enslavers, recapture, but especially maroon women's Civil War–era decisions to vacate the swamp after the war's end—as one former maroon woman put it, because they "heered de news, dat de [negroes] all b'longed ter darselves now"—meant that, over time, a notable number of women who had once inhabited the Dismal Swamp reentered dominant society, bringing with them insurgent knowledge, resolve, fugitive practice, and experience.[3] During the Age of Revolution, enslaved women like Phebe and Jude, who aided organized rebellion shaped by strategic commune with Tidewater wetlands, emerged on the other side of their roles in these conspiracies with heightened political consciousness both of the danger of plotting Black political opposition and of the greater possibilities for transformative collective resistance and movements—a sentiment and a mindfulness that would have reverberated in their wake for generations. Despite punitive violence and their own failings as maroons, captured maroon women—women like the unnamed mother who found herself and her two children detained in the Newbern jail after seven years in the swamp; women like Tamar, who, not yet recovered from the birth of her third baby in the swamp, was discovered, "taken," and ultimately sold to numerous owners away from her two remaining children; and women like Maria and the two unnamed women at Snaky Swamp, who were caught skirting the recesses of the swamp's edge—each may have returned to the world of Black captivity and carcerality with steadfast and undeterred insights about evasion and noncompliance.[4] Any prevailing determinations these women held about movement and defiance, woods, and swamps would have helped shape new futures, since what they shared with their communities in the aftermath of their fugitive and insurgent acts likely impacted and inspired others.

A manumitted writer and abolitionist by the 1850s and 1860s, Harriet Jacobs never let go of her fugitive convictions, and she spent the rest of her life moving and fighting against the same forces of racist and patriarchal injustice that had once led her to believe that flight into Snaky Swamp was "less dreadful" than suffering the white men of Edenton, North Carolina.[5] In 1862, Jacobs left the train station in Philadelphia and headed to Alexandria, Virginia, to provide much-needed aid to Union "contraband" camps there containing formerly enslaved people who, believing these stations to be spaces of safety and freedom, had fled their enslavers to reach them. In her published report, "Life Among the Contrabands," Jacobs denounced the continued raced and gendered injustices she witnessed, and despite her finding that these camps were "most wretched" in their privation, grief, illness, and death, she wrote of "beautiful," loving, and "intelligent" women and mothers there who sometimes let out "a shout of joy" among kin, and who could be found making "home for all."[6] Fugitive and maroon women who moved through the Dismal Swamp to reach Union lines nearby in Suffolk, Norfolk, and at Fort Monroe, Virginia, may have continued to support and encourage their families and communities in the same ways. Mary, who moved with four children through the woods and swamps of Nansemond County to flee enslavers in Southampton, Virginia; Lucy Wiggins, who fled her enslaver in Gates County, North Carolina, with her husband and daughter; and Larinda, who left her maroon outpost in the Dismal Swamp with her baby and husband by her side, may have been among those women who, as the historian Thavolia Glymph has written, transformed these camps into "neighborhoods" and also into "political meeting grounds" against pervasive harm and unfinished freedom.[7]

As to the longer-lasting and uncaptured maroon women of the remotest swamps—women like Pamba and Venus who could have lived and died in the Dismal Swamp—they, too, left a legacy of insurgent meaning and direction. Through hard-won public history, long-standing local memory, and thanks to the eternal energy of their refusals and movements written into waters, trees, and earth, the assertions of deep swamp maroon women and men remains etched into the surviving swamp. Though centuries of draining, logging, canal construction, and intercoastal travel have caused the present-day Dismal Swamp to have shrunk to just a fraction of its original sprawling size of over one million acres, the very ecological intensity that aided and sheltered deep swamp maroons remains undeniable to anyone who encounters it, and the history of maroon women and their communities can still be seen and felt in the places where they once moved and lived.[8]

Today, the public can engage the swamp and learn about the African descendants who shaped its significance in a number of ways. Whether driving on major throughways such as highway US-58 along the northern remaining swamp in Suffolk, Virginia, or traveling east of what is left of the swamp along US-17 and the Great Canal—between Chesapeake, Virginia, and South Mills, North Carolina—the dense woods, cypress knees, and flooded grounds adjacent to these major roads are hard to ignore. Those interested in learning more about the swamp's history and social significance can visit the Great Dismal Swamp National Wildlife Refuge in Suffolk, Virginia, which since 2012 has featured an "Underground Railroad Education Pavilion" that includes information about the diverse maroons whose historic communities and escapes have made the swamp a space of resistance and freedom. Since 2008, the public has also been able to enter into the swamp on raised boardwalks and educate themselves about its history of marronage at exhibits in the Visitors Center at the Dismal Swamp State Park, in South Mills. Both these sites, as well as the Dismal Swamp Canal Trail in Chesapeake, Virginia—completed in 2006 as a recreational space for hiking, biking, running, and kayaking—were opened as designated historic sites within the National Park Service's Underground Railroad Network to Freedom program. These accomplishments owe much to the leadership of descendants of enslaved people as well as to a small group of scholars (chiefly Daniel Sayers and members of the GDSLS), who agitated for and compelled the cooperation of the US Fish and Wildlife Service, the North Carolina Department of Environment and Natural Resources, and the City of Chesapeake beginning as early as 2003.[9] Since that time, continued community activism and calls for greater efforts to protect and preserve the swamp's cultural and ecological value have led to initiatives like those organized by the Great Dismal Swamp Stakeholder Collaborative, to act against the interlocking threats of marginalized and oppressed peoples' historical erasure and unending capitalist extraction imperiling the swamp's ecology through climate change, pollution, and continued development and infrastructure projects. Formed in 2019, this stakeholder collective brings together local community members, agencies, and organizations like the Great Dismal Swamp National Wildlife Refuge, the Wilderness Protection Society, the Association for the Study of African American Life and History, the Environmental Justice Oral History Project, the Nansemond Indian Nation, the Meherrin Tribe, and a number of invested academic scholars and local historians. The Great Dismal Swamp StoryMap project, launched in 2023, is one of the collective's efforts to increase protections for the swamp's natural environment and rich cultural history by telling the stories of its human inhabitants, including Venus and other Black women, who moved through and consorted with the swamp to elevate their lives and those of their families and communities.[10] Other public-facing projects, such as the City of Chesapeake's planned Historical Village at the Dismal Swamp and the Chesapeake National Recreation Area, bring fuller narratives about marronage, deep swamp maroon women, and their ecological bonds with the swamp to greater public visibility in the surviving swampscape. The National Park Service is currently working to support these stakeholder efforts by designating and incorporating them within the Great Dismal Swamp National Heritage Area, which has announced it will bring even greater conservation and education to the region.[11] This designation is expected to be formalized by 2027, though these efforts must now confront the Trump administration's March 2025 Executive Order entitled "Restoring Truth and Sanity to American History," which aims to erase public historical narratives that pose "corrosive ideology," or, more directly, that expose how "the United States [has] used race to establish and maintain systems of power, privilege, and disenfranchisement."[12]

Beyond these recent, yet tentative strides, the legacy of maroon women and men continues to give the swamp insurgent meaning through descendants' memories—independent of any state efforts to make visible this history in the surviving swamp's commemorative landscape. Local descendants of enslaved people in swamp-adjoining towns like Suffolk, Hobson, and Smithfield, Virginia, have long remembered and passed on stories of their ancestors who courted the swamp in flight, resistance, and marronage. In 2015, one lifelong resident of the historic Black oystering village of Hobson, located at the northern edge of the historic swamp, recalled that during the tumultuous final years of Jim Crow, her own elders encouraged her with stories of a "thriving" community of "runaway slaves" who built houses on dry land farther into the swamp and who enjoyed peace and community control, protected by the fact that "everything else around them was marsh."[13] At seventy-four years of age, a descendant in Smithfield and Suffolk shared that her grandmother spoke of swamp maroons who preferred to "breathe through reeds and submerge under water to hide from their masters" than return to slavery. Another of her elders kept the memory of maroon life alive when he explained to her that maroons made beds in trees, called "cocoons," for occupancy and concealment during the day while pillaging and foraying by night.[14]

Black women's lives as maroons and life-givers to multigenerational maroon communities in the Dismal Swamp continue to inscribe it with insurgent meaning through generational remembering and through the indestructible spirit and energy that their historic motions archived into the living swampscape itself. The present swamp's indiscernibly deep, peaty black water that continues to hide a mass of submerged, entangled vines and tree roots, for example, is a record of maroon tenacity and sheer determination that to move through the environmental difficulties of a swamp was less challenging than chattel slavery. The swamp reed—through which to breathe when submerged under water to avoid detection or hide from pursuers—becomes a text on ingenious maroon strategies of evasion. The living trees (many of which are old enough to have beckoned and sheltered fugitives and maroons) and the insects, animals, and dense and verdant brush that continue to give the swamp life also document the sensorial, affective, spiritual, and political collaborations and encounters between fugitive African descendants and the historic swamp. Guided by historical inquiry, "descendant knowledge," and memory, the current swamp's ecological vibrancy and natural environment is itself readable as a crucial record, alive and humming with Black refusal, autonomy, creative worldmaking, and the movements and imperatives of the women, children, and men who chose to make it an insurgent space of home and freer life.[15]

The women whose responses to raced and gendered constriction, limits, and violence give life to these pages may not have known that they were thinking, acting, and plotting in ways that were connected to and shared with others across the Atlantic world and the African Diaspora—but they were. The uncapturable instincts of African and African-descendant women who invariably protested and rejected external claims to their labor and bodies took root in the shaping of enslaved and maroon communities, just as they also helped make possible collective insurgent movement and rebellion against slaveholding regimes—wherever the rule of the chattel principle fell. Enslaved women who everywhere set forward their feet—to breathe more deeply in forests and on grounds giving way to creeks, rivers, and swamps—were foremothers of a lasting tradition of Black women seeking and creating the space in which to demand and assert their own interests, claim their own peace, declare their place and value in worlds beyond commodification and capital, and engender and commune in environments conducive to their safety, health, pleasure, enjoyment, and truth. The audacity of such artful women, whose daily acts of noncompliance, impudence, and refusal to still themselves or to remain when, where, and how they were ordered and expected to be is a tradition that knows no borders or bounds. In the words of the poet, scholar, and activist Alexis Pauline Gumbs, there have always been so many "nameless women in unknown places laughing and looking sideways at each other," moving waywardly, errantly, yet decisively in fugitive motions that escape and defy those worlds unable or unwilling to hold them.[16] Nameless women—like the Black Water maroon woman who in 1818 moved stealthily in support of her "band of ruffians"—share impulse and conviction with women such as the late Assata Shakur, who, 150 years later, also chose fugitive flight, evasion, and outlawry against state capture and imprisonment. Hunted and accused of being the "bandit queen" of the Black Liberation Army—an underground militant group thought to be responsible for plundering, robbing banks, and using deadly force against police officers in the 1970s—Shakur broke free from prison in 1979 and thereafter likened herself to a maroon, explaining that she drew courage from runaway slaves and "people like Harriet Tubman and all those people who got away from slavery." She continued to sustain herself in flight from the "whip, chain, and cell" of the carceral state through her elected exile in Cuba, until the time that she passed away and transitioned in September 2025.[17] Black women seeking peace among birds, trees, water, and fresh air; those who have planted seeds, raised, and nurtured gardens and plots; women who dared move their "work-worn, sexually abused bodies" to escape, rest, and indulge in nature's bounty and spiritual connectedness have also continued to do so in slavery's wake. Women like Augusta Savage, Zora Neal Hurston, Fannie Lou Hamer, June Jordan, and Octavia Butler are among those who have given language to Black women's universal ecological rumination, relating, and stewardship within this liberatory and insurgent tradition of imagining and creating, or as Alice Walker put it, the "magic" of transforming "whatever rocky soil" into rich and beautiful works of art.[18] Tidewater women, who in these very ways helped make the Dismal Swamp a beacon of transhistorical insurgent potential, were among the first to breathe life into the spatially and temporally boundless Black radical tradition of fugitivity, marronage, worldmaking, and refusal.

They will not be the last. So long as injustice, fractional freedom, and the intersections of raced, gendered, and economic harm continue to shape and affect Black women's lives, the insurgent choices, decisions, and actions of enslaved, maroon, and rebel women will continue to matter and resonate as exemplary and instructional in current struggle and political movement. Previously untold stories about Black women's fugitivity, marronage, and rebellion merit our attention and need to be told so that we can more fully appreciate the range of Black women's ongoing contributions to building cultures and

Lake Drummond, Great Dismal Swamp National Wildlife Refuge, Suffolk, Virginia.
(Photo by the author, 2022.)

Great Dismal Swamp Canal and Dismal Swamp
Canal Trail, Chesapeake, Virginia.
(Photo by the author, 2022.)

Great Dismal Swamp Canal, Dismal Swamp State Park,
South Mills, Camden County, North Carolina.
(Photo by the author, 2013.)

politics of resistance as well as the myriad ways Black women have always been invested in and essential to manifesting both everyday resistance and overtly oppositional movements. The history of Black women whose certain motions made a vast swamp a place of healing, love, defensive strategy, and alternative life and community is a blueprint filled with plans, directions, and tactics for making possible worlds where all Black life matters. That Black women modeled active reclamation of their bodies and selves against unimaginable constraints, repurposed their energy and labor as key links in liberatory networks, embraced reciprocal violence, rearranged and redirected time and space in the service of their families and entire collectives and communities they cared about—all the while providing crucial knowledge about the life-saving potential of physical and spiritual communion with ecologies, land, and waterscapes—can and should give guidance to present and future movements. If unjust policing, surveillance, and carceral violence; imposed socio-political borders; continued hunting and persecution of migrants, refugees, fugitives, or "illegal" people; constricting dominant expectations of sex, reproduction, and gender; and ongoing capitalist accumulation and environmental extraction that disproportionately exploit Black people and Black spaces are to continue, the insights from these movements pioneered by so many Black women in and around the formidable Dismal Swamp will continue to offer invaluable logistic road maps to plotting viable alternatives.

Freedom may well be a place tied and connected to one's relationships to land and ground, but the discovery and arrangements of life-giving routes, resources, ritual, and self-serving community remain contingent on creative and persistent forward movement.[19] Each of the named and nameless Tidewater women who gave insurgent meaning to the Great Dismal Swamp knew well the importance of moving differently, out, and away, and they did so in emboldening motions that inched closer to freedoms not yet realized. Women like Harriet Tubman—whose dying words, "I go away to prepare a place for you," assured the work and service of women's unending motion—shared with Tidewater rebel, fugitive, and maroon women in this knowledge that futures of safety, peace, vitality, and justice would require their own trekking and drive.[20] The legacy of such women informs and empowers present movements now gathering momentum from Black women's vision, gifts, and stamina, revealing what worlds of Black life and sociality against placelessness, degradation, and harm might yet be possible today and in the days ahead.

ACKNOWLEDGMENTS

This book is a product of wise and seasoned elders and recent ancestors whose stories about youth and life in Jim Crow Southern towns and rural homesteads captivated and transformed my thinking from an early age. The recollections all four of my grandparents imparted about old childhood friends, neighbors, trouble, play, incomparable food, music, their closeness to nature and agrarian life and labor, deeply cutting and life altering injustice, distinct traits and personalities of their parents, and trace memories of other foremothers and forefathers are testament to the power inherent in our ability to tell our stories and to retrieve them. That some of my grandparents' stories begin with elders who were themselves once enslaved shows, too, how close the history of slavery is to our lives, how its lessons and traditions shape and color how we understand ourselves, and how closely knit together our stories are, despite the passing of time. In this light, my grandparents' memories and stories are not so far removed from the ordinary and extraordinary, harrowing, and triumphant lived experiences of the fugitive, maroon, and enslaved women, men, and children who asserted themselves and their rights and values when they gave insurgent meaning to the Great Dismal Swamp in an earlier age. The pages in this book are part of this tradition of storytelling, and I owe everything I have written to griots who knew and who taught that Black people like the women centered in this study deserve our collective attention and commemoration.

There is no better home for *This Insurgent Ground* than the unprecedented collection of books to be published in the University of North Carolina's

Black Women's History series. I am full of gratitude for the vision, time, and energy that the series editors Daina Ramey Berry, Ashley Farmer, and Talitha LeFlouria have spent establishing this new intellectual base devoted to Black women and our stories, upheld by the capacious and inventive methodologies we have created to find and see ourselves, and those before us, at any point in history. This work owes much to their careful feedback and review of my project, and to their invitation to participate in the series' annual incubator as an inaugural awardee. Workshopping chapter drafts during the incubator was instrumental to the evolution of this study. I am indebted to Jessica Marie Johnson and Tamika Nunley, who gave so much in reading multiple drafts, both as interlocutors during the incubator and outside of the workshop. A special thank-you is certainly owed Dawn Durante—the most compassionate, scrupulous, giving, and attentive editor I have ever known.

So many other colleagues and friends read versions and portions of this work, and my appreciation knows no bounds. For their critical and generous attention to some of my earliest drafts, I must thank the late and forever treasured Julie Saville, as well as the incredibly incisive and insightful Allyson Hobbs, Jakeya Caruthers, and Marisa Fuentes. Sasha Turner, Thavolia Glymph, SJ Zhang, Shauna Sweeney, Micah Khater, and Hayley Negrin also read and carefully engaged with parts of this work and provided invaluable suggestions. I am grateful to Adam McNeil, whose reading of the basis of just one of this book's chapters led to an explosion of elevating and enriching feedback following the airing of our New Books Network in African American Studies dialogue on "Armed in the Great Swamp." I am indebted to JT Roane for all his sincere readership and support, thoughtful questions and ideas, and the burgeoning canon in Black Ecologies scholarship he articulates and assembles, from which this work benefits and to which it stands in direct conversation.

The Africana Studies family at the University of Delaware have supported me throughout my writing—personally, intellectually, and professionally. Wunyabari Maloba, Kimberly Blockett, Cheryl Hicks, Monica Coleman, and Alicia Fontnette have been especially supportive and generous with their time in reviewing and engaging with works in progress, and in their warm reminders to hold space for rest, relief, breaking bread, and celebrating all the little victories.

Without my own time and experience spent consulting and trekking the living, surviving Dismal Swamp, this book would not be. Fortunately, this study is enlightened and enlivened by the opportunity American University archaeologist Daniel Sayers provided me to "meet" the swamp and to traverse its peaty waters as part of his Great Dismal Swamp Landscape Study (GDSLS). Dan did not know me when I joined his dig during its last year thirteen years ago, but since that time, his unwavering support and counsel as well as the wealth of excavated material evidence and interpretive possibility his project keeps on giving have exceptionally impacted this work. I am also grateful to fellow GDSLS contributor Brent Morris, for sharing sources, reading, and engaging drafts of this book as it unfolded over the span of a decade. During the dig, Mark Hamilton—now a lifelong friend—made me laugh despite the swarms of mosquitoes, fist-sized water-walking spiders, and inescapable ticks and snakes. I am truly thankful for his friendship. Other Dismal Swamp scholars and Tidewater local historians Christy Hyman, Cassandra Newby-Alexander, Eric Sheppard, and Therbia Parker provided precious source evidence and exchange about the swamp itself, its enslaved laborers, the lifeways of maroons, and descendant knowledges that helped me grasp the social meaning of these wetlands. Finally, nobody read more iterations of this book in part, in full, with a critical, meticulous, and painstaking eye for record interpretation, context, scope, and argumentation as well as to guard me against my own errata than Marcus Peyton Nevius. Comrade in the 2013 GDSLS crew, I cannot thank him enough for the level of time, care, and support he gave to ensuring this book exists.

Ula Taylor, Stephen Small, Carolyn Finney, Charles Daniel Dawson, Carla Shedd, and Manning Marable breathed life into this work with the truest investments of mentorship and backing. At the University of California–Berkeley: Zach Manditch-Prottas, Essence Harden, Selina Makana, Brukab Sisay, Charisse Burden-Stelly, Amani Morris, Jarvis Givens, Michael Myers II, Christina Bush, Kim McNair, John Mundell, Rob Connell, Grace Gipson, and Kelley Fanto Deetz individually and collectively showed encouragement, affirmation, and friendship that I will cherish always. At Columbia University: Akilah Reynolds and Kendall Bassard had no doubts, even when I ate the fears. I value our sisterhood immeasurably, and I know you are only ever a call away. Friends who knew this book was in me decades ago—Marika Hinds, Ruthy Aguilera, and especially Courtney Laine McCrary—have suffered my chatter on related subjects since the age of six. I thank you.

To my immense Bay Area family and kin: Benjamin, Richmond, Hedgspeth, Huie, Mahoney, Knox, and Hardy family. I love and thank you. Cousin Rosalind McGary blessed this book with beautiful and stirring original cover art. No one else could have given this project the face and spirit of women and Tidewater wetlands we now behold. Majadi Hardy spent many hours discussing this work with me, from which it has improved in breadth and depth, and I am ever grateful. I could always count on Danielle Benjamin to bring water and light when the seeds I sought to plant struggled to sprout and grow. Samari Hardy Benjamin will always be—giver of strength to me. My parents, David and Maria Benjamin, have given me the greatest inheritance of all—the consciousness and the will to harness "lessons from history" toward truth, justice, and the worlds we actually want to see and live in.

Jurdon Golden, you old-timer—the man's sacrifices and unswerving faith and belief in this work, and in me, are matched by no other. I am infinitely grateful. Though their cheerful little souls remained curious, encouraged, and excited, Amiri and Sage felt the weight of what it meant to have their mother pulled away to research and write each of these pages, for which I am filled with gratitude, and am eternally beholden to their love and their patience.

NOTES

ABBREVIATIONS

CP	Colonial Papers, 1630–1778, Library of Virginia, Richmond, Virginia
CS-LVRV	Condemned Slaves and Free Blacks Executed or Transported, 1779–1865, Library of Virginia, Richmond, Virginia
DSLC	Dismal Swamp Land Company Records, 1665–1832, Rubenstein Library, Duke University, Durham, North Carolina
LVRV	Library of Virginia, Richmond, Virginia
NCSA	North Carolina State Archives, Raleigh
RES-LVRV	Runaway and Escaped Slaves Records, 1794–1863, Library of Virginia, Richmond, Virginia

INTRODUCTION

1. "Mary Pope," in Blassingame, *Slave Testimony*, 455–57.

2. Hartman, *Scenes of Subjection*, 266–67.

3. This "something else" is Katherine McKittrick's extrapolation of Sylvia Wynter's notion of "demonic grounds." See McKittrick, *Demonic Grounds*, 122–23. Saidiya Hartman has also named young Black women's art of living in the face of "surveillance, arrest, punishment, and confinement" an "insurgent ground" by which they created "beautiful experiments" of quotidian rebellion, "waywardness, refusal, mutual aid, and free love" in early twentieth century Philadelphia and New York City. This book agrees that it is through this insurgent ground of radical imagination, "the refusal to be governed," and movement elsewhere (physically and metaphysically) that the promise of freer, more livable worlds and futures resides. See Hartman, *Wayward Lives*, xiv–xv.

4. By no means a comprehensive list, a few of these works that have shaped this book include J. Morgan, *Reckoning with Slavery*, 16; J. Morgan, *Laboring Women*; Berry and Gross, *Black Women's History*; Bay et al., *Toward an Intellectual History*; Fuentes, *Dispossessed Lives*; Turner, *Contested Bodies*; J. Johnson, *Wicked Flesh*; Nunley, *Demands of Justice*; Dunbar, *Never Caught*; Eddins, "'Rejoice!"; Spillers, "Mama's Baby, Papa's Maybe."

5. J. Morgan, *Reckoning with Slavery*, 7.

6. Byrd, "Earliest Passage Through the Dismal Swamp"; N. S. Shaler, "General Account of the Fresh-Water Morasses of the United States, with a Description of the Dismal Swamp District of Virginia and North Carolina," in Powell, *Tenth Annual Report*, 255–339; Leaming, *Hidden Americans*, 222; Sayers, *Desolate Place*, 105; Nevius, *City of Refuge*, 3; Morris, *Dismal Freedom*, 2.

7. Byrd, "Proposal to Drain the Dismal Swamp," 522; Byrd, "Earliest Passage Through the Dismal Swamp," 594. In the eighteenth and early nineteenth century, "desart" or "desert" meant any "uninhabited and uncultivated tract of country," or "any wild, uninhabited region, including forest-land." See Berland, *Dividing Line Histories*, 267.

8. Bilby and N'Diaye, "Creativity and Resistance," 54.

9. Ismail Rashid highlights communities of Africans (the Bullom, Baga, and Temne) that resisted transatlantic trade and enslavement through resistant strategies that included marronage and violent rebellion. See Rashid, "Devotion to the Idea of Liberty," 132–51. Chapters on flight and marronage from captivity in West Africa's coastal holding cells that "pre-figured Maroon societies of the Americas" are explored in two chapters in Gad Heuman's *Out of the House of Bondage*, 2–3, 11–33.

10. Price, *Maroon Societies*, xi–xii.

11. Aptheker, "Maroons Within the Present Limits," 167; Price, *Maroon Societies*, 2–3, 4, 105; A. Thompson, *Flight to Freedom*, 9; Eddins, *Rituals, Runaways*, 279.

12. That these writers used other terms besides *maroons* should not suggest that marronage was altogether unknown. As the scholar Jarvis Givens has shown, by the end of the nineteenth century, Black educators including Edward A. Johnson, and soon after, Leila Amos Pendleton and Carter G. Woodson, wrote of the maroons of Palmares, Brazil, Suriname, and even the Dismal Swamp, as "prescriptive theme[s] of black self-determination" against continuous racial violence and disenfranchisement. See Givens, *Fugitive Pedagogy*, 139–54.

13. Gabriel Debien is responsible for this traditional categorization of marronage into two classifications: *petit* (less enduring, small group, or solitary marronage where maroons "did not go very far from the plantation from which they fled), and *grand* (populous, long-term, sustained flight and self-government with "no intention of ever returning"). See Gabriel Debien, "Marronage in the French Caribbean," in Price, *Maroon Societies*, 107. (Debien's article was first published as "Le marronage aux antilles françaises au XCIIIe siècle," *Caribbean Studies* 6, no. 3 (1966): 3–44.)

14. White Southerners wanted no likeness between the groups of so-called runaways outlying in southern woods and swamps and the warring maroons of Latin America and the Caribbean, who were so disruptive to the social and economic machinations of colonial slavery that they forced European imperial powers to bend and adhere to many of their terms, through negotiations and formal treaties, recognizing maroon sovereignty and land rights. Southern slaveholders knew that colonists offered these treaties to maroons in Jamaica, Cuba, Ecuador, Mexico, Hispaniola, Colombia, Brazil, and Suriname—a result of often years-long

wars fought against "revolted negroes." See Price, *Maroon Societies*, 3–4; A. Thompson, *Flight to Freedom*, 308–15. Maroons were also considered a "plague" as their numbers steadily climbed, quickly reaching the hundreds and the thousands in many Atlantic world locales. For example, by the 1730s, maroons in Suriname had reached a population of "between a thousand and several thousand" strong. See de Groot, "Comparison Between the History," 174. The maroons of Palmares, Brazil reached a population of "about twenty thousand." See Roger Bastide, "The Other Quilombos," in Price, *Maroon Societies*, 193. Demographic factors in slaveholding British North America and the United States seldom enabled such numbers, as most people of African descent in most places and at most times were outnumbered by whites.

15. Diouf, *Slavery's Exiles*, 313.

16. Edmund Jackson, "The Virginia Maroons," *Liberty Bell*, January 1, 1852.

17. Aptheker, "Maroons Within the Present Limits"; Aptheker, "Additional Data on American Maroons," 452–60.

18. Aptheker, "Maroons Within the Present Limits," 167.

19. Debien wrote that grand marronage was marronage "in the true sense." See Debien, "Marronage in the French Caribbean," in Price, *Maroon Societies*, 107. Thirteen years later, Eugene D. Genovese subscribed to Debien's classification of marronage when he wrote that Southern maroons "typically huddled in small units and may be called 'maroons' only as a courtesy." See Genovese, *From Rebellion to Revolution*, 77. Michael Mullin also wrote of the "absence of a maroon dimension in the South." See M. Mullin, *Africa in America*, 61. John Hope Franklin and Loren Schweninger confirmed that "in virtually every state there were gangs of ten to twenty outlying slaves," also called maroons, though these "reached only a few hundred members (with the exception of those in the Great Dismal Swamp . . . which numbered several thousand)." See Franklin and Schweninger, *Runaway Slaves*, 86. Gwendolyn Midlo Hall has offered a chapter on the maroons of Bas du Fleuve in Spanish colonial Louisiana. See G. Hall, *Africans in Colonial Louisiana*, 201–36. See Lockley, *Maroon Communities in South Carolina*. Works on flight and marronage in Florida—though sometimes conflating autonomous marronage in wilderness spaces with "negro forts" established in protected Spanish and British territories—include Mulroy, *Freedom on the Border*; Rivers, *Rebels and Runaways*; Millet, *Maroons of Prospect Bluff*. Diouf's *Slavery's Exiles* is the first and only comprehensive study of marronage in British North America and the United States. As for the maroons of Virginia and North Carolina, books written exclusively on Dismal Swamp maroons include Sayers, *Desolate Place for a Defiant People*; Nevius, *City of Refuge*; Morris, *Dismal Freedom*; Leaming, *Hidden Americans*. Contributions to academic journals include Maris-Wolf, "Hidden in Plain Sight"; Peixotto, "Wetlands in Defiance"; Benjamin Golden, "'Armed in the Great Swamp.'" Dissertations include Austin, "Morass of Resistance"; Goode, "Engaging the Tools of Resistance"; and Benjamin Golden, "Through the Muck and Mire."

20. Price, *Maroon Societies*, 1; Fouchard, *Haitian Maroons*, 248.

21. The ways the enslaved, fugitives, and maroons saw, thought about, utilized, and experienced the built and natural environment has also been referred to as "the black landscape," "slave geographies," and the "black cognitive landscape." See Ginsburg, "Escaping Through a Black Landscape," 52.

22. Diouf, *Slavery's Exiles*, 5–6.

23. Aptheker, "Maroons Within the Present Limits," 167. A useful summary of hemispheric maroon warfare can be found in Price, *Maroon Societies*, 6–9.

24. Despite current debates that "fear permeated the experience of maroons," fear should not monopolize historical interpretation, especially when considering the totality of maroon lifeways and insurgent worldmaking. While the pages that follow will show that fear played a significant role in the lives of rebels and maroons who understood well the guarantees of punitive violence for marronage and rebellion, they will also show that fear did not dictate all, and that there are many other ways to view and think about fugitive and maroon strategy and action. See Nevius, "Global Warfare,"" 546.

25. See Hyman, "To Render a Landscape of Trauma."

26. See Leaming's *Hidden Americans*. See also P. Stewart, "Review of Hugo Prosper Leaming, *Hidden Americans*," 666–67.

27. Sayers, *Desolate Place for a Defiant People*, 22, 140.

28. Nevius, *City of Refuge*, 6.

29. Morris, *Dismal Freedom*, 113; Sayers, *Desolate Place for a Defiant People*, 115–16.

30. Camp, *Closer to Freedom*, 3, 6.

31. Trouillot, *Silencing the Past*, 72.

32. J. Morgan, *Reckoning with Slavery*, 209. Elizabeth Fox-Genovese has suggested, for example, that if "we are to believe our sources," Black women in the American South "did not participate in large numbers, if at all, in the smaller but explicitly military insurrections that punctuated the eighteenth and early nineteenth centuries." In Fox-Genovese's estimation, "Revolt seems to have become even more a specialized political and insurrectionary male responsibility." See Fox-Genovese, "Strategies and Forms of Resistance," 145, 153.

33. J. Morgan, *Reckoning with Slavery*, 215, 229, 232.

34. hooks, *Feminist Theory from Margin to Center*, xi.

35. D. White, *Ar'n't I a Woman*, 15.

36. Holden, *Surviving Southampton*, 7–8.

37. Jennifer Morgan describes motherhood within the context of racial chattel slavery as "plundered," reduced to "goods or wealth taken," and structurally situated as "naturally and reasonably commodified." See J. Morgan, *Reckoning with Slavery*, 217.

38. *Virginia Gazette*, October 26 to November 2, 1739; Franklin and Schweninger, *Runaway Slaves*, 212; G. Mullin, *Flight and Rebellion*, 104, 113–14.

39. Camp, *Closer to Freedom*, 2. Gerald Mullin has also defined the covert end of this continuum as "inward-directed rebelliousness," which included "attacks on crops, stores, tools, and overseers, as well as deliberate laziness, feigned illness, and truancy." See G. Mullin, *Flight and Rebellion*, 81. See also Bauer and Bauer, "Day to Day Resistance," 388–419.

40. Eugene Genovese contends that "revolt against slavery generally took the form of simple revolt against unbearable exploitation," and that most revolts "had a restorationist or isolationist, rather than a revolutionary, content." See Genovese, *From Rebellion to Revolution*, xiv.

41. Hine, "Rape and the Inner Lives of Black Women," 912.

42. Glymph, *Out of the House of Bondage*, 44.

43. Holden agrees that "resistance and rebellion existed along a continuum that assumes that both men and women participated in strategies of both resistance and rebellion because of their connectedness within the enslaved community." See Holden, *Surviving Southampton*, 7.

44. Camp, *Closer to Freedom*, 7.

45. *Norfolk Herald*, June 23, 1818.

46. Orlando Patterson, "Slavery and Slave Revolts," in Price, *Maroon Societies*, 279.

47. Benjamin Golden, "'Armed in the Great Swamp,'" 4.

48. Hening, *Statutes at Large*, 481–82.

49. Rebecca Hall's definition of revolt (the former) stands here in contrast with Herbert Aptheker's more stringent one (the latter). See R. Hall, "Not Killing Me Softly," 4; Aptheker, *American Negro Slave Revolts*, 162. In an effort to bring greater visibility to Black women's contributions to insurrection and revolt, R. Hall and, more recently, Nikki M. Taylor agree that revolt should be defined as the "organized, coordinated, violent, or lethal acts of resistance that are motivated by unbearable exploitation or injustice." See N. Taylor, *Brooding Over Bloody Revenge*, 6. Here, I agree, but suggest that interpreting marronage as a distinct form of organized rebellion removes physical violence as a requirement in determining what can constitute insurrection or revolt. Consistent with R. Hall and N. Taylor, the premise of revolt stems from oppositional acts that are lethal to the vitality of slaveholders and slavery.

50. Blassingame, *The Slave Community*, 215–16; Genovese, *Roll, Jordan Roll*, 588.

51. Finch, *Rethinking Slave Rebellion in Cuba*, 142–43.

52. Farmer, *Remaking Black Power*, 5.

53. Finch, *Rethinking Slave Rebellion in Cuba*, 143. Ashley Farmer emphasizes "how Black women consistently positioned themselves on the organizational and intellectual frontlines" before and during the Black Power era. During this movement, women embodied and enacted "calls for armed self-defense and community control without the leadership or protection of men." Farmer, *Remaking Black Power*, 10, 65. Jasmin A. Young's examination of Civil Rights activist Gloria Richardson's "highly controversial refusal to publicly denounce armed resistance" also "disrupts the assumption that armed resistance was primarily the domain of Black men." See Young, "Gloria Richardson, Armed Self-Defense," 213–14. Though not framed by questions about gender, see also Cobb, *This Nonviolent Stuff'll Get You Killed*. In two books, Ula Taylor reveals how Black women's personal and political priorities shaped the Black nationalist Universal Negro Improvement Association and the Nation of Islam behind front-facing men such as Elijah Muhammad and Marcus Garvey. See U. Taylor, *Promise of Patriarchy*; U. Taylor, *Veiled Garvey*. Kellie Carter Jackson highlights enslaved, fugitive, and manumitted abolitionist women who "were not afraid to use violent force to protect themselves and their loved ones." See Carter Jackson, "'Dare You Meet a Woman,'" 271. In her books, Carter Jackson also points to the ways the use of force and "violent resistance did not belong to men alone." See Carter Jackson, *We Refuse*; and Carter Jackson, *Force and Freedom*. Thavolia Glymph's body of work asserts that Black women engaged in quotidian rebellions as well as in organized conspiracies and armed collective movement, such as the case of Rose's leadership in insurrection with the "armed negroes" of Pineville, South Carolina in 1865. See Glymph, *Out of the House of Bondage*; and Glymph, "Rose's War," 502. For more on women's coordinated contributions to Black rebellion during the Civil War, see Glymph, *Women's Fight*. Few studies focus explicitly on women and premeditated, collective rebellion during slavery in British North America and the United States. Those that do include Terborg-Penn, "Black Women in Resistance"; R. Hall, *Wake*; R. Hall, "Not Killing Me Softly'"; Holden, *Surviving Southampton*; Taylor, *Brooding Over Bloody Revenge*.

54. Diouf's consideration of gender stops at her discussion of the low numbers of fugitive women, their deterrents to marronage, and the challenges borderland women faced—spanning a total of three pages. See Diouf, *Slavery's Exiles*, 89–92. Based primarily on the work of

Diouf, Aptheker, and other historians previously noted, Karen Cook Bell's book on women and fugitivity in Revolutionary America documents maroon women's "declaration of independence in the swamps and woods of Virginia, North Carolina, Louisiana, South Carolina, Georgia, and Florida." She does this in the space of one chapter. The chapter concludes that maroon women "unabashedly claimed the liberty denied to them and fundamentally transformed their lived experience," but it is not invested in providing analysis of the political, social, or economic implications of women's movements, motivations, or possible roles within their communities. See Cook Bell, *Running from Bondage*, 137–59. Jennifer Morgan's chapter, "'Treacherous Rogues': Locating Women in Resistance and Revolt," includes a section entitled "Marooning Women," that names the gendered dynamics of marronage, alongside revolt, an "equally alarming space of refusal." This exploration sits with examples of women maroons in the Spanish colonies and British Caribbean, though its careful analysis of maroon women's "profound rejection of the totalizing logic of hereditary racial slavery" and critique of the assumed masculinist nature of marronage is useful and applicable to British North America and the United States. J. Morgan, *Reckoning with Slavery*, 228–37.

55. Works by SJ Zhang explore archives, marronage, gender, and reproduction in both North America (Spanish colonial Louisiana) and the French Caribbean. See Zhang, "Simarrona"; Zhang, "Mulâtresse Solitude"; and Zhang, "What Cecelia Knew." In the context of revolutionary Saint-Domingue, Crystal Eddins reveals how African-descended women were instrumental actors in the revolutionary struggle as providers of "sacred protection to male rebels; nurses; producers of rebel armies' provisions . . . couriers of weapons and ammunition; spies; and partners to their military husbands," but also as maroons—"bridge leaders" in resistive networks both before and during revolution—who refused exhaustive labor and the exploitation of their bodies "to the detriment of their reproductive health." See Eddins, "'Rejoice!,'" 563, 576; Eddins, *Rituals, Runaways*, 101, 145, 279, 288–89. Shauna J. Sweeney posits "market marronage"—Black women's fugitivity in illicit "spheres of production and exchange" she identifies as a "distinct form of enslaved resistance bound up with black women's unique ability to carve out a modicum of economic independence" in Jamaica's internal market system. Sweeney, "Market Marronage," 198, 200; Gottlieb, "Queen Nanny"; Gottlieb, *Mother of Us All*. Studies on maroon women, resistance, and the Dutch and Spanish colonies include Laurent-Perrault, "Esclavizadas"; Landers, "Founding Mothers"; and de Groot, "Maroon Women as Ancestors."

56. Genovese, *Roll, Jordan Roll*, 591; Patterson, "Slavery and Slave Revolts," 288.

57. While maroon women in the Dismal Swamp supported the use of force to sustain and defend themselves and their communities in the recorded instances of 1709–10, 1811, 1818, and 1823, maroon women in the Caribbean and Latin America were similarly embracing armed resistance against colonial chattel slavery. For example, in French Guiana, between 1802 and 1806, maroon women in a community called Maripa set their former plantation on fire before taking to the "forests and waterways" where they actively helped fight French troops, successfully, for years. See Moitt, "Slave Women and Resistance," 247. In 1748, "all the Negroes and Negresses" in another maroon group in French Guiana were reported to have been readied and "equipped with axes and machetes." See Bush, *Slave Women in Caribbean Society*, 70. In perhaps the first study devoted entirely to challenging the "age old plantocratic view that female marronage was almost non-existent," Alvin O. Thompson explores the diverse roles of maroon women in the Caribbean, including those engaged in "military and

paramilitary roles," such as Zeferina of the Urubu maroons in Bahia; Romaine la Prophetesse, Marie-Jeanne, and Henriette Saint-Marc in Saint-Domingue; Nanny of the Windward Maroons in Jamaica; and "150 Black women who fought more valiantly than men" in Colombia. See A. Thompson, "Gender and Marronage," 262, 273–76. Despite her obvious pregnancy, the maroon woman Solitude of Guadalupe was instrumental to armed resistance against the French militia in the year 1802. Although there is no history book yet published in English about her, French works highlight her resistive leadership and contributions to marronage. See Gautier, *Les Soeurs de Solitude*; Zhang, "Mulâtresse Solitude." See also Hurley, "Solitude."

58. Refer to the chapter titled "The Diminution of the Diaspora," in Robinson, *Black Marxism*, 72–73, 130–66. Daniel Sayers also notes that the maroons of the Dismal Swamp were part of a tradition of "radical action." See Sayers, "Marronage Perspective," 141.

59. Sayers, "Marronage Perspective," 124.

60. Jennifer Morgan's book follows the key question: "How might the experience of enslaved women have given rise to a Black radical tradition . . . that was rooted in the intersections between birth and commodification?" See J. Morgan, *Reckoning with Slavery*, 16, 233. Tamika Nunley's work also asks how the Southern penal system and Black women's criminalized resistive acts against gendered chattel slavery and racial capitalism gave shape and meaning to the Black radical tradition. See Nunley, *Demands of Justice*, 14–15. Similarly, Aisha Finch attributes the gendered terrain of insurgency throughout the Cuban rebellions of 1841–44 to a "black political consciousness" shared differently by both women and men, rooted in a tradition of Black radicalism. See Finch, *Rethinking Slave Rebellion in Cuba*, 81, 250.

61. Crystal Eddins defines the Black radical tradition as the "multigenerational struggle against interlocking systems of oppression that re-shaped life in the Americas," to which she finds the "reproductive justice advocacy" of maroon women in eighteenth century Haiti to be exemplary as just one of manifold ways women engendered the roots of Black radicalism. Eddins, "'Rejoice!,'" 564, 575.

62. Robinson, *Black Marxism*, 121–22. Marisa Fuentes has defined fugitivity in the context of slavery as a subversion of "the very paradigm of enslavement—immobility, disembodiment, violation—and [the creation of] an alternative self" in rival worlds. See Fuentes, *Dispossessed Lives*, 17. J. T. Roane's enunciation of insurgent Black social life and his theory of Black plotting articulates how Black communities assembled and inhabited dark agoras, "forms of gathering and shadowing and terrorizing the colonial state to create the conditions for Black social life," where sociality is understood as irreducible to the terror that calls Black experience into existence. Roane, *Dark Agoras*, 47. See also Roane, "Plotting the Black Commons," 249, 251–52.

63. Campt, *Image Matters*, 79; Sharpe, *In the Wake*, 20.

64. Givens, *Fugitive Pedagogy*, 10–11; Campt, *Image Matters*, 79–80.

65. Neil Roberts calls for "scholars interested in understanding both normative ideals of freedom and the origin of those ideals" to understand marronage (and in principle, fugitivity) as a "useful heuristic device" forged in a specific historical context, though holding "normative value" and "trans-historical utility." See Roberts, *Freedom as Marronage*, 4, 10, 13, 173. In her incisive offering of a world beyond policing, Celeste Winston examines "shared moments of Black flight across time" to show how the framework of fugitivity and marronage serves "not as a descriptive rehearsal of anti-Black violence" but as a way to conceive how to live differently in the present and engender new worlds and critical interventions. Winston's book responds to Roberts's call for scholars to "reorient our epistemology of freedom around

marronage" and flight by situating its histories within ongoing radical Black struggle and fugitivity against anti-Black police violence. See Winston, *How to Lose the Hounds*, xvi–xvii, 2. In their edited volume, *On Marronage*, a Black studies critique of antiblackness, P. Khalil Saucier and Tyron P. Woods point to the "ongoing necessity and dynamism of black marronage from the slavocracy through to the present day," as central to ongoing Black political contestation and the Black radical tradition. See Saucier and Woods, *On Marronage*, 10–11.

66. Ford, "Close-Up," 110–14; Moten, *The Undercommons*, 19.

67. Winston, *How to Lose the Hounds*, 3.

68. Roberts, *Freedom as Marronage*, 128. "Waterscapes," including swampscapes, are expressions of the ways "freshwater and saltwater systems actively informed" Black lives, but also the ways people of African descent "enlisted water as a player in historical drama." See Dawson, *Undercurrents of Power*, 4–5.

69. McKittrick, *Demonic Grounds*, xxii–xxv.

70. Roane, *Dark Agoras*, 21, 45.

71. Blum, "Power, Danger, and Control," 248.

72. This work is particularly indebted to the leading work of Justin Hosbey and J. T. Roane. See Hosbey et al., *Blackecologies*; Hosbey et al. "Introduction: Global Black Ecologies," 1–10; Hosbey and Roane, "Totally Different Form of Living," 68–73; Hosbey and Roane, "Mapping Black Ecologies." Refer also to J. T. Roane's extensive bibliography on Black ecological thought and praxis, particularly in the post-emancipation era. Roane, *Dark Agoras*, 7–8; Clark, *Reclaiming Stolen Earth*; Moulton, "Towards the Arboreal Side-Effects"; Moulton and Salo, "Black Geographies and Black Ecologies"; Lethabo King, *Black Shoals*, 9, 32; Dawson, *Undercurrents of Power*; M. White, *Freedom Farmers*; Finney, *Black Faces, White Spaces*; Smith, *African American Environmental Thought*; Glave and Stoll, *"To Love the Wind and the Rain"*; Hare, "Black Ecology."

73. Some notable exceptions include Silkenat, *Scars on the Land*; Nelson, "Hidden Away"; Allewaert, "Swamp Sublime"; Wilson, *Shadow and Shelter*; M. Stewart, *What Nature Suffers to Groe*. None of these consider the implications of gender or Black female subjectivity. Katherine McKittrick's work is foundational to disrupting these gaps in the scholarship concerning Black women. Her influential book called for long-past due attention to Black women's conceptualization and creation of geographies through embodied and intersectional struggle. McKittrick's *Demonic Grounds* has inspired recent and forthcoming work by Black feminist literary ecocritics Carlyn Ena Ferrari and Chelsea M. Frazier, who trailblaze in centering "Black Women's Ecologies" and "Black Feminist Ecological Thought," through their engagement with Black women's literary and artistic visions and articulations of nature. See McKittrick, *Demonic Grounds*; Ferrari, "On Black Women's Ecologies"; Ferrari, *Do Not Separate Her from Her Garden*; Frazier, "Black Feminist Ecological Thought"; and Frazier, "Troubling Ecology."

74. Finch, *Rethinking Slave Rebellion in Cuba*, 12.

75. Vanessa Holden posits silence as an opening for further interpretation, rather than grieving it as an obliterating force preventing a richer, fuller historical interpretation of women's roles in rebellion. Holden, *Surviving Southampton*, 84, 120. Similarly, Jessica Marie Johnson offers the "null value": "a mechanism for naming archival silences" that "imbues absence with disruption and possibility" instead of accepting documentation at face value and ignoring women completely. Johnson's null value affirms interpretive opportunity "before reading the

bias grain for 'marking this space of indeterminacy.'" J. Johnson, *Wicked Flesh*, 13, 135. Marisa Fuentes's history of enslaved women in colonial Barbados raises Black women's lives beyond "fleeting glimpses" or "ephemeral archival presences" while arguing that archival violence, uneven power, dispossession, and the silences they produce are part of the narration of Black women's history—not the end of it. See Fuentes, *Dispossessed Lives*, 1–7. See also Hartman, "Venus in Two Acts," 1; Hartman, *Scenes of Subjection*, xxxvii, 10–11.

76. Bryant, *36th Infantry United States Colored Troops*, 19–20.

77. *Logain County News*, September 16, and September 23, 1863.

78. Camp, *Closer to Freedom*, 7, 117–18.

CHAPTER 1

1. Moses Grandy, "Narrative of Moses Grandy," in Andrews, *North Carolina Slave Narratives*, 159, 175–77, 180, 182.

2. Before intensive postbellum draining, deforestation, and industrialization, the swampland known as the Great Dismal Swamp reached the ends of the counties of Princess Anne, Norfolk, Nansemond, and Isle of Wight in Virginia, and Camden, Currituck, Perquimans, Pasquotank, Chowan, and Gates in North Carolina. Refer to map 1 for an image of the pre–Civil War Dismal Swamp and its associated Tidewater counties alongside its present-day lesser expanse. See Davis, *Great Dismal Swamp*, 23; Leaming, *Hidden Americans*, 222; Sayers, *Desolate Place for a Defiant People*, 20, 92; Sayers, "Scission Communities and Social Defiance," 185; Nevius, *City of Refuge*, 3.

3. Sylviane Diouf estimates hundreds of maroons lived in the swamp, with "certainty." Diouf, *Slavery's Exiles*, 210–12. Without providing an explanation for his estimate, Herbert Aptheker states that "about two thousand" lived in swamp. See Aptheker, "Maroons Within the Present Limits," 168. Leaming agrees that "some two thousand" lived in the swamp across these years, but he also fails to explain how he arrives at this conclusion. Leaming, *Hidden Americans*, 221. Sayers reasonably suggests that "it makes perfect sense that thousands of maroons inhabited the swamp." See Sayers, *Desolate Place for a Defiant People*, 88. At the height of the formal abolition movement of the nineteenth century, the abolitionist Edmund Jackson received reports from a reputable Norfolk merchant that "the value of slave property lost in the swamp, at one and a half million dollars . . . would give near forty thousand as the population of the swamp"—though this, he advised, was "quite too large" an estimate. See Edmund Jackson, "The Virginia Maroons," *Liberty Bell*, January 1, 1852, 149.

4. Hartman, "Venus in Two Acts," 12. See also Patterson, *Slavery and Social Death*.

5. Smith, *African American Environmental Thought*, 19. Nathan Hare's groundbreaking "Black Ecology" introduces the framework of "Black ecology" to name the ways Black community vitality in the 1960s and 1970s was spatialized but also directly connected to ties between structural racism and the environment—particularly as he prescribes the "decolonization of the black race" against overcrowding, lack, pollution, and extractivism within Black (urban) space and communities. See Hare, "Black Ecology," 2–8. Neil Roberts has pointed to the ways that land, including its environmental foundation as a source of "assemblies, trees, vitamins, food," is integral to political movement and fugitivity because "the experience of communion between an agent and the land generates flight," and Black agents have long "associated land

with freedom." See Roberts, *Freedom as Marronage*, 128–29. In his articulation of an "ethic of marronage" in twentieth-century emancipatory Black US-based movements, Adam Bledsoe has highlighted connections between maroon relationships to land and to nature during slavery, and the spatial and environmental demands made by the Gullah-Geechee of South Carolina, Georgia, and Florida to preserve and protect their ancestral coastal marshlands (including their cultural and social ties to "farming, fishing, hunting"); and the Black Panther Party's "geopolitical" imperatives and "respatialization" of urban land and space toward Black autonomy, community wellness, and uplift. See Bledsoe, "Marronage as a Past and Present Geography in the Americas," 41, 43.

6. Roane, "Plotting the Black Commons," 249, 251–52. Saidiya Hartman has defined "fungibility" as "the replaceability and interchangeability endemic to the commodity"—in other words, it is the expendability of captive Africans and African descendants rendered chattel that dispossesses them from all "other signs of value." See Hartman, *Scenes of Subjection*, 28–29.

7. Benjamin Golden, "Trouble in the Water."

8. Moulton and Salo, "Black Geographies and Black Ecologies," 157, 161.

9. Camp, *Closer to Freedom*, 7; Holden, *Surviving Southampton*, 25. Aisha Finch argues that in Cuba, the "rival geography became the insurgent geography" as enslaved women and men "found ways to shape their worlds" and contemplated ways to unmake geographies of surveillance and control, fashioning instead "insurgent collectives across the rural landscape" during the rebellions of 1843 and 1844. See Finch, *Rethinking Slave Rebellion in Cuba*, 51–53, 63, 66, 71, 78. Yuko Miki posits enslaved and maroon "insurgent geographies"—the political "practice" of claim making and reconfiguring rights to space where "flight became a transformative force that destabilized these very configurations." For Miki, insurgent geographies in São Mateus, northern Brazil, laid the "groundwork for undoing slavery's grasp." See Miki, "Fleeing into Slavery," 508, 512, 517, 528. Diouf has termed the maroon landscape the "world" established by a "whole range of maroon life" that evolved across interconnected areas throughout the border and hinterlands. Diouf, *Slavery's Exiles*, 5–9. The social ecologist Andreas Malm has argued that "wilderness was a premise for emancipation," and he points to the "strategic logic of maroon ecologies," or maroon vanguardism against slavery and capitalism through symbiosis with "wild and barren" lands that "whites dared not tread." Malm, "In Wildness Is the Liberation of the World," 13, 15–16, 21. Becca Peixotto terms the intricate "wet- and drylands" constituting the Great Dismal Swamp the "wetlands of defiance" to conceive of the ways "marginal lands became a refuge" for those "marginalized by an enslavement system," who chose instead to act against their own exploitation and oppression. Peixotto, "Wetlands in Defiance," 21–22, 32. Lennox Honychurch attributes Dominica's rainforests and forested highlands—or "forests of freedom"—as central to sustaining the maroon landscape and to late eighteenth-century maroon insurgency on the British island. See Honychurch, *In the Forests of Freedom*.

10. Moulton and Salo, "Black Geographies and Black Ecologies," 160, 164, 166, 168–69. Justin Hosbey, Hilda Lloréns, and J. T. Roane agree that "African and African diasporic ingenuity and cultivation" of "world-making and life sustaining coordinates" against environmental and geographic precarity are interventions and practices situated within traditions of "insurgent ecocriticism" and, more broadly, Black radicalism. See Hosbey et al., "Introduction: Global Black Ecologies," 1, 5, 8. Yahnick Marshall rightly calls for the "radical thought"

imbued through maroon worldmaking, critique, and "clairvoyance" about colonialism and the "moribund racist experiment" to be brought to the center of analyses on the "territorialization of human beings" as well as to Black intellectual history itself. See Yahnick Marshall, "An Appeal: Bring the Maroon to the Foreground in Black Intellectual History," Black Perspectives, June 19, 2020, www.aaihs.org/an-appeal-bring-the-maroon-to-the-foreground-in-black-intellectual-history/.

11. For example, there is a rich tradition of Black women writers, artists, and activists who imagine, depict, and give language to Black women's ecological rumination, critical engagement, and environmental futures. The work of women like Alice Walker, Augusta Savage, Fannie Lou Hamer, Zora Neal Hurston, June Jordan, Dionne Brand, Octavia Butler, and Anne Spencer indicates the deep and far-reaching roots and branches of such a legacy. Yet, an obvious dearth of sincere scholarly attention to gendered Black spatialities and Black women's ecological thought and praxis persists. Katherine McKittrick's influential *Demonic Grounds* expanded Sylvia Wynter's "demonic grounds" and called for scholars of Black spatialities to reorient analysis to Black women's geographies and to apply Black feminist approaches to the study of race and geography. See Wynter, "Unsettling the Coloniality of Being/Power/Truth/Freedom," 257–337. More recently, Chelsea Frazier has continued to urge that the "prevailing disciplinary and theoretical frameworks for comprehending black feminist subjectivity and its integral relationship to world/land/territory/earth ethics are impoverished." She turns to the work of Black women writers and artists such as Octavia Butler and Wangechi Mutu who "effectively *trouble ecology*" by offering "transgressive visions" and "critical attention on black female subjectivity and resistive notions of ecological relationality." See Frazier, "Troubling Ecology," 40, 43, 46.

12. Carlyn Ferrari defines "ecopoetics" as an analytical framework that encourages exploring the place of the natural world in Black women's lives, whereas Black women's ecological consciousness "offers alternative expansive visions of Black womanhood" and being. See Ferrari, *Do Not Separate Her from Her Garden*, 2, 8.

13. Frazier, "Black Feminist Ecological Thought."

14. Ferrari, *Do Not Separate Her from Her Garden*, 2, 9–11.

15. Blum, "Power, Danger, and Control," 263.

16. Rediker, *Slave Ship*, 155; Brown, *Good Wives, Nasty Wenches*, 107–8.

17. Gomez, *Exchanging Our Country Marks*, 20–21.

18. McCartney, "Study of the Africans and African Americans on Jamestown Island," 87–88; E. Morgan, *American Slavery, American Freedom*, 171.

19. Hening, *Statutes at Large*, 170.

20. Jennifer Morgan reads against the language of the 1662 law—also known as *partus sequitur ventrem*, or "offspring follows belly"—and finds a naming of "mixed-race children as excess, as both circulating and unregulated, and ultimately a source of chaos" if the political, ideological, and economic indeterminacy of unregulated racial mixture was not "fixed." See J. Morgan, "*Partus sequitur ventrem*," 2–6. Melanie Newton has pointed out that *partus sequitur ventrem* became "customary legal practice for British Caribbean slaveholders to assume that the principle of enslavement through the maternal line could apply to anyone who had an enslaved female African or Indian ancestor." Newton, "Returns to a Native Land," 116.

21. Block, *Rape and Sexual Power*, 80–84.

22. Saidiya Hartman writes of the violence of the historical archive of slavery, produced in the "economy of theft and the power over life," that renders the lives of captive women and girls "objects of power," "cargo, inert masses, and *things*" (emphasis added) excluded from subjectivity and representation. Hartman, "Venus in Two Acts," 10. Hortense Spillers's crucial work theorizes the captive body as a "thing" dispossessed and absented from a subject position, or an object of "*being* for the captor." The captive body as "thing" is, however, distinct from her readings of the "flesh," where flesh "carries" the captive body "to the frontiers of survival" and generates a primary narrative—a "text for living and for dying, and a method for reading both." See Spillers, "Mama's Baby, Papa's Maybe," 67–68. Jennifer Morgan has similarly shown that within the context of Atlantic slavery, Black women's bodies—beyond their capacities for productive and reproductive labor—were fundamentally marked as spatial objects essential in the symbolic colonial imaginary of the rights to settle, claim, and possess lands and their natural resources. She writes that European men's "urge for discovery of new lands was inextricable from the language of sexual conquest," or the violable meanings attached to the female African body. See J. Morgan, *Laboring Women*, 16–17.

23. Cecelski, *Waterman's Song*, 5.

24. Sawyer, *America's Wetland*, 1–6; Peixotto, "Wetlands in Defiance," 19–20.

25. Sawyer, *America's Wetland*, 4. Though the word "dismal" was once commonly used in the seventeenth and eighteenth centuries as a term simply meaning swamp or morass, the appellation of "Dismal Swamp" to name this particular morass was popularized by Col. William Byrd II of Westover—one of the leading Commissioners of the Council of Virginia between 1710 and 1744 and surveyor in the expedition to determine the border between Virginia and North Carolina in 1728. Following the expedition, the term "dismal" would also reflect growing colonial and slaveholding frustration with the insubordinate swamp ecology. Davis, *Great Dismal Swamp*, 44; Leaming, *Hidden Americans*, 222; Morris, *Dismal Freedom*, 42.

26. Negrin, "Return to the Yeokanta/River," 525.

27. Kirby, *Poquosin*, 8.

28. Sayers, *Desolate Place for a Defiant People*, 14, 20.

29. Brown, *Dismal Swamp Canal*, 17–19; Kirby, *Poquosin*, 6; Morris, *Dismal Freedom*, 21–22.

30. Rountree and Taukchiray, *Manteo's World*, 122, 131–37; Griffin, *Ante-Bellum Elizabeth City*, 3; Kirby, *Poquosin*, xii.

31. Negrin, "Return to the Yeokanta/River," 525–28.

32. Negrin, "Return to the Yeokanta/River" 529.

33. Rountree, *Pocahantas's People*, 8; Rountree, *Manteo's World*, 44, 47.

34. Negrin, "Return to the Yeokanta/River," 528.

35. Rountree, *Pocahantas's People*, 8–9. Rountree also writes that within Indigenous Tidewater communities, "no forcing of women was allowed." See Rountree, *Mateo's World*, 45. Indigenous women thus resisted the conjoined colonial claims to the use and access of the wetlands as well as to their own bodies.

36. Negrin, "Return to the Yeokanta/River," 533–39.

37. For example, the divination systems and spiritualities of the Alusi for Ndi Igbo, the Orisa for the Yoruba, the Ntrw for ancient Kemet, the Nkisi for the Bakongo, and the Vodun for the Fon are "all expressions of nature as sacred, yet concretely experienced, in the day-to-day interactions between human beings and local ecologies." See Densu, "Omenala," 41. See also Clark, *Reclaiming Stolen Earth*, 37–51; Karenga, *Maat*, 389.

38. Smith, *African American Environmental Thought*, 14; Eddins, *Rituals, Runaways*, 42; Wells-Oghoghomeh, *Souls of Womenfolk*, 173, 177, 224–27; Rucker, *River Flows On*, 1–14, 146; Gomez, *Exchanging Our Country Marks*, 56–57, 111; Wynter, "Jonkonnu in Jamaica," 34–48.

39. Carter, "Other Worlds, Nowhere," 160, 164, 169.

40. Thornton, *Africa and Africans*, 17–21.

41. As such, the connective capacity, movement, joining, and meaning of water in Black life has served as a framework of analysis that has long occupied a space in Black intellectual life and the history and study of the African Diaspora. For example, Edward Kamau Brathwaite's "tidalectics" posits water and the touching of oceans as the ever-moving "continuum" of diasporic dialogue against dialectical fragmentation or absence in the African Diaspora. Brathwaite, *ConVERSations with Nathaniel Mackey*, 34. More recently, against traditional terra-centric approaches to history, Kevin Dawson has turned to the "waterscapes of the African Diaspora" to comprehend Black traditions and identity in the history of the Atlantic world shaped by undercurrents, sacred waters, and maritime and aquatic cultures. Dawson, *Undercurrents of Power*, 1. Tiffany Lethabo King has offered that Native studies and Black diaspora studies should not only be concerned with landscapes or oceanic geographies, but that these studies should also consider the shoal—"a space of liminality, indeterminacy, and location of suture" between land and water and an important lens by which to understand transit, exchange, struggle, and domination. Lethabo King, *Black Shoals*, 4–5. Rebecca Hey-Colón asserts the "spiritual currents" of saltwaters and sweetwaters as unbound archives of connectivity and the meeting of Afro-diasporic religious traditions. Hey-Colón, *Channeling Knowledges*, 13–15. See also Gilroy, *Black Atlantic*, ix–39; Tinsley, "Black Atlantic, Queer Atlantic," 191–215.

42. Gomez, *Exchanging Our Country Marks*, 111.

43. R. Thompson, *Flash of the Spirit*, xv, 72–75, 79.

44. Wells-Oghoghomeh, *Souls of Womenfolk*, 180.

45. Gomez, *Exchanging Our Country Marks*, 118–20; Mustakeem, *Slavery at Sea*, 129; Smallwood, *Saltwater Slavery*, 185–86.

46. For example, in Haitian Vodou, the *lwa*, or ancestral spirits of the water, include an ancient water serpent and his rainbow wife Ayida Wèdo; a woman with a fish tail, Lasirèn; and a spirit called Simbi of the water, among others, whose presence in the waters enslaved people in Saint-Domingue interacted with "helped break the physical, mental, and spiritual bondage" of slavery. See Hey-Colón, *Channeling Knowledges*, 12.

47. Michael Gomez points to the affinity West Africans and West Central Africans alike had for rivers and suggests that this African precedent had no little bearing on African American traditions of water rites, water immersion, and baptisms in the United States South. See Gomez, *Exchanging Our Country Marks*, 273.

48. Vickers, "On Swampification," 1676; Silkenat, *Scars on the Land*, 125.

49. Tiffany Lethabo King has argued that Black embodied errantry, ingenuity, reinvention, and fugitivity were symbolic contestations of British colonial conceptions of Blackness and the natural world as expendable commodities, and as such, remain symbols of "unstable borders, processes, and the shifting power relations that inspired key renderings of eighteenth-century British plantation landscapes." Lethabo King, *Black Shoals*, 110, 120. Elsewhere, she writes that "Black bodies in flux are dynamic and kinetic sites" that, when in motion, "enable diverse ecological forms and cycles"—particularly transitory waterways—to "work together

rhythmically" in ways that disrupt colonial regimes of domination and control. See Lethabo King, "Racial Ecologies," 71, 74.

50. Leaming, *Hidden Americans*, 224; Sayers, *Desolate Place for a Defiant People*, 87.

51. P. Morgan, *Slave Counterpoint*, 58–71; G. Mullin, *Flight and Rebellion*, 6; Sidbury, *Ploughshares into Swords*, 58.

52. "Letter of the Surry County Court," March 24, 1709, Box 144, Folder 20, CP-LVRV. See also Palmer, *Calendar of Virginia State Papers*, 1:129; McIlwaine, *Executive Journals*, 242.

53. Byrd, *History of the Dividing Line*, 26–27, 34.

54. Lefler and Powell, *Colonial North Carolina*, 195–97; "Lord Culpeper to Lords of trade and Plantations," December 12, 1681, in Fortescue, *Calendar of State Papers*, 11:155; "Letter from Lieutenant Governor Alexander Spotswood to the Laurence Hyde, Earl of Rochester," July 30, 1711, in Saunders, *Colonial Records of North Carolina*, 1:798; F. Johnson, *Tales from Old Carolina*, 41, 153.

55. Morris, "'Running Servants and All Others,'" 92–95; Morris, *Dismal Freedom*, 22, 26–27, 37–39; Leaming, *Hidden Americans*, 61, 124, 179–82, 223–24; Hadden, *Slave Patrols*, 32–33; G. Mullin, *Flight and Rebellion*, 110–11.

56. Powell, *North Carolina Through Four Centuries*, 105, 112; Hadden, *Slave Patrols*, 32. Hadden estimates that in the 1720s, there were only two thousand Black people in the colony while there were a total of between four thousand and five thousand white people.

57. Cecelski, *Waterman's Song*, 4, 8, 11; P. Morgan, *Slave Counterpoint*, 48.

58. Sayers, *Desolate Place for a Defiant People*, 2–3, 87, 114. Consistent with this evidence, Sayers argues that "after 1680 or so" the swamp's population consisted of "mostly African American Maroons." Leaming notes that by the 1730s, most colonists "thought of the maroons of the Dismal Swamp as Black, rather than Indian or white." See Leaming, *Hidden Americans*, 231.

59. Cecelski, *Waterman's Song*, 5–8.

60. Grandy, "Narrative of Moses Grandy," in Andrews, *North Carolina Slave Narratives*, 159, 176.

61. Smith, *African American Environmental Thought*, 5; Blum, "Power, Danger, and Control," 249.

62. David Hunter Strother, "The Dismal Swamp," *Harper's Monthly*, September 1856, 448; "The Game of the Dismal Swamp," *Forest and Stream*, 38, no. 21 (May 5, 1892): 420; "The Dismal Swamp and Its Occupants," *Natural Science News*, 1, no. 31 (October 1895): 146; Diouf, *Slavery's Exiles*, 223–24; Sayers, *Desolate Place for a Defiant People*, 107; Leaming, *Hidden Americans*, 222; Sawyer, *America's Wetland*, 156; Silkenat, *Scars on the Land*, 138; Morris, *Dismal Freedom*, 22; US Fish and Wildlife Service, "Great Dismal Swamp Wildlife Refuge," accessed September 2024, www.fws.gov/refuge/great-dismal-swamp/species.

63. David Hunter Strother, "The Dismal Swamp," *Harper's Monthly* 13 (1856): 450. Daniel Sayers's Great Dismal Swamp Landscape Study (GDSLS) and archaeological survey found that raised ridges of forested dry land throughout the swamp's interior, or mesic islands, can range in size from "approximately one acre to thirty-nine acres," and "come in clusters or groupings in which the distances between islands are relatively limited (anywhere from about 50 feet to 1,500 feet of swamp [water] separating two given landforms)." Sayers, *Desolate Place for a Defiant People*, 22–23.

64. Edmund Jackson, "The Virginia Maroons," *Liberty Bell*, January 1, 1852, 145.

65. Grandy, "Narrative of Moses Grandy," in Andrews, *North Carolina Slave Narratives*, 176.

66. Jacobs, *Incidents in the Life of a Slave Girl*, 126–27.

67. William Byrd, "The History of the Dividing Line betwixt Virginia and North Carolina Run in the Year of Our Lord 1728," in Berland, *Dividing Line Histories*, 109, 372; Byrd, "Earliest Passage Through the Dismal Swamp," 594.

68. Smyth, *A Tour in the United States of America*, 64, 147–48.

69. "Some Account of the Great Dismal Swamp," *Literary Magazine and American Register* 3, no. 18 (March 1805): 170.

70. Sharla Fett points to the Black American "notion of a spiritually enlivened landscape" in the United States South. See Fett, *Working Cures*, 77–78.

71. Blum, "Power, Danger, and Control," 249–55.

72. Bass, "Mojo," 384–86.

73. Dawson, *Undercurrents of Power*, 192–93.

74. Mellon, *Bullwhip Days*, 191.

75. *Edenton (NC) Gazette*, March 2, 1819.

76. Cowan, *Slave in the Swamp*, 62; Camp, *Closer to Freedom*, 6, 60; Givens, *Fugitive Pedagogy*, 28.

77. Cowan, *Slave in the Swamp*, 62.

78. "Peter Randolph, a Former Virginia Slave," in Mintz, *African American Voices*, 142–43.

79. Grandy, "Narrative of Moses Grandy," in Andrews, *North Carolina Slave Narratives*, 171.

80. Alexis Wells-Oghoghomeh points to a range of spiritual and ancestral powers that animated the natural world and gave it meaning, rooted in African Indigenous cosmology, including the symbology and mythology of birds, whose ability to fly often elevated their status and significance among other animals. Wells-Oghoghomeh, *Souls of Womenfolk*, 164–65. Ideas connecting birds in flight to the freedom due Black people can be found in other slave narratives. For example, James Curry, formerly enslaved in North Carolina, remembered that he "would look at the birds as they flew over [his] head or sung their free songs upon the trees, and think it strange that, of all God's creatures, the poor negro only was held in bondage." See James Curry, "Narrative of James Curry, A Fugitive Slave," *The Liberator*, January 10, 1840.

81. Camp, *Closer to Freedom*, 6–7.

82. The once-solitary Cuban maroon Esteban Montejo, for example, "remember[ed] well the birds in the woods." He recalled, "I became accustomed to hearing them. I really believed they were watching out for me." Barnet, *Biography of a Runaway Slave*, 53–55.

83. Bayley, *Narrative of Some Remarkable Incidents*, 9–11.

84. Cowan, *Slave in the Swamp*, 63.

85. Smith, *African American Environmental Thought*, 24, 27.

86. Blum, "Power, Danger, and Control," 261.

87. "Adeline Crump," in Federal Writers' Project, *Slave Narratives*, 11:84, 204.

88. "John Brown (b. 1860)," in Perdue et al., *Weevils in the Wheat*, 62.

89. This account is taken from Blum, "Power, Danger, and Control," 261.

90. Blum, "Power, Danger, and Control," 256–57; Wells-Oghoghomeh, *Souls of Womenfolk*, 136–38.

91. Fett, *Working Cures*, 5.

92. "May Satterfield (b. 1861)," in Perdue et al., *Weevils in the Wheat*, 244, 246.

93. "Sarah Louise Augustus, Age 80 Years," in Federal Writers' Project, *Slave Narratives*, 11:51, 54.

94. Mellon, *Bullwhip Days*, 95–96; "Marrinda Jane Singleton (b. 1840)," in Perdue et al., *Weevils in the Wheat*, 267–68; Wells-Oghoghomeh, *Souls of Womenfolk*, 212.

95. Mellon, *Bullwhip Days*, 97–98; Blum, "Power, Danger, and Control," 257.

96. Grandy, "Narrative of Moses Grandy," in Andrews, *North Carolina Slave Narratives*, 170.

97. F. Johnson, *Tales from Old Carolina*, 47–48. One visitor to the swamp wrote in 1881 that the swamp is a "perfect magazine of medicinal barks and roots and herbs." See Alfred Trumbull, "Through the Dismal Swamp," *Frank Leslie's Popular Monthly* 2, no. 4 (April 1881): 409.

98. Benjamin Golden, "'Very Fond of Spirituous Liquors,'" 14, 19–20.

99. Goode, "Engaging the Tools of Resistance," 219, 241–45.

100. Eddins, "'Rejoice!,'" 562, 574; A. Thompson, "Gender and Marronage in the Caribbean," 274; Price, *Maroon Societies*, 331; Terborg-Penn, "Black Women in Resistance," 197, 199–201; Bush, *Slave Women in Caribbean Society*, 73–77, 155.

101. Trumbull, "Through the Dismal Swamp," 409.

102. Ledoux, *Princess Anne*, vi, 39, 68–71.

103. This position builds from Chelsea Frazier's assertion that "it is normal, appropriate, and bewitching to witness [Black women] luxuriate in [their] environments and that these resources that we call 'nature' are available—not just for our work—but for Black women's leisure, healing, and living!" See Frazier, "Black Feminist Ecological Thought."

104. "Mrs. Louise Jones (b. ca. 1855)," in Perdue et al., *Weevils in the Wheat*, 186.

CHAPTER 2

1. Walsh, *From Calabar to Carter's Grove*, 9–12, 20–21, 47–49.

2. "Isle of Wight County Records," 312; Walsh, *From Calabar to Carter's Grove*, 15; Haverty King, *Historical Notes on Isle of Wight County*, 437.

3. A conflicting record written by Mary in 1778 states with greater confidence that Nelly was the daughter of "Zeny," or, likely, the "Zenith" that also appears here. It is possible that the ailing Robert Burwell confused these lineages while adding to his 1772 will, which he amended in order to include Mary, whom he married at the end of December 1774. If so, this would suggest that Venus lived with only one sister in the home—Rachel. "Isle of Wight County Records," 312. *Virginia Gazette*, July 10, 1778.

4. Washington, *Papers of George Washington*, 271–73; Royster, *Fabulous History*, 82–83; Morris, *Dismal Freedom*, 58, 60.

5. Nevius, *City of Refuge*, 26; Royster, *Fabulous History*, 96–97.

6. Legal Records, 1665–1832, Folder 1, Box 6, DSLC.

7. Byrd, "Proposal to Drain the Dismal Swamp," 521–24.

8. "Jacob Collee to David Jamison, Esquire," December 26, 1784, Correspondence, 1688–1791, Folder 1, Box 7, DSLC.

9. Shingles were an essential wood product and a staple in the construction of houses, buildings, farmsteads, plantations, and growing local townships.

10. Royster, *Fabulous History*, 98; Morris, *Dismal Freedom*, 62; Nevius, *City of Refuge*, 26.

11. Adventurers for Draining the Dismal Swamp, "Ledger A, 1750–1772: pg. 194," May 3, 1766, George Washington Financial Papers Project, accessed August 18, 2024, http://financial.gwpapers.org/?q=content/ledger-1750-1772-pg194.

12. Byrd, "Proposal to Drain the Dismal Swamp," 523; Thorne Kent, *Swampers*, v.

13. Hartman, "Venus in Two Acts," 1–2, 8. Barbara Bush adds that as the slave trade expanded, "European perceptions of the 'African woman' condensed into three homogenizing but contradictory stereotypes; the wanton 'whore,' romanticized as the 'Sable Venus'; the passive drudge subordinated to lazy, dominant African men as slaves, or in polygamous marriages; and the powerful 'witch' who metamorphosed into the rebellious slave 'she devil.'" See Bush, "'Daughters of Injur'd Africk,'" 675. Daniel Sayers alludes to this pervasive sexual economy as it may have pertained to Burwell's Venus in writing that the name was "a code word for sexual activities." Sayers, *Desolate Place for a Defiant People*, 191.

14. Washington, *Papers of George Washington*, 314–15; Royster, *Fabulous History*, 98; Morris, *Dismal Freedom*, 62; Nevius, *City of Refuge*, 26.

15. "Jacob Collee to David Jaimeson, Esq.," December 12, 1782, Correspondence, 1688–1791, Folder 1, Box 7, DSLC.

16. *Virginia Gazette*, June 23, 1768; October 6, 1768; April 13, 1769; Washington, *Papers of George Washington*, 315; "Jacob Collee to David Jamison, Esquire," December 26, 1784, Correspondence, 1688–1791, Folder 1, Box 7, DSLC; Royster, *Fabulous History*, 147; Morris, *Dismal Freedom*, 63–64; Nevius, *City of Refuge*, 26–28.

17. For example, DSC officials reported that another "likely Negro fellow by the name of Tom" had "been out almost two years" in 1782 but was caught in 1784 after four years of marronage, alongside Lewis who was caught around the same time, after sixteen months of marronage. See "Jacob Collee to David Jaimeson, Esq.," December 12, 1782; "Jacob Collee to David Jamison, Esquire," December 26, 1784; "John Driver," August 26, 1786; "John Driver to David Jameson," September 24, 1789, all in Correspondence, 1688–1791, Folder 1, Box 7, DSLC. See also Royster, *Fabulous History*, 147; Nevius, *City of Refuge*, 30.

18. Byrd, "Proposal to Drain the Dismal Swamp," 524; "Memo of Wills Cooper," February 1783, Correspondence, 1688–1791, Folder 1, Box 7, DSLC.

19. Brent Tarter and Dictionary of Virginia Biography, "Robert Burwell (1720–1777)," *Encyclopedia Virginia*, accessed September 1, 2024, https://encyclopediavirginia.org/entries/burwell-robert-1720-1777.

20. William Byrd, "The History of the Dividing Line betwixt Virginia and North Carolina Run in the Year of Our Lord 1728," in Berland, *Dividing Line Histories*, 103, 109, 372; Byrd, "The Earliest Passage Through the Dismal Swamp," 597; *Virginia Gazette*, December 5, 1771; *Virginia Gazette*, January 30, 1772; *Virginia Gazette*, April 2, 1772; "Isle of Wight County Records," 312.

21. Grandy, "Narrative of Moses Grandy," in Andrews, *North Carolina Slave Narratives*, 169.

22. Royster, *Fabulous History*, 98.

23. *Virginia Gazette*, December 5, 1771; *Virginia Gazette*, January 30, 1772; *Virginia Gazette*, April 2, 1772.

24. W. Johnson, *Soul by Soul*, 215.

25. Franklin and Schweninger, *Runaway Slaves*, 98.

26. Camp, *Closer to Freedom*, 35–39.

27. Nevius, *City of Refuge*, 55–57.

28. Diouf, *Slavery's Exiles*, 89. Exceptions to these "extremely rare" opportunities for women to leave the plantation include permission granted to midwives, or for "truly special occasions." See also Camp, *Closer to Freedom*, 30–32, 34, 38.

29. Cheryl LaRoche has called this lack of socio-geographical knowledge and experience "spatial illiteracy," which Black women often overcome by escaping in groups. See LaRoche, "Coerced but Not Subdued," 61.

30. Franklin and Schweninger, *Runaway Slaves*, 239, 251; William Byrd, "July, 1710," in *Secret Diary of William Byrd*, 199; Moses Roper, "A Narrative of the Adventures and Escape of Moses Roper, from American Slavery," in Andrews, *North Carolina Slave Narratives*, 46.

31. Camp, *Closer to Freedom*, 33, 42, 57–58; Cook Bell, *Running from Bondage*, 32, 48, 85.

32. This does not mean that enslaved men were not valued and respected in their communities, or that they did not feel tied to or committed to their families and their children. This also does not mean that no women or mothers chose to become permanent or far-removed fugitives. The point remains that these gendered factors amount to the advantages of being male in a patriarchal society, and as a result, more men had greater ability and opportunity to practice enduring forms of flight and fugitivity in greater numbers and with greater frequency than women.

33. Franklin and Schweninger, *Runaway Slaves*, 212; Camp, *Closer to Freedom*, 38.

34. The classification of borderland marronage refers to those maroons who lived in woods and swamps nearby, bordering, and adjoining slaveholding towns and the broader plantation world. *Petit* marronage, can be defined as short-term flight toward wilderness spaces, "without intending to remain indefinitely in flight or to escape permanently." See Nevius, *City of Refuge*, 7.

35. Franklin and Schweninger, *Runaway Slaves*, 98; Camp, *Closer to Freedom*, 54.

36. Similar trends are found throughout the Atlantic world. Gad Heuman has shown that in Barbados, between the years 1807 and 1834, 63.5 percent of the people running away were men, and 36.5 percent were women. See Gad Heuman's chapter, "Runaway Slaves in Nineteenth-Century Barbados," in Heuman, *Out of the House of Bondage*, 4, 98. Barbara Bush reports that over 60 percent of absconders in the Caribbean were men. Bush, *Slave Women in Caribbean Society*, 64–65. Michael Mullin estimates that between the 1730s and 1805, female "runaways" made up 11 percent of all escapees in Virginia, 24 percent in Jamaica, 21 percent in South Carolina, 34 percent in Barbados, and 18 percent in Georgia. See M. Mullin, *Africa in America*, 290.

37. *Virginia Gazette*, December 5, 1771; *Virginia Gazette*, January 30, 1772; *Virginia Gazette*, April 2, 1772.

38. Franklin and Schweninger, *Runaway Slaves*, 211–12.

39. M. Mullin, *Africa in America*, 290.

40. Franklin and Schweninger, *Runaway Slaves*, 211–12.

41. Parker, *Running for Freedom*, 69, 106.

42. LaRoche, "Coerced but Not Subdued," 58–59; Fox-Genovese, *Within the Plantation Household*, 304; Wood, *Black Majority*, 240.

43. Parker, *Running for Freedom*, 6.

44. Thorne Kent, *Swampers*, v.

45. "Jordan Johnson (b. 1848)," in Perdue et al., *Weevils in the Wheat*, 160.

46. "Susan Mabry (b. 1850)," in Perdue et al., *Weevils in the Wheat,* 199; "Jane Arrington, 84 Years Old," in Federal Writers' Project, *Slave Narratives,* 11:45–47.

47. "Elizabeth Sparks (b. 1841)," in Perdue et al., *Weevils in the Wheat,* 274–75.

48. "Mrs. Fannie Berry, (b. 1841)," in Perdue et al., *Weevils in the Wheat,* 45.

49. Grandy, "Narrative of Moses Grandy," in Andrews, *North Carolina Slave Narratives,* 166.

50. "Elizabeth Sparks (b. 1841)," in Perdue et al., *Weevils in the Wheat,* 274.

51. "Mrs. Katie Blackwell Johnson (b. 1860)," in Perdue et al., *Weevils in the Wheat,* 161–62.

52. "Mrs. Minnie Fulkes," in Federal Writers' Project, *Slave Narratives,* 17:11.

53. Jacobs, *Incidents in the Life of a Slave Girl,* 88, 96, 106–9, 112–13, 126–27; "$100 Reward," *American Beacon,* July 4, 1835.

54. Grandy, "Narrative of Moses Grandy," in Andrews, *North Carolina Slave Narratives,* 166.

55. Jacobs, *Incidents in the Life of a Slave Girl,* 96.

56. Walsh, *From Calabar to Carter's Grove,* 211; Royster, *Fabulous History,* 150; Brent Tarter and Dictionary of Virginia Biography, "Robert Burwell (1720–1777)," *Encyclopedia Virginia,* accessed September 20, 2024, https://encyclopediavirginia.org/entries/burwell-robert-1720-1777.

57. "To Be Sold," *Virginia Gazette,* May 16, 1771.

58. *Virginia Gazette,* December 5, 1771; January 30, 1772; and April 2, 1772; "Isle of Wight County Records," 312.

59. *Virginia Gazette,* July 10, 1778.

60. Franklin and Schweninger, *Runaway Slaves,* 211.

61. Diouf, *Slavery's Exiles,* 91; Cook Bell, *Running from Bondage,* 11.

62. *Elizabeth-City Star and North-Carolina Eastern Intelligencer,* August 10, 1833.

63. *North Carolina Journal,* January 13, 1799.

64. *North Carolina Minerva and Raleigh Advertiser,* September 4, 1803.

65. A. Thompson, "Gender and Marronage in the Caribbean," 265–67; Eddins, "'Rejoice!,'" 570.

66. For example, the French colonist M. L. E. Moreau de Saint-Méry described the abduction of Anne—an enslaved housekeeper—by the maroon leader Kébinda during a maroon raid in Saint-Domingue. Saint-Méry reported that Anne had to be "tied up and pulled along by force" by the man, in order for her to join him. See M. L. E. Moreau de Saint-Méry, "The Border Maroons of Saint-Domingue: Le Maniel," in Price, *Maroon Societies,* 137.

67. Bell Cook, *Running from Bondage,* 83–84.

68. Camp, *Closer to Freedom,* 7, 47–48, 51.

69. "Mrs. Fannie Berry, (b. 1841)," in Perdue et al., *Weevils in the Wheat,* 34.

70. "Cornelia Carney, (b. 1838)," in Perdue et al., *Weevils in the Wheat,* 66–67.

71. Redpath, *Roving Editor,* 289–91.

72. "$50 Reward," *Edenton (NC) Gazette,* February 1, 1811.

73. "$30 Reward," *Old North State,* August 4, 1849.

74. "$20 Reward," *Democratic Pioneer,* January 5, 1858.

75. *Herald of Freedom,* March 27, 1799.

76. "25 Dollars Reward," *Edenton (NC) Gazette,* June 16, 1808.

77. "$50 Reward," *Spirit of the Age,* March 15, 1854.

78. Berry and Gross, *A Black Women's History of the United States,* 78.

79. Douglass, "The Heroic Slave," 190–92.

80. Grandy, "Narrative of Moses Grandy," in Andrews, *North Carolina Slave Narratives*, 176.

81. Walsh, *From Calabar to Carter's Grove*, 46; Byrd, "April, 1709," "May, 1709," in *Secret Diary of William Byrd*, 28–30.

82. Byrd, "April, 1709," "May, 1709," "June, 1710," "July, 1710," "November, 1710," in *Secret Diary of William Byrd*, 28–30, 195–97, 199, 202, 254, 257.

83. "$20 Reward," *Old North State*, February 24, 1849.

84. "Seventy-Five Dollars Reward," *American Beacon and Commercial Diary*, October 8, 1816.

85. *Norfolk Herald*, March 20, 1800.

86. "$10 Reward," *Edenton (NC) Gazette*, March 24, 1829.

87. "Ten Dollars Reward, Will be Given for the Apprehension and Securing of Negro Woman Pendar," *American Beacon and Commercial Diary*, August 8, 1817.

88. *Norfolk Herald*, July 8, 1800.

89. *Norfolk Herald*, June 9, 1803.

90. "Run-Away," *Raleigh Star*, September 13, 1810.

91. "Runaway from the Subscriber, About 12 or 15 Days Ago, a Negro Girl, Maria," *American Beacon and Commercial Diary*, October 2, 1817.

92. Hunter, *Bound in Wedlock*, 6, 80–83.

93. *Virginia Gazette*, December 5, 1771; January 30, 1772; April 2, 1772; February 18, 1773.

94. Walsh, *From Calabar to Carter's Grove*, 207–9; *Virginia Gazette*, February 18, 1773.

95. "Thirty Dollars Reward," *Free Press*, November 28, 1826.

96. "100 Dollars Reward," *Edenton (NC) Gazette*, May 11, 1819.

97. *Norfolk Herald*, August 11, 1803.

98. "$10 Reward," *Edenton (NC) Gazette*, July 13, 1831.

99. "20 Dollars Reward," *Edenton (NC) Gazette*, June 9, 1818.

100. "20 Dollars Reward," *Edenton (NC) Gazette*, April 27, 1808; "10 Dollars Reward," *Edenton (NC) Gazette*, May 7, 1827.

101. "Isle of Wight County Records," 312; "Marriages," *Virginia Gazette*, January 7, 1775.

102. *Virginia Gazette*, July 10, 1778; "Isle of Wight County Records," 312; Walsh, *From Calabar to Carter's Grove*, 211–12, 214; Brent Tarter and Dictionary of Virginia Biography, "Robert Burwell (1720–1777)," *Encyclopedia Virginia*, accessed October 1, 2024, https://encyclopediavirginia.org/entries/burwell-robert-1720-1777.

103. Bell Cook, *Running from Bondage*, 61.

104. Hodges, *Black Loyalist Directory*, xii; Bell Cook, *Running from Bondage*, 80; Morris, *Dismal Freedom*, 70–71.

105. Hodges, *The Black Loyalist Directory*, xi–xiv, xix.

106. Hodges, *The Black Loyalist Directory*, xi–xiv, xix, 183–85, 188–89.

107. *Virginia Gazette*, July 10, 1778; "Isle of Wight County Records," 312.

108. Walsh, *From Calabar to Carter's Grove*, 214; *Virginia Gazette*, July 10, 1778; "Isle of Wight County Records," 312.

109. "Forty Dollars Reward," *Edenton (NC) Gazette*, May 8, 1827.

110. "Five Dollars Reward," *Elizabeth-City Star and North-Carolina Eastern Intelligencer*, July 21, 1827.

111. Daniel Sayers asserts that Venus and Jack "both fled to the morass." Sayers, *Desolate Place for a Defiant People*, 89. Ted Maris-Wolf suggests the same. See Maris-Wolf, "Between

Slavery and Freedom," 43. Although Brent Morris misses the 1778 posting in the *Virginia Gazette* and incorrectly suggests that Jack Dismal was listed in the 1783 *Nesbit* registration book, he does agree that Venus, at least, "may have finally found her permanent freedom." See Morris, *Dismal Freedom*, 64, 71.

112. The Dismal Swamp Company came to an end in 1814 but was then reincorporated by the efforts of the Dismal Swamp Land Company. See Royster, *Fabulous History*, 342, 423; Nevius, *City of Refuge*, 28–37, 42, 55–56; Morris, *Dismal Freedom*, 76; Bell Cook, *Running from Bondage*, 144–45. Descriptions of some of the youngest boys hired to perform the grueling work of digging ditches and canals in the swamp include the following: "Stephen the property of Archibald Brinkly of Nansemond County, Virginia hired by Willis S. Riddick of said county and by him registered as one of his hands in the Dismal Swamp. Stephen is dark brown about twelve years old high round forehead, scar on the left side of the forehead and two scars on the right. He stands without shoes four feet 3 ¼ inches." Similarly, "Isaac the property of Mills Riddick deed of Suffolk Virginia and hired the present year by Willis S. Riddick of said county Nansemond Virginia and by him registered as one of the hands in the Dismal Swamp. Isaac is about ten years old without scars of any kind. Shows his teeth a little when his mouth is shut. Is four feet one inch high with shoes off." Entries entered March 2, 1847, in Fouts, *Registration of Slaves to Work in the Dismal Swamp*, 11.

113. State of North Carolina, *Laws of the State of North Carolina*. For just one record evidencing persistent flight plaguing canal and lumber companies even well after this 1847 law, see *Democratic Pioneer*, May 6, 1856.

CHAPTER 3

1. Less enduring *petit* maroons "did not go very far from the plantation from which they fled, but remained on its edges," pillaging, stealing, and committing other crimes to subsist. See Gabriel Debien, "Marronage in the French Caribbean," in Price, *Maroon Societies*, 107. Diouf has defined borderland maroons as those living and operating at the borders between Southern wilderness and cities, towns, farms, and plantations. Diouf, *Slavery's Exiles*, 10. With respect to the Great Dismal Swamp, Morris has defined fringe maroons as those who "settled at the edge of the swamp, strategically situated for easy access to both the interior of the swamp and outside world if and when they needed it." See Morris, *Dismal Freedom*, 97. Elsewhere, I have referred to these "fringe" maroons as peripheral swamp maroons. Benjamin Golden, "'Armed in the Great Swamp,'" 5.

2. Warfare here, including "guerilla warfare," is defined as spontaneous, organized, and/or irregular small group combat, including raids, ambush, sabotage, and attack and retreat against a less flexible, and often, arrogantly unsuspecting authority.

3. Williams, "Colonel George Blow," 435. This account refers to the activities of a "most daring and lofty villain"—the "self styled runaway" General Sampson—operating near the Dismal Swamp in Sussex and Southampton Counties. See also Schwarz, *Twice Condemned*, 276.

4. *Edenton (NC) Gazette*, May 11, 1819.

5. F. Johnson, *Tales from Old Carolina*, 155–56; Morris, *Dismal Freedom*, 82–83.

6. *Argus of Western America*, March 10, 1824; *North Carolina Free Press*, May 7, 1824; *Norfolk and Portsmouth Herald*, June 24, 1824; *Fayetteville Weekly Observer*, May 20, 1824. For more

on this group of maroons, see also Morris, *Dismal Freedom*, 86–87; Diouf, *Slavery's Exiles*, 240–41; Schwarz, *Twice Condemned*, 276–77; Parramore, *Southampton County Virginia*, 70–71.

7. Franklin and Schweninger, *Runaway Slaves*, 211–12; Diouf, *Slavery's Exiles*, 89; Cook Bell, *Running from Bondage*, 17.

8. In the context of (urban) slavery, Tiya Miles has aptly defined the force of violence as tripartite: "the force of physical violence, the force of psychological threat, the force of intimidating brick, stone, and iron environments," or the force of geographies of captivity and control. See Miles, *All That She Carried*, 170. Elizabeth Hinton has argued that twentieth-century violent eruptions and rebellions are instructive because they "did not represent a wave of criminality, but a sustained insurgency" brought on by unmet needs and an "inevitable" historical trend against injustice. See Hinton, *America on Fire*, 7, 14–15. Other works that emphasize anti-Black violence as a continued fixture in Black life include Lindsey, *America, Goddam*; and Sharpe, *In the Wake*. See also Hannah-Jones et al., *1619 Project*.

9. Fanon, *Wretched of the Earth*, 61, 94.

10. Nikki Taylor has referred to enslaved women's deliberate violence as "reciprocating *mercilessness*." See N. Taylor, *Brooding Over Bloody Revenge*, 58. Tamika Nunley and Vincent Brown agree that slavery and "slave trade catalyzed ongoing diasporic warfare." See Nunley, *Demands of Justice*, 145; Brown, *Tacky's Revolt*, 4. Marcus Nevius adds that the constancy of slave revolts and related practices of marronage evidence how exchanges in global warfare—including slave resistance and European retaliation and military efforts at prevention—provide an important context for the study of Atlantic world slavery. See Nevius, "Global Warfare," 538; and Williams, *Negroes with Guns*. Kwame Nkrumah has argued that "revolutionary warfare is the logical, inevitable answer to the political, economic and social situation" preventing independence and liberation from enemy control. See Nkrumah, *Handbook of Revolutionary Warfare*, 42.

11. In her discussion of fugitive and free Black violent resistance and militant abolitionism, Kellie Carter Jackson has argued that we should examine both Black women's and Black men's use of force as the "politics of protective violence"—the community-centered employment of force to protect "all vulnerable people" and "ultimately promote the overthrow of slavery." See Carter Jackson, "'Dare You Meet a Woman,'" 271. See also Carter Jackson, *Force and Freedom*, 8–9. Jasmin Young makes a similar argument as to the value of armed defense as "the protection of human life, dignity and property through the use of force to counter violence inflicted by others." See Young, "Gloria Richardson, Armed Self-Defense," 216–17.

12. Holden, *Surviving Southampton*, 5.

13. Gross, *Hannah Mary Tabbs*, 151.

14. Deborah Gray White notes that enslaved women used force much as enslaved men did. Though she also acknowledges that "women chose violent resistance, particularly that which involved fisticuffs, less often than did men." See D. White, *Aren't I A Woman*, 78. For work on enslaved women and everyday resistance, see Camp, *Closer to Freedom*.

15. Glymph, *Out of the House of Bondage*, 36–37, 67; Bouton, *Setting Slavery's Limits*, 60–63, 89–114; Taylor, *Brooding Over Bloody Revenge*, 8–9.

16. "Mrs. Fannie Berry (b. 1841)," in Perdue et al., *Weevils in the Wheat*, 36.

17. Wyndham Robertson Executive Papers, 1836–1837, Accession 43097, Box 1, Folder 1, State Records Collection, LVRV. Black women who chose defensive violence against slavery

and sexual assault were routinely criminalized and executed. See Nunley, *Demands of Justice*, 92–93. Another prime example is explored in McLaurin, *Celia*.

18. "Catharine Miles," 1798, Executed, Box 1, Folder 15, CS-LVRV.

19. "H. Dougherty Estate," 1821, Executed, Box 2, Folder 20, CS-LVRV.

20. Taylor, *Brooding Over Bloody Revenge*, 36, 50.

21. "Thomas Lawson," 1803, Executed, Box 2, Folder 2, CS-LVRV.

22. "From the *Norfolk Herald*," *New York Evening Post*, August 7, 1818.

23. *Commonwealth*, July 17, 1863; *Freeman's Record*, March 1865.

24. Edda L. Fields Black uses Harriet Tubman's count of 756 enslaved people freed during the raid. See Fields Black, *Combhee*, 352. See also Dunbar, *She Came to Slay*, 74, 91–93.

25. A paw is a graspable, handheld weapon with iron prongs, intended to be used at close encounter. Still, *Underground Railroad*, 99.

26. Another interpretation of her exclamation is that, looking the promise of capture squarely in the face, she dared her would-be captor, "Shoot!, shoot!! shoot!!!" Still, *Underground Railroad*, 124–25.

27. Still, *Underground Railroad*, 124–29.

28. Michel Rolph Trouillot points to the ways dominant records and archives work hard to "repress the unthinkable"—above all, that Africans and African descendants were capable of "[formulating] strategies for gaining and securing freedom." This unthinkability applies even more to Africans and African descendants who are women and girls. See Trouillot, *Silencing the Past*, 72–73.

29. "West Turner (b. 1842)," in Perdue et al., *Weevils in the Wheat*, 288–89.

30. "Poquosin" is the early seventeenth-century English spelling of the Algonquian word meaning "swamp-on-a-hill." "Pocosin" became the standard spelling and a colloquialism for swamp into the nineteenth century. See Kirby, *Poquosin*, xii.

31. Jarrett, *Wiley Blackwell Anthology of African American Literature*, 1:436n142.

32. Benjamin Golden, "'Armed in the Great Swamp,'" 1, 11, 16, 18, 25; Olmsted, *A Journey*, 77–78.

33. *Edenton (NC) Gazette*, March 22, 1811; J. Morgan, *Reckoning with Slavery*, 235.

34. *Edenton (NC) Gazette*, March 22, 1811.

35. *Edenton (NC) Gazette*, November 18, 1807; October 5, 1808. Aptheker points to "fire and other casualties" that exacerbated a pre-existing, general sense of unrest amongst the white inhabitants of Edenton in 1807 and 1808, leading to heightened vigilance and policing of Black mobility. Aptheker, *American Negro Slave Revolts*, 145. See also Morris, *Dismal Freedom*, 80–81.

36. Edward Fentress enslaved two people in 1810. See James, "Slave Owners in Princess Anne County, Virginia," 55.

37. "Catharine," April 6, 1835, Box 1, Folder 2, RES-LVRV.

38. Eaves, *Sexual Violence and American Slavery*; Berry and Harris, *Sexuality and Slavery*.

39. *Edenton (NC) Gazette*, March 22, 1811.

40. Diouf, *Slavery's Exiles*, 177; G. Hall, *Africans in Colonial Louisiana*, 216–19.

41. Diouf, *Slavery's Exiles*, 178–79; G. Hall, *Africans in Colonial Louisiana*, 226–27.

42. Diouf, *Slavery's Exiles*, 168; G. Hall, *Africans in Colonial Louisiana*, 232.

43. *Evening Post*, July 11, 1827; *Evening Post*, July 12, 1827. See also Aptheker, "Maroons Within the Limits," 177.

44. *Edenton (NC) Gazette*, March 22, 1811.

45. James Henry Hammond, "Plantation Records for Silver Bluff," October 16, 1835, James Henry Hammond Papers, South Caroliniana Library, University of South Carolina, Columbia, South Carolina.

46. "Lindsey Faucette, 86 Years Old, Ex-Slave," in Federal Writers' Project, *Slave Narratives*, 11:304.

47. Glymph, *Out of the House of Bondage*, 80, 84–90.

48. Yellin, "Incidents Abroad," 159; Benjamin Golden, "'Armed in the Great Swamp,'" 2.

49. Jacobs, *Incidents in the Life of a Slave Girl*, 126.

50. Jacobs, *Incidents in the Life of a Slave Girl*, 125–26.

51. F. Johnson, *Tales from Old Carolina*, 37–38.

52. Jacobs, *Incidents in the Life of a Slave Girl*, 179.

53. Jacobs, *Incidents in the Life of a Slave Girl*, 126–27.

54. *Norfolk Herald*, June 23, 1818. See also *New York Evening Post*, July 7, 1818. In Princess Anne County, it was not unusual for disgruntled poor white men to consort with, aid, or fail to report maroon activities and whereabouts. See Bouton, *Setting Slavery's Limits*, 121–25. See also Morris, *Dismal Freedom*, 83; Benjamin Golden, "'Armed in the Great Swamp,'" 23.

55. *Norfolk Herald*, June 23, 1818.

56. Knight, *Black Elders*, 4; Terborg-Penn, "Black Women in Resistance," 190, 202. Barbara Bush also notes that "women, especially older women . . . wield great power and influence" as spiritual, political, and military leaders in the social organization of African and African descendant communities across the Diaspora. See Bush, *Slave Women in Caribbean Society*, 68.

57. Patterson, "Slavery and Slave Revolts," xvi.

58. Gottlieb, *Mother of Us All*, xvi; Kopytoff, "Maroons of Jamaica," 208.

59. Thicknesse, *Memoirs and Anecdotes of Philip Thicknesse*, 74.

60. Aptheker, *American Negro Slave Revolts*, 91; Parramore, *Cradle of the Colony*. See also Porter, *County Government in Virginia*, 178–79.

61. *Norfolk and Portsmouth Herald*, October 5, 1813. There was good reason for authorities to suspect maroon collusion with the British. Following the last colonial Virginia Governor, John Murray, Lord Dunmore's Proclamation of 1775, which offered freedom to enslaved people joining force with British Loyalists, there were "indications that maroons made up a not-insignificant portion of Dunmore's troops." See Morris, *Dismal Freedom*, 68–71; Leaming, *Hidden Americans*, 233–39.

62. "Negro Hunt," *Pittsburgh Weekly Gazette*, January 5, 1819; *American Beacon*, December 17, 1818; *Baltimore Patriot*, December 21, 1818; *Pittsburgh Weekly Gazette*, January 5, 1819.

63. The "murderous Mingo" is referenced in Forrest, *Historical and Descriptive Sketches*, 445–46.

64. "Petition of Princess Anne County citizens," December 1–11, 1818, Oversize file on the trial of Mingo, Princess Anne County, CS-LVRV; Bouton, *Setting Slavery's Limits*, 126; Morris, *Dismal Freedom*, 84; Benjamin Golden, "'Armed in the Great Swamp,'" 23.

65. "Petition of Princess Anne County Citizens," December 1–11, 1818, Oversize file on the trial of Mingo, Princess Anne County, CS-LVRV; Princess Anne County Minute Book, February 19, 1819, LVRV.

66. Princess Anne County Minute Book, February 19, 1819, LVRV; "Letter to the Sheriff," December 7, 1818, Oversize file on the trial of Mingo, Princess Anne County, CS-LVRV; Benjamin Golden, "'Armed in the Great Swamp,'" 23.

67. "Negro Hunt," *Pittsburgh Weekly Gazette*, January 5, 1819; *American Beacon*, December 17, 1818; *Baltimore Patriot*, December 21, 1818; *Pittsburgh Weekly Gazette*, January 5, 1819.

68. *Edenton (NC) Gazette*, March 2, 1819; *American Beacon*, February 20, 1819. For more about Mingo's activities and demise, see "Murder and Robbery," *Alexandria Herald*, December 9, 1818; *Clarion and Tennessee State Gazette*, December 29, 1818; *American Beacon*, December 17, 1818; *Baltimore Patriot*, December 21, 1818; Coroner's Inquisitions, February 1819, Princess Anne County, LVRV; Oversize Accession Number 41737, Box 11, James Patton Preston Executive Papers, 1816–1819, LVRV; Benjamin Golden, "'Armed in the Great Swamp,'" 23–24; Bouton, *Setting Slavery's Limits*, 121–28; Morris, *Dismal Freedom*, 83–85.

69. *New York Evening Post*, June 30, 1823; "Deposition of Nelson and James," Accession Number 42046, Box 2, James Pleasant's Executive Papers, 1823, LVRV.

70. *Norfolk Herald*, June 29, 1818. This is the same Wilson Butt of Great Bridge who in 1802 reported that rebels in the Easter Rebellion had "embodied in large companies, armed, in the Great Swamp." See chapter 4, this volume, and "Negroes Again Troublesome!!!" *Norfolk Herald*, June 15, 1802.

71. *Norfolk Herald*, June 29, 1818.

72. "Deposition of Nelson and James," Accession Number 42046, Box 2, James Pleasant's Executive Papers, 1823, LVRV.

73. "A Serious Subject," *Norfolk Herald*, May 12, 1823. See also *New York Evening Post*, May 15, 1823; *Vermont Journal*, June 2, 1823. For accounts centering Bob Ferebee, none of which makes mention of Maria, see Benjamin Golden, "'Armed in the Great Swamp,'" 24–25; Morris, *Dismal Freedom*, 85–86; Aptheker, "Maroons Within the Present Limits," 177; Bogger, *Readings in Black and White*, 3–4; Sayers, *Desolate Place for a Defiant People*, 104; Bouton, *Setting Slavery's Limit*, 123; Schwarz, *Twice Condemned*, 276–77; Harding, *There Is a River*, 72–73.

74. "Will of Robert Butt," March 17, 1803, in Gable and Bonney, *Norfolk County Virginia Will Book 4*, 8; "Deposition of Nelson and James," Accession Number 42046, Box 2, James Pleasant's Executive Papers, 1823, LVRV.

75. "Will of Herbert Brothers," September 24, 1814, in Gable and Bonney, *Norfolk County Virginia Will Book 4*, 162.

76. "Deposition of Nelson and James," Accession Number 42046, Box 2, James Pleasant's Executive Papers, 1823, LVRV.

77. The deposition of Nelson, Maria's husband, states that at the fence, Maria told Nelson and James that "Mrs. Butt" told her that Manning was dead. This is a perplexing detail, as it suggests that the mistress of the house was inclined toward protecting, harboring, or otherwise aiding Maria against capture. This is not an impossibility, as there is some evidence that slaveholding white women assisted fugitives. Take for example, the "kind lady," described by Harriet Jacobs as being "unlike the majority of slaveholders' wives"—who agreed to conceal Jacobs for a time in the attic of her own home. Jacobs, *Incidents in the Life of a Slave Girl*, 111.

78. *New York Evening Post*, May 15, 1823; *New York Evening Post*, May 29, 1823; *New York Evening Post*, June 30, 1823; "Trials of Lewis and Jasper," May 31, 1823, Norfolk County, Box 4, CS-LVRV.

79. "A Serious Subject," *Norfolk Herald*, May 12, 1823. See also *New York Evening Post*, May 15, 1823.

80. "A Serious Subject," *Norfolk Herald*, May 12, 1823; Aptheker, "Maroons Within the Present Limits," 176.

81. *New York Evening Post*, May 29, 1823; Morris, *Dismal Freedom*, 85; *Norfolk and Portsmouth Daily Advertiser*, August 11, 1825; "Deposition of Nelson and James," Accession Number 42046, Box 2, James Pleasant's Executive Papers, 1823, LVRV.

82. "Trials of Lewis and Jasper," May 31, 1823, Norfolk County, Box 4, CS-LVRV; *New York Evening Post*, May 12, 1823; *New York Evening Post*, May 29, 1823; *New York Evening Post*, June 5, 1823; *New York Evening Post*, June 30, 1823.

83. *New York Evening Post*, May 29, 1823.

84. "Deposition of Nelson and James," Accession Number 42046, Box 2, James Pleasant's Executive Papers, 1823, LVRV.

85. "Trial of Bob Ferebee," June 1823, Princess Anne County, CS-LVRV.

86. *New York Evening Post*, May 29, 1823.

87. "Ten Dollars Reward," *American Beacon and Commercial Diary*, August 9, 1817. The ad does not specify which Butt she escaped from; however in 1803, a "Negro girl Racheal" was bequeathed to Arthur Lee Butt by his father, Nathaniel Butt Sr., alongside "two Negro boys Jack and Harry," Nathaniel's house and plantation, and "a part of the woodland running on a line down the swamp." If the "girl" Racheal (distinct from "Negro woman," a descriptive also used in the will to describe others) was nine years old when the will was written, she would have been twenty-three or twenty-four when the ad was written for the return of "Rachel" in 1817. See "Will of Nathaniel Butt, Sr.," June 16, 1803, in Gable and Bonney, *Norfolk County Virginia Will Book* 4, 30–31.

88. *Norfolk Herald*, March 19, 1803.

89. *Norfolk Herald*, March 1, 1803.

90. "Thirty Dollars Reward," *American Beacon and Commercial Diary*, December 8, 1818.

91. Virginia Historical Society, "Journals of the Council of Virginia in Executive Sessions, 1737–1763," *Virginia Magazine of History and Biography* 15, no. 4 (April 1908): 379–80.

92. Gross, *Hannah Mary Tabbs*, 161.

CHAPTER 4

1. Insurrection, organized rebellion, and revolt are used synonymously.

2. Parent, *Foul Means*, 152; Morris, *Dismal Freedom*, 47; Leaming, *Hidden Americans*, 225; Benjamin Golden, "'Armed in the Great Swamp,'" 14; Egerton, "'Fly Across the River,'" 87–110; Nevius, *City of Refuge*, 48–52. While historians such as Douglas Egerton have referred to the 1802 Easter Rebellion as a "slave conspiracy," others, such as Sally Hadden refer to it as a rebellion. See Hadden, *Slave Patrols*, 143, 147. This work names the Easter Rebellion of 1802 and treats the insurgent movements involving enslaved, fugitive, and maroon networks across the swampscape in 1802 as plotting, conspiracy, *and*—fundamentally—rebellion.

3. Vanessa Holden has argued that rebellion, revolt, and survival are best understood by centering communities not merely as "backdrops for resistive action," but as the "genesis of resistive action." See Holden, *Surviving Southampton*, 7.

4. Haverty King, *Historical Notes on Isle of Wight County*, 432–60.

5. "Letter of the Surry County Court," March 24, 1709, Box 144, Folder 20, CP-LVRV. See also Palmer, *Calendar of Virginia State Papers*, 1:129.

6. Morris, *Dismal Freedom*, 36. Parent agrees that this group of insurgents and maroons "conspired to escape by force of arms and settle in the North Carolina frontier of the Great Dismal Swamp." See Parent, *Foul Means*, 151.

7. McIlwaine, *Journals of the House of Burgesses of Virginia*, 270.

8. "Letter of Philip Ludwell," March 19, 1709, Box 144, Folder 20, CP-LVRV.

9. Middle Plantation, established in 1632 and subsequently known as Williamsburg, formed Middletown Parish of James City County in 1648. In 1674, Middletown Parish joined with Marston Parish (initially established within the limits of York County) and together formed Bruton Parish. See Goodwin, *Historical Sketch of Bruton Church*, 11.

10. "Order of Edmund Jenings," March 20, 1709, Box 144, Folder 20, CP-LVRV.

11. "Letter of the Surry County Court," March 24, 1709, Box 144, Folder 20, CP-LVRV. See also Palmer, *Calendar of Virginia State Papers*, 1:129.

12. McIlwaine, *Executive Journals*, 234, 573–74. See also, "Proclamation [against the] Illegal, Unusual and Unwarrantable Concourses, Meetings and Assembling Together of Negro, Mulatto, and Indian Slaves," March 29, 1709 [1710], London 5/1316, 166–69, Colonial Office, Public Record Office, Library of Congress.

13. Palmer, *Calendar of Virginia State Papers*, 1:129, 161; McIlwaine, *Executive Journals*, 234, 242.

14. Palmer, *Calendar of Virginia State Papers*, 1:130.

15. Palmer, *Calendar of Virginia State Papers*, 1:129–30.

16. Two weeks prior, Jenings wrote a letter to the Virginia Lords of Trade, dated April 4, 1710, in which he stated: "A conspiracy of Negroes discovered intended insurrection to have been on Easter day—two of the chief have been tried and found guilty and will be executed." The two in question were likely Scipio and Salvadore, executed the following month. See William Noel Sainsbury, Vol. III, 142, Virginia Manuscripts, British Public Record Office, LVRV.

17. McIlwaine, *Executive Journals*, 235–36.

18. Shortly after Alexander Spotswood was appointed Lieutenant Governor of Virginia in the spring of 1710, "there sprang up the rumor of a slave conspiracy in Surry County." See Bruce, *History of Virginia*, 301. See also Hening, *Statutes at Large*, 537–38; McIlwaine, *Journals of the House of Burgesses of Virginia*, 270.

19. McIlwaine, *Executive Journals*, 575.

20. McIlwaine, *Executive Journals*, 242–43, 246. The diary kept by William Byrd II, who was present at the council held at Williamsburg on April 18 and 21, 1710, reveals that several of the council enjoyed drinking French wine at Jenings's house the night before they "directed the negroes to be arraigned for high treason" the following day. In between references to drinking and carousing with some of the council and "persuading" an unwilling girl to "go with [him] into [his] chambers," Byrd's April 21 entry dismissively states that "two of the negroes were tried and convicted for treason." After witnessing Salvadore and Scipio's trial and sentencing, Byrd's normative lack of regard for such violence helps situate the actions, risks, and motives of the insurgents both at the bar and still at large. See Byrd, "April 1710," in *Secret Diary of William Byrd*, 167–69.

21. "Letter of Philip Ludwell," March 19, 1709, Box 144, Folder 20, CP-LVRV. McIlwaine, *Executive Journals*, 235; Palmer, *Calendar of Virginia State Papers*, 1:129.

22. "Order of Edmund Jenings," March 20, 1709, Box 144, Folder 20, CP-LVRV; Palmer, *Calendar of Virginia State Papers*, 1:129; McIlwaine, *Executive Journals*, 236.

23. "Order of Edmund Jenings," March 20, 1709, Box 144, Folder 20, CP-LVRV.

24. Martin, *Divided Mastery*, 27–28; P. Morgan, *Slave Counterpoint*, 272, 490.

25. Aptheker, *American Negro Slave Revolts*, 169–71; Parent, *Foul Means*, 152–53; Leaming, *Hidden Americans*, 225, 230; Morris, "'Running Servants and All Others,'" 95; Morris, *Dismal Freedom*, 47, 56.

26. "Letter of Philip Ludwell," March 19, 1709, Box 144, Folder 20, CP-LVRV.

27. "Order of Edmund Jenings," March 20, 1709, Box 144, Folder 20, CP-LVRV.

28. Parent, *Foul Means*, 151–52.

29. Palmer, *Calendar of Virginia State Papers*, 1:129.

30. Although one can rarely be certain what designations or terms such as "Angola," or "Bambara" meant in their eighteenth-century contexts, Gwendolyn Midlo Hall has noted that English slave traders "referred to all of West Central Africa as Angola and English-language documents . . . tended to list all West Central Africans as Angolans." G. Hall, *Slavery and African Ethnicity in the Americas*, 37, 46. People labeled "Bambara," were usually those who came from the Senegambia region. See Caron, "'Of a Nation Which the Others Do Not Understand,'" 99–100, 102–3, 115. Finally, the fairly common name Mingo is thought to be of West African origin, but it could also be a derivative of the Algonquian word "mingwe," meaning "stealthy" or "treacherous." Mingo may also suggest Spanish influence as the abbreviation of "Domingo"—or those born on Sunday. See Morris, "'Running Servants and All Others,'" 96–97.

31. By the 1710s and 1720s, Africans from the Bight of Biafra (mostly Igbos) dominated in the trade into Virginia, making up 57 percent of the African-based population. By the 1730s, "changes in the regional foci of the British trade" meant that captives from Senegambia and Angola "came to rival, and indeed surpass, the Bight of Biafra as supplying regions." See P. Morgan, *Slave Counterpoint*, 62–64.

32. Arthur Cotterell, scholar of ancient and precolonial civilizations, writes that the Ovambo people declare the significance of Pamba through the expression: "The mother of pots is a hole in the ground; the mother of people is god." See Cotterell, *Dictionary of World Mythology*, 255.

33. J. Johnson, *Wicked Flesh*, 79–105.

34. J. Morgan, "*Partus sequitur ventrem*," 1–17.

35. McIlwaine, *Journals of the House of Burgesses of Virginia*, 240. Regarding Virginia, Michael Gomez writes, "The slave population accelerated with the chartering of the Royal African Company in 1672, so that a population that grew very slowly at first (23 in 1625; 300 by 1650) was greatly augmented by importations of more than 1,000 Africans per year by the end of the seventeenth century." As a result, "the African-based population in Virginia grew from 12,000 in 1708 to 120,156 in 1756." See Gomez, *Exchanging Our Country Marks*, 20–21.

36. Palmer, *Calendar of Virginia State Papers*, 1:129; McCartney, "Study of the Africans and African Americans," 87–88.

37. Palmer, *Calendar of Virginia State Papers*, 1:129.

38. McIlwaine, *Executive Journals*, 573.

39. "Letter from Lieutenant Governor Alexander Spotswood to the Laurence Hyde, Earl of Rochester," July 30, 1711, in Saunders, *Colonial Records of North Carolina*, 1:798. See also Morris, *Dismal Freedom*, 47.

40. Diouf, *Slavery's Exiles*, 40; Morris, "'Running Servants and All Others,'" 98.

41. McIlwaine, *Executive Journals*, 574.

42. Diouf, *Slavery's Exiles*, 48. Similarly, across the colonial South, nearly two-thirds of African maroons fled in groups of two or more, and nearly one-third of Africans ran in groups of five or more. See Franklin and Schweninger, *Runaway Slaves*, 232.

43. "Letter from the Pitt County Committee of Safety," July 15, 1775, in Saunders and Clark, *Colonial and State Records of North Carolina*, 94–95; Martin, *History of North Carolina*, 353–55.

44. Palmer and McRae, *Calendar of Virginia State Papers*, 5:333–39.

45. Flournoy, *Calendar of Virginia State Papers*, 10:120–23. Rebecca Hall's dissertation provides an excellent summary and analysis of this plot and the previously ignored roles of Celia, Hannah, and the unnamed woman therein. See R. Hall, "Not Killing Me Softly," 1–3.

46. Terborg-Penn, "Black Women in Resistance," 195–96.

47. Bush, "'Daughters of Injur'd Africk,'" 691.

48. McIlwaine, *Executive Journals*, 234.

49. This uprising is also referred to as the "Chesapeake Rebellion" of 1730. It was probably the greatest mass entry of people marooning into the Dismal Swamp until the revolutionary period beginning in the 1770s. Brickell, *Natural History of North-Carolina*, 357. See also Parent, *Foul Means*, 159–62; Morris, *Dismal Freedom*, 55–56; Nevius, *City of Refuge*, 15.

50. Cecelski, *Waterman's Song*, 28–29.

51. This is the argument of Julius Scott, *Common Wind*; Sidbury, *Ploughshares into Swords*, 60; Jordan, *White Man's Burden*, 149–53. See also Alexander, *Fear of a Black Republic*.

52. Brown, *Tacky's Revolt*, 8, 239.

53. McRae, *Calendar of Virginia State Papers*, 6:651. For more references to the influence of Haiti on this insurrectionary plot, see McRae, *Calendar of Virginia State Papers*, 6:453, 470, 490, 571; Palmer and McRae, *Calendar of Virginia State Papers*, 5:542, 547, 625.

54. Palmer and McRae, *Calendar of Virginia State Papers*, 5:534–35, 540–43, 546–47, 551, 555, 585, 624–25; McRae, *Calendar of Virginia State Papers*, 6:452–53, 470, 475, 488–90, 493–94, 523–24, 547, 551–52, 649–52.

55. McRae, *Calendar of Virginia State Papers*, 6:547; Palmer and McRae, *Calendar of Virginia State Papers*, 5:542; "Letter from Petersburg, Virginia, May 17, 1792," *Boston Gazette and the Country Journal*, June 4, 1792.

56. "Letter from Petersburg, Virginia, May 17, 1792," *Boston Gazette and the Country Journal*, June 4, 1792. In early August 1793, a letter discovered on a street in Yorktown (between James City and Warwick Counties) revealed insurgent plans to orchestrate simultaneous attacks against the Tidewater slavocracy. The author of the letter, "Secret Keeper Richmond," addressed the "Secret Keeper Norfolk" but also wrote of other secret keepers and coconspirators as far away as Charleston, South Carolina, and assured that "we will be in possession of the whole country in a few weeks." A rare insight into the fundamental intentions of organizing violent rebellion, the letter also encourages and instructs: "Don't be feared have a good heart fight brave and we will get free." See "A Letter from and to Slave Rebels," in Aptheker, *Documentary History*, 28.

57. "Letter from Petersburg, Virginia, May 17, 1792," *Boston Gazette and the Country Journal*, June 4, 1792; Palmer and McRae, *Calendar of Virginia State Papers*, 5:625; McRae, *Calendar of Virginia State Papers*, 6:470, 547. For more on the events comprising the plot of 1792–1793, see Benjamin Golden, "'Armed in the Great Swamp,'" 11–14; Morris, *Dismal Freedom*, 73–75; Leaming, *Hidden Americans*, 247–49.

58. Northampton County Court Book, July 2, 1792, LVRV. Palmer and McRae, *Calendar of Virginia State Papers*, 5:625.

59. Northampton County Court Book, July 2, 1792, LVRV. McRae, *Calendar of Virginia State Papers*, 6:453, 572.

60. Cecelski, *The Waterman's Song*, 139.

61. McRae, *Calendar of Virginia State Papers*, 6:461–64, 521, 542–44.

62. McRae, *Calendar of Virginia State Papers*, 6:521, 542–44.

63. McRae, *Calendar of Virginia State Papers*, 6:543, 547.

64. SJ Zhang has written that captured and incarcerated insurgent women like Cecelia—a convicted maroon woman of the Bas du Fleuve maroons of Spanish colonial Louisiana—knew that their "potential to produce another enslaved person, another laborer" was "exactly the power" to "wield briefly," to assert, and to leverage with in order to protect and prolong their lives. See Zhang, "What Cecelia Knew," 158, 169.

65. Holden, *Surviving Southampton*, 3, 36–37.

66. Flournoy, *Calendar of Virginia State Papers*, 9:138, 147.

67. Flournoy, *Calendar of Virginia State Papers*, 9:141–42, 149–50.

68. Flournoy, *Calendar of Virginia State Papers*, 9:148, 150.

69. Flournoy, *Calendar of Virginia State Papers*, 9:150.

70. Sidbury, *Ploughshares into Swords*, 90; Egerton, *Gabriel's Rebellion*, 22, 30, 50, 68–69, 111, 177.

71. Flournoy, *Calendar of Virginia State Papers*, 9:143.

72. Flournoy, *Calendar of Virginia State Papers*, 9:150, 169.

73. Flournoy, *Calendar of Virginia State Papers*, 9:165.

74. Nikki Taylor and Rebecca Hall agree. See N. Taylor, *Brooding Over Bloody Revenge*, 4–5, 184–85. See also R. Hall, "Not Killing Me Softly," 33–34. Herbert Aptheker notes only that "Gabriel's wife, Nanny, was active, too." Aptheker, *American Negro Slave Revolts*, 220. Gerald Mullin also acknowledges that "Gabriel's wife, Nanny, told a black man 'that 1000 Men were to meet her husband,'" to begin the rebellion, but offers no further consideration. See G. Mullin, *Flight and Rebellion*, 150.

75. Egerton, *Gabriel's Rebellion*, 53; Sidbury, *Ploughshares into Swords*, 90.

76. Sidbury, *Ploughshares into Swords*, 90. Nikki Taylor has rightfully pointed out that Sidbury, "instead of assuming that the comment was a reflection of Woolfolk's personal, misguided views about women, contends that the rebels as a group may not have trusted Black women as policy." See Taylor, *Brooding Over Bloody Revenge*, 185.

77. Egerton, *Gabriel's Rebellion*, 53.

78. Flournoy, *Calendar of Virginia State Papers*, 9:141–43, 151.

79. Flournoy, *Calendar of Virginia State Papers*, 9:152. David Cecelski writes that "slave bateaumen, flatboat hands, and raftsmen" were common in Tidewater ports. "Bateaux" were "square-ended, flat-bottomed scows," or dinghies. See Cecelski, *Waterman's Song*, 43.

80. Flournoy, *Calendar of Virginia State Papers*, 9:144–46, 149, 151, 159, 164–65, 171. Sidbury certainly thinks so. See Sidbury, *Ploughshares into Swords*, 91–92.

81. Flournoy, *Calendar of Virginia State Papers*, 9:146, 154, 164.

82. Flournoy, *Calendar of Virginia State Papers*, 9:154–55.

83. *Kentucky Gazette*, November 3, 1800.

84. Morris, *Dismal Freedom*, 77; Sidbury, *Ploughshares into Swords*, 264–65. See also Egerton, *Gabriel's Rebellion*, 178; Leaming, *Hidden Americans*, 251–52.

85. The Virginia-born abolitionist Martin Delany published *Blake: or the Huts of America* in 1859. The novel, which sometimes corroborates content with notes alluding to factual basis, ventures into the Dismal Swamp, where the central character, Blake, finds "Virginia and North Carolina's boldest black rebels." The maroons there held "Nat Turner, Denmark Veezie, and General Gabriel . . . in sacred reverence," and considered them "the greatest men who ever lived." See Delany, *Blake*, 112–14.

86. Flournoy, *Calendar of Virginia State Papers*, 9:159, 160.

87. A prime example is the mountain-dwelling maroons of Le Maniel, Haiti, who helped Black elites and the enslaved launch what would become the only "successful" revolt in the hemisphere. See Fouchard, *Haitian Maroons*, 292–95. Fouchard argues that "the linkage between marronage and the events of 1791 is a historic fact," pointing to the prior recidivism of several key leaders, the simultaneous destruction of thousands of plantations, and the rise of marronage in Haiti leading up to the revolution. He estimates that some 25,000 maroons were fighting in the revolution by 1792, at a time when the enslaved population was more than 500,000.

88. More recently, Crystal Eddins has shown that while not "wholly dictated" by marronage, the "uprising was laid through maroon reclamation, organization, and the embodiment of a socio-political critique of the plantation system," and that the revolution "benefitted from maroon bands and ritual leaders at important moments of its unfolding." See Eddins, *Rituals, Runaways*, 279, 298.

89. Orlando Patterson has written about the leading role of Leeward and Windward Maroons in slave revolts and colonial warfare in Jamaica. See Patterson, "Slavery and Slave Revolts," 246–92.

90. Egerton, *Gabriel's Rebellion*, 111.

91. Flournoy, *Calendar of Virginia State Papers*, 9:173.

92. Flournoy, *Calendar of Virginia State Papers*, 9:262–63.

93. Flournoy, *Calendar of Virginia State Papers*, 9:263–67, 270–75. A letter written by Frank Goode, one of the insurrectionists, informs that plans were to "begin at Jude's Ferry and put to death every man on both sides of the river to Richmond" (274).

94. Flournoy, *Calendar of Virginia State Papers*, 9:279–80.

95. "Phebe's Trial," April 23, 1802, Halifax County Court Order Book, LVRV.

96. Flournoy, *Calendar of Virginia State Papers*, 9:294; Egerton, *Gabriel's Rebellion*, 141.

97. Egerton, "'Fly Across the River,'" 91; "Sancho's Trial," April 23, 1802, Halifax County Court Order Book, LVRV.

98. "Sancho's Trial," April 23, 1802; Egerton, *Gabriel's Rebellion*, 124.

99. Many enslavers gave enslaved people Easter Monday and Easter Sunday as days of rest and leisure. See Genovese, *Roll, Jordan, Roll*, 576.

100. Egerton, "'Fly Across the River,'" 94–97. Though he readily admits that Sancho was directly influenced by the conspiracy begun in Henrico County in 1800, Egerton argues that the Halifax plot of 1802, at least initially, provided the "leadership" of the unfolding Easter Rebellion. Given the lack of evidence that this is so, it is perhaps more useful to consider how the varied plots arising between the 1800 conspiracy and the winter of 1802 were

multidirectional, reflexive movements and exchanges of insurrectionary ideas and plans, not fixed as emanating from any one place. This is particularly salient, as stirrings in the Norfolk region and in other places predate the making of plans in Halifax. Water, and all that it moves and channels, rarely, if ever moves merely in one direction. Flournoy, *Calendar of Virginia State Papers*, 9:173, 262–63.

101. "Phebe's Trial," April 23, 1802, Halifax County Court Order Book, LVRV.

102. Taylor, *Brooding Over Bloody Revenge*, 61.

103. Egerton, *Gabriel's Rebellion*, 140. Egerton is the only historian to note Phebe's involvement in the Easter Rebellion of 1802. He offers a brief paragraph discussing her trial, citing only her trial record in the Halifax County Court Order Book. It is unclear how he concludes that Phebe was a "house servant" of Daniel Price, or how he finds that Abram was among the witnesses who spoke against her, as there is no record of either claim.

104. "Phebe's Trial," April 23, 1802, Halifax County Court Order Book, LVRV; Personal Property Tax Lists, 1800–1812, Film 2024564, Image Group 7919006, Family History Library, accessed January 2024, www.familysearch.org/en/search/catalog/776119.

105. Halifax County Plea Book pp. 23, 24, February 24, 1804, Film 31928, Image Group 8572483, accessed January 2024, www.familysearch.org/search/catalog/401169; Halifax County Will Book 6, pp. 615–16, February 27, 1804, Film 31863, Image Group 7676118, accessed January 2024, www.familysearch.org/en/search/catalog/417646.

106. For example, in May 1802 the testimony of Lewis, a literate enslaved ferryman who worked the rivers connecting Nottoway, Dinwiddie, and Richmond, implicated at least three others in this wing of the plan that was to "kill the inhabitants of Richmond and burn the city." But by June 1802, Lewis escaped from custody as he was being escorted out of Richmond to appear in other trials being held in Petersburg, Goochland, and Nottoway County courts. Despite a persistent search, there is no indication of Lewis's recapture. See Egerton, *Gabriel's Rebellion*, 141–43. See also, Flournoy, *Calendar of Virginia State Papers*, 9:298.

107. Benjamin Golden, "'Armed in the Great Swamp,'" 16; Morris, *Dismal Freedom*, 79–80; Aptheker, *American Negro Slave Revolts*, 230; Leaming, *Hidden Americans*, 250; Diouf, *Slavery's Exiles*, 259; Sayers, *Desolate Place for a Defiant People*, 103–4; Bogger, *Readings in Black and White*, 1–8; Johnston, *Race Relations in Virginia*, 34–36.

108. Flournoy, *Calendar of Virginia State Papers*, 9:286–87.

109. Marcus Nevius has illuminated how white fear of enslaved and maroon violence is not only a part of the system of slavery but also part of a global history of slave resistance, Atlantic slavery, and empire. As Nevius shows, across the broader Atlantic world, white fear shaped not only capitalist and imperialist interest but also the records left behind in the aftermath of enslaved people's conspiracies to rebel and revolt, usually in the form of rumors or exaggerations meant to incite control and heightened vigilance through fear mongering. As is clear in the rebellions surrounding the Great Dismal Swamp, the famous Tacky's Revolt of 1760–61 in Jamaica, and other rebellions across the hemisphere, these fears were also rooted in the very real actions and insurgent potential of African descendants. See Nevius, "Global Warfare," 538, 548–49. See also Brown, *Tacky's Revolt*, 7–13; Benjamin Golden, "'Armed in the Great Swamp,'" 6–8.

110. Flournoy, *Calendar of Virginia State Papers*, 9:293, 296; Parramore, Stewart, and Bogger, *Norfolk: The First Four Centuries*, 119–21, 129.

111. Egerton, *Gabriel's Rebellion*, 135–37.

112. Roeber, *New England Woman's Perspective*, 307–8.

113. Flournoy, *Calendar of Virginia State Papers*, 9:293, 296, 299–300.

114. Parramore et al., *Norfolk*, 120–21.

115. Flournoy, *Calendar of Virginia State Papers*, 9:304–5.

116. Roeber, *New England Woman's Perspective*, 316.

117. "Authentic Particulars of the Late Intended Insurrection of the Negroes," *Alexandria Advertiser*, May 18, 1802.

118. "More About the Negroes," *Virginia Gazette*, June 2, 1802. See also *New York Herald*, June 2, 1802; *Raleigh Register*, June 1, 1802; Byrd, *North Carolina Slaves*, 55.

119. "More About the Negroes," *Virginia Gazette*, June 2, 1802; "Extract from a Letter from Elizabeth City, North Carolina, dated May 12, 1802," *Eastern Herald*, June 7, 1802. See also *Commercial Advertiser*, May 24, 1802; Byrd, *North Carolina Slaves*, 55–57; Morris, *Dismal Freedom*, 79; Diouf, *Slavery's Exiles*, 260–61. Because Diouf pays less attention to the ecology and geography of the pre–Civil War Dismal Swamp, she underestimates the massiveness and impact of the Tidewater swamp and thus erroneously denies the connection between Tom Copper and the Dismal Swamp. Diouf also misses that the activities of Copper are connected to the larger Easter Rebellion of 1802.

120. Pasquotank County Court Minute Book, 1802, North Carolina State Archives, Raleigh, North Carolina. Perquimans County Slave Records, 1759–1864, Insurrection Among the Slaves, 1802–1803, NCSA; "More About the Negroes," *Virginia Gazette*, June 2, 1802.

121. Byrd, *North Carolina Slaves*, 261.

122. Pasquotank County Court Minute Book, 1802.

123. Byrd, *North Carolina Slaves*, 262.

124. *Raleigh Register*, July 6, 1802; Byrd, *North Carolina Slaves*, 53; "Letter from Willis Riddick," June 6, 1802, Perquimans County Slave Records, NCSA; Flournoy, *Calendar of Virginia State Papers*, 9:307.

125. *Raleigh Register*, July 6, 1802. Douglas Egerton is the only historian to acknowledge Jude's role in the Easter Rebellion. Though, he did so without offering more than "the terrified woman confessed" that she had instructed her daughter to take the letter and then hid it herself. Egerton, *Gabriel's Rebellion*, 144.

126. "Testimony of Fitts' Fed," Bertie County Slave Collection, 1802 Conspiracy, NCSA; Byrd, *North Carolina Slaves*, 53, 55; "Letter from Willis Riddick," June 6, 1802, Perquimans County Slave Records, NCSA.

127. *Raleigh Register*, July 6, 1802.

128. "Testimony of Fitts' Fed," Bertie County Slave Collection, 1802 Conspiracy, NCSA; Flournoy, *Calendar of Virginia State Papers*, 9:307.

129. Excerpted from a letter of intelligence written and signed by one of the insurgents, "J. L. C." Bertie County Slave Collection, 1802 Conspiracy, NCSA.

130. Some enslavers permitted the enslaved to keep small cotton patches of their own, or to cultivate small amounts of cotton for their own use, which could explain why Jude kept a barrel containing cotton in her cabin. See Penningroth, *Claims of Kinfolk*, 48–49.

131. Genovese, *Roll, Jordan, Roll*, 563.

132. Harriet Jacobs spent her early childhood years enslaved by a "kind mistress" who taught her to "read and spell." See Jacobs, *Incidents in the Life of a Slave Girl*, 4–5.

133. "Letter from Willis Riddick," June 6, 1802, Perquimans County Slave Records, NCSA.

134. Flournoy, *Calendar of Virginia State Papers*, 9:306–7.

135. Egerton, *Gabriel's Rebellion*, 145.

136. "Letter from Willis Riddick," June 6, 1802, Perquimans County Slave Records, NCSA; *Raleigh Register*, July 6, 1802; "Examination of Witnesses for the State," Bertie County Slave Collection, 1802 Conspiracy, NCSA.

137. "Examination of Witnesses for the State."

138. Kay and Carey, "Slave Runaways in Colonial North Carolina," 18–19.

139. Flournoy, *Calendar of Virginia State Papers*, 9:308; "Negroes Again Troublesome!!!" *Norfolk Herald*, June 15, 1802. In the end, at least twenty-five men from both Virginia and North Carolina were executed, and at least nineteen were transported out of the country. See Benjamin Golden, "'Armed in the Great Swamp,'" 21.

140. Forret, *Slave Against Slave*, 264–65, 312, 337.

CHAPTER 5

1. Sayers, *Desolate Place for a Defiant People*, 22, 25, 116, 118, 120; Diouf, *Slavery's Exiles*, 221.

2. Sayers, *Desolate Place for a Defiant People*, 115; Morris, *Dismal Freedom*, 95.

3. *New York Evening Post*, May 15, 1823.

4. This illicit market is the subject of Marcus Nevius's unprecedented study, *City of Refuge*.

5. For example, in Jamaica, "about three hundred men, women, and children" of the Windward Maroons marched across dense woods and treacherous mountains to join the then safer home of the maroons on the Leeward side of the island. See Patterson, "Slavery and Slave Revolts," 269. In Suriname, men, women, and children were—with "masterly maneuver"—prepared to retreat to other locations, which they did under the threat of attack, carrying with them weapons and food, while the "unfathomable marsh" refuge they lived in helped to hinder their pursuers. Captain J. G. Stedman, "Guerilla Warfare: A European Soldier's View," in Price, *Maroon Societies*, 307, 311. Stedman's article was originally published in his *Narrative of a Five-Years' Expedition*, 106–21.

6. Scholars of the Dismal Swamp agree that cross-swamp interaction did happen, and that "reciprocity networks linked deep swamp communities." See Morris, *Dismal Freedom*, 124; Sayers, *Desolate Place for a Defiant People*, 105.

7. A. Thompson, "Gender and Marronage in the Caribbean," 262–89.

8. For a discussion of hierarchical and "heterarchical" power shared between enslaving men and women in the paternalistic slaveholding US South, see Jones-Rogers, *They Were Her Property*, 70–71.

9. D. White, *Ar'n't I a Woman*, 22. In her essay on the economic, political, spiritual, and military authority of matrilineal West African societies and the tradition of the Asante Queen Mother, Beverly Stoeltje expounds that when it comes to African conceptions of gender, "the terms *duality* and *parallel* do not imply equality or sameness, but *complementarity*, a term that refers to differences that mutually complement each other, to different parts, each of which represents a lack in the other that is needed to complete the whole." See Stoeltje, "Asante Queen Mothers," 44.

10. Price, *Saramaka Social Structure*, 46.

11. I owe the framing of this chapter a great debt to the late Rosalyn Terborg-Penn, who in 1986 first wrote of Black women's insurgent contributions and leadership in their communities as the work and value of "hearthstones." See Terborg-Penn, "Black Women in Resistance," 195, 199.

12. "Sketches in Color," *Putnam's Magazine* 4 (December 1869): 741–46.

13. J. Morgan, *Reckoning with Slavery*, 223; Wells-Oghoghomeh, *Souls of Womenfolk*, 73; Turner, "Nameless and the Forgotten," 16–19.

14. "Sketches in Color," 742.

15. Eddins, "'Rejoice!,'" 563–64.

16. J. Morgan, *Reckoning with Slavery*, 233.

17. "Sketches in Color," 742. For more on burial rites and the ritual expression of emotions and maternal bereavement see Wells-Oghoghomeh, *Souls of Womenfolk*, 156.

18. Miki, "Fleeing into Slavery," 523.

19. *Virginia Gazette*, December 5, 1771; January 30, 1772; April 2, 1772; February 18, 1773.

20. King, *Stolen Childhood*, 233–34.

21. Grandy, "Narrative of Moses Grandy," in Andrews, *North Carolina Slave Narratives*, 176.

22. McLean, "Yankee Tutor in the Old South," 62.

23. Roome, *Southward in Roamer*, 36.

24. "The Dismal Swamp," *The Sun*, April 17, 1845; "Fire in the Dismal Swamp," *The Jeffersonian* (Charlotte, NC), May 2, 1845.

25. *Logain County News*, September 16, 1863; September 23, 1863.

26. King, *Stolen Childhood*, xxi–xxii.

27. *Logain County News*, September 23, 1863.

28. William Byrd, "The History of the Dividing Line betwixt Virginia and North Carolina Run in the Year of Our Lord 1728," in Berland, *Dividing Line Histories*, 89.

29. Redpath, *Roving Editor*, 293.

30. Olmsted, *A Journey*, 77.

31. T. M., "For the Republican," *Petersburg Republican*, October 10, 1820; "Singular Relation," *American Masonic Register, and Ladies and Gentlemen's Magazine*, January 1, 1821; Warner, *Authentic and Impartial Narrative*, 34–35; Tragle, *Southampton Revolt of 1831*, 298.

32. Olmsted, *A Journey*, 77.

33. "Mrs. Louise Jones (b. ca. 1855)," in Perdue et al., *Weevils in the Wheat*, 185; Blum, "Power, Danger, and Control," 259.

34. King, *Stolen Childhood*, 58; Trumbull, "Through the Dismal Swamp," 409.

35. "Allen Crawford (b. 1835)," in Perdue et al., *Weevils in the Wheat*, 74; "Mrs. Candis Goodwin (b. 1857)," in Perdue et al., *Weevils in the Wheat*, 107.

36. Benjamin Golden, "Through the Muck and Mire," 126.

37. Grandy, "Narrative of Moses Grandy," in Andrews, *North Carolina Slave Narratives*, 168; King, *Stolen Childhood*, 114.

38. Sayers, *Desolate Place for a Defiant People*, 118, 120–21, 127, 135; Morris, *Dismal Freedom*, 109–10; Diouf, *Slavery's Exiles*, 220–21; Nevius, *City of Refuge*, 55–57.

39. Frederick Street, "In the Dismal Swamp," *Frank Leslie's Popular Monthly*, March 1903, 530; "Peat in the Dismal Swamp," *DeBow's Review*, October 1867, 371.

40. Ledoux, *Princess Anne*, 41, 49.

41. Morris, *Dismal Freedom*, 110; Diouf, *Slavery's Exiles*, 221–22.

42. Morris, *Dismal Freedom*, 106.

43. Diouf, *Slavery's Exiles*, 132; Morris, *Dismal Freedom*, 117.

44. For references to disputes amongst enslaved communities see: Forret, *Slave Against Slave*, 6–7; D. White, *Ar'n't I a Woman*, 151. Disputes and dissension were guarantees in maroon life that were mediated by maroons across the Atlantic world. See Price, *Maroon Societies*, 16–18.

45. Morris, *Dismal Freedom*, 118.

46. Despite English colonial interference, this is an enduring tradition. Stoeltje, "Asante Queen Mothers," 51–53.

47. Knight, *Black Elders*, 3, 14, 31, 78, 83.

48. Morris, *Dismal Freedom*, 119.

49. Wells-Oghoghomeh, *Souls of Womenfolk*, 134–36.

50. Grandy, "Narrative of Moses Grandy," in Andrews, *North Carolina Slave Narratives*, 176.

51. *Logain County News*, September 23, 1863.

52. "Mrs. Marriah Hines (b. 1835)," in Perdue et al., *Weevils in the Wheat*, 141.

53. King, *Stolen Childhood*, 175.

54. "Rev. W. P. Jacobs (b. 1852)," in Perdue et al., *Weevils in the Wheat*, 157.

55. Bush, *Slave Women in Caribbean Society*, 70; Thicknesse, *Memoirs and Anecdotes*, 73.

56. For a more elaborative description of the near impossibility of accessing and entering deep swamp maroon settlements, see Morris, *Dismal Freedom*, 116.

57. Bush, *Slave Women in Caribbean Society*, 70.

58. A. Thompson, "Gender and Marronage in the Caribbean," 275.

59. de Groot, "Comparison Between the History," 174.

60. J. G. Stedman, "Guerilla Warfare: A European Soldier's View," in Price, *Maroon Societies*, 296, 309–11.

61. Sayers, *Desolate Place for a Defiant People*, 129–31, 133–34, 138, 140, 148, 153, 178, 185; Morris, *Dismal Freedom*, 114–15.

62. Morris, *Dismal Freedom*, 115–16, 128–29.

63. F. Johnson, *Tales from Old Carolina*, 163.

64. Arnold, *Great Dismal Swamp and Lake Drummond*, 7–8.

65. *Logain County News*, September 16, 1863.

66. Strother, "The Dismal Swamp," *Harper's Monthly* 13 (1856): 446, 452–53.

67. Morris notes that deep swamp maroons may have "seldom" sent out expeditions to foray but did "maintain connections with trusted men and women still enslaved on labor camps" and canals who would "occasionally" exchange with them. Women were probably the least likely community members to participate in these rare efforts. See Morris, *Dismal Freedom*, 115, 117.

68. Alvin Thompson rightly asserts that "gender equality did not prevail" in maroon societies in the Caribbean. See A. Thompson, "Gender and Marronage in the Caribbean," 263. Similarly, Yuko Miki has pointed to gendered division of labor within the quilombolas of Brazil as one example of the ways male maroons circumscribed maroon women's freedoms. See Miki, "Fleeing into Slavery," 525–26.

69. A. Thompson, "Gender and Marronage in the Caribbean," 263.

70. "Sketches in Color," 741.

71. *Logain County News*, September 23, 1863; T. M., "For the Republican," *Petersburg Republican*, October 10, 1820; "Singular Relation," *American Masonic Register, and Ladies and Gentlemen's Magazine*, January 1, 1821. Frederick Street corroborates that maroons lived "thirty years or more" in the Dismal Swamp "depending chiefly for both food and clothing, on the 'coons." See Street, "In the Dismal Swamp," 530. See also, F. Johnson, *Tales from Old Carolina*, 162; Diouf, *Slavery's Exiles*, 225.

72. Sayers, *Desolate Place for a Defiant People*, 121, 127.

73. Heath, "Space and Place Within Plantation Quarters," 169–71; Samford, "Engendering Enslaved Communities," 157–59.

74. Smyth, *Tour in the United States of America*, 65; Morris, *Dismal Freedom*, 111.

75. Leaming, *Hidden Americans*, 279; Edmund Ruffin, "Observations Made During an Excursion to the Dismal Swamp," *Farmers' Register* 4, no. 9 (January 1, 1837): 519.

76. A. Thompson, "Gender and Marronage in the Caribbean," 277.

77. Nwokeji, "African Conceptions of Gender," 56.

78. Gomez, *Exchanging Our Country Marks*, 93, 96.

79. "Louisa Adams," in Federal Writers' Project, *Slave Narratives*, 11:6; "Ex-Slave Story," in Federal Writers' Project, *Slave Narratives*, 11:184; "Robert Hinton," in Federal Writers' Project, *Slave Narratives*, 11:438.

80. Cook Bell, *Running from Bondage*, 143. Diouf and Morris hint at the same. See Diouf, *Slavery's Exiles*, 89; Morris, *Dismal Freedom*, 111. Sayers agrees that "gardens were most likely" kept within settlements. Sayers, *Desolate Place for a Defiant People*, 107.

81. Grandy, "Narrative of Moses Grandy," in Andrews, *North Carolina Slave Narratives*, 159, 176.

82. Goode, "Engaging the Tools of Resistance," 219, 241–45; Morris, *Dismal Freedom*, 111.

83. *Logain County News*, September 23, 1863; "Mrs. Mollie Booker (b. 1850)," in Perdue et al., *Weevils in the Wheat*, 55.

84. Olmsted, *A Journey*, 78; "Mrs. Sis Shackelford (b. 1854)," in Perdue et al., *Weevils in the Wheat*, 252.

85. Moulton and Salo, "Black Geographies and Black Ecologies," 160.

86. Eddins, "'Rejoice!,'" 562, 574; A. Thompson, "Gender and Marronage in the Caribbean," 274; Price, *Maroon Societies*, 331; Terborg-Penn, "Black Women in Resistance," 197, 199–201; Bush, *Slave Women in Caribbean Society*, 73–77, 155.

87. Wells-Oghoghomeh, *Souls of Womenfolk*, 173–74.

88. Fett, *Working Cures*, 3, 5, 95–100.

89. *Logain County News*, September 23, 1863.

90. Pybus, "'One Militant Saint,'" 1–9; Morris, *Dismal Freedom*, 121; Bell Cook, *Running from Bondage*, 103.

91. "George W. Harris," in Federal Writers' Project, *Slave Narratives*, 11:372.

92. "Mrs. Marrinda Jane Singleton (b. 1840)," in Perdue et al., *Weevils in the Wheat*, 267–68.

93. Trumbull, "Through the Dismal Swamp," 409.

94. F. Johnson, *Tales from Old Carolina*, 199–200.

95. Ledoux, *Princess Anne*, vi, 39, 68–71.

96. Trumbull, "Through the Dismal Swamp," 409.

97. Sayers, *Desolate Place for a Defiant People*, 115–16.

98. Sayers, *Desolate Place for a Defiant People*, 116; Morris, *Dismal Freedom*, 116.

99. The field of Atlantic world slavery owes the important concept of the "three bodies" to the life work and study of Stephanie Camp. See Camp, *Closer to Freedom*, 67–68. Similarly, Daina Ramey Berry reflects this point about embodied and experienced internal struggle through the concept of "soul values," or the many ways enslaved people understood their own worth against external and imposed exploitative values. Berry is rightfully concerned about how enslaved people "valued themselves by recognizing that they could be enslaved in body yet free in their souls." See Berry, "Soul Values and American Slavery," 202. Sergio A. Lussana adds that the "reclaimed body" is a "site of resistance to slavery." See Lussana, *My Brother Slaves*, 55.

100. Trumbull, "Through the Dismal Swamp," 408–9.

101. These artifacts date from the period 1620–1860. Sayers, *Desolate Place for a Defiant People*, 140, 148, 152, 178, 184, 188; Goode, "Engaging the Tools of Resistance," 118–19, 123.

102. Olmsted, *A Journey*, 75.

103. Price, *Maroon Societies*, 11. Observing the Saramaka maroons in Suriname, the English soldier Captain John Stedman noted that "the palm-tree wine they have always in plenty; they procure it by making deep incisions of a foot square in the fallen trunk, where the juice being collected, it soon ferments by the heat of the sun; it is not only a cool and agreeable beverage, but sufficiently strong to intoxicate." Stedman, *Narrative of a Five-Years' Expedition*, 119.

104. Goode, "Engaging the Tools of Resistance," 219, 241–45.

105. "May Satterfield (b. 1861)," in Perdue et al., *Weevils in the Wheat*, 244, 246; "Deposition of Nelson and James," Accession Number 42046, Box 2, James Pleasant's Executive Papers, 1823, LVRV.

106. Hersey, *Rest Is Resistance*, 132–34.

107. William Aitchison and James Parker Account Book, 1763–1804, Accession Number 12992, Albert and Shirley Small Special Collections and University of Virginia, Charlottesville, Virginia, 51.

108. Carter Jackson, *We Refuse*, 208–9.

109. Tara A. Bynum highlights the use of and need for recognizing Black interiority beyond suffering—"those good feelings" such as "joy, excitement, or enthusiasm"—as "a necessary antecedent to public and resistive acts," and as a creative "source of human action." See Bynum, *Reading Pleasures*, 1–2. For other explorations of how pleasure, positive feeling, and enslaved and Black interiority works against "the din of pain," see Judd, *Feelin*, 15. See also Lindsey and Johnson, "Searching for Climax," 169–95.

110. Carter Jackson, *We Refuse*, 227.

111. To this point, W. E. B. Du Bois wrote that Black people "are filled with laughter and delicious chuckling. They enjoy themselves; they enjoy jokes; they perpetuate them on each other and on white folk." See Du Bois, "Humor of Negroes," 8.

112. "Interview of Mrs. Minnie Fulkes," in Federal Writers' Project, *Slave Narratives*, 17:12.

113. "Rev. Ishrael Massie (b. 1849)," in Perdue et al., *Weevils in the Wheat*, 209–10.

114. Jacobs, *Incidents in the Life of a Slave Girl*, 128–30. Another example of maroon laughter, mockery, pleasure, and delight in refusing and resisting slaveholders comes from Captain John Stedman's account of the maroons of Suriname who he found "hallooing" with "more mirth that [Stedman] had been witness to for some time." The subject of their humor was the colonists' promises to them of "life, liberty, victuals, drink, and all they wanted," if only

the maroons would surrender and comply. Stedman notes that in response to this offer, the maroons replied, "with a loud laugh," that they wanted nothing from them, could better feed the colonists than the other way around, and that the colonists were "to be pitied more than they." Such enjoyment and pleasure often precedes and nurtures a politics of resistance. See J. G. Stedman, "Guerilla Warfare: A European Soldier's View," in Price, *Maroon Societies*, 310; and Stedman, *Narrative of a Five-Years' Expedition*, 114, 117.

115. Roane, "Plotting the Black Commons," 247.

EPILOGUE

1. *Cambridge Democrat*, October 3, 1849; Dunbar, *She Came to Slay*, 23, 39.

2. "Harriet Tubman, Interviewed 1859–1865," in Blassingame, *Slave Testimony*, 460–61.

3. "Sketches in Color," *Putnam's Magazine*, December 1869, 742.

4. Grandy, "Narrative of Moses Grandy," in Andrews, *North Carolina Slave Narratives*, 176–77.

5. Jacobs, *Incidents in the Life of a Slave Girl*, 126–27. See also Yellin, *Harriet Jacobs*.

6. Harriet A. Jacobs, "Life Among the Contrabands," *The Liberator*, September 5, 1862, 3.

7. "Mary Pope," in Blassingame, *Slave Testimony*, 455–57; Bryant, *36th Infantry United States Colored Troops in the Civil War*, 19–20; *Logain County News*, September 16, 1863; September 23, 1863; Glymph, *Women's Fight*, 249.

8. Sayers writes that the swamp is "perhaps 10%" of its original size. See Sayers, "Scission Communities," 185; Sayers, *Desolate Place for a Defiant People*, 20, 92; Leaming, *Hidden Americans*, 222; and US Fish and Wildlife Service, "Great Dismal Swamp National Wildlife Refuge: The Great Dismal Swamp and the Underground Railroad," Great Dismal Swamp National Wildlife Refuge, accessed February 7, 2026, https://npshistory.com/brochures/nwr/great-dismal-swamp-ugrr.pdf.

9. Benjamin Golden, "Through the Muck and Mire," 99–111.

10. Great Dismal Swamp Stakeholder Collaborative, "GDSSC at a Glance," accessed March 13, 2025, www.gdssc.org/.

11. Julie Bell, "Great Dismal Swamp National Heritage Area Feasibility Project," National Park Service, accessed March 15, 2025, https://parkplanning.nps.gov/projectHome.cfm?projectID=119003.

12. President Donald J. Trump, Executive Order, "Restoring Truth and Sanity to American History," The White House, March 27, 2025, www.whitehouse.gov/presidential-actions/2025/03/restoring-truth-and-sanity-to-american-history/.

13. Benjamin Golden, "Through the Muck and Mire," 128, 131.

14. Benjamin Golden, "Through the Muck and Mire," 132.

15. Jackson, *Speaking for the Enslaved*, 14.

16. Gumbs, *Spill*, xi.

17. Christian Parenti, "Assata Shakur Speaks from Exile: PostModern Maroon in the Ultimate Palenque" (interview), AssataShakur.org, October 24, 2000, www.assatashakur.org/maroon.htm.

18. Walker, "In Search of Our Mothers' Gardens," (1974), in *In Search of Our Mother's Gardens: Womanist Prose*, 233, 241.

19. Ruth Wilson Gilmore argues that "freedom is a place"—the basis of an abolitionist future recognizing the imperative of people's relationships to land, space, and power. Gilmore, "Abolition Geography," 227.

20. Larson, *Bound to the Promised Land*, 289.

BIBLIOGRAPHY

PRIMARY SOURCES

Manuscript Collections

Albert and Shirley Small Special Collections Library, University of Virginia, Charlottesville, Virginia
Library of Congress, Washington, DC
  Colonial Office, Public Record Office, 1709–1710
Library of Virginia, Richmond, Virginia
  Colonial Papers, 1630–1778
  Condemned Slaves and Free Blacks Executed or Transported, 1779–1865
  Coroner's Inquisitions, Princess Anne County
  Halifax County Court Order Book, 1802
  James Patton Preston Executive Papers, 1816–1819
  James Pleasant's Executive Papers, 1823
  Northampton County Court Book, 1792, 1800
  Princess Anne County Minute Book, 1819
  Runaway and Escaped Slaves Records, 1794–1863
  Virginia Manuscripts, British Public Record Office
    Sainsbury Transcripts
  State Records Collection
    Wyndham Robertson Executive Papers, 1836–1837
North Carolina State Archives, Raleigh, North Carolina
  Bertie County Slave Collection
  Pasquotank County Court Minute Book, 1802
  Perquimans County Slave Records, 1759–1864

Rubenstein Library, Duke University, Durham, North Carolina
Dismal Swamp Land Company Records, 1665–1832
Correspondence, 1688–1791
Legal Records, 1665–1832
South Caroliniana Library, University of South Carolina, Columbia, South Carolina
James Henry Hammond Papers

Periodicals

Alexandria Advertiser
Alexandria Herald
American Beacon (Norfolk, VA)
American Beacon and Commercial Diary
American Masonic Register, and Ladies and Gentlemen's Magazine
Argus of Western America
Baltimore Patriot
Boston Gazette and the Country Journal
Cambridge Democrat
Clarion and Tennessee State Gazette
Commonwealth
Commercial Advertiser
DeBow's Review
Democratic Pioneer (Elizabeth City)
Eastern Herald
Edenton (NC) Gazette
Elizabeth-City Star and North-Carolina Eastern Intelligencer
Farmer's Register
Fayetteville Weekly Observer
Forest and Stream
Frank Leslie's Popular Monthly
Free Press (Tarborough, NC)
Freeman's Record
Harper's Monthly
Herald of Freedom (Edenton, NC)
The Jeffersonian
The Liberator
Liberty Bell
Literary Magazine and American Register
Logain County News
Natural Science News
New York Evening Post
New York Herald
Norfolk Herald
Norfolk and Portsmouth Daily Advertiser
Norfolk and Portsmouth Herald
North Carolina Free Press
North Carolina Journal
North Carolina Minerva and Raleigh Advertiser
Old North State
Petersburg Republican
Pittsburgh Weekly Gazette
Putnam's Magazine
Raleigh Register
Raleigh Star
Spirit of the Age (Raleigh, NC)
The Sun
Vermont Journal
Virginia Gazette

Books

Andrews, William L., ed. *North Carolina Slave Narratives: The Lives of Moses Rore, Lunsford Lane, Moses Grandy, and Thomas H. Jones*. University of North Carolina Press, 2003.
Aptheker, Herbert, ed. *A Documentary History of the Negro People in the United States*. Vol. 1., *From Colonial Times Through the Civil War*. Citadel, 1951.

Arnold, Robert. *The Great Dismal Swamp and Lake Drummond: Early Recollections and Vivid Portrayals of Amusing Scenes.* Green, Burke and Gregory, 1888. www.loc.gov/resource/gdcmassbookdig.dismalswamplakedooarnod/?sp=7.

Barnet, Miguel. *Biography of a Runaway Slave.* Translated by W. Nick Hill. Curbstone Press, 1994. https://archive.org/details/biographyofrunawooooeste/page/n5/mode/2up.

Bayley, Solomon. *A Narrative of Some Remarkable Incidents in the Life of Solomon Bayley, Formerly a Slave, in the State of Delaware, North America; Written by Himself, and Published for His Benefit.* Harvey and Darton, 1825. https://docsouth.unc.edu/neh/bayley/bayley.html.

Beecher Stowe, Harriet. *Dred: A Tale of the Great Dismal Swamp.* Phillips, Sampson, 1856.

Berland, Kevin Joel, ed. *The Dividing Line Histories of William Byrd II of Westover.* University of North Carolina Press, 2013.

Blassingame, John W., ed. *Slave Testimony: Two Centuries of Letters, Interviews, Speeches, and Autobiographies.* Louisiana State University Press, 1977.

Brickell, John. *The Natural History of North-Carolina; with an Account of the Trade, Manners, and Customs of the Christian and Indian Inhabitants.* 1737. Reprint, Johnson Reprint Corporation, 1969. https://archive.org/details/naturalhistoryof03bric/page/n3/mode/2up.

Byrd, William. *History of the Dividing Line, and Other Tracts: From the Papers of William Byrd, of Westover, in Virginia, Esquire.* Vol. 1, *History of the Dividing Line.* Richmond, VA, 1866. https://archive.org/details/historyofdividino2byrd/page/n3/mode/2up.

Byrd, William, III, ed. *North Carolina Slaves and Free Persons of Color: Perquimans County.* Heritage Books, 2006.

Byrd, William. *The Secret Diary of William Byrd of Westover, 1709–1712.* Edited by Louis B. Wright and Marion Tinling. Dietz Press, 1941.

Delany, Martin. *Blake; or, The Huts of America.* Edited by Floyd J. Miller. *1859. Reprint,* Beacon Press, 1970.

Douglass, Frederick. "The Heroic Slave." In *Autographs for Freedom,* compiled by the Rochester Ladies' Anti-Slavery Society, 174–239. John P. Jewett, 1853.

Federal Writers' Project. *Slave Narratives: A Folk History of Slavery in the United States from Interviews with Former Slaves.* Vol. 11, *North Carolina,* Pt. 1, Adams–Hunter. Work Projects Administration, 1941. www.loc.gov/resource/mesn.111/?st=gallery.

Federal Writers' Project. *Slave Narratives: A Folk History of Slavery in the United States from Interviews with Former Slaves.* Vol. 11, North Carolina, Pt. 2, Jackson–Yellerday. Work Projects Administration, 1941. www.loc.gov/resource/mesn.112/?st=gallery.

Federal Writers' Project. *Slave Narratives: A Folk History of Slavery in the United States from Interviews with Former Slaves.* Vol. 17, *Virginia, Berry–Wilson.* Work Projects Administration, 1941. www.loc.gov/resource/mesn.170/?st=gallery.

Flournoy, H. W., ed. *Calendar of Virginia State Papers, and Other Manuscripts, January 1, 1799–December 31, 1807,* Vol. 9. Richmond, Virginia, 1890. https://hdl.handle.net/2027/hvd.32044020396693.

Flournoy, H. W., ed. *Calendar of Virginia State Papers, and Other Manuscripts, January 1, 1808–December 31, 1835,* Vol. 10. Richmond, Virginia, 1892. https://hdl.handle.net/2027/hvd.32044097931315.

Forrest, William S., ed. *Historical and Descriptive Sketches of Norfolk and Vicinity: Including Portsmouth and the Adjacent Counties . . . of Interest in Eastern Virginia.* Lindsay and Blakiston, 1853. https://archive.org/details/historicaldeooforr/page/n9/mode/2up.

Fortescue, J. W., ed. *Calendar of State Papers, Colonial Series.* Vol. 11, *America and West Indies, 1681–1685.* H. M. Public Record Office, 1898. https://archive.org/details/sim_great-britain-public-record-america-and-the-west-indies_1681-1685/mode/2up.

Fouts, Raymond Parker. *Registration of Slaves to Work in the Dismal Swamp: Gates County, North Carolina, 1847–1861.* GenRec Books, 1995.

Hening, William Waller. *The Statutes at Large; Being a Collection of All the Laws of Virginia from the First Session of the Legislature, in the Year 1619*, Vol. 2. R. and W. and G. Bartow, 1823. https://hdl.handle.net/2027/hvd.hxh5u4.

Hodges, Graham Russell. *The Black Loyalist Directory: African Americans in Exile After the American Revolution.* Garland Publishing, 1996.

Jacobs, Harriet. *Incidents in the Life of a Slave Girl.* First Signet Classic Printing, 2000.

Jarrett, Gene Andrew, ed. *The Wiley Blackwell Anthology of African American Literature.* Vol. 1, *1746–1920.* John Wiley and Sons, 2014.

Ledoux, Albert R. *Princess Anne: A Story of the Dismal Swamp and Other Sketches.* Looker-On Publishing, 1896.

Lockley, Timothy, ed. *Maroon Communities in South Carolina: A Documentary Record.* University of South Carolina Press, 2009.

Longfellow, Henry Wadsworth. *The Poetical Works of Henry Wadsworth Longfellow.* Ticknor and Fields, 1866.

McIlwaine, H. R. *Executive Journals of the Council of Colonial Virginia.* Vol. 3, *May 1, 1705–October 23, 1721.* Davis Bottom, Superintendent of Public Records, 1928.

McIlwaine, H. R. *Journals of the House of Burgesses of Virginia, 1702/3–1705, 1705–1706, 1710–1712.* Colonial Press, E. Waddey, 1912.

McRae, Sherwin. *Calendar of Virginia State Papers.* Vol. 6, *August 11, 1792 to December 31, 1793.* A. R. Micou, 1886. https://books.google.com.na/books?id=9kgOAAAAIAAJ.

Mellon, James, ed. *Bullwhip Days: The Slaves Remember.* Grove Press, 1988.

Mintz, Steven, ed. *African American Voices: A Documentary Reader, 1619–1877.* Wiley-Blackwell, 2009.

Nkrumah, Kwame. *Handbook of Revolutionary Warfare: A Guide to the Armed Phase of the African Revolution.* International Publishers, 1960.

Gable, Sharon Rea, and Truitt M. Bonney. *Norfolk County Virginia Will Book 4, 1802–1817.* Published by the authors, Suffolk, VA, 2009.

Olmsted, Frederick Law. *A Journey in the Seaboard Slave States: With Remarks on Their Economy.* 1856. Reprint, Arcadia Press, 2017. https://archive.org/details/journeyinseaboarolms/page/n7/mode/2up.

Palmer, William, ed. *Calendar of Virginia State Papers, and Other Manuscripts, 1652–1781, Preserved in the Capitol at Richmond*, Vol. 1. R. F. Walker, 1875. www.google.com/books/edition/Calendar_of_Virginia_State_Papers_and_Ot/pKwFAAAAQAAJ.

Palmer, William, and Sherwin McRae, eds. *Calendar of Virginia State Papers, and Other Manuscripts, from July 2, 1790, to August 10, 1792, Preserved in the Capitol at Richmond*, Vol. 5. Rush U. Derr, 1885. https://hdl.handle.net/2027/hvd.32044097931299.

Parker, Freddie L. *Running for Freedom: Slave Runaways in North Carolina, 1775–1840*. Garland Publishing, 1993.

Perdue, Charles L., Jr., Thomas E. Barden, and Robert K. Phillips, eds. *Weevils in the Wheat: Interviews with Virginia Ex-Slaves*. University Press of Virginia, 1976.

Powell, J. W. *Tenth Annual Report of the United States Geological Society to the Secretary of the Interior*. Part 1, *1888–1889*. Washington, D.C., 1890. https://doi.org/10.3133/ar10_1.

Redpath, James. *The Roving Editor, or, Talks with Slaves*. 1859. Reprint, Negro University Press, 1968. www.loc.gov/item/11011700/.

Roome, Henry Clay. *Southward in Roamer: Being a Description of the Inside Route from New York to Florida*. Ruddler Publishing, 1907.

Saunders, William L., ed. *Colonial Records of North Carolina*. Vol. 1, *1662 to 1712*. P. M. Hale, 1886. https://archive.org/details/colonialrecordsoo1nort/page/n5/mode/2up.

Saunders, William L., and Walter Clark, eds. *The Colonial and State Records of North Carolina*. Vol. 10, *1662–1790*. 1886. Reprint, Broadfoot Publishing, 1993.

Smyth, John F. D. *A Tour in the United States of America: Containing an Account of the Present Situation of That Country* . . . . Vol. 2. G. Robinson, 1784. https://hdl.handle.net/2027/hvd.hxj3rq.

State of North Carolina. *Laws of the State of North Carolina, Passed by the General Assembly at the Session of 1846–1847*. Thomas J. Lemay, Printer, 1847. https://digital.ncdcr.gov/Documents/Detail/laws-of-the-state-of-north-carolina-passed-by-the-general-assembly-1846-1847/1952514?item=2010624.

Stedman, J. G. *Narrative of a Five-Years' Expedition, Against the Revolted Negroes of Surinam . . . from the Year 1772, to 1777*. J. Johnson and J. Edwards, 1813.

Still, William. *The Underground Railroad: A Record of Facts, Authentic Narratives, Letters*. People's Publishing, 1879. https://archive.org/details/undergroundrailroolcstil/page/n7/mode/2up.

Thicknesse, Philip. *Memoirs and Anecdotes of Philip Thicknesse, Late Lieutenant Governor of Land Guard Fort, and Unfortunately Father to George Touchet, Baron Audley*. William Jones, 1790. https://hdl.handle.net/2027/uc2.ark:/13960/t4pk08c1p.

Thorne Kent, Harriette. *Swampers: Free Blacks and the Great Dismal Swamp*. H. T. Kent, 1999.

Tragle, Henry Irving, ed. *The Southampton Revolt of 1831: A Compilation of Source Material*. University of Massachusetts Press, 1971.

Warner, Samuel. *Authentic and Impartial Narrative of the Tragical Scene Which Was Witnessed in Southampton County (Virginia) on Monday the 22d of August Last* . . . . Warner and West, 1831.

Washington, George. *The Papers of George Washington*. Vol. 7, *January 1761–June 1767*. Edited by W. W. Abbot and Dorothy Twohig. University Press of Virginia, 1990.

Wells Brown, William. *Clotel; or, The President's Daughter: A Narrative of Slave Life in the United States*. Partridge and Oakey, 1853. https://docsouth.unc.edu/southlit/brown/summary.html.

SECONDARY SOURCES

Books, Book Chapters, and Essays

Alexander, Leslie M. *Fear of a Black Republic: African Americans, Haiti, and the Brith of Black Internationalism*. University of Illinois Press, 2022.

Aptheker, Herbert. *American Negro Slave Revolts*. International Publishers, 1983.

Bass, Ruth. "Mojo." In *Mother Wit from the Laughing Barrel: Readings in the Interpretation of Afro-American Folklore*, edited by Alan Dundes, 380–87. University Press of Mississippi, 1990.

Bay, Mia, Farah J. Griffin, Martha S. Jones, and Barbara D. Savage, eds. *Toward an Intellectual History of Black Women*. University of North Carolina Press, 2015.

Berry, Daina Ramey, and Kali Nicole Gross. *A Black Women's History of the United States*. Beacon Press, 2021.

Berry, Daina Ramey, and Leslie Harris, eds. *Sexuality and Slavery: Reclaiming Intimate Histories in the Americas*. University of Georgia Press, 2018.

Bilby, Kennet, and Diana Baird N'Diaye. "Creativity and Resistance: Maroon Culture in the Americas." In *1992 Festival of American Folklife*, 54–61. Washington, DC: Smithsonian Institution, 1992. https://folklife-media.si.edu/docs/festival/program-book-articles/FESTBK1992_27.pdf.

Blassingame, John. *The Slave Community: Plantation Life in the Antebellum South*. Oxford University Press, 1979.

Block, Sharon. *Rape and Sexual Power in Early America*. University of North Carolina Press, 2006.

Bogger, Tommy. *Readings in Black and White: Lower Tidewater Virginia*. Portsmouth Public Library, 1982.

Bouton, Christopher H. *Setting Slavery's Limits: Physical Confrontations in Antebellum Virginia, 1801–1860*. Lexington Books, 2020.

Brathwaite, Edward Kamau. *ConVERSations with Nathaniel Mackey*. We Press, 1999.

Brown, Alexander Crosby. *The Dismal Swamp Canal*. Norfolk County Historical Society of Chesapeake, 1970.

Brown, Kathleen M. *Good Wives, Nasty Wenches, and Anxious Patriarchs: Gender, Race, and Power in Colonial Virginia*. University of North Carolina Press, 1996.

Bruce, Philip Alexander. *History of Virginia*. Vol. 1, *Colonial Period, 1607–1763*. American Historical Society, 1924. https://archive.org/details/historyofvirgini01bruc/page/n7/mode/2up.

Bryant, James K., II. *The 36th Infantry United States Colored Troops in the Civil War: A History and Roster*. McFarland, 2012.

Brown, Vincent. *Tacky's Revolt: The Story of an Atlantic Slave War*. Harvard University Press, 2020.

Bush, Barbara. *Slave Women in Caribbean Society, 1650–1838*. Indiana University Press, 1990.

Bynum, Tara A. *Reading Pleasures: Everyday Black Living in Early America*. University of Illinois Press, 2023.

Camp, Stephanie. *Closer to Freedom: Enslaved Women and Everyday Resistance in the Plantation South*. University of North Carolina Press, 2004.

Campt, Tina M. *Image Matters: Archive, Photography, and the African Diaspora in Europe.* Duke University Press, 2012.

Carter, J. Kameron. "Other Worlds, Nowhere (or, The Sacred Otherwise)." In *Otherwise Worlds: Against Settler Colonialism and Anti-Blackness,* edited by Tiffany Lethabo King, Jenell Navarro, and Andrea Smith, 158–210. Duke University Press, 2020.

Carter Jackson, Kellie. *Force and Freedom: Black Abolitionists and the Politics of Violence.* University of Pennsylvania Press, 2019.

Carter Jackson, Kellie. *We Refuse: A Forceful History of Black Resistance.* Hachette Book Group, 2024.

Cecelski, David. *The Waterman's Song: Slavery and Freedom in Maritime North Carolina.* University of North Carolina Press, 2001.

Clark, Jawanza Eric. *Reclaiming Stolen Earth: An Africana Ecotheology.* Orbis Books, 2022.

Cobb, Charles E. *This Nonviolent Stuff'll Get You Killed: How Guns Made the Civil Rights Movement Possible.* Duke University Press, 2015.

Cook Bell, Karen. *Running from Bondage: Enslaved Women and their Remarkable Fight for Freedom in Revolutionary America.* Cambridge University Press, 2021.

Cotterell, Arthur. *A Dictionary of World Mythology.* Oxford University Press, 1986.

Cowan, William Tynes. *The Slave in the Swamp: Disrupting the Plantation Narrative.* Routledge, 2005.

Davis, Hubert J. *The Great Dismal Swamp: Its History, Folklore, and Science.* Cavalier Press, 1962.

Dawson, Kevin. *Undercurrents of Power: Aquatic Culture in the African Diaspora.* University of Pennsylvania Press, 2018.

de Groot, Silvia W. "A Comparison Between the History of Maroon Communities in Surinam and Jamaica." In *Out of the House of Bondage: Runaways, Resistance and Marronage in Africa and the New World,* edited by Gad Heuman, 173–84. Frank Cass, 1986.

Diouf, Sylviane A. *Slavery's Exiles: The Story of the American Maroons.* New York University Press, 2014.

Dunbar, Erica Armstrong. *Never Caught: The Washingtons' Relentless Pursuit of their Runaway Slave, Ona Judge.* Simon and Schuster, 2017.

Dunbar, Erica Armstrong. *She Came to Slay: The Life and Times of Harriet Tubman.* Simon and Schuster, 2019.

Eaves, Shannon C. *Sexual Violence and American Slavery: The Making of a Rape Culture in the Antebellum South.* University of North Carolina Press, 2024.

Eddins, Crystal Nicole. *Rituals, Runaways, and the Haitian Revolution: Collective Action in the African Diaspora.* Cambridge University Press, 2022.

Egerton, Douglas R. *Gabriel's Rebellion: The Virginia Slave Conspiracies of 1800 and 1802.* University of North Carolina Press, 1993.

Fanon, Frantz. *The Wretched of the Earth.* Présence Africaine, 1963.

Farmer, Ashley D. *Remaking Black Power: How Black Women Transformed an Era.* University of North Carolina Press, 2017.

Ferrari, Carlyn Ena. *Do Not Separate Her from Her Garden: Anne Spencer's Ecopoetics.* University of Virginia Press, 2022.

Fett, Sharla M. *Working Cures: Healing, Health, and Power on Southern Slave Plantations.* University of North Carolina Press, 2002.

Fields Black, Edda L. *Combhee: Harriet Tubman, the Combahee River Raid, and Black Freedom Struggle During the Civil War*. Oxford University Press, 2024.

Finch, Aisha. *Rethinking Slave Rebellion in Cuba: La Escalera and the Insurgencies of 1841–1844*. University of North Carolina Press, 2015.

Finney, Carolyn. *Black Faces, White Spaces: Reimagining the Relationship of African Americans to the Great Outdoors*. University of North Carolina Press, 2014.

Forret, John. *Slave Against Slave: Plantation Violence in the Old South*. Louisiana State University Press, 2015.

Fouchard, Jean. *The Haitian Maroons: Liberty or Death*. Edward W. Blyden Press, 1981.

Fox-Genovese, Elizabeth. "Strategies and Forms of Resistance: Focus on Slave Women in the United States." In *In Resistance: Studies in African, Caribbean, and Afro-American History*, edited by Gary Okihiro, 143–65. University of Massachusetts Press, 1986.

Fox-Genovese, Elizabeth. *Within the Plantation Household: Black and White Women of the Old South*. University of North Carolina Press, 1988.

Franklin, John Hope, and Loren Schweninger. *Runaway Slaves: Rebels on the Plantation*. Oxford University Press, 1999.

Fuentes, Marisa J. *Dispossessed Lives: Enslaved Women, Violence, and the Archive*. University of Pennsylvania Press, 2016.

Gautier, Arlette. *Les Soeurs de Solitude: Femmes et esclavage aux Antilles du XVII au XIX siècle* [The Sisters of Solitude: Women and slavery in the West Indies from the 17th to the 19th century]. Presses Universitaires de Rennes, 2010.

Genovese, Eugene D. *From Rebellion to Revolution: Afro-American Slave Revolts in the Making of the Modern World*. Louisiana State University Press, 1979.

Genovese, Eugene D. *Roll, Jordan Roll: The World the Slaves Made*. Vintage Books, 1976.

Gilmore, Ruth W. "Abolition Geography and the Problem of Innocence." In *Futures of Black Radicalism*, edited by Gaye T. Johnson and Alex Lubin, 225–40. Verso, 2017.

Gilroy, Paul. *The Black Atlantic: Modernity and Double Consciousness*. Harvard University Press, 1993.

Ginsburg, Rebecca. "Escaping Through a Black Landscape." In *Cabin, Quarter, Plantation: Architecture and Landscapes of North American Slavery*, edited by Clifton Ellis and Rebecca Ginsburg, 51–66. Yale University Press, 2010.

Givens, Jarvis R. *Fugitive Pedagogy: Carter G. Woodson and the Art of Black Teaching*. Harvard University Press, 2021.

Glave, Dianne D., and Mark Stoll, eds. *"To Love the Wind and the Rain": African Americans and Environmental History*. University of Pittsburgh Press, 2005.

Glymph, Thavolia. *Out of the House of Bondage: The Transformation of the Plantation Household*. Cambridge University Press, 2008.

Glymph, Thavolia. *The Women's Fight: The Civil War's Battles for Home, Freedom, and Nation*. University of North Carolina Press, 2020.

Gomez, Michael. *Exchanging Our Country Marks: The Transformation of African Identities in the Colonial and Antebellum South*. University of North Carolina Press, 1998.

Goodwin, William Archer Rutherfoord. *Historical Sketch of Bruton Church, Williamsburg, Virginia*. Franklin Press, 1903.

Gottlieb, Karla. *The Mother of Us All: A History of Queen Nanny, Leader of the Windward Jamaican Maroons*. Africa World Press, 2000.

Gottlieb, Karla. "Queen Nanny of the Jamaican Maroons: A Study of Women's Leadership in the Caribbean." In *Women in Caribbean Politics*, edited by Cynthia Barrow-Giles, 3–13. Ian Randle Publishers, 2011.

Griffin, William A. *Ante-Bellum Elizabeth City: The History of a Canal Town.* Roanoke Press, 1970.

Gross, Kali Nicole. *Hannah Mary Tabbs and the Disembodied Torso: A Tale of Race, Sex, and Violence in America.* Oxford University Press, 2016.

Gumbs, Alexis Pauline. *Spill: Scenes of Black Feminist Fugitivity.* Duke University Press, 2016.

Hadden, Sally E. *Slave Patrols: Law and Violence in Virginia and the Carolinas.* Harvard University Press, 2001.

Hall, Gwendolyn Midlo. *Africans in Colonial Louisiana: The Development of Afro-Creole Culture in the Eighteenth Century.* Louisiana State University Press, 1992.

Hall, Gwendolyn Midlo. *Slavery and African Ethnicities in the Americas: Restoring the Links.* University of North Carolina Press, 2005.

Hall, Rebecca. *Wake: The Hidden History of Women-Led Slave Revolts.* Simon and Schuster, 2021.

Hannah-Jones, Nikole, Caitlin Roper, Ilena Silverman, and Jake Silverstein, eds. *The 1619 Project: A New Origin Story.* One World, 2021.

Harding, Vincent. *There Is a River: The Black Struggle for Freedom in America.* Harcourt Brace, 1981.

Hartman, Saidiya. *Scenes of Subjection: Terror, Slavery, and Self-Making in Nineteenth-Century America.* Oxford University Press, 1997.

Hartman, Saidiya. *Wayward Lives, Beautiful Experiments: Intimate Stories of Intimate Upheaval.* W. W. Norton, 2019.

Haverty King, Helen. *Historical Notes on Isle of Wight County.* Isle of Wight County Board of Supervisors, 1993.

Heath, Barbara. "Space and Place Within Plantation Quarters in Virginia, 1700–1825." In *Cabin, Quarter, Plantation: Architecture and Landscapes of North American Slavery*, edited by Clifton Ellis and Rebecca Ginsburg, 156–76. Yale University Press, 2010.

Hersey, Tricia. *Rest Is Resistance: A Manifesto.* Hachette Book Group, 2022.

Heuman, Gad J. *Out of the House of Bondage: Runaways, Resistance and Marronage in Africa and the New World.* Frank Cass, 1986.

Hey-Colón, Rebecca L. *Channeling Knowledges: Water and Afro-Diasporic Spirits in Latinx and Caribbean Worlds.* University of Texas Press, 2023.

Hinton, Elizabeth. *America on Fire: The Untold History of Police Violence and Black Rebellion Since the 1960s.* Liveright Publishing, 2021.

Holden, Vanessa M. *Surviving Southampton: African American Women and Resistance in Nat Turner's Community.* University of Illinois Press, 2021.

Honychurch, Lennox. *In the Forests of Freedom: The Fighting Maroons of Dominica.* Papillote Press, 2017.

hooks, bell. *Feminist Theory from Margin to Center.* South End Press, 1984.

Hunter, Tera W. *Bound in Wedlock: Slave and Free Black Marriage in the Nineteenth Century.* The Belknap Press of Harvard University Press, 2017.

Hurley, E. Anthony. "Solitude." In *Dictionary of Caribbean and Afro-Latin American Biography*, edited by Franklin W. Knight and Henry Louis Gates Jr., 299–300. Oxford University Press, 2016.

Hyman, Christy. "To Render a Landscape of Trauma: Deep Mapping a Historical Landscape of Domination—the Great Dismal Swamp." In *Ideas in Unexpected Places: Reimagining Black Intellectual History*, edited by Brandon R. Byrd, Leslie M. Alexander, and Russell Rickford, 263–75. Northwestern University Press, 2022.

Jackson, Antoinette. *Speaking for the Enslaved: Heritage Interpretation at Antebellum Plantation Sites*. Left Coast Press, 2012.

Johnson, F. Roy. *Tales from Old Carolina: Traditional and Historical Sketches of the Area Between and About the Chowan River and Great Dismal Swamp*. Johnson Publishing, 1965.

Johnson, Jessica Marie. *Wicked Flesh: Black Women, Intimacy, and Freedom in the Atlantic World*. University of Pennsylvania Press, 2020.

Johnson, Walter. *Soul by Soul: Life Inside the Antebellum Slave Market*. Harvard University Press, 1999.

Johnston, James Hugo. *Race Relations in Virginia and Miscegenation in the South, 1776–1860*. University of Massachusetts Press, 1970.

Jones-Rogers, Stephanie E. *They Were Her Property: White Women as Slave Owners in the American South*. Yale University Press, 2019.

Jordan, Winthrop. *White Man's Burden: Historical Origins of Racism in the United States*. Oxford University Press, 1974.

Judd, Bettina. *Feelin: Creative Practice, Pleasure, and Black Feminist Thought*. Northwestern University Press, 2023.

Karenga, Maulana. *Maat, the Moral Ideal in Ancient Egypt: A Study in Classical African Ethics*. University of Sankore Press, 2006.

King, Wilma. *Stolen Childhood: Slave Youth in Nineteenth-Century America*. Indiana University Press, 2011.

Kirby, Jack Temple. *Poquosin: A Study of Rural Landscape and Society*. University of North Carolina Press, 1995.

Knight, Frederick C. *Black Elders: The Meaning of Age in American Slavery and Freedom*. University of Pennsylvania Press, 2024.

LaRoche, Cheryl Janifer. "Coerced but Not Subdued: The Gendered Resistance of Women Escaping Slavery." In *Gendered Resistance: Women, Slavery, and the Legacy of Margaret Garner*, edited by Mary E. Frederickson and Delores M. Walters, 49–76. University of Illinois Press, 2013.

Larson, Kate Clifford. *Bound to the Promised Land: Harriet Tubman, Portrait of an American Hero*. Random House, 2009.

Laurent-Perrault, Evelyn. "Esclavizadas, cimarronaje y la ley en Venezuela, 1760–1809." In *Demando mi libertad: Mujeres negras y sus estrategias de resistencia en la Nueva Granada, Venezuela y Cuba*, edited by Aurora Vergara Figueroa and Carmen Luz Cosme Puntiel, 77–108. Universidad Icesi, 2018.

Leaming, Hugo Prosper. *Hidden Americans: Maroons of Virginia and the Carolinas*. Garland, 1995.

Lefler, Hugh, and William S. Powell. *Colonial North Carolina: A History*. Charles Scribner's Sons, 1973.

Lethabo King, Tiffany. *The Black Shoals: Offshore Formations of Black and Native Studies.* Duke University Press, 2019.

Lethabo King, Tiffany. "Racial Ecologies: Black Landscapes in Flux." In *Racial Ecologies,* edited by Leilani Nishime and Kim D. Hester Williams, 65–75. University of Washington Press, 2018.

Lindsey, Treva B. *America, Goddam: Violence, Black Women, and the Struggle for Justice.* University of California Press, 2022.

Lussana, Sergio A. *My Brother Slaves: Friendship, Masculinity, and Resistance in the Antebellum South.* University Press of Kentucky, 2016.

Martin, Francois-Xavier. *History of North Carolina: From the Earliest Period,* Vol. 2. A. T. Penniman, 1829. https://archive.org/details/historyofnorthca_02mart/page/n9/mode/2up.

Martin, Jonathan D. *Divided Mastery: Slave Hiring in the American South.* Harvard University Press, 2004.

McCartney, Martha W. *A Study of the Africans and African Americans on Jamestown Island at Green Spring, 1619–1803.* National Park Service and Colonial Williamsburg Foundation, 2003. https://archives.indianapolis.iu.edu.

McKittrick, Katherine. *Demonic Grounds: Black Women and the Cartographies of Struggle.* University of Minnesota Press, 2006.

McLaurin, Melton A. *Celia, a Slave.* Avon, 1999.

Miles, Tiya. *All That She Carried: The Journey of Ashley's Sack, a Black Family Keepsake.* Random House, 2021.

Millet, Nathaniel. *The Maroons of Prospect Bluff and Their Quest for Freedom in the Atlantic World.* University Press of Florida, 2015.

Moitt, Bernard. "Slave Women and Resistance in the French Caribbean." In *More Than Chattel: Black Women and Slavery in the Americas,* edited by David Barry Gaspar and Darlene Clark Hine, 239–58. Indiana University Press, 1996.

Morgan, Edmund S. *American Slavery, American Freedom: The Ordeal of Colonial Virginia.* W. W. Norton, 1975.

Morgan, Jennifer L. *Laboring Women: Reproduction and Gender in New World Slavery.* University of Pennsylvania Press, 2004.

Morgan, Jennifer L. *Reckoning with Slavery: Gender, Kinship, and Capitalism in the Early Black Atlantic.* Duke University Press, 2021.

Morgan, Philip D. *Slave Counterpoint: Black Culture in the Eighteenth-Century Chesapeake and Lowcountry.* University of North Carolina Press, 1998.

Morris, J. Brent. *Dismal Freedom: A History of the Great Dismal Swamp.* University of North Carolina Press, 2022.

Morris, J. Brent. "'Running Servants and All Others': The Diverse and Elusive Maroons of the Great Dismal Swamp." In *Voices from Within the Veil: African Americans and the Experience of Democracy,* edited by William Alexander, Cassandra Newby-Alexander, and Charles Ford, 85–112. Cambridge Scholars Press, 2008.

Moten, Fred. *The Undercommons: Fugitive Planning and Black Study.* Minor Compositions, 2013.

Mullin, Gerald W. *Flight and Rebellion: Slave Resistance in Eighteenth Century Virginia.* Oxford University Press, 1972.

Mullin, Michael. *Africa in America: Slave Acculturation and Resistance in the American South and the British Caribbean, 1736–1831*. University of Illinois Press, 1995.
Mulroy, Kevin. *Freedom on the Border: The Seminole Maroons in Florida, the Indian Territory, Coahuila, and Texas*. Texas Tech University Press, 1993.
Mustakeem, Sowande' M. *Slavery at Sea: Terror, Sex, and Sickness in the Middle Passage*. University of Illinois Press, 2016.
Nelson, Megan Kate. "Hidden Away in the Woods and Swamps: Slavery, Fugitive Slaves, and Swamplands in the Southeastern Borderlands, 1739–1845." In *"We Shall Independent Be": African American Place Making and the Struggle to Claim Space in the United States*, edited by Angel David Nieves and Leslie M. Alexander, 251–72. University Press of Colorado, 2008.
Nevius, Marcus P. *City of Refuge: Slavery and Petit Marronage in the Great Dismal Swamp, 1763–1856*. University of Georgia Press, 2020.
Nunley, Tamika Y. *The Demands of Justice: Enslaved Women, Capital Crime, and Clemency in Early Virginia*. University of North Carolina Press, 2023.
Parent, Anthony S., Jr. *Foul Means: The Formation of a Slave Society in Virginia, 1660–1740*. Omohundro Institute for Early American History, 1996.
Parramore, Thomas C. *Cradle of the Colony: The History of Chowan County and Edenton, North Carolina*. Edenton Chamber of Commerce, 1967.
Parramore, Thomas C. *Southampton County Virginia*. University Press of Virginia, 1978.
Parramore, Thomas C., Peter C. Stewart, and Tommy L. Bogger. *Norfolk: The First Four Centuries*. University Press of Virginia, 1994.
Patterson, Orlando. "Slavery and Slave Revolts: A Sociohistorical Analysis of the First Maroon War, 1665–1740." In *Maroon Societies: Rebel Slave Communities in the Americas*, edited by Richard Price, 246–92. Johns Hopkins University Press, 1996.
Patterson, Orlando. *Slavery and Social Death: A Comparative Study*. Harvard University Press, 1982.
Penningroth, Dylan C. *The Claims of Kinfolk: African American Property and Community in the Nineteenth-Century South*. University of North Carolina Press, 2003.
Porter, Albert O. *County Government in Virginia: A Legislative History, 1607–1904*. Columbia University Press, 1947.
Powell, William S. *North Carolina Through Four Centuries*. University of North Carolina Press. 1989.
Price, Richard. *Maroon Societies: Rebel Slave Communities in the Americas*. Johns Hopkins University Press, 1996.
Price, Richard. *Saramaka Social Structure: Analysis of a Maroon Society in Surinam*. Institute of Caribbean Studies, 1975.
Rashid, Ismail. "A Devotion to the Idea of Liberty at Any Price: Rebellion and Antislavery in the Upper Guinea Coast in the Eighteenth and Nineteenth Centuries." In *Fighting the Slave Trade: West African Strategies*, edited by Sylviane A. Diouf, 132–51. Ohio University Press, 2003.
Rediker, Marcus. *The Slave Ship: A Human History*. Penguin Books, 2007.
Rivers, Larry Eugene. *Rebels and Runaways: Slave Resistance in Nineteenth-Century Florida*. University of Illinois Press, 2012.

Roane, J. T. *Dark Agoras: Insurgent Black Social Life and the Politics of Place.* New York University Press, 2023.

Roberts, Neil. *Freedom as Marronage.* University of Chicago Press, 2015.

Robinson, Cedric J. *Black Marxism: The Making of the Black Radical Tradition.* University of North Carolina Press, 1983.

Rountree, Helen C. *Pocahantas's People: Powhatan Indians of Virginia Through Four Centuries.* University of Oklahoma Press, 1990.

Rountree, Helen C., and Wesley D. Taukchiray. *Manteo's World: Native American Life in Carolina's Sound Country Before and After the Lost Colony.* University of North Carolina Press, 2021.

Royster, Charles. *The Fabulous History of the Dismal Swamp Company: A Story of George Washington's Times.* Alfred A. Knopf, 1999.

Rucker, Walter C. *The River Flows On: Black Resistance, Culture, and Identity Formation in Early America.* Louisiana State University Press, 2006.

Samford, Patricia. "Engendering Enslaved Communities on Virginia and North Carolina's Eighteenth- and Nineteenth-Century Plantations." In *Engendering African American Archaeology: A Southern Perspective,* edited by Jillian E. Galle and Amy L. Young, 151–76. University of Tennessee Press, 2004.

Saucier, P. Khalil, and Tyron P. Woods. *On Marronage: Ethical Confrontations with Antiblackness.* Africa World Press, 2015.

Sawyer, Roy T. *America's Wetland: An Environmental and Cultural History of Tidewater Virginia and North Carolina.* University of Virginia Press, 2010.

Sayers, Daniel O. *A Desolate Place for a Defiant People: The Archaeology of Maroons, Indigenous Americans, and Enslaved Laborers in the Great Dismal Swamp.* University Press of Florida, 2014.

Sayers, Daniel O. "Scission Communities and Social Defiance: Marronage in the Diasporic Great Dismal Swamp, 1660–1860." In *The Limits of Tyranny: Archaeological Perspectives on the Struggle Against New World Slavery,* edited by James A. Delle, 177–212. University of Tennessee Press, 2015.

Schwarz, Philip J. *Twice Condemned: Slaves and the Criminal Laws of Virginia, 1705–1865.* Louisiana State University Press, 1988.

Scott, Julius. *The Common Wind: Afro-American Currents in the Age of the Haitian Revolution.* Verso, 2018.

Sharpe, Christina. *In the Wake: On Blackness and Being.* Duke University Press, 2016.

Sidbury, James. *Ploughshares into Swords: Race, Rebellion, and Identity in Gabriel's Virginia, 1730–1810.* Cambridge University Press, 1997.

Silkenat, David. *Scars on the Land: An Environmental History of Slavery in the American South.* Oxford University Press, 2022.

Smallwood, Stephanie. *Saltwater Slavery: A Middle Passage from Africa to American Diaspora.* Harvard University Press, 2008.

Smith, Kimberly K. *African American Environmental Thought: Foundations.* University Press of Kansas, 2007.

Stewart, Mart A. *What Nature Suffers to Groe: Life, Labor, and Landscape on the Georgia Coast, 1680–1920.* University of Georgia Press, 2002.

Stoeltje, Beverly. "Asante Queen Mothers: A Study in Female Authority." In *Queens, Queen Mothers, Priestesses, and Power: Case Studies in African Gender*, edited by Flora Edouwaye S. Kaplan, 41–71. New York Academy of Sciences, 1997.

Taylor, Nikki M. *Brooding Over Bloody Revenge: Enslaved Women's Lethal Resistance*. Cambridge University Press, 2023.

Taylor, Ula Y. *The Promise of Patriarchy: Women and the Nation of Islam*. University of North Carolina Press, 2017.

Taylor, Ula Y. *The Veiled Garvey: The Life and Times of Amy Jacques Garvey*. University of North Carolina Press, 2002.

Terborg-Penn, Rosalyn. "Black Women in Resistance: A Cross-Cultural Perspective." In *In Resistance: Studies in African, Caribbean, and Afro-American History*, edited by Gary Okihiro, 188–209. University of Massachusetts Press, 1986.

Thompson, Alvin O. *Flight to Freedom: African Runaways and Maroons in the Americas*. University of the West Indies, 2006.

Thompson, Robert Farris. *Flash of the Spirit: African and Afro-American Art and Philosophy*. Random House, 1984.

Thornton, John. *Africa and Africans in the Making of the Atlantic World, 1400–1800*. Cambridge University Press, 1998.

Trouillot, Michel Rolph. *Silencing the Past: Power and the Production of History*. Beacon Press, 1995.

Turner, Sasha. *Contested Bodies: Pregnancy, Childrearing, and Slavery in Jamaica*. University of Pennsylvania Press, 2019.

Turner, Sasha. "The Nameless and the Forgotten: Maternal Grief, Sacred Protection, and the Archive of Slavery." In *Motherhood, Childlessness and the Care of Children in Atlantic Slave Societies*, edited by Camillia Cowling, Maria Helena Pereira Toledo Machado, Diana Paton, and Emily West, 13–31. Routledge, 2020.

Walker, Alice. *In Search of Our Mother's Gardens: Womanist Prose*. Harcourt, 1983.

Walsh, Lorena S. *From Calabar to Carter's Grove: The History of a Virginia Slave Community*. University Press of Virginia, 1997.

Wells-Oghoghomeh, Alexis. *The Souls of Womenfolk: The Religious Cultures of Enslaved Women in the Lower South*. University of North Carolina Press, 2021.

White, Deborah Gray. *Ar'n't I a Woman? Female Slaves in the Plantation South*. W. W. Norton, 1999.

White, Monica. *Freedom Farmers: Agricultural Resistance and the Black Freedom Movement*. University of North Carolina Press, 2018.

Williams, Robert F. *Negroes with Guns*. Marzani and Munsell, 1962.

Wilson, Anthony. *Shadow and Shelter: The Swamp in Southern Culture*. University Press of Mississippi, 2006.

Winston, Celeste. *How to Lose the Hounds: Maroon Geographies and a World Beyond Policing*. Duke University Press, 2023.

Wood, Peter. *Black Majority: Negroes in Colonial South Carolina, 1670 Through the Stono Rebellion*. Alfred A. Knopf, 1974.

Yellin, Jean Fagan. *Harriet Jacobs: A Life*. Basic Civitas Books, 2004.

Yellin, Jean Fagan. "Incidents Abroad: Harriet Jacobs and the Transatlantic Movement." In *Women's Rights and Transatlantic Antislavery in the Era of Emancipation*, edited by Kathryn Kish Sklar and James Brewer Stewart, 158–72. Yale University Press, 2008.

Zhang, SJ. "Mulâtresse Solitude, heroine de la resistance." In *Colonisations: Notre Histoire à Nous*, edited by Pierre Singaravélou, 750–51. Seuil, 2023.

Journal Articles

Allewaert, M. "Swamp Sublime: Ecologies of Resistance in the American Plantation Zone." *PMLA* 123, no. 2 (March 2008): 340–57.

Aptheker, Herbert. "Additional Data on American Maroons." *Journal of Negro History* 32, no. 4 (October 1947): 452–60.

Aptheker, Herbert. "Maroons Within the Present Limits of the United States." *Journal of Negro History* 24, no. 2 (April 1939): 167–84.

Bauer, Raymond, and Alice Bauer. "Day to Day Resistance." *Journal of Negro History* 27, no. 4 (October 1942): 388–419.

Benjamin Golden, Kathryn. "'Armed in the Great Swamp': Fear, Maroon Insurrection, and the Insurgent Ecology of the Great Dismal Swamp." *Journal of African American History* (Winter 2021): 1–26.

Benjamin Golden, Kathryn. "Trouble in the Water: Maroon Arrangements of an Insurgent Ecology." *Blackecologies* (2023): 40–45. https://globalracialjustice.rutgers.edu/sites/default/files/2023-08/ISGRJ%20Blackecologies%208_17final.pdf.

Benjamin Golden, Kathryn. "'Very Fond of Spirituous Liquors': Alcohol and Fugitive Black Life in the Slaveholding South." *Slavery and Abolition: A Journal of Slave and Post-Slave Studies* 45, no. 2 (2024): 242–63.

Berry, Daina Ramey. "Soul Values and American Slavery." *Slavery and Abolition: A Journal of Slave and Post-Slave Studies* 42, no. 2 (2021): 201–18.

Bledsoe, Adam. "Marronage as a Past and Present Geography in the Americas." *Southeastern Geographer* 57, no. 1 (Spring 2017): 30–50.

Blum, E. D. "Power, Danger, and Control: Slave Women's Perceptions of Wilderness in the Nineteenth Century." *Women's Studies* 31 (2002): 247–65.

Bush, Barbara. "'Daughters of Injur'd Africk': African Women and the Transatlantic Slave Trade." *Women's History Review* 17, no 5 (December 2008): 673–98.

Byrd, William. "The Earliest Passage Through the Dismal Swamp" (ca. 1728–1737). *Farmer's Register* 4, no. 10 (February 1, 1837): 593–99.

Byrd, William. "Proposal to Drain the Dismal Swamp" (ca. 1728–1737). *Farmer's Register* 4, no. 9 (January 1837): 521–24.

Caron, Peter. "'Of a Nation Which the Others Do Not Understand': Bambara Slaves and African Ethnicity in Colonial Louisiana, 1718–60." *Slavery and Abolition: A Journal of Slave and Post-Slave Studies* 18, no. 1 (1997): 98–121.

Carter Jackson, Kellie. "'Dare You Meet a Woman': Black Women, Abolitionism, and Protective Violence, 1850–1859." *Slavery and Abolition: A Journal of Slave and Post-Slave Studies* 42, no. 2 (2021): 269–92.

de Groot, Silvia W. "Maroon Women as Ancestors, Priests and Mediums in Surinam." *Slavery and Abolition: A Journal of Slave and Post-Slave Studies* 7, no. 2 (September 1986): 160–74.

Densu, Kwasi. "Omenala: Toward an African-Centered Ecophilosophy and Political Ecology." *Journal of Black Studies* 49, no. 1 (2018): 29–52.

Du Bois, W. E. B. "The Humor of Negroes." *Mark Twain Quarterly* (Fall–Winter 1942); reprinted (Spring 1998).

Eddins, Crystal. "'Rejoice! Your Wombs Will Not Beget Slaves!' Marronage as Reproductive Justice in Colonial Haiti." *Gender and History* 32, no. 3 (October 2020): 562–80.

Egerton, Douglas R. "'Fly Across the River': The Easter Slave Conspiracy of 1802." *North Carolina Historical Review* 68, no. 2 (April 1991): 87–110.

Ferrari, Carlyn Ena. "On Black Women's Ecologies." *Blackecologies* (2023): 37–38. https://globalracialjustice.rutgers.edu/sites/default/files/2023-08/ISGRJ%20Blackecologies%208_17final.pdf.

Ford, James Edward. "Close-Up: Fugitivity and the Filmic Imagination." *Black Camera* 7, no. 11 (Fall 2015): 110–14.

Frazier, Chelsea M. "Black Feminist Ecological Thought: A Manifesto." *Atmos Magazine*, October 1, 2020. https://atmos.earth/political-landscapes/black-feminist-ecological-thought-essay/.

Frazier, Chelsea M. "Troubling Ecology: Wangechi Mutu, Octavia Butler, and Black Feminist Interventions in Environmentalism." *Critical Ethnic Studies* 2, no. 1 (Spring 2016): 40–72.

Glymph, Thavolia. "Rose's War and the Gendered Politics of a Slave Insurgency in the Civil War." *Journal of the Civil War Era* 3, no. 4 (December 2013): 501–32.

Hare, Nathan. "Black Ecology." *Black Scholar* 1, no. 6 (April 1970): 2–8.

Hall, Rebecca. "Not Killing Me Softly: African American Women, Slave Revolts, and Historical Constructions of Racialized Gender." *Freedom Center Journal* 2 (2010): 1–48.

Hartman, Saidiya. "Venus in Two Acts." *Small Axe* 26 (June 2008): 1–14.

Hine, Darlene Clark. "Rape and the Inner Lives of Black Women in the Middle West." *Signs* 14, no. 4 (Summer 1989): 912–20.

Hosbey, Justin, Hilda Lloréns, and J. T. Roane. "Introduction: Global Black Ecologies." *Environment and Society* 13, no. 1 (2022): 1–10.

Hosbey, Justin, and J. T. Roane. "Mapping Black Ecologies." *Current Research in Digital History* 2 (August 2019). https://doi.org/10.31835/crdh.2019.05.

Hosbey, Justin, and J. T. Roane. "A Totally Different Form of Living: On the Legacies of Displacement and Marronage as Black Ecologies." *Southern Cultures* 27, no. 1 (Spring 2021): 68–73.

Hosbey, Justin, J. T. Roane, Emeralda Rutledge, and Teona Williams, eds. *Blackecologies* (2023). https://globalracialjustice.rutgers.edu/sites/default/files/2023-08/ISGRJ%20Blackecologies%208_17final.pdf.

"Isle of Wight County Records." *William and Mary Quarterly* 7, no. 4 (April 1899): 205–315.

James, Edward W. "Slave Owners in Princess Anne County, Virginia." *William and Mary Quarterly* 3, no. 1 (July 1894): 52–60. www.jstor.org/stable/1915503.

Kay, Marvin L. Michael, and Lorin Lee Carey. "Slave Runaways in Colonial North Carolina, 1748–1775." *North Carolina Historical Review* 63, no. 1 (January 1986): 1–39.

Landers, Jane. "Founding Mothers: Female Rebels in Colonial New Granada and Spanish Florida." *Journal of African American History* 98, no. 1 (Winter 2013): 7–23.

Lindsey, Treva B., and Jessica Marie Johnson. "Searching for Climax: Black Erotic Lives in Slavery and Freedom." *Meridians* 12, no. 2 (2014): 169–95.

Malm, Andreas. "In Wildness Is the Liberation of the World: On Maroon Ecology and Partisan Nature." *Historical Materialism* 26, no. 3 (2018): 3–37.

Maris-Wolf, Ted. "Hidden in Plain Sight: Maroon Life and Labor in Virginia's Dismal Swamp." *Slavery and Abolition: A Journal of Slave and Post-Slave Studies* 34, no. 3 (2013): 446–64.

McLean, Robert. "A Yankee Tutor in the Old South." *North Carolina Historical Review* 47, no. 1 (January 1970).

Miki, Yuko. "Fleeing into Slavery: The Insurgent Geographies of Brazilian Quilombolas (Maroons), 1880–1881." *The Americas* 68, no. 4 (April 2012): 495–528.

Morgan, Jennifer L. "*Partus sequitur ventrem*: Law, Race, and Reproduction in Colonial Slavery." *Small Axe* 22, no. 1 (March 2018): 1–17.

Moulton, Alex A. "Towards the Arboreal Side-Effects of Marronage: Black Geographies and Ecologies of the Jamaican Forest." *Environment and Planning E: Nature and Space* 6, no. 1 (May 2022): 3–23.

Moulton, Alex A., and Inge Salo. "Black Geographies and Black Ecologies as Insurgent Ecocriticism." *Environment and Society: Advances in Research* 13 (2022): 156–74. https://doi.org/10.3167/ares.2022.130110.

Negrin, Hayley. "Return to the Yeokanta/River: Powhatan Women and Environmental Treaty Making in Early America." *Environmental History* 28, no. 3 (July 2023): 522–53.

Nevius, Marcus P. "Global Warfare, Conspiracy Scares, and Slave Revolts in a World of Fear." *William and Mary Quarterly* 78, no. 3 (July 2021): 537–50.

Newton, Melanie J. "Returns to a Native Land: Indigeneity and Decolonization in the Anglophone Caribbean." *Small Axe* 41 (July 2013): 108–22.

Nwokeji, G. Ugo. "African Conceptions of Gender and the Slave Traffic." *William and Mary Quarterly* 58, no. 1 (January 2001): 47–68.

Peixotto, Becca. "Wetlands in Defiance: Exploring African-American Resistance in the Great Dismal Swamp." *Journal of Wetland Archaeology* 17, no. 1 (September 2017): 18–35.

Pybus, Cassandra. "'One Militant Saint': The Much Traveled Life of Mary Perth." *Journal of Colonialism and Colonial History* 9, no. 3 (Winter 2008): 1–9.

Roane, J. T. "Plotting the Black Commons." *Souls* 20, no. 3 (July–September 2018): 239–66.

Roeber, A. G. "A New England Woman's Perspective on Norfolk, Virginia, 1801–1802: Excerpts from the Diary of Ruth Henshaw Bascom." *Proceedings of the American Antiquarian Society* 88, no. 2 (1979): 277–325. www.americanantiquarian.org/proceedings/44517621.pdf.

Sayers, Daniel O. "Marronage Perspective for Historical Archaeology in the United States." *Historical Archaeology* 46, no. 4 (2012): 135–61.

Spillers, Hortense. "Mama's Baby, Papa's Maybe: An American Grammar Book." *Diacritics* 17, no. 2 (Summer 1987): 65–81.

Stewart, Peter C. Review of Hugo Prosper Leaming, *Hidden Americans: Maroons of Virginia and the Carolinas. William and Mary Quarterly* 53, no. 3 (July 1996): 666–67.

Sweeney, Shauna J. "Market Marronage: Fugitive Women and the Internal Marketing System in Jamaica, 1781–1834." *William and Mary Quarterly* 76, no. 2 (April 2019): 197–222.

Thompson, Alvin O. "Gender and Marronage in the Caribbean." *Journal of Caribbean History* 39, no. 2 (2005): 262–89.

Tinsley, Omise'eke Natasha. "Black Atlantic, Queer Atlantic: Queer Imaginings of the Middle Passage." *GLQ: A Journal of Lesbian and Gay Studies* 14, nos. 2–3 (2008): 191–215.

Vickers, Morgan P. "On Swampification: Black Ecologies, Moral Geographies, and Racialized Swampland Destruction." *Annals of the American Association of Geographers* 113, no. 7 (2023): 1674–81.

Williams, Gary M. "Colonel George Blow: Planter and Political Prophet of Antebellum Sussex." *Virginia Magazine of History and Biography* 90, no. 4 (October 1982): 432–55.

Wynter, Sylvia. "Jonkonnu in Jamaica." *Jamaica Journal* 4 (1970): 34–48.

Wynter, Sylvia. "Unsettling the Coloniality of Being/Power/Truth/Freedom: Towards the Human, After Man, Its Overrepresentation—An Argument." *CR: The New Centennial Review* 3, no. 3 (2003): 257–337.

Young, Jasmin A. "Gloria Richardson, Armed Self-Defense, and Black Liberation in Cambridge, Maryland." *Journal of African American History* 107, no. 2 (Spring 2022): 212–37.

Zhang, SJ. "Simarrona: Beyond Etymologies Towards a Poetics of Unlearning." *Small Axe* 71 (July 2023): 122–27.

Zhang, SJ. "What Cecelia Knew: Reading Reproduction and Marronage in Records of Recapture." *History of the Present* 14, no. 1 (April 2024): 156–73.

Dissertations and Theses

Austin, Karl M. "The Morass of Resistance During the Antebellum: Agents of Freedom in the Great Dismal Swamp." PhD diss., American University, 2017.

Benjamin Golden, Kathryn. "Through the Muck and Mire: Marronage, Representation, and Memory in the Great Dismal Swamp." PhD diss., University of California, Berkeley, 2018.

Goode, Cynthia. "Engaging the Tools of Resistance: Enslaved Africans' Tactics of Collective and Individual Consumption in Food, Medicine, and Clothing in the Great Dismal Swamp." PhD diss., American University, 2018.

Kopytoff, Barbara. "The Maroons of Jamaica: An Ethnohistorical Study of Incomplete Polities, 1655–1905." PhD diss., University of Pennsylvania, 1973.

Maris-Wolf, Edward Downing. "Between Slavery and Freedom: African Americans in the Great Dismal Swamp, 1763–1863." Master's thesis, College of William and Mary, 2002.

INDEX

www.ingramcontent.com/pod-product-compliance
Lightning Source LLC
LaVergne TN
LVHW090834031026
849361LV00018B/167
* 9 7 8 1 4 6 9 6 9 7 9 7 0 *